REKINDLING T

The Truth
About Swimming with Dolphins

www.RekindlingTheWaters.com

REKINDLING THE WATERS

The Truth About Swimming with Dolphins

Leah Lemieux

Matador
9 De Montfort Mews
Leicester LE1 7FW, UK
Tel: (+44) 116 255 9311 / 9312
Email: books@troubador.co.uk
Web: www.troubador.co.uk/matador

ISBN 978-1848760-578

A Cataloguing-in-Publication (CIP) catalogue record for this book
is available from the British Library.

Typeset in 11pt Book Antiqua by Troubador Publishing Ltd, Leicester, UK
Printed in the UK by TJ International, Padstow, Cornwall

Matador is an imprint of Troubador Publishing Ltd

For Juan
& All those trapped behind human barriers

& in memory of
Bia, Sebastian
Mimi & Mum

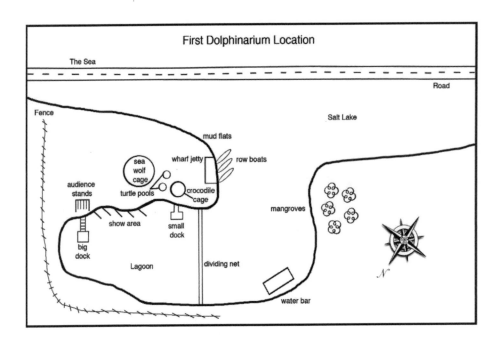

First Dolphinarium Location

The Sea

Road

Fence

Salt Lake

mud flats

wharf jetty

row boats

sea wolf cage

crocodile cage

turtle pools

audience stands

mangroves

show area

small dock

big dock

dividing net

Lagoon

N

water bar

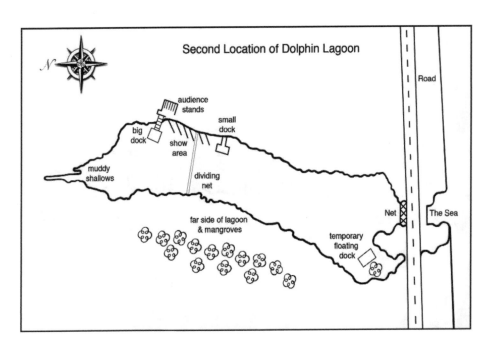

Second Location of Dolphin Lagoon

N

Road

audience stands

big dock

small dock

show area

muddy shallows

dividing net

The Sea

Net

far side of lagoon & mangroves

temporary floating dock

CONTENTS

ACKNOWLEDGEMENTS

First of all, I must send out my thanks to the Cubano Dolphins: Juan, Bia, Sebastian, Choney, Christine, Unior, Li & Bi without whom this book would never have been written.

Deepest thanks go to Dr. Mark McCutcheon, for his keen, merciless and brilliant editing, Camilla Singh for her support, company and beautiful photos, Beata Pillach for her dedicated help throughout the early years of struggle, Dan Finnigan for his invaluable assistance with the website and Carmen Victor for the wonderful maps.

Further thanks for assistance from those dedicated folks who work tirelessly on behalf of cetaceans: Dr. Naomi Rose of HSUS for her time, patience and encyclopedic knowledge of cetacean issues; Cathy Williamson and WDCS, Ric & Helene O'Barry, Bill Rossiter, Ruth (Sea Lady) Samuels, Margaux Dodds and Marine Connection, Dr. Toni Frohoff, Dr. Monika Wilke, Suzanne Chisholm, Cathy Kinsmen.

Thank you also to Ute Margreff & Reailtin, Wade & Jan Doak, Dr. Marc Bekoff, Dr. Denise Herzing, Graham Timmins, Keith Buchanan, Rick $pill, Derrick Jensen, Dr. Rachel Smolker, Jim Nollman, Dr. Hal Whitehead, Dr. Howard Gardner, Dr. Brenda McCowan, Dr. Frans de Waal, Dr. Peter Beamish, Cara Sands, Elizabeth Harley, Terry Whittaker, Lory Kenyan and Brendal in Abaco. Also, the late Ben White & Laura Scott, both of whom played quiet, but essential roles.

Deepest appreciation to Mr. Peter S. Beagle and Connor Cochran of Conlan Press; David Sylvian and Richard Chadwick of Opium Arts Ltd.; Mr. Jeremy Thompson at Matador; and to Lisa Hannigan and Bernadette Barrett.

Closer to home I must thank Earth Mammas Michelle Martin and Tara Treanor, Heidi Cameron & Kirsty Spencer; Sarah Marcus, Wendy Postma, Jen Cornish, Mike Leznoff, Paul & Aidyl Jago, Enver Sali, Andrew Roberts, Walter Willems, Mischa Chicoine, Bob Beamish, The Nommo, Natalie Kruger, Mandy, Tony, Y Mamma Louisa; My family Martin, Anne-Marie, Marc & Sheila Lemieux, Sirius and Pesto! Last, but never least, my sweet Bowie bird and all the Wild Ones....

PREFACE

"A time comes when silence is betrayal."
Dr. Martin Luther King Jr.

Since antiquity dolphins have possessed an undeniable and compelling appeal for the human species, surfacing gracefully in our art, mythologies and literature, creating a liquid imprint upon our psyches, which in recent years has intensified, inspiring everything from new age fervor to multi-million dollar theme parks. In our profit-driven age, suppliers are never far behind demand, and discovering people will eagerly pay exorbitant sums for the opportunity to get close, enterprises offering captive "dolphin encounters" can now be found in most tropical tourist-frequented locales. Enticed and lulled by the promise of proximity, millions of people annually swarm to aquariums, marine parks and dolphin-swim venues to pursue an infamous mystery: To caress that shining skin and perhaps glimpse what lingers behind the dolphins' curving, archaic smile.

However desperately our affinity with the natural world needs reaffirming, we must be wary that in our enthusiasm to seek and foster such connection, we do not in the same breath become a part of its desecration and undoing. Such cause for concern is embodied by these lucrative "Swim-With-the-Dolphins" attractions mushrooming throughout the US, Caribbean, Mexico, and various other vacation destinations, cashing in on the human hunger for close contact with these powerfully charismatic creatures.

Growing numbers of people are starting to realize that in caging wild things for our convenience and forcing them into our confines, something most precious is irretrievably lost — a treasure we claim to value above all others – *freedom*. Even as enthusiasm for "swimming with dolphins" grows, millions of people are increasingly objecting to the idea and practice of keeping dolphins captive. The resulting controversy has become volatile, impassioned and intensely polarized.

Commercial practices insist they represent perfectly acceptable opportunities for the public to fraternize with fleet, exotic marine creatures – while critics maintain that capturing and imprisoning such sentient, far-ranging beings for public amusement and corporate gain demonstrates unacceptable approval towards something *intrinsically* and ethically wrong.

In this way, the ineffable lure of the dolphin has become an apt symbol: Of the terrible harm that can result from blindly pursing our desires – and the rising voices of those who advocate compassion and freedom. I have plunged deep into the fraught waters of this clouded, ethical debate and its far-reaching implications. This is the story of what I found there.

Rekindling the Waters reflects on twenty years of unique experience, advocacy and study, chronicling the trials of a particular family of dolphins held captive at a popular tourist destination in Cuba. In sharing the story of the Cubano Dolphins' troubled lives, losses and struggles at the hands of their human captors and visitors, I wish to make people aware of the *truth* – of the ruinous and exacting toll extracted for fleeting human pleasure. Trapped behind human barriers, exquisite tenderness, suffocating heartbreak, colliding conflict and flickering hope, etch an indelible portrait of the suffering that lies behind the dolphins' smile. Only when people come to understand and empathize with this detrimental reality, will their participation in such harmful activities cease. In taking a closer look at the very *real* effects of certain seemingly harmless choices, we see how even a whimsical or well-earned holiday excursion can support horrendous suffering.

My time among the dolphins has taught me that some things, though they may be sold, can never be bought. Some things hold value beyond measure: Unconditional aid in adversity; a kindly presence when lost, tired, afraid or grieving; the unveiled look in love's eye and the trust of a wild heart, aligned by choice, with one's own, as an equal, and as a friend. Most of all, they have shown me the true value of Freedom – *freedom* of *choice*. These are inestimable treasures and their loss is devastating. How ironic, with so much talk of freedom and liberty; with so much righteousness in the air – that we routinely steal that which means most from others without a even a thought.

Dolphins enslaved by greedy corporate entities are indicative symptoms of a much deeper and insidious malady; one that could claim us all – a grievous lack of awareness, respect and regard for *life*

– human, animal and ecosystem. Whether we recognize it or not – we are all interconnected, and whether we choose to acknowledge it or not, atrocities continue—and it is we ourselves who make them possible. Marine parks and captive dolphin-swim attractions are fueled by tourist dollars, without which, they will go extinct.

The liquid passage through my life, of the ocean's most lucent, sought-after creatures, has lifted me up to touch and take part in a vast kinship and through an incredible alchemy, I have in a fashion, become that which I love. I owe a life debt and I have a story to tell. *Rekindling the Waters* is *Their* story, a story to *rekindle* kinship, by immersing us in the lives of *Other* – so that *Other* becomes *Us*.

Hope for a better future lies in shifting the underlying attitudes responsible for our destructive ways and it begins with *realization*. As hearts and minds open – positive reaction and global restoration follows. As one of the world's most beloved and beleaguered creatures, it is perhaps appropriate that dolphins serve as an illuminating focal point in helping to achieve this end.

CHAPTER ONE

OCEAN ARDOR

"We're of the going water and the gone
We are of water in the holy land of water"
Kate Bush, *The Jig of Life**

Irecognized destiny when it swam up and looked me in the eye. Beyond banal and reassuringly safe human borders, *something* waited for me to hear the call, and accept the summons…

I cannot remember a time when I did not love dolphins. Inexplicably riveting, impossibly familiar, any glimpse held me spellbound, with swelling sea waves of joy as they came flashing across the flickering television screen, leaving a trail of goose bumps in their wake.

A typical sylph, slight and agile, I was forever climbing trees, scraping knees; pursuing grasshoppers and snowflakes with equal relish; balancing flower petals on my tongue, or smelling the folded paper secrets of maple keys. A perpetually tussled look clung to me, which has not faded with age. I still come in from the garden with leaves or rain in my hair. In winter, driven to indoor amusements once the icy seep of snow percolated into my mittens and socks, my mother, an artful raconteur, often read to me. While my extremities thawed, I became quietly wed to this hieratic magic; tales of distant isles, sailing ships and abysmal serpents on the high seas, tumbling from the pages.

The only real dolphins for miles around were at Marineland. Commercial jingles and shiny magazines handed out at the turnstiles promised dynamic, cheerful dolphins, leaping in joyous precision — cartoon characters made flesh. Sitting in the distanced stands, the music trumpeted and suddenly the dolphins appeared, twirling and hoop jumping to the

* from the album, *The Hounds of Love*. (1985)

1

accompaniment of the park's grandiose theme song. To my innocent eyes, every arc, every spin was perfect, their curving smiles demonstrating obvious delight.

After the show, we went to watch the dolphins through the underwater window. Here, the dolphins no longer jumped for joy; instead, they paced in endless circles. In the false, watery light, without the glamour of tawdry theatrical distraction, the sight of the circling dolphins made me feel uneasy. Nose sprinkled with summer's freckles pressed to the glass, I watched as they passed blindly by only inches away, going round and round. Despite their proximity, the dolphins felt even farther away than when I'd been up in the stands and in a pure, unworded child's way, I understood that even though they were right in front of me, those dolphins were hardly there at all.

Even with all the attractions and distractions the marine park offered, I left feeling a little shadowed and saddened, though my parents put it down to too much sun after a long, exciting day. All the way home the dolphins circled in my head, as they had in the tank. I tried humming the marine park's bubbly show tune, but it rang empty and hollow in my ears. Shaking my latest acquisition, a glass globe filled with snowflakes and dolphins, brought no comfort either and I remained silent and pensive the entire journey home.

I was perhaps seven, when my Grandmother brought me to Cuba for the first time. Stepping off the plane onto a windy runway lined with coconut palms, the heavy humidity of the tropics wrapped itself around me, singing into my skin. I wore a blue-flowered dress, off the shoulder style, balancing with cute concentration along a curb while awaiting our luggage. My memory of the long bus-ride from Havana has become blur of sun-kissed, earth-toned faces with dancing eyes, expressively gesturing, positively trilling as they spoke. The smells of bright blooms and cigars blended with a thousand others, novel and dizzying. Our bus, crowded with loquacious Cubans, clunking luggage and flustered chickens, bumped along to the thrumming of a guitar's Spanish aiguilette, giving me the impression I had suddenly become part of a riotous gypsy caravan.

I awoke before the sun that first morning, listening to the wondering sounds of an unfamiliar dawn through the ocean's ceaseless whispers. Enormous gnarled, long-needled pine trees guarded the beach. My feet were bare and I had to step carefully to avoid the tiny, prickly pine cones scattered over the winding roots. The sand was soft and pale and rather cool, leading in gentle, frozen ripples to the misted whispering of the waves. It was still so early, the ocean and the sky had not yet decided what color they were going to be.

I paused, hypnotized; the Sea lay before me, almost undulating, surreal, like some great grey mythical beast. A sweet, salt-breeze reached invisibly out, touching my cheek and stirring my hair. The waves entreated softly, luring me to follow some latent, magnetic path over the sand to stand before the ever-shifting water's edge. Gulls uttered long wails overhead. Looking at last upon the ocean, a sea-secret rose to over-flowing in me, so that I felt I must become water myself and melt into it... Tentatively, I stepped forward... with this aqueous meeting, came the knowledge that there would be others.

Though it encompassed only a couple of weeks, that first childhood visit to Cuba became a lifetime in itself, offering a fresh stream of experiences, which remained at once immediate and dreamy. Days fell past, my skin grew dark and I never wanted to leave that place. Mornings were spent gathering shells left by the receding tide and scampering after crotchety crabs hiding amongst the flotsam and twiggy footprints of sea birds. With my grandmother, I waded through tropical gardens laden with flowers and swimming with scent, escaping the sultry heat in the airy, marble-cool of hotel halls.

I also came to know some of the ocean's different moods and guises: Wild and ominous, the frothing waves causing the earth to tremble, as they cast themselves ashore in sobs of foam, or pensive and quiescent, blanketed in seeping mist. But it was the days of inexorable sunlight, when the water held a scintillating spectrum of pale inviting aquamarine, smoothing into deeper layers of teal and peacock that would haunt me for years with a sharp longing to return. Every day that ocean held me, imbuing my spirit with the enormity of its shifting swelling strength and I was certain I would shrivel like a fallen leaf if I ever left.

But the final hour stole upon me, standing disparate on the sand, feet shod and locked away from all conversation with earth and water, gazing at the glinting Sea one last time. The idea of the flight, of home, of school and snow remained an impossible reality, while I looked upon that sparkling oceanic plain. As I was ushered onto the bus, the tropical warmth was swallowed up by a sterile, air conditioned chill, and with a grinding moan the bus lurched into gear and I was carried away—away from all that had so easily, so naturally replaced my entire world.

CHAPTER TWO

IMPACT OF PROXIMITY

"It was thy kiss, love, made me immortal."
Margaret W. Fuller, *The Dryad Song*

The length of my childhood I dreamed of that Cuban Sea, but it wasn't until my sixteenth year that I finally returned. Revisiting my old haunts, I discovered the passage of time had left things much as I remembered — as if change itself became languorous in Cuba's sleepy, tropical heat. Threading my path down to the sea, I again navigated the hoary twisting roots of the beach's sentinel pines (still barefoot), placing a quiet hand against the corrugated bark in greeting, before moving to stand once more before the jeweled water, breathless. Powerful currents; memories, saved all these years, released back into the great wellspring

I waited for the waves to invite me in, finding this ocean chillier than memory told. Cupping the pale water to splash and run in gleaming rivulets over my face, the sharp, salt-taste awakened a fierce joy and laughing, I surrendered myself to the sea with relish and abandon.

I had returned to Cuba carrying a single and urgent question. Locating the hotel's tour guide, I made my inquiry: Where could wild dolphins be found along the coast? Shaking her head regretfully, the tour guide explained that dolphins were no longer seen along these shores. This disparaging news produced a shock of disbelief — how could such an immaculate, azure ocean fail to harbor dolphins? I had come so far and waited so long, secretly certain that reunion with this tropical Elysium would at last realize my dream: to swim among wild dolphins. Only later would I discover that dolphins had indeed once frequented this coast, but after many of their number had been captured and sent away to aquariums, the remnants had fled to less perilous waters.

Almost as an afterthought, the tour guide added that just a little ways down the peninsula, there was a lagoon set up with some sort of dolphin show. The idea of a dolphin show didn't really interest me, but with no other alternatives, the possibility of proximity eventually drew me to investigate.

I paid exactly one dollar at the entrance. Thatched huts offered cold drinks and ice cream, but I drifted past these unseeing, searching through a forest of surging shoulders for the glint of water ahead. Emerging from the gaudy throngs, I discovered a large, rounded lagoon, edged with rocks and containing dark, weedy green water. This dim brine surprised me — naturally I'd expected to find the dolphins frolicking in the same oceanic turquoise I had so recently and so ecstatically engaged.

On the still water I counted four dolphins, silver drops, languidly dipping and diving. The sight of them, so close, so impossible, so long dreamed of — struck me past blood and bone, bolting to my very core. An immediate urge to slip into the olivaceous water followed, capturing my breath unexpectedly. It was unequivocal — I should be with *Them*. Quelling this sudden presumption, I instead settled on the rocks, as close to the dolphins as I dared, riveted and aching with their liquid beauty.

Unlike those around me, I did not whistle, hoot, yell or clap, choosing to remain respectfully silent. I knew they were not fish. No, *not* fish. Something else — something else entirely. I did not know what exactly they were. I'm still not sure — but they've become inextricably caught up within the most profound elements of what I am. What I've been.

The show began with blaring music and blurry words over the crackling loud speakers, but despite the battering of this atrocious racket, I held my perch by the water's edge. Piercing blasts from the trainer's whistle sent the dolphins, nodding and chattering, to perform a slew of embarrassingly silly activities. But every time they leapt, curving like scimitars with the sun raging along their mirrored sides, I felt myself smitten anew, trembling with the power of their true presence, somehow disguised by those ridiculous antics.

After the show, while people milled around with their iced goodies dripping into the dirt, I remained by the water unable to take my eyes from them. Every movement the dolphins made struck a chord, the resonation dizzying, their grace almost painful in its rendering. Rising to exhale explosively from the hole crowning its domed head and pausing to regard me momentarily, I felt the searing impact of a dolphin's dark eyes upon my own. Recognizing this potency, I rose, turning my back — knowing if I gazed on them even one moment longer, I would do something foolish.

Wading through the loitering tourists, I sought a trainer — someone — *anyone* to whom I might voice all the wordless questions suddenly fluttering blindly behind my eyes. But then I realized I couldn't speak anyway, remaining silenced by the sight of them. So I returned to the ocean's dusk, seething and shivering; phantom dolphins appearing in every wave and hollow, swimming before this unknown swoon.

I returned to the dolphinarium lagoon on a day threatening rain, imagining such unfriendly weather might keep the crowds at bay, but arriving at the closed gate, I found the place deserted and empty. Pacing the damp dirt road, I strained to catch a glimpse of the dolphins in their dim water between the abandoned kiosks, their nearness beckoning unbearably. Some scent of intuition led me along the fence outlining the lagoon's curving bulge and so I happened upon a break in the barrier. Sitting on a pile of stones contentedly hugging my knees, I watched the dolphins from across the lagoon. Their movements seemed subdued, their silvered skin reflecting only the sky's drab pewter, instead of sunny splendor. A squall of rain blew in, leaving me damp and shivering, yet determined in my vigil.

Clad in a windbreaker, ball cap and jeans, a trainer appeared carrying plastic buckets. I watched as the trainer fed the dolphins — until he looked up, noticing me there. Though I wasn't really inside the enclosure, I felt a sudden knot in my belly, worrying he might insist I leave. Instead, he waved — so I responded in kind. It began to rain harder, but I just couldn't tear myself from the sight of the dolphins, so I remained as I was. Glancing up again, the trainer paused in his work, and after a moment of reflection (a moment that would change my life), he beckoned to me.

Momentarily confused, I turned to look over my shoulder — but seeing no other, I turned back. Emphatically, he pointed to me, beckoning again, motioning for me to go back round the lagoon to the entrance. The trainer welcomed me in at the gate, the kind lines of his weathered face crinkling in a smile. He appeared forty-something, sporting a typical Cuban moustache and dark, unruly curls. Regarding my sopping person with amicable amber eyes, he told me in broken English that his name was Umberto. I liked him immediately. He was just finishing up a training session, and casually invited me to follow along. Silent and unbelieving, I trailed Umberto's sauntering gait, coming to stand behind the partition separating the dolphin dock from shore, where a faded wooden sign declared "No Passa."

I couldn't take my eyes off the dolphins; their least movement sent me brimming over with hushed wonder. Tossing dead fish into their open mouths, Umberto introduced us: *Juan*, the smaller one, with a shark bite scar on his back; and *Unior*, the bigger male with a notch in his beak*—a curious,

---

* It is likely this injury resulted from a violent capture as it appears consistent with damage caused by net entanglement.

Meeting Juan.

old injury. *Christine* and *Choney*, the two female dolphins who performed in the show, had been fed earlier from the larger dock in the show area.

Nodding encouragingly, Umberto motioned for me to join him on the dock — I must have floated, settling down on the wobbling platform before the two dolphins. Joy is ever the state for miraculous happenings. Taking up the empty fish buckets, Umberto stood to leave and looking down as I rose to follow, he smiled warmly and invited me to *stay. There.* With *Them.* At the candid look of disbelief on my face, his grin widened — and then Umberto, who I would learn was the easy-going sort, just turned and strolled off without a backward glance.

And so I entered the Cubano Dolphins' story.

Juan and Unior: Looking at them, I thought I might disintegrate with rapture at their opalescent proximity. Despite this internal rejoicing, I remained mute and still, all eyes, absorbing each minute, curving detail; every pace and glance. Alone or together, the dolphins would glide up, regarding me with their unfathomable eyes. I had never in my life been so entirely captivated by anything, taking in their shining with all my senses, until they dove, arching away into the murky water, leaving a circle of stillness where they'd been. Despite the decidedly dubious water, a powerful urge to follow them into the unknown cloudy depths tugged at me. *Not yet.*

Appearing from the fog below, Unior, the larger dolphin with the notch, reappeared, drifting closer, otherworldly eyes appraising. The unexpected intimacy of this incorporeal caress left me suddenly shy and lowering my gaze, I felt myself flush. When I looked up again, he was still watching me. To encourage rapport I lay down, chin resting on my wrists, eyes level with the dolphins' just above the water. I so wanted to reach out and touch that glorious, luminescent skin, but already I understood it was not my decision. The choice to close the distance between us was *theirs*, not mine.

The sky may have remained overcast, but their presence bathed me in a curiously encompassing light. Hours passed in their company, entranced, watching them, trying to understand what they were, of themselves and to me.

Umberto returned with the dolphins' late afternoon meal, and perceiving the fish buckets, I realized my time had flown. The trainer kindly helped me wobble ashore — I had forgotten I had legs. Though I doubt he understood most of it, Umberto endured my profuse thanks, beaming beneficently. In his charmingly stilted accent he told me that every afternoon the dolphins had several hours of "free time" and that I was welcome to visit whenever I liked. Overwhelmed by this invitation, I barely managed a coherent promise of return. Then I returned to the Sea; vast enough to contain my sudden overflow, still aglow, reflecting their radiance.

So, the wandering afternoon hours almost invariably found me among the dolphins. Over time I began to learn the subtle differences between the four dolphins who initially appeared very much alike. Unior (YOO-nee-or), the older male with the notched snout and sleepy eyes, was the largest and palest, seeming at once bold and mellow. Juan (hw-ON), the younger, smaller male had eyes like ebony pools and wore crescent scars on his back, where a shark had once held his body in its not inconsiderable jaws. Christine, the larger female, was the darkest, sable more than silver. Then there was Choney (rhyming with Johnny); she was different — *diffident*. Slender and fey, this most delicately lined dolphin seemed either reserved or indifferent, hanging back behind the others when she came round at all.

To my eyes they moved like music, permeated with exquisite inflections, and I, unsuspecting pupil, waited and watched, trying to resolve these impossible creatures glimmering before me. I saw nothing resembling the eager squeaking of "Flipper" — nor the equally cartoonish hoop-leaping, ball-balancing, tail-stuttering antics of the Marineland dolphins. Up close these creatures were all smooth grace and knowing eyes and more self-

Unior & Christine.

possessed than anyone I'd ever met. I would kneel on the dock before them, like an offering on an altar, wondering if silence and prayer would lead to acceptance — or revelation.

One afternoon, Unior chose his moment. Surfacing before me, I had no way of knowing what he was about to do. After a moment's pause, he eased forward and nudged my elbow with his blunt beak. *Contact.* My eyes never left his. Unmissably subtle, he slid forward and gently repeated the gesture. In response, I placed my open palm on the water between us, like a question. Unior considered this gesture a moment and then lightly brushed my offered fingertips. I remained absolutely still, only a slight intake of breath betraying my expanding wonder. Drifting before me Unior studied my reaction leisurely, before dipping beneath the murky water. He returned almost immediately with Juan alongside, again nudging my fingers, more boldly now. Taking this cue, Juan then echoed Unior's gesture himself!

This was the first lesson the dolphins taught me, which I will never forget: A sense of *trust* must develop before the initiation of *contact.* Instinctively I understood *choice* was integral in this matter. (I also learned that the colloquialism, *'monkey see, monkey do'* quite applies to creatures outside the primate family!) Christine proved just as inquisitive as the two male dolphins, but from the start, Choney set herself apart. While she marked the progression of these initial tactile investigations, Choney remained unmoved to come in so close herself. I would learn that this dolphin's trust was not to be won so easily. Not at all.

At length, I joined the dolphins in their dubiously turbid water. Though at home in their element, next to the dolphins' speed and soaring grace, I couldn't help but feel a little frog-like. Without a diving mask the water took on the clarity of green tea once submerged, obscuring the dolphins until they surfaced. However, a symphony of creaks and whistles echoed clearly all around me, leaving their movements to my imagination as they careened around making excited pinging sounds. For the time being, I enjoyed a closer rapport with the dolphins just lying on the dock, head resting on my hands, eye to eye.

I rose to meet my last day in Cuba with defiant disbelief. It seemed impossible to leave this life; the heavy sustenance of the tropical air; the sea, which I wore like an immense, aqueous skin; rising each morning to tread the familiar strand, a curving trail of footprints stretching out behind me in the sand. And the dolphins — already integral, past precious — too new for this sudden sundering. They had awoken places in me I hadn't known existed; places sylvan and spring-fed in their presence.

Amid numb farewells, Umberto was thanked for the thousandth time. I drank a last moment with the dolphins, wondering if it would carry me through the dolphin-less desert ahead — and with a promise of return, I did leave. But I was a different creature now, awakened to a thirst that neither fresh nor salt water could assuage. Beyond any doubt, I *knew* I would return to pursue and kindle this oddly ordained ember.

CHAPTER THREE

MINGLE

"Girl of green waters, liquid as lies…
Rolling her porpoise thighs alone
Her smooth mouth moons among the tides…"
Laurie Lee, *Song of the Sea*

Thirst. That is what it was. An avid, parched voracity for deeper understanding; a search that led me past months of study and speculation, wandering library aisles, poring over articles and periodicals between teetering towers of carefully chosen books. Moonlight, rippling with nebulous, delphic intimations, crept into my restless dreams, laced in the sultry spice of tropical breezes.

I discovered dolphins had been cherished by the ancient Greeks: Oppian, Herodotus, Ovid, Aelian, Pliny and Plutarch all wrote in their praise. In ancient Greece, killing a dolphin was considered a desecration of the sacred before the gods, an offense punishable by death.

I never ceased inhaling information — some of it useful — and some of it not nearly so…

"Belonging to the great and ancient family of mammals called Cetaceans, dolphins are actually tiny, toothed whales; roughly thirty varying species… *Tursiops truncatus*, the Bottlenose dolphin, enjoys a wide distribution in the world's oceans, inhabiting almost every kind of marine habitat in tropical and temperate seas… The reproductive organs are tucked away within the body, the mammary glands located on either side of the genital slit, below the navel… The brain of the bottlenose dolphin is larger than that of man…"

The delineation of their streamlined physiognomy became the recitation of a familiar haiku: peduncle-dorsal-fin-blowhole-melon-rostrum-pectoral-fin-fluke. But *none* of this evoked the reality of their smooth grace, their lithe lilt, the cantillation of their eyes on mine or the sudden actuality of their breathing. And none of it explained why they caused these strange lyrical tremors inside of me — or why they always had.

This search, driven by a desire to move *closer* to these creatures through the venue of collected literature, almost invariably left me gazing at my subjects through a *barrier* every bit as real as the glass at any aquarium. Months would eventually run into years, absorbing the gathered erudition on the species, so much of which remains undiscovered. I *knew*, that beyond the coarse matter of natural history, the distance of ancient poetry, the clinical probe of biological science, or even the passing pique of occasional anecdotes, there were certain integral illuminations that remained unwritten in the collective tome of human knowledge — things that might yet be learned by a patient scribe, in their willing presence.

A year passed and all of it faded, faced with that first rending stab of aqua; the ardis of an incurable arrow, standing again before that sparkling Cuban Sea. I felt the heaviness, the dullness of living on land, and knew I could never be fully complete without the water.

Still, essential questions hovered ominously, threatening with distended, venomous stingers: Would Umberto remember me and invite me back among the dolphins? Would the way remain open, as it had been once before? Unable to bear the idea of refusal, I remained taut and strained until the moment of fond greeting across the painted gate, met with Umberto's familiar, sleepy face and crinkled smile. Rather than navigating the parting estrangement of an entire year, it was almost as if we had spoken only the previous week. Completing our light banter, I gestured inquiringly towards the lagoon where so much wonder had been awoken. Nodding with absent-minded benevolence, Umberto ushered me towards the water, reminding me that the dolphins were on "free time" until the afternoon shows.

Remaining tense, though now with growing excitement rather than deep worry, I settled down on the damp dock to await their appearance with tremulous expectation. As if riding the silent wave of my internal exhilaration, Juan and Unior surfaced, rising up from memory's halls where they had glimmered since the moment I had left them. Watching them turn their exquisite, pellucid faces this way and that, regarding me first with one eye and then the other, I dared wonder if they might remember me.

With a vaporous exhalation Christine materialized from below, squeezing herself between Juan and Unior, without the least trace of reticence. From behind her curving hematite bulk, Choney peeped out, hanging back behind the others. Arms open, I received the three dolphins, crowding forward for caresses, intoxicated not only by the sea-smoothness of their skin and the raven warmth of their eyes on mine, but by the inevitable naturalness of it all.

Engulfed in their presence — at the dream somehow become real yet again — I shivered with delight. This unexpected, welcoming proximity awoke and stirred great internal tides; sifting, gathering, silently, irrevocably binding essences; paths chosen, promises made, though I did not know it. Yet I was aware, only just, of my emerging part in something vast, sweeping me up with a glorious, cyclonic unfolding of wings.

Slipping into the turbid water among them, I found the swim-fins I had acquired aided my abilities immensely, though amid their aqueous virtuosity, I remained a happily resigned neophyte.

Fifty million years ago, the dolphins' ancestors had appeared more terrestrial than I, but beckoned by some natant song, they had returned to the primordial womb, immaculately streamlined and perfected over evolutionary aeons. Fur was replaced with a layer of insulating blubber, its thickness varying with seasonal temperature fluctuations; nostrils migrated to the top of their skulls to form a blowhole; forelimbs modified into paddle-like pectoral fins used for steering, while the rear limbs gradually vanished, leaving only remnant pelvic bones, nestled deep within the body cavity. Powerful crescent tail flukes provided propulsion with vertical thrust, rather than the lateral swish of fish, and from their backs arose thorn-like dorsal fins, to act as maneuvering stabilizers. For millions of years they'd remained virtually unchanged, lifted to a liquid pinnacle, faultlessly sculpted by their chosen element, masters of the submerged realm. Hovering and gleaming before me, Nature's polished work was humbling.

Without a diving mask, the lagoon and its contents remained opaque and mysterious, but a continuous symphony of trills, whistles and creaks assured me I was far from alone, undulating through the green soup-like water. These sounds I now knew, were produced in the complex nasal passages just beneath the blowhole, emitted and focused through the melon — that lens of rounded, fatty tissue on the forehead — and used by the dolphins for both communication and navigation. These clicking sounds could decode a considerable amount of information, revealing details of size, distance and texture, furnishing the dolphins with a sort of acoustic X-ray vision so sensitive they could detect an object about the size of a plum from seventy-two meters away! The whole process, known as echolocation or sonar comprised the dolphins' most vital, primary sense, and is considered the most advanced sound capability on earth.

To my ears the sound pulses they emitted while echolocating sounded like creaking door hinges, or buzzing of various intensities. Locking on a target, the dolphins' clicks would rise in pitch, these higher frequencies providing more detailed sonic-image resolution, while indicating the intensity of their interest. Scientists suspect that it is via the lower jaw, possibly the teeth, that the reflected echoes are received, directed to the inner ear bones by fatty tissues and interpreted by the extensive auditory centers in the dolphins' formidable brain. Apparently these rapidly analyzed echoes provide such rich and detailed perception, that the dolphins' sense of sight, though more than comparable to the human visual interpretation of light, has become almost secondary. Easily transmitted in darkness and traveling 4.7 times faster through the dense medium of water, sound is the perfect underwater communication system, also making nocturnal activity and deep or murky waters available to dolphins. While their supple skin demonstrated an amazing awareness to the slightest touch, I would find it was also extremely sensitive to vibrational sound, effectively transforming their entire bodies into tympanic sensors. With my sense of sight so limited in the murky lagoon, my imagination was left to paint its own whimsical images; dolphins spiraling rapidly around me, effortlessly navigating the fog, swift as thought unbound.

A willing and patient pupil, my education among the dolphins continued, building on what they had taught me during my previous visit — contact only at their discretion, following the establishment of trust. The depths, the nuances and the obscure complexities among them would shed their voluminous veils only slowly over the years. Yet I loved just to watch them, Juan, Unior, Christine and Choney — watch them slither and curve on the water and suddenly vanish, quiet as a ripple, to continue their unknowable errands in the dim reaches below. They seemed to mirror the mysterious liquid subtlety of water in their ways, as if millennia within the oceans had permeated them profoundly on every level through the distill of some aqueous acquiescence.

One of the ways in which the dolphins forged and maintained the bonds between us was through avenues of play. An example I came to refer to as the "*pec-pat*" — short for pectoral-fin-patty-cake game — where, with a sort of "gimme five" gesture, the dolphins offered first one and then the other pectoral fin to meet with my palm (an almost universal gesture shared by socializing dolphins). Christine was initially the most enthusiastic with this exchange, wiggling her pec-fins vigorously and bobbing brightly while I dissolved in helpless hiccups of laughter. Though initially appearing somewhat facile, these repetitive gestures belied, I sensed, something very important at work and eventually I would learn that dolphins use these same established methods to befriend one another as well.

Except for Choney's careful reticence, the daily progression of trust,

Traveling with Juan & Unior.

contact and relationship through our games was noticeable. But there were many layers to the familiarity forming between us, not all of which I could entirely grasp. During quieter moments, the dolphins' cryptic, musing gaze sometimes lingered on mine. My mentors regarded me with tacit, non-committal countenances, as I faced them in an interminable pose of attentiveness; almost impossible to translate the innocuous wordless immensity between us.

The dolphins' rhythmic compositions changed quickly and quietude might suddenly transform into curious "dolphin tumults;" all four of them excitedly exploding out of the water, leaping, splashing and churning the surface of the lagoon with rushing foam. Heads, tails and fins would momentarily protrude with the roll of their shining bodies amongst one another, while a cacophony of decidedly odd sounding expletives escaped into the air. I had no idea if this was the result of disagreements, high spirits, hanky panky, or some other less-identifiable urge, but I promised myself to investigate further once a dive mask was procured.

In addition to sporadic training sessions, three daily shows punctuated my time among the dolphins. Far from resembling anything fun or interesting, the repetitive routine of flips and hoops quickly became the most tedious and boring part of the day. Watching the dolphins over time, I began to suspect they might feel similarly. I noticed it was not uncommon for Choney and Christine to quit performing halfway through the show, evincing a certain disinterest or perhaps disdain in the whole repetitive and tawdry performance. It gave me pause for thought.

Time bled away, leaving me sitting spellbound before a swelling sunset, knowing this would be my last night to wander and bathe beneath the stars' scintillating multitudes. Sighing into the water amongst the dolphins, I tried to absorb and imprint every detail of their splendor, though I was already familiar with the way any true image of them fatally fled my memory, emerging only upon reunion. After my last, parting caresses, Juan, Christine, Unior and Choney all lined up facing the net, which blocked them from the watery expanse beyond the lagoon, gazing with muted despondence past the barrier. A melancholy snapshot of parting memory.

CHAPTER FOUR

REALIZATIONS OF PERIL

"It's the kind of thing that no human being should be involved in."
Dr. Ken Norris

In the light spring rain, the streets glistened like the tiled backs of enormous reptilians. Standing in the spattered reflections of the street lamps, I watched people gathering before the stoic bulk of the Euclid Theater. It was busier than I had imagined — this milling crowd, drawn by an affiliative interest in dolphins.

Soon after my return from Cuba, a friend had brought to my attention a tiny ad, squatting in the back of some metropolitan magazine, indicating the existence of a local dolphin conservation society. I called the listed number and learned that this organization was poised to host a downtown Earth Day event featuring a presentation on the topic of dolphins! So here I was, watching my misted breath rise toward the blanketed night sky, breathing in the softening smell of earth mingled with wet pavement. Wrapped in a mantle of growing curiosity and unaware of what lay before me, I entered the arid theater to secure a seat in the cavernous auditorium. The lights dimmed, transforming the people around me into silhouettes, as the surrounding murmurs staggered into a final hush.

Without the least trace of trepidation, our hostess, an ample and bright brunette, took the podium. Progressing rapidly through perfunctory pleasantries, she proceeded to announce that the previous year, while making a documentary film, she had obtained footage that she was eager to bring to our collective attention. Dolphins being the topic of her film, she had headed to the nearest place they could be found: Marineland marine park — the same one from my childhood.

Informing the trainers of her enthusiastic project, she happily found herself invited on a special "behind the scenes" tour, which culminated as she was brought camera in hand, into a darkened warehouse where the "retired" animals not currently being used in public shows were kept. As the dull electric bulbs flickered on and huge fans began to whir, we looked upon a dingy scene; the echoing grey interior of a warehouse containing a small, shallow concrete pool. Drawing nearer, the camera revealed its contents: A single orca whale with a bent, disfigured dorsal fin, floating motionless at the surface, and dwarfed by its inert companion, an equally listless and flaccid-finned dolphin.

Seemingly unaffected by this abject sight, the blithe trainer gave the names of the orca and dolphin as "Junior" and "Duke", respectively. Moving up to the pool's edge, the camera revealed Duke's heavily scarred body, a dorsal fin bent over from endless circling and his eyes, puckered from chlorine and milky with cataracts. Neither Duke nor Junior showed much inclination to stir under the dim lights, and I looked upon the aimless floating of the sickly, leaden pair with expanding melancholy. Little could have been further from the popular image of exuberant dolphins riding blue sea waves or majestic orca whales leaping against the magnificent Pacific Northwest.

Asked why Duke and Junior were housed in a warehouse instead of with the other whales and dolphins, the trainer answered that Duke had been deemed "too ugly" to participate in the dolphin show and already cramped conditions had left the park without anywhere else to put the "excess" orca whale. So they remained in a tiny chlorinated pool — in live storage. Disturbed by what she had seen, our hostess decided to contact a dolphin conservation group in the U.S. to make inquiries into her rising concern over a situation that somehow seemed so very wrong. She quickly learned that outdated, substandard conditions and treatment in marine parks were common and that certain organizations focused solely in tackling this issue and making the public aware of the problem.

Introducing, *Deconstructing the Flipper Myth 101*: With the arrival of the popular television show "Flipper," public enthusiasm for dolphins rose dramatically. Suddenly hotel swimming pools, petting pools, aquariums, marine parks, and traveling circus shows were all clamoring for dolphins to leap, spin, flip and line their owners' pockets with money. Dolphin shows quickly became a lucrative business.

"Flipper" helped create a rather Disney-like portrait of dolphins as jolly, friendly, helpful, perpetually smiling creatures, eager to interact with man as his best friend in the sea. However, "Flipper" was no more an actual dolphin, than Mickey a mouse, being rather a façade, constructed for entertainment — and profit. *Real* dolphins were revealed to be free spirited, far roaming wild creatures that generally prefer the company of their own kind, when given the choice. In order to bring them before a paying public, they had to be chased down and forcibly removed from their families and communities.

Like just about everyone else there, I had never realized this fact, and certainly marine parks weren't eager to draw attention to this aspect of the industry. In captivity, little mention is made of how the dolphins got there or what their natural lives were like, because this would highlight the vast differences between freedom and captive life, and lead to awkward questions. Tricks, costumes, charismatic trainers and loud music distract audiences from contemplating small, stark, concrete enclosures.

Reviewing my own memories, so much was suddenly coming clearly into disturbing focus... I had been twelve the last time I'd been to Marineland with my family. I had begun to notice the listlessness of the animals and the ugliness of the place, while the blaring show held nothing, except the actual grace of the dolphins themselves. Watching them through the underwater window, still swimming in endless circles, I remembered suddenly seeing several dolphins gang up on another. As the swirling ball of dolphins drew nearer, I saw to my twelve-year-old horror, that they all had their bright pink penises out and with them were vehemently bludgeoning the unfortunate in their midst. Here were my favorite creatures, invariably portrayed as seamless, sexless, smiling, cartoon-like critters — beating the crap out of one of their own with their erections! I couldn't have imagined a more violent and disturbing scene! We hadn't returned to the place after that and I hadn't wanted to.

As the presentation progressed, I found myself furnished with more grim facts, about which I simply had no idea. Apparently it wasn't uncommon for trainers to force dolphins to perform by withholding food until hunger forced them to bow to human demands. Despite years of "captive breeding programs" dolphins were *still* being taken from the wild and even with veterinary care their life spans were often drastically reduced. When "Nemo" or "Flipper" or "Squirt" died, another dolphin would take his place and name — and the show would go on. However, as news of traumatic captures, high mortality rates and cramped conditions were being revealed, public attitude was beginning to change — indeed, I could feel it changing all around me.

I felt my own eyes opening and I did not like what I saw. But now I grasped the very things that had left me feeling so uneasy watching those captive dolphins as a child. Though these sea-circuses liked to tote themselves as having "educational value" that couldn't be matched or gleaned in any other way, watching those dolphins endlessly circle in their tiny tank hadn't taught me that they could travel up to forty miles a day or shown me how they might work in choreographed discipline to capture schools of fish. Seeing dolphins and orcas repetitively hoop-jumping, ball balancing, begging for dead fish and ferrying trainers around on their backs hadn't taught me anything. Deprived of all *choice* in food, companions or surroundings and with any accurate representation of normal behavior, life span, habitat or social structure severely compromised, MIS-education might be a more apt description of what marine parks offered. Despite their propaganda, years of public exposure to live captive dolphins had not translated into practical action or heightened ecological awareness, failing to directly churn out armies of folk inspired to protect the world's oceans and its creatures.

It was an ugly realization — these marine attractions actually *desensitized* people to the cruelty of the situation right under their noses! That this cruelty wasn't immediately and *glaringly* obvious to even the most casual observer in a marine park, perfectly demonstrated the danger. Like so much suffering and injustice in the world, it all boiled down to money. Drawn by dolphins' natural allure, millions of people were paying substantial sums to gain entrance to these marine parks, which ultimately exploited both people and dolphins. Theme parks, our hostess proclaimed, were for rides, roller coasters, cotton candy and thrills — not places to try and sensitize people to the plight of wild animals. Instead, marine parks endorsed the idea that there's nothing wrong with capturing and confining intelligent, far-ranging wild creatures for the rest of their shortened lives and forcing them to do inane tricks for dead fish. How could this tarnished spectacle teach people about compassion, respect or conservation?

With popularity and attendance waning in some places, a problem had arisen: What to do with unwanted dolphins from parks that closed? As it turned out, several projects had already established that captive dolphins could be rehabilitated and released back into the wild. Excited that another option existed for dolphins like Duke, our hostess had returned to Marineland with a proposal that might allow the unfortunate and unwanted dolphin a second chance at life. If Duke, after twenty years of captivity, proved unsuitable for re-adaptation to the wild, he might at least have the dignity of being retired into spacious natural surroundings with real sunlight, salt water and companionship. But Marineland had refused to even consider the option.

Undaunted, our hostess sought support for Duke, at a provincial and federal level — only to discover that legislation governing conditions at marine parks or aquariums was virtually non-existent. So, she joined efforts with several other animal welfare organizations in drafting a "Canadian

Cetacean Protection Act," to raise standards of care at existing aquariums and marine parks, ban the import and export of cetaceans and implement the rehabilitation, release or retirement of unwanted dolphins or whales.

And here she was, asking that if we truly cared for dolphins and their well-being, to avoid supporting marine parks, sea circuses and aquariums that held cetaceans. Our hostess had done her work well. Keeping dolphins and whales in glorified swimming pools was clearly *wrong*. The matter was settled.

After a short recess, the audience reconvened for the second half of the evening's presentation. Standing behind the narrow podium, our hostess introduced her guest speaker as Sam LaBudde, a young biologist working for an environmental organization called Earth Island Institute. Leaning his lank form over the microphone, Sam cleared his throat, dark hair falling into his serious eyes.

"Does anyone here know about the connection between the tuna-fishing industry and the deaths of *millions* of dolphins?" he asked the assembly. To the ensuing silence he replied: "*That's* why I'm here." The lights dimmed further as Sam started a film, which he narrated himself.

It had long been known, he told us, that yellow-fin tuna (a most prized fish, commanding top dollars), often swim beneath pods of dolphins. Traveling at the surface, dolphins are much easier to detect than the tuna far below and fishermen discovered one of the fastest, ways to catch record amounts of large, yellow-fin was to encircle families of dolphins. Small coastal boats have been replaced with huge, hi-tech seiner-ships that can scoop up entire shoals of fish. In laden, leaden tones, Sam explained how the dolphins are hunted by lookouts in helicopters, sent up from platforms aboard the gigantic tuna seiners. Once sighted, speedboats are dispatched from the mother ship, to chase the dolphins, sometimes for hours, in a relentless, coordinated assault. In order to keep the dolphins from scattering and escaping, explosives are thrown to further panic and disorient them. Sam reminded us, what horrendous effects these explosives would have on creatures whose livelihoods depend on their finely tuned acoustic senses. Exhaustion finally forces the dolphins to slow to a halt, huddling together in terror, while the ship's gigantic seine net, almost a mile long and over 300ft deep, is deployed, encircling them. With their target surrounded, the net is pulled closed, like a huge drawstring purse, trapping both tuna and dolphin within in. Then the immense net is hauled in, using a giant winch on board known as the power block.

These tuna fishing practices have been responsible for the deaths of over *seven million* dolphins! Inexact figures, Sam informed us, were due to the remote areas where the killing takes place and the poor to non-existent records of dolphin fatality kept by the tuna fishers. The death toll, he said, might even be as high as *ten million*.

1972 saw the passage of the US Marine Mammal Protection Act (MMPA), which stated: "*...it shall be the immediate goal that the incidental kill or serious injury of marine mammals permitted in the course of commercial fishing operations be reduced to insignificant levels approaching zero mortality...*"

But almost before the "ink was dry", congress submitted to the powerful economic and political lobby of the tuna industry and began to water the MMPA down, permitting the US tuna fleet an astonishing annual kill quota of *20,500* dolphins, labeled quite misleadingly as an "incidental take." Because the dolphins are *intentionally* located, chased and encircled in the tuna nets, Sam expressed difficulty in conceding how this could be construed as "incidental." Judging by the angry murmurs of the audience, it appeared I was not the only one who agreed with his determination. Far from reducing the dolphin death toll to zero, this *kill-quota* completely overturned the protective law, confirmed by scientific observers on board US tuna boats, many of whom described an on-going dolphin slaughter, far worse than anyone had feared.

Unwilling to accede even to this weakened and lax legislation, much of the US tuna fleet simply "went foreign" and continued catching tuna on dolphins under other flags (Panama, Mexico, Venezuela etc.), thereby escaping *any* policing of their fishing methods. As the completely unregulated foreign fleet swelled in ranks, an ever-skyrocketing number of dolphins continued to die in tuna nets.

Reliable death statistics from the foreign fleet remained difficult to gather; so Sam LaBudde had gone undercover aboard a Panamanian tuna boat to covertly film the full horror of the killing. He knew film footage was needed to reveal the shocking truth of dolphins dying in tuna nets, in order to provoke public outcry and action.

And here it was.

With a sickening slither growing in my entrails, I watched panic-stricken dolphins whipping across ocean waves, fleeing for their lives, pursued by roaring speedboats. I saw them rounded up in the tuna nets, saw what happened when canopies formed in the nets, trapping hundreds of dolphins beneath the heavy mesh. The blue water churned white as the dolphins struggled and fought to breathe from beneath the deadly netting, their shrill, thin cries rending the air, tearing soft gasps of horror and shock from the audience. Unable to wrench my eyes from the frantic scene of brutal suffering, my sight blurred until the tears steamed unchecked down my face. The images that followed burned in my mind and would return to haunt my dreams for years.

Helpless, I watched their strength give out, watched them drown and die in a marine holocaust. In smote silence I saw panicked dolphins charge the net, throwing themselves at freedom and instead become tangled and twisted; watched them dragged aloft as the huge net was inexorably winched in. I saw dolphins, hanging only by a delicate pectoral fin, twisting and thrashing until the extremities were ripped from their bodies and they tumbled, mutilated and bleeding back into the water only to be tangled and lifted again. Stunned, I watched a slender spinner dolphin, hopelessly wrapped in netting, struggling for its life as it was drawn inevitably toward the massive power block, where it was slowly fed through the winch and crushed alive. The sleek body, now reduced to rubbery mangled flesh, tumbled down on top of the net pile, all the life crushed out of it. I could only imagine those last moments of terror and agony. Another shot depicted dead, crippled and dying dolphins strewn on the ship's deck and then the Captain, walking up to one of them still jerking in agonized death throes, took out a knife and began cutting it open. This exquisite creature, with a brain the size of our own—being carved up for steak. *Suffocatingly* profane.

With several hundred dolphins remaining in the net, crew members began pushing dead dolphins over the net's cork-line. One guy held a tiny newborn dolphin over his head like a trophy football, before tossing it into the water where sharks were eagerly converging. After twenty to thirty minutes of removing dead dolphins from the net, Sam informed us that the catch was revealed — only *a single* yellow-fin tuna. For this, hundreds of dolphins had perished in agony, right before my eyes. For a tuna sandwich.

The searing images continued: a mother dolphin, ejected from the tuna net, hovering over her dead infant, floating lifeless on the sea, her face pointed to the sky as if in silent supplication. Though voiceless, that dolphin's rending, ululation tolled powerfully through the stricken audience.

Sam continued his grim narration, informing us that the drastic death rates did not count those dolphins that are maimed or mortally wounded and thrown over the nets to the waiting sharks. Those that escape and survive might be chased and netted as many as three times a day by the tuna fleet, causing unimaginable stress, especially on the young and pregnant or nursing mothers. The *worst* part of it all, Sam told us, was that these horrendous deaths were completely *needless* — purse-seining in the areas where tuna associate with dolphins accounting for only a mere five percent of the world's tuna catch. There was no excuse for the killing — yet it's almost unavoidable when setting tuna nets on dolphins.

Actions speak louder than any palliative words, and the only thing the tuna industry appeared to have conclusively proved was that in presuming both dolphins and tuna were nothing more than resources to be ruthlessly stripped, it would willingly drive them from the face of the earth for profit.

However, the unmistakable and horrifying images of Sam's film were indeed jolting the public into action, igniting tremendous outcry, boycott, press and now — *change*! Star-Kist Seafood, the world's biggest tuna canner, had just announced they would no longer sell any tuna caught by encircling and thereby killing dolphins! Not only was *this* a victory, but other major canneries were likely to follow suit, if only to keep up appearance. (Indeed, they did.)

Sam reminded us that it was only a battle, not the war that had been won, pointing out that Star-Kist certainly hadn't done this out of the kindness of its corporate heart. Rather, this was a response to public boycott — this was just good business, and because of that, environmental groups would continue to monitor the situation.

"Ultimately," he reminded us, "the power lies with the conscious choices made by the consumer — *YOU.*"

There was a digestive pause before a monsoon of applause thundered through the auditorium. This night had turned out nothing like I had expected and I felt deeply inspired to try and help make a difference. Ignoring these scalding discoveries simply wasn't an option.

CHAPTER FIVE

DEATH OF A STAR

"Since I was cut from the reed bed I have made this crying sound.
Anyone separated from someone he loves understands what I say.
Anyone pulled from a source, longs to go back."
Rumi

After navigating through the crush and swirl of Miami's hazed heat, we began the sweltering drive down the Florida Keys — I was on a mission of discovery.

I had joined with the local dolphin conservation society and offered my assistance in raising public awareness about marine parks and the dolphin-tuna issue, and in doing so, I came to learn much more about the global dangers facing cetaceans. As the sub-tropical summer progressed, a heated topic of discussion arose in conservation circles regarding the business of "Swim-with-the-Dolphins" attractions. Many of these popular and lucrative enterprises flaunted themselves as so-called *"semi-captive"* facilities by virtue of the natural lagoons or sea pens within which they kept dolphins for the public to swim with. As the debate raged, it seemed some people felt this kind of captive facility was acceptable, perhaps even beneficial (and it was rumored, voluntary on the part of the dolphins), while others maintained that capturing and keeping such sentient, far-ranging creatures for *any* kind of public amusement or gain demonstrated *unacceptable* approval towards something intrinsically and ethically wrong.

In examining my own feelings on the matter, I found them uncharacteristically clouded. If these places resembled the Cubano Dolphins' spacious and sunny lagoon — they were a far cry from Marineland's concrete tanks. I imagined — or rather hoped — that these Swim-With dolphins must, for the most part, be content with their lot and the human affection lavished upon them. However, having never had the privilege of meeting any wild dolphins for comparison, I had to concede that my judgment in the matter could very well be lacking balanced perspective. I knew I needed to rectify this, so when an opportunity presented itself to join an excursion to the Florida Keys, the premise of which was to compare encounters with both wild and supposedly "semi-captive" dolphins, I leapt at the invitation.

It had been my search for *wild dolphins* that had led me to the Cubano Dolphins. Had I instead found one of those magical places with which the world was secretly, sacredly speckled, where wild dolphins might allow humans into their midst, I would likely have never bothered seeking out any shabby dolphin show. But I had, and ever since then, the landscape of my life had been internally heaving.

So I here I was, on a journey to seek the truth of this matter for myself. Our first investigative stop was a dolphin-swim facility on Key Largo. Despite my initial excitement, taking in our surroundings had an almost immediate cooling effect on my mood. The entire place owned a feeling of dingy decrepitude: Opaque grey-green water, rust-stained concrete walls, towering chain-link fences and there, in the drab brine before us, the torpid dip of dolphins. They seemed so out of place, with the sun mirrored over their bowed backs and the stoic walls rising so forbiddingly high up all around them — a dolorous vista, which left me besmeared with a feeling of oily unease.

One of the dolphins drifted over, regarding us with doe-like eyes. The coy candor of her gaze seemed to beckon in an open invitation to break the rules and transgress the understood limit; to pass the barrier, and *dare* to come closer… I didn't though, shaking my head to clear it of the siren-strains. *What was it in their presence that sang so ardently to me?* The dolphin herself, quiescent and curved upon the water's stagnant surface, seemed to be studying our group with lingering deliberation. The frozen smile revealed nothing.

The next day dawned, unearthing an unknown passion — boats and sailing. Unencumbered by any landmass, we skimmed away from Key West, plunging out into the Gulf of Mexico, seeking the wild dolphins. Flying over the sweet waves, the sails rounded with a clean wind, tangling my hair with frenzied glee in the sunshine. This effortless speed with which we foraged onwards over the ocean's rich scintillation was only the first of the day's delights.

My initial glimpse of wild dolphins was a mere flash and fall of minute dorsal fins; dots on the water, growing more distinct as they drew closer. Spirits soared to gull-shaming heights on board. Two of them came to float and waver before the bow: Liquid. Perfect. Unfettered. The dream's portal entered, others came to drift and shimmer before us like heat-mirages, while I sang and suffered with the trifling distance which prevented me from melting into their midst. They shone and faded before my starved sight; undulating upon inconceivable errands, their passage a lyrical vibrato through the water's layered harmonies.

At last cut adrift beneath the sea's tepid azure, I glanced up to see two dolphins, mirroring one another in faultless symmetry, gliding towards me. The brief caress of their eyes upon my own caused an electric ripple of impossible recognition. In moments they were gone, merging into the insubstantial turquoise mist ringing my submerged vision, yet that brilliant instant shared between us, lingered. That one glance had smote the possibility of anything other than an intensely *aware* intelligence behind those unearthly eyes. Those two entities, imbued with strange luminosities had peered, not at, but *into* me, and though fleeting, their egress imparted an aqueous afterglow; a memory of exotic, dappled *Presence*.

Sailing on through spume and spray, the dolphins flickered in the tropical haze; smoky ghosts, now faint on the periphery, now opalescent before me. Glimpses. When delphic whim decreed, I immersed once more in the tourmaline flux. Was it the same pair that came to drift for those immortal moments beside me?

Back aboard, swaying easily with the boat's reel and toss, I faced the sun, enmeshed now in dusk's rosy blankets, eyes remaining wed to the water — too soon terra firma would receive us. Life on land was too solid, too immutable to provide balm for the longing of my suddenly pensive soul. Sail away, sail away…

Upon our return to the Key Largo dolphin-swim attraction, we were met with a forty-minute speech delivering general facts about the dolphins and how to behave with them in the water. Here I learned nothing new — nothing that could not be found in a child's book. But this mandatory and soulless recital was the *key* excuse for keeping these dolphins captive in the first place – "educating the public. "I was *not* impressed.

Introduced into a pen containing six dolphins, the first realization was like a slap — the stale water was so shallow! After being unfettered among the wild dolphins, nothing could have been more immediately obvious. Compared with the ocean, this meager fifteen feet seemed hardly a puddle — so how must it seem to the dolphins, pacing the same fences, day after day?

Descending to explore my cramped surroundings, several gracile forms came arcing through the ambient, green light towards me. The dolphins, after scanning proficiently with prickling ultrasonics, brushed up against me, nudging elbows and knees with Zen insouciance. Certainly, they were bolder — or rather more acclimatized to swimmers than the Cubano Dolphins. At their invitation, I twirled and twined synchronously alongside their fluent forms. Though the dolphins' proximity could not fail to induce hypnotic delight — it was impossible for me to ignore the note of discord in the place.

Bleached and blonded, the tanned, bland trainers had assured us that the underwater gates found in all the pens were regularly opened, allowing the dolphins to explore the concrete sea channels beyond the tall fences, and even presenting them with the option to leave, should they desire to do so. With smug and vapid finesse, the trainers insisted that "their dolphins" unfailingly returned of their own accord, because they adored their visiting fans so very, very much. Polished crocodile smiles for all.

Having noticed the underwater gate at one end of the iron fence, I swam over for a closer look. At this, one of the dolphins came up alongside me and after a weighty pause (collecting my complete attention with the silent magnitude of her disenchanted eye), moved forward and began pulling on the chain-lock! Suspending this action a moment and seeming to mark with grim satisfaction the terrible realization dawning in my eyes, the dolphin then resumed pulling determinedly on the chains which separated her from freedom. A deliberate message, heart wrenching in its obvious plea:

Let me free
We are sisters, you and I

Meeting the betrayed gaze, I took hold of the chain myself, yanking on it with all my impotent strength, while the dolphin looked on. I would have sold my life if it would have bought their freedom, if it could have erased the wounded look in that dolphin's eye. Almost immediately, a trainer who had been monitoring the pen's occupants from the sidelines, descended upon us, the plastic smile strained, near to cracking, warning me not to touch the gate, as it would agitate the dolphins. Small wonder. It had become apparent (to me), that the dolphins were *already* agitated with their situation.

Leaving the water, I could not bring myself to look back — and see their helplessness and lack of recourse so starkly revealed. Unlike the dolphins, *I* could walk away…

The following day, we went to examine another captive dolphin-swim attraction, this one on Grassy Key — to discover its *true* climate. After the pure, effortless spontaneity of my encounters at sea, the jostling tourists, piercing trainers' whistles and buckets of dead fish served only to dissolve any last dim vestiges of puny and artificial glory. The dolphins themselves (and there were many), seemed so despondent and listless when not sitting erect to await a deceased herring. Where was the fey toss and slide of the wild dolphins? Drowned. Abandoned. Forgotten.

Here, they were forced to look to humans for companionship, for food, for any break in the boredom and it was painfully clear how much of their dignity and majesty had been stolen from them. The wild dolphins needed nothing from any human, their sovereignty and mystery remaining intact. It was *this*, which made any moment they kept one's company so poignant and precious. Even in the supposed spaciousness of these "sea pens," every dolphin I saw was reduced, floating on the water's slick, sickly surface, stifled and inert with boredom, unless begging for dead fish from their jailers. It was eerie and the squeals of delighted tourists and bubbly commands of the trainers echoing over the flat water did nothing to cloak it.

At the end of this gloomy tour, we were invited down onto one of the docks to meet several of the dolphins. Three males, without any female company. One of them, with lucent, immaculate skin and particularly soulful eyes, was introduced as Natua, or Nat. A "very special celebrity dolphin," we were informed, who loved the camera and had been in several commercials and films. Nat, we were told, liked to paint and later, looking at one of his creations, I thought the arching indigo and turquoise streaks ironically reminded me of nothing so much as wild dolphins. Nat, was the facility's crown jewel, the most people-loving dolphin of them all — which only made his story all the more hurtful.

A few years later, during a daily swim program, poor, people-loving Natua, was interacting with a couple and had cut between the paddling pair, at which the woman became distressed. The man reacted with unconscionable violence, by *punching* Nat in the head! In response to this unprecedented attack, Natua swung his head round, breaking several of his assailant's ribs on contact. (Of course, if he'd wanted to, Nat could easily have smashed the guy into unobtrusive bits. But he hadn't.)

Predictably, the man raised a fuss, threatening to press charges and all the miserable like — despite the fact that it was his own aggression that provoked the incident. But it was the dolphin who had to pay — *with his life*. Natua was put into solitary confinement, alone, without other dolphins, or the human attention he was used to having lavished upon him. Labeled: "dangerous" and "aggressive" because human lives are routinely placed in jeopardy in these captive-swim places to turn a profit.

Poor Natua — the Star, once so beloved; gregarious, interactive, the center of that tiny, caged solar system. A *Star*, forsaken and never even understanding why… Prolonged sadness is a sure killer of dolphins — more deadly than any shark and nowhere to run. Natua died, not long after the

Natua.

incident. Some said it was a tumor, grown to the size of a basketball within his desolate body; others said it was a liver infection. The facility refused to reveal particulars. Perhaps those responsible for the dolphin felt some shame — while their coffers continued to over-flow with the eager, unseeing public's money. Cold Hard Cash. One more sad story; a drop in sorrow's seas, so many would I come to hear.

Voyaging once more into the Gulf of Mexico, everything remained fresh, despite the heavy tropical heat. Just the clean potency of the sea and the sky, allowing me to temporarily forget the recent and troubling sights. This ocean was completely free of the melancholy film that coated the captive dolphin-swim parks.

Quick-silvered shadows found us, haunting the bow with rippling cadence. I was transfixed. Each time one of the dolphins, curving on its supple side gazed up at me, I felt as though some kind of electricity were exciting my core. It was the candor of contact with those eyes, at once exact and ineffable; a hidden spring, brimming over with strange affinities. Released again into the malachite waters, six dolphins appeared. *The Liquid Six*. In moments, I was surrounded: smoothly encapsulated on all sides, above and below. Enfolded, flower-like; they, magnolia petals, all glimmer and resplendence. Suspended moments of unity, outwardly expressed, inwardly profound, the Liquid Six left me wondering in their wake.

A ripening sunset revealed it was time almost to turn back. At the eleventh hour, my hovering hope was answered and a last glimpse of the wild dolphins granted before their diluvial world was left for land.

Gliding by in pairs and trios through the long, dappled slant of the late afternoon, they came to meet us. Everything beneath the waves was hung with a fey glamour, bathed in lotic light. A delphic dyad coalesced: Oberon and Titania, leading their bejeweled retinue, seeming to nod in some unspoken agreement, before allowing me to drift along among them, burnished, sunny sides close enough to touch.

Drawn beneath the water, across an unknown threshold, I tasted this humbling, otherworldly collusion, ingested the fire of communion and saw myself reflected in the eye of a foreign and formidable intellect…But as the sun stole inevitably toward the blushing horizon, they began to fade, slipping between wandering sunbeams, nebulous in the half-light, drawing from me the silent sigh, *take me with you…* Heedless, they drifted on, melting into evening's copper-stained swells.

All praise, I broke the surface, lifting my arms to the wind in a final keen of exultation and farewell. As if in impossible response, a dolphin sang into the air, hanging for an elongated instant against the sanguine sky, before vanishing into velvet indigo. The power of this striking image ignited the certainty of an irrevocable verdict:

THIS, I understood, was where dolphins belong.
No walls
No nets
No fences
No pens
Free among the rash elements!

This was and always would be the only true sojourn of the Dolphin and *this*, I saw, was what no enclosure or aquarium could ever hold or hope to show people. Here, all around me, surpassing any argument, was the infinite and undeniable reason why it was **wrong,** why it was a *lie* that there could ever be any man-made replacement for the world's immeasurable oceanic expanses.

There was a final return to the Key Largo attraction, pre-booked into our itinerary before our trip's completion, and we found ourselves grappling with the idea of returning to the dreary place. Whether I went or not, they already had my money — still the internal debate raged. I went in the end, though some of the group chose not to. Some whisper of intuition led me.

Hovering and submerged, I stared at the chain-link fence as several dolphins arced towards me. Before their great, shinning eyes, I couldn't help but wonder that they held any good will or curiosity towards the species that had caught and caged them. Looking upon them I understood how this journey had fulfilled its intended purpose. The wild dolphins had left their mark; the lesson had been taught, leaving me with some true grasp of what was forever lost to those trapped behind human barriers, however soft or subtle those barriers might sometimes seem. I knew now unequivocally why, be it sea pen or pool — capturing and confining these creatures was indeed *intrinsically wrong.*

But people see what they want to see — or are told to see: dolphins, ethereal, ever-smiling and unanimously eager to enjoy human company. Awash in the gratification of their own experiences and perceived connection, most never pause to reflect on the ruinous and exacting toll inevitably paid by the *dolphins* for fleeting human pleasure. The loss of an irreplaceable life in the boundless oceans; friends, family, lovers, children, community, the splendor of the hunt — simple *freedom of choice* — *stolen!*

Glowing stories of peoples' marvelous and magical dolphin-swim experiences fail to carry credence — that its all worthwhile — fail to make it acceptable to steal these creatures away from everything precious to them, to snatch them from their oceanic birthright and cage them for human delight and amusement. Though certain dolphins, in certain situations, appear willing to give of themselves in certain ways — this in no way denotes benediction upon those who would *TAKE* from them. An endless stream of enthusiastic, thrill-seeking humans availing themselves to the pleasure of the dolphins' innately enchanting company can never replace what they've lost. *No* amount of human affection can truly justify doing this to them.

Looking up from these tumbling, igneous thoughts, I found one of the dolphins had appeared before me. Meeting that recondite, obsidian gaze, I saw the truth of it all reflected there, and suddenly I felt such a terrible *shame* for my species. Yet, together the two of us rose to graze the surface for breath. Descending, we were joined by the other five dolphins. Opening ranks, they invited me into their midst and curiously, for a few moments they held the exact formation *The Liquid Six* had taken in the sea. Synchronous, curving through the water, we rose as one to respire.

Then I saw the other two — restrained in an adjoining pen, sweet, solemn faces pressed up against the steel fence, watching. My heart almost burst with the wrenching sight of those wistful countenances peering through the bars. Rushing over, distress sent me surging back and forth along the iron barrier, the dolphins pacing my every move. They called, and heart-wrung, I answered. At last, we halted regarding each other through the divide.

What could I do? What power could give them their lives back? Their *real* lives. It was time to go, reluctantly relinquishing their pitiful company, perishing inside. Yet one of them lingered, gazing up at me. How could I just walk away? My recent epiphany told me I could not simply abandon them — not without first making a pact, a whispering promise:

"I will try to help."

CHAPTER SIX

MORE ANCIENT THAN WORDS

"Drink to me only with thine eyes,
And I will pledge thee with mine."
Ben Jonson.

Cornered between dilemma's difficult horns, I struggled with a bitter decision. Though I longed to continue my initiation among the Cubano Dolphins, the naked facts reined me in. Like the captives in the Florida Keys, the Cubano Dolphins were enslaved, living stolen lives, and their situation stood for everything I had come to abhor. Thus far, I had been Umberto's guest, and so, exempt from any entry fee at the Cuban dolphinarium — but I couldn't assume this arrangement would necessarily persist throughout future visits. In refusing to support a calculating system growing obese on the dolphins' unwilling misfortune, I was only too aware of what I'd have to do if money were demanded from me at the dolphinarium's gate. The resolution tore and scalded — I would have to turn my back on Juan, Unior, Choney and Christine forever. As a matter of profound principle, I couldn't knowingly contribute to this machine of misery.

I returned to Cuba in autumn and unable to stay the dreaded verdict, I went straight to the dolphinarium to settle the matter at once. As ever, Umberto reacted to my unannounced return as if he had seen me only the week before and again I found myself ushered past the ticket wicket, tacitly graced once more as his guest. Amid our greetings, my private euphoria momentarily eclipsed the news Umberto was relating.

Suddenly I realized what the trainer was telling me: In May, only two months after my previous visit, Choney had given birth. Though her tiny infant was born lively and healthy, only days after it had come into the world, her baby had somehow become tangled in the net and drowned! I blanched at this terrible news, unable to formulate a response — something so precious, lost before I had even known of it — and Choney, herself so young and slight, at only the tender age of ten. How had this loss affected her? Yet I couldn't help but wonder what kind of life the little one had been spared, born bereft of freedom.

Of course it was only a matter of time before Choney or Christine conceived again and I inquired what would stop the same thing from occurring once more? Thus pressed, the trainer told me that there were no plans in place to prevent further tragedies. Nothing would be done. It was difficult for me to grasp this Siberian attitude, but in time I would learn that such "details" were often left to sort themselves out — or rather unravel at will.

There was no need to wonder if the dolphins remembered me. Christine, Juan, Choney and Unior all appeared at the swaying dock to greet me, their presence more radiant than ever memory allowed. Choney however, soon withdrew from our party, gliding away to brood alone by the net. Was she haunted by the empty space beside her that should have contained a tiny, fifing infant?

Soon after the dolphin show, I made another unwanted discovery when I found Juan and Unior being trained to tow tourists around on their dorsal fins for "dolphin rides." Looking on with a darkening countenance, I recalled an article I had come across several years previously in some accursed magazine or other, describing a dream come true: "swimming with dolphins in sunny Florida." Breathless, I had poured over the dreamy description of the encounter among the "shining, smiling, majestic sea mammals", which had climaxed with a "ride", pulled on a dolphin's fin. In light of what I now knew, the memory made me cringe. But before me was the result of millions of others sharing exactly this same fabricated dream: Juan and Unior, piggybacking tourists for their supper. I left them that first day feeling helplessly protective and undeniably downcast.

At the end of each day, I would join Umberto and the rest of the dolphinarium staff on the Cuban bus, heavy with the smell of sweet cigar smoke. Held in the late afternoon's heat, bumping and jolting along in the belly of the rumbling, dusty bus and lulled by the lilting chatter around me, I'd feel the seeping ache of limbs immersed in cool water most of the day. Watching the shore breeze by out the open window, I imagined I saw dolphins in every folded wave, in every creased shirt. Wind blown and salt burnished, my meager possessions abandoned in a soggy pile on the adobe villa's bathroom floor, I'd fly straight back to the sea; drifting through the warm swells to roll in a cloud of the day's happenings, until the sun sank, stealing the last copper stain from the waves.

Every possible moment was spent with the dolphins, unless they were involved with training and tourists, both of which I instinctively avoided associating myself with. At their perceived invite, I would join Juan, Christine and Unior in the turbid water to twirl and dive alongside their sleekness. Always, they encouraged me to dive deeper and hold my breath longer — better teachers of aqueous movement could not be found. Though I found joy in every instant of their companionship, I remained aware of a constant sadness — they were not free. There were reminders everywhere, not the least among them Choney, who so often chose to spend much of her time alone, drifting with her face pressed to the net, a small silver lump seeming wrapped in a fog of private melancholy.

Unior remained the most forward in his inquires. Several times he caught me snoozing on the dock between swims (trying to regain some warmth), and lightly clopped me on the head, before ducking cheekily below the water. At Unior's insistence, I lent him my limbs to investigate, which he did by mouthing — running his powerful jaws up and down an arm or leg. Fortunately, he was usually very reserved with his tickly teeth. Though dolphins' sense of smell is thought to have all but vanished through evolution, they retain a good sense of taste and are thought to be able to pick up chemical cues from the water. While Unior may have been exploring me in this way, I came to perceive these interactions as a sort of test of trust. Despite the rows of pointed dentition, I did not hesitate in delivering the desired limb into the expectant jaws, whenever any of the dolphins requested such sharing.

Juan was less forward, seeming a rather contemplative observer. He would drift close by, studying me, leaning his face this way and that, regarding me with one eye and then the other. In fact, as the initial days progressed, the two of us came to spend quite a lot of time in one another's company, drifting side by side in the water. Juan dissipated my initial shyness, inviting my hesitant hands against the subtle silks of his sides, flank, chest, belly and back. *Wondrous* skin. None of the many attempts at describing the limpid qualities of dolphins' skin have ever quite captured the indescribable charms of sumptuous contact and so, it must join the annals of their inherent mystery and allure.

Curving alongside me just so, Juan seemed to invite me to dance. The two of us took to exploring the lagoon together, and at his side, I ventured right down through layers of temperature and verdure to the dim, silty floor of the lagoon twenty feet below. Sometimes the other dolphins joined us, and watching as they flew through the water all around me, tumbling, rolling, curving, standing on their heads, they taught me to use the space and dimension their element afforded. They seemed to take tremendous joy in their weightless freedom — and indeed, before their capture, they must have known nothing else. I also absorbed something of signal and syncopation — and began to glimpse and understand how their movements were a communication in itself. Like dancers, flourishing and arching their bodies, high spirits, tensions, joyous abandon and brooding melancholy were all sensuously conveyed, and though it seemed utterly artless and effortless, I knew they were aware of it; consciously, *purposefully* expressing themselves through grace, breath and movement. It was no less astonishing to find myself invited into their capricious dances!

But not all was dancing and diving. I also came to learn a great deal about how the dolphin's lives were imposed upon and dictated by human greed, ignorance and dominance. I saw how this weighted down their fleet spirits, and left them staring out through the net at the setting sun, enveloped in an air of grave disconsolation at the end of each day.

As I came to know the cast of characters that punctuated the dolphins' days, the lot of a life in captivity was revealed first hand, in squalid and serrated detail. I met Iago, the head trainer, hulking and dark in countenance and mood. He was the slave driver, the one who deprived the dolphins of food, day after day, to bend their wills. *He* was the reason I came to dread the "swim-with-the-dolphins" sessions that now followed almost every show. Iago would arrive at the small dock, barking out orders at Juan and Unior and issuing repeated ear-splitting blasts on his whistle. More often than not, he quickly degenerated into abrasive screaming and I was galvanized to find it was not uncommon for him to remove his shoe in order to strike the dolphins if they hesitated or disobeyed him!

My appalled protestations, far from deterring the trainer, would send him further into snarling rage, causing the dolphins to suffer even more. I had no power to stop him. The dolphinarium's manager, preferred to stay closeted away in some little cubby hole, indifferent, leaving daily decisions regarding the dolphins and their treatment to the head trainer — Iago.

Umberto, my friend, incontestably sweet natured (though absent minded), was certainly not about to initiate any confrontation with intimidating Iago, so that just left Benicio, the third trainer. Stalwart and stubborn, he was the dolphins' only hope of defense, the only one who would stand up to Iago's tyranny. Though he was always being reprimanded for crossing the fiend on their behalf, Benicio had a way with the dolphins and could get them to work when everyone else failed. Things tended to fall apart when he was away, and so he was never fired, despite Iago's unceasing lies, complaints and tantrums.

Benicio I found, truly cared for the dolphins. He was a knowledgeable

wellspring of information and spoke a number of languages, including
English. A friendship ensued, but there were certain things about which we
would never see eye to eye. Benicio could never understand that though he
was a kind jailer — he was still a jailer. He firmly believed that the dolphins
should never be beaten or deprived of food and he always looked towards
their health, but he just didn't understand why keeping them captive, even
under the best possible conditions was *wrong*. The ethics of it eluded him —
that their loss of personal freedom and the suffering derived thereby, was
hardly different than what he, himself would experience, were he
unrightfully thrown in jail, though kept clothed and fed. In time, an ironic
insight came to me as I realized how many Cubans considered themselves
unhappy captives in their own country.

However, in a way, as the years went by, I became almost glad, for if
Benicio had ever experienced a sudden rush of realization and left the
dolphins to Iago's "tender mercies" their lives, I think, would have become
unbearable. So Benicio remained a sort of champion, fighting to make their
lives more tolerable and for this, I will always be deeply thankful.

Juan continued to seek my company and we were to spend many long hours
just drifting together, as if lost in a mutual reverie. Often, he vocalized in low,
murmuring moth-hushed tones — and thus whispered to, I sighed. Peering
into his dark eyes, I caught glimpses, incomparably poignant, of something
I could not name. Those nebulous, limpid pools held something radiant as
it was intangible, and thus linked, he poured his strange incandescence into
me; an experience both alien and intimate, beyond anything I had ever dared
conceive. Among the hidden jewels revealed to me during our long, liquid
gazes, were the dolphin's pupils; shaped like two inverted black teardrops.
I had never read of this in any book. The effect was startlingly strange and
yet undeniably beautiful — all of them had those hauntingly aware,
otherworldly eyes.

Many times I woke from these rhapsodies to find both Choney and Unior
drifting close by, watching our interactions with something akin to fascination.
They made no move to interfere, yet their attentions were held for a long time.
As I became more familiar with the dolphins' low tolerance for that which they
deemed uninteresting, their unbroken scrutiny became a clear indication of
something extraordinary unfolding between Juan and I — something
experienced, rather than understood — sweeping me up far from any echo of
shore. I had never imagined such things could unfold under a blue sky.

One afternoon, Benicio appeared for a training session with Juan and
Unior, and asked if I would go over to the bigger dock and visit with

Juan & I.

Christine and Choney to distract them from disrupting the males, as they were so often fond of doing. I agreed only to try. The two of them were already there, waiting for me. Most pleased, I settled down to meet Christine's offered pec-fin with my palm, as she'd made it clear that she remembered this pec-pat ritual from previous visits. As always, Choney hung back, watching over Christine's shoulder. And then it happened — Choney slid forward and made contact: a simple nudge on the wrist.

I lay my open palm on the water and hesitantly, Choney lay her chin there, until my touch came to rest on the shivering softness under her jaw. She had waited until the moment spoke to her, before choosing to offer her quiet gift of touch and trust. The invisible boundary surpassed, each passing moment saw the slight dolphin becoming bolder, rolling and turning to encourage further caresses. Even as I reveled in this new level of relationship, I had to wonder, what had precipitated this change in Choney?

After the last show, it was time for the day's final "dolphin-swim" session. However it wasn't long before Juan and Unior both just stopped working. Puzzled at their unusual behavior, Benicio was unsure what to make of it. When Iago arrived, followed by a flock of eager, jabbering tourists, things took a turn for the worse. The little dock was flooded with people, all trying to imitate the trainers' hand signals, attempting to order the dolphins to jump, or sing, or rise up out of the water and "kiss" their sun burnt faces. But amid the commotion, Juan and Unior continued to refuse all commands. Infuriated, Iago started screaming at the dolphins, attempting to beat them with a sandal in his obscene rage and Benicio's immediate interjection, ignited a ferocious argument.

Wisely, Juan and Unior fled the scene. I followed suit, retreating round to the channel that connected the dolphin's lagoon to the larger salt lake beyond it. Staring out over the water, I waited for the wretched scene unfolding behind me to cease. I wondered how the lake connected to the ocean. Tides and sea life found their way into the dolphin's lagoon — could dolphins ever find their way out to oceanic freedom from the lake? Was escape *possible?*

Not until the flurry and fester of tourists and training had subsided did I return to the dock. All four dolphins swept me up amongst them and together we parted the silted waters. Moving in perfect time among them in this manner had an almost immediately calming effect after the recent nastiness, and I wondered if our synchronous travels affected them similarly.

Juan and I soon slowed to gaze upon one other. In the presence of those great, star gathering eyes, I felt myself both dissolved and replenished. With gentle hands, I smoothed his skin, as if to rid it of recent unhappy memories. Benicio appeared, announcing the imminent arrival of the bus. Espying a rosy flower growing in the dust, he plucked it from its place and with exaggerated gallantry presented it to me. Juan looked on. A moment later, with a flourish of his own, Juan presented me with a small, yellow, ovaline leaf. So much can be said without uttering a word.

Every morning, stepping through the coolness of the long shadows, I came to greet the four dolphins on the little wavering dock. I was delighted to find Choney no longer keeping herself aloof, though her inclusion in the morning greetings amended the collective dynamic, as the slight (and no longer shy) dolphin now added her avid efforts, pushing all the others aside to solicit contact! Christine, uttering an audible snort of derision and flourishing her flukes, usually departed as if refusing to dignify such rudeness with reply, while Juan wisely kept out of Choney's reach, patiently waiting off to one side. Unior however, didn't give up so easily, coming up under or beside little Choney, using his bulk to push her aside. Once it became clear that this ploy did very little to displace his feisty mate, he usually resorted to nipping at her tail — provoking a strenuous stream of protestations and sometimes an ensuing chase.

With visibility hardly ever more than eight feet (or a dolphin length), much of their doings remained mysterious, as when Unior surfaced suddenly before me, completely draped in a great shawl of seaweed, pausing just long enough to catch my astonishment, before re-submerging to continue his strange doings.

Yet everywhere, motes of illumination fell, where once so much had appeared opaque. With Juan curving around me, I was initiated into the midst of their mysterious "dolphin-tumults", where amongst them, I would dive and twirl in the shrouded depths before bursting up through the surface to see them leaping against the sun. I found these revelries dimmed only by the barrier of my exhaustion — how I wished for their endurance — to be able to fly effortlessly up out of the water with them! Another of ten thousand sighs...

These fleet, unfettered moments, with the dolphins' nebulous silhouettes streaming against the sunbeams, I found reminiscent of the wild dolphins — but in their captive state, it could never last. Always the whistles would blow, the music would blare and the tourists coagulate in the stands, ready for the show to begin. And still Unior and especially Juan refused to work, despite the sometimes harsh rebukes they received. Our days always ended with the four dolphins in a row, faces pressed against the net, staring out past the barrier. Hungry for life.

However our mornings began, it was not until after the show, when Iago conducted the "dolphin-swims" (or *tourist-hauls,* as I came to call them), that the pervading mood for the day would be revealed. In addition to this thrice-daily wretchedness, Iago sometimes brought people down on the docks while the rest of the staff had afternoon siesta, in order to pocket the money he solicited. One such incident stood out as particularly abrasive:

After a morning of cajoling and flirting, Iago appeared, followed by one of the many dissolute flesh pots he often carried on with. Both Juan and Unior initially refused all contact with the woman's grasping, fuchsia talons. Using leftover scraps of dead fish that Iago had withheld earlier, she began trying to lure the dolphins over to her, only to refuse them the fish and instead try to grab their dorsal fins. Wanting no part of this, the dolphins retreated again. Further (well-earned) insult came when (for a ragged shred of fish held up), Juan refused to touch his face to hers in the parody of a "kiss." In irate response to this dismissal, the woman tried, in a reviling fit of peevishness, to *kick* him! Compounding this appalling display of human manners, Iago then began yelling at Juan and Unior, threatening their refusal of his commands. Only when the fish was used up — and the dolphins gone, did the repugnant pair retreat from the dock.

I would see these sorts of scenarios repeated many times, always leaving me sick and aching with bitter anguish at my inability to shield my companions from the miserable situation they endured. Once their tormenters were gone, I would slip quietly into the water beside Juan to offer him my apologies. More than once, he responded by gliding straight to the net and pulling on it with mighty vigor! I was all too familiar with this gesture, having seen it before. He wanted *out!* I responded the only way I could, looking him straight in the eye and pulling on the net myself, to tell him I understood and felt exactly the same.

The dolphins' moods often remained tarnished after these incidents, yet the flowing multitudes, drawn by the lure of their fixed smiles, remained ignorant of what sorrows troubled the silver wonders before them. I studied the crowds for even *one* person to approach them with an iota of respect or understanding, but all were pushing blindly forward, eager for a chance to touch, to grab, to fondle the dolphins — no thoughts for anything but the expectant gratification of being pulled through the water like some mockery of a Greek legend on a dolphin's fin. The irony was rending; that the dolphins' own innate charm drew people to pay money to get close to them — inspiring the greedy and heartless to steal so many from their undersea communities, to forever twirl, nod and squeak before ignorant crowds. And I knew it would never stop — not until realization of the dolphins' reality caused minds and hearts to change. So, I began to take every opportunity to answer people's questions, working quietly to leave them with something of true substance, about which to think.

The end of November brought rain and chilled winds, which made the water of the dolphins' lagoon seem warmer. Rain meant most tourists relinquished outdoor activities for fruity cocktails in hotel lounges. Relieved of their regular burden of human company, I found the dolphins' spirits generally improved with the stormy weather, bringing vivacious moods, racing, chasing and leaping as they cut frothy furrows through the drab water.

Lured to Juan's side by the tilt of his beloved face on the grey water, we began a slow, sensuous dance in the rain. Our moods matched the subdued air, and together with our faces close, we watched the rain falling. Our communion was broken by the blast of music over the loudspeakers, announcing the commencement of the dolphin show, to the almost abandoned grounds. A rude awakening.

Afterwards, while picking my way along the rocky edge of the lagoon back towards the small dock, I glanced up to find Christine and Choney, keeping pace with me. The force of their gaze gave me pause; they were *trying* to get my attention. Then I saw what they were up to — somehow, they had got hold of one of the swim fins I'd left on the dock! Realization perceived, the two dolphins began to ham up their act before my pretense of indignance, larking and gamboling about with the stolen item in a most hilarious manner. Attempting to stifle my growing mirth, I retrieved the other fin, to wave meaningfully at them while fixing the gleeful pair with my best fish-eye. To no avail! Between giggles, I played the part of the cross dupe, while Choney and Christine jauntily paraded their abducted prize before me. Having enjoyed their joke, the duo relented and finally cast the swim fin ashore, where, still chuckling, I retrieved it.

But these sunny moments were heavily impinged upon. Iago, on the tail end of a week-long drinking binge, was seething in the depths of a mood black and foul, even for him. He had been showing up late, eyes bloodshot, stinking and unmistakably hung-over, every day. During the next dolphin-hauling session, he began treating Juan and Unior so horrendously, even modest Umberto was moved to protest! Benicio was livid and a fistfight almost erupted between them right on the dock. Instead, snarling and cursing, Iago retreated, taking the majority of the dolphins' fish with him. This practice was not uncommon, and I discovered the dolphins were being deprived of much of their allotted food in this way.

These excessive joys and sorrows took their toll on me, and a day came when I could not bring myself to face what lay before me at the dolphinarium. Pensive and weary, I chose to remain in the sea, to drift and swim in an attempt to refuel my worn spirit. Even in so brief a time, that place had left me utterly fatigued — how did the dolphins endure it? Realizing the bitter answer, even the ocean's balm dimmed — Juan, Unior, Christine and Choney had *no choice.* Amid the troubled waves, tears and rain were indistinguishable.

Early the next morning, I received a call from Benicio, telling me that during my absence the previous day, Juan had refused to eat, or allow anyone close to him. Butterflies of concern pounding in my breast, I all but flew to the lagoon. With Benicio looking on, I knelt tentatively down on the dock. Juan came up to greet me along with the other three dolphins, just as he had every other morning. The trainer's puzzlement increased, as Juan readily swallowed the fish he was offered. There was no sign of his earlier behavior. Choney, Christine and Unior soon dispersed upon errands of their own, while Juan remained quietly in the water beside me. Lightly describing unknown hieroglyphs across his silken sides, I wondered what transpired behind the precious umbra of his gaze; what secrets his silence kept.

During the show, I watched closely as Benicio conducted Unior and Juan through their repertoire of tricks. After only a minute or two, Juan ceased to work, deigning instead, to drift at the side of the dock, looking up at me where I waited on shore. However, immediately upon *Iago's* arrival, Juan turned and fled to the far side of the lagoon, hiding himself behind the bigger dock!

So, the villain is revealed! Not surprising, of course, but what, I wondered, could Iago have done that was so much more awful than his usual monstrous behavior? All attempts involving whistles and fish buckets failed to dislodge Juan from his refuge. Finally, at a loss, Benicio asked me to take an entire mackerel and swim over to the dolphin and see if I couldn't lure him out, while he waited, wet-suit clad, floating out in the middle of the lagoon with the remainder of Juan's fish in a bucket.

A little hesitantly, I embarked across the lagoon, hoping Juan would not flee my approach. He did not, and I was able to glide to a halt along side him. With a soft caress of greeting, I peered into his shadowed face, trying mutely to offer some comfort while seeking to understand his distress. Declining the fish, Juan continued to accept my touch, but would not be coaxed from his spot. And so, leaning my cheek against his, I wound a protective arm over his scarred back to hold and lull him. Very slowly, I felt the tension easing from his body. Curving against my solace, he kept his eyes, brimming with indigo secrets, on mine. The sight of him, so furtive and uncertain, brought stinging pangs of helpless and protective fury.

When at last a reluctant Juan finally consented to accompany me out into the lagoon, where Benicio still waited, he continued to keep his side pressed to mine, seeking to perpetuate the balm and support of nearness. Exchanging a meaningful glance with the trainer, I shared my observations regarding a probable connection between Juan's disturbed behavior, and some unknown and nefarious act of Iago's. After Juan, with progressive vigor, swallowed the contents of the fish bucket, Benicio returned to shore, for a little word with the peccant Iago.

Eventually Juan's spirits seemed to rise, and when he was ready, we joined the other dolphins and the five of us descended to soar and climb in the privacy of the dim water. Flickering with them in sublime synchrony, I again became aware of that palpable infusion of the group's unity and strength. I was within their mystery and had never been more at home.

Then, with a smooth arc, Juan diverted my path, leading me towards the net before angling purposefully downward. There, shrouded in the dark water Juan revealed to me with a flourish, what were unmistakably the beginnings of a hole in the net's mesh! I could see the ropes had been frayed and cut in strategic spots and now the barrier's tattered wound was almost big enough for a dolphin to slip through! *A hole! A plan of escape!* Feeling the thickness of the rope and realizing they had nothing but their peg-like teeth to saw through it, I understood the magnitude of the task undertaken. Still, it would only be a matter of time — escape *was* possible! Silent and suddenly brimming with hope, I sent out my thanks out to Juan for the trust of this shared secret.

Time again, for training and tourists. Juan abandoned the dock after one flipper shake, lots of screaming from Iago, and no food, heading straight to the net where he remained, with his back to everyone. When it was all over and done for the day, he still held the same attitude. Kneeling on the dock, I called softly to him, aware how my voice strained with worry, but he would not come. The following morning Juan still floated there alone, his face pressed to the barrier. I can only imagine how hungry he must have been. But when I surfaced alongside him, gently nudging and seeking to distract him from his melancholy, he became elusive. Downhearted, I returned to the dock, looking up to see a swelling crowd of people watching, filming, staring and pointing. The sight made me want to flee — but there was nowhere to go.

Then I felt a caress slide across my shoulder blades — Juan. Side by side, we turned our backs on the crowd's clamor. Juan lay his silken cheek against the water, seeking to hold my gaze and I felt myself delicately drawn...into the aqueous hollows of a dolphin's inner seas. In those nacreous, unsounded depths, he and I seemed to speak in a language far more ancient and universal than any worldly words. Lost in his unwavering, sun-dappled gaze, I felt as though I might dissolve into the mysterious fire of his secret, ineffable core. I was in over my head.

Shrill whistles and raucous music woke us from our mutual trance. Show time. With much distress, I looked on as Juan refused Iago's commands and again delivered himself to the net, to stare mournfully out past it. Strangely, Unior would not stop staring at me. It became eerie. A persistent inkling told me it had something to do with Juan, and though I could almost see the gears turning in his head, I found myself unable to imagine what he might be thinking. Whatever Unior's thoughts, Juan and I were becoming inseparable, seeking one another's companionship at every available moment. Through it all, the other dolphins continued to evince much curiosity and interest over our exchanges. But always the burgeoning wonder was immolated by the daily shows and the wretchedness that inevitably followed. This place had become both the delight and the horror of my existence.

On my last morning, Unior, Choney and Christine all came to greet me on the dock as part of our morning ritual — only Juan failed to join us, which was unusual. My concern over his manifest absence was temporarily eclipsed as Choney became especially insistent, pushing Christine and Unior back, to collect my complete attention herself. Today however, neither Christine nor Unior were giving up so easily, and much tussling, whistling and squawking erupted before me. Despite her delicate size, Choney was commandeering the prized position of front and center, against the two larger dolphins, seeming intent on prolonging a *very* focused pec-pat game. In fact, I began to wonder if perhaps "game" were not too idle a word to attach to such intense behavior.

Afterward, while Iago and his vociferous entourage presided over the usual grotesque happenings, I settled on the bigger dock to write, trying to ignore the ache of my heart and the snarling brutalities that echoed amid tourist laughter from the scene across the lagoon. Poor, poor Juan. As if transported by my thoughts of him, the dolphin suddenly appeared before me! Sighing, I delivered myself to his dark gaze as he gently rested his head in my hands. Across the lagoon, I could see that Christine had taken Juan's place, hauling tourists, shaking fins and planting false, forced kisses on over-rouged faces. But for the moment, Juan and I were free.

He led me on a slow tour around the perimeter of the lagoon. I had never realized the beauty to be found around its edges until our tour du jardin. Together we sailed among jeweled fish, flickering lazily through sun-speckled filaments, candy-like shrimp snapping, anemones undulating poisonous, tentacled cilia, colored corals and flowing sea flowers. We saw blue crabs, testily waving their claws, tiny frog-eyed gobies, alert and sail-backed and a host of other beasties skittering for cover, as our floating cloud-shadows momentarily dimmed the sunken seascape below us.

Having finished their tourist-related duties, Unior and Choney joined us for the completion of the circuit. At their inclusion, Juan, with eyes bright, began to bestir himself around me in a restless manner. A moment later, Unior also began sliding against me in sensuous request for caresses, expertly pacing Juan and I as we dove and spiraled, still making flirtatious bids for my attention, eyes half-lidded, pec-fins outstretched in a plea for caresses.

Curving against the dim sea floor, Juan signaled to me with a meaningful glance and a nod, and in perfect synchrony, the two of us began to speed upwards. I broke the surface to see Juan soar into the air above me, twisting to smash against the water in a spectacular breach! The splash was terrific — and then he flew up anew to breach again and again and *again,* throwing himself upon the water with mighty abandon! Completing his magnificent display, Juan glided up royally to collect me at his side. I was mute with awe at his show of vigor and power — wondering if it hadn't been a message for Unior to back off. But Juan wasn't done yet. Once more, he led me down to dim depths and on his cue we again raced to the surface. This time, he arched high and noble in a series of stunning leaps, all around me! Spell bound, my very breath was stolen. Perhaps content with my reaction Juan then swam right into my overwhelmed arms. It took a moment before I realized a great clamoring lay behind us. Turning, I beheld another day's crowd, snapping photos, filming and yammering excitedly. Regarding this uncouth sight a moment, Juan led me away with him.

At length, the chill of the water crept under my skin and shivering furiously, I realized I would have to leave Juan's humid embrace long enough to recollect some warmth in the last of the fading sun. My mind was swimming with thoughts of the dolphin and the meaning this unforeseen bond come to life between us. Even suffused with the strange radiance of his nearness, I remained wary of becoming blinded by it. If there was one thing the dolphins had shown me, it was something of the true wildness of their enigmatic essence. To impress a human outlook or response upon them, would blind me to their true nature. Fact, I had found, was far stranger than fiction.

In the final moments of my visit, the dolphins gathered round, but I had eyes only for Juan. I could not imagine days without him, apart from him. I didn't know how to say good-bye, and so I simply immersed into his gaze, shadowed and luminous. Though I remained unable to name what I sensed there, it had, through some inscrutable alchemy, become part of me. At last, somehow, I tore myself away, stumbling and blinded in the last rays of the setting sun, my eyes feeling full of cobwebs.

CHAPTER SEVEN

SOLSTICE

"A lyric of love, which words cannot tell."
George William Curtis

Reeling from the recent wonder, still enwreathed within a remnant nimbus of lotic light and shadow, I had to catch my balance — returning to my sobering work with the conservation society.

We'd already caught wind that a connection existed between Marineland and Cuba, and I'd returned with information confirming this. I'd discovered that about five years previously, Marineland had collaborated with a team from a Cuban aquarium, and captured dolphins from Varadero — the very same shores I had so recently returned from! Marineland had dwindled down to only *four* dolphins, Duke and three other remaining 'old timers' from my childhood, and the park needed its ailing stock replenished with fresh blood.

Over the years I would see film footage of dolphin captures and speak with people once responsible for orchestrating them. This violent procedure begins by chasing down a family of dolphins in speedboats, corralling them in shallow water and encircling them in nets. Like most marine parks, Marineland was hunting for small, unmarked dolphins, three-to-seven years old — children and youngsters — these being the "cutest" and the easiest to manage, bully and train.

During that Varadero capture, I was told older dolphins repeatedly tore holes in the nets and held them down, sacrificing their freedom to allow the young and mothers with infants to escape. These bigger, older, battered and scarred dolphins were rejected and released, but the men continued their efforts. In order to subdue, sequester and select their prey, they leapt bodily upon the struggling captives to wrangle them, fighting and crying, into the boat for closer examination.

In the sheer panic this violence provokes, dolphins often ram the nets, blindly trying to flee, and in minutes can become hopelessly tangled and drown. The lucky ones, deemed too large or old may be dumped back into the water — those less fortunate will never see family or freedom again. The resulting trauma of this separation (especially for mothers and young) in such social and sensitive beings is never taken into consideration, nor the effects of depletion on local dolphin populations, as families and communities are brutally wrenched apart by these raids. Over several days, seventeen dolphins were captured along that stretch of Cuban coastline, decimating the Varadero peninsula's resident wild dolphin population. Before such captures, the sight of dolphins surfing and feeding just off shore was not uncommon — and afterwards, almost unheard of.

The Cuban military took several dolphins for their own nefarious purposes and two went to a Cuban aquarium. Marineland took *eight*. The remaining two captives, I had come to know well — they were Christine and Choney (then only about six years old). *This* was the reprehensible truth of how they had come to the lagoon where I met them — and in a bizarre coincidence, Marineland was responsible for their capture. Would people still be as eager to attend these places if they knew what the dolphins had been through? Had I known the *real* cost, I could never have paid that first paltry, laden, dollar at the gate — I would have fled, sickened and saddened, back to the Sea.

Now, I wondered if certain tides ever carried a melancholy taste of home to the Cubano Dolphins? Yet the other dolphins that had been sent to Marineland had fared far worse, locked away in cramped, chlorinated, concrete tanks. No more sunshine, no more moonlight, no more warm wild wind or waves, no more stars — ever again. Small wonder then, that in the five years since their capture and incarceration at Marineland, half of those Cuban-caught dolphins had already died (and in another five years, *only two* survivors would remain). There was no statement a marine park, corporation or government could issue that could excuse such wrongs or erase the tragic and untimely deaths and suffering of those dolphins. And so our determined efforts to educate the public continued.

Amid such grim work (that circuitously concerned them), I missed the Cubano Dolphins. I was determined to discover more about the Cuban dolphin slave trade, and so long as I remained exempt from demands for monetary support, I could safely return to the Cuban dolphinarium, which I did in spring.

My relationship with the dolphins possessed an atemporal ambiance, which superseded any rifts of absence — for the most part they picked up right where they'd left off with me. I arrived to find Unior, Christine, Choney and

Juan all drifting in a row, facing out through the net in the same melancholy pose I had left them, five months before — only now I knelt in morning's cool shadows instead of evening's fading heat. I had hoped to find that Juan's net-vandalizing ploys had succeeded, releasing them into the much larger salt lake, or even the ocean beyond — but nothing appeared to have changed.

Espying my arrival, three dolphins roused themselves, gliding over: Christine, sable and broad with her wide, Bedouin eyes; Unior, with his pirate squint and notched rostrum; and just behind them, slender, falcon-eyed and immaculate, Choney — a triplicate wave of welcome, sliding and splashing into my arms!

However, Juan had chosen to remain alone at the net and his absence troubled me. Lifting my gaze across the water, I glimpsed the sullen, silver dome of his head, stirring the surface. Suddenly, like a drawn sword, Juan rose up almost his entire length out of the water, right up, as if to climb right over the netting! Unable to find either a means of escape, nor sustain the height of his position, he repeated this sudden burst, releasing harsh, ugly, bitter sounds each time he fell back into the water. Progressing to a peak of apparent frustration, Juan rose up again and pulled vigorously and repeatedly on the be-slimed barrier with his jaws!

Immediately I slipped into the water, determined to attend his distress, but he refused to meet my concerned countenance, continuing instead, to pull defiantly on the net. To this I responded with a pledge of buoyant support — pulling on the net myself, with a mighty conviction, of which he took note. Slowly, heavily, Juan lifted his unmistakably unhappy gaze onto mine; dark pools of melancholy fire.

Conversing later with Umberto and Benicio, I learned that Juan rarely bothered with any of his trained behaviors or pulling tourists on his dorsal fin. Instead, he seemed to spend most of his time brooding by the net, pulling on it and devising a succession of holes, which Benicio, with regular vigilance, continuously found and patched. Neither Iago's brutality, nor Benicio's patient cajoling, had been able to turn Juan from his ways. However, for the time being, Benicio had arranged to oversee the "swim-with-the-dolphins" business, rather than Iago, thus significantly reducing the daily quotient of yelling, abuse and wretchedness — respective relief.

I reunited with Juan after the day's last tourists had gone. His spirits seemed to have risen, as evidenced by his curving presence, nibbling and nudging to tempt further caresses. Supple skin, having never known snow; sumptuous, opiate, marred only by the Saturnian shark-bite scars on his back. Each morning I found him pacing the net, famished and forlorn, or rebellious and raging; always miserable, always pulling at the barrier, seeking a way

Juan & I, with Unior looking on.

out. Yet silent patience never failed to lead him from his confined edge, at last relinquishing his misery for companionship. Always, it began with my gesture mirroring his — pulling on the net.

It was now rare to see Juan join the other dolphins on their jaunts about the lagoon, or as they erupted into their curious bouts of rapid chasing and splashing. Still, those celebratory moods seemed contagious, and while the others sheared watery furrows all around us, Juan sprang to life, rearing out of the water and nudging me playfully as I responded in kind. Together we'd swirl and spiral in the nubiferous depths, he, curving around me spiritedly, offering the sliding caress of his ivory teeth, never leaving the faintest scratch upon my limbs. Sometimes Unior (perhaps no longer content to observe from the sidelines), would rush amongst us, overtaking his rival and attempting to collect my caresses himself. If, during our helical flights in the dim water, I mistook Unior for Juan, the larger male appeared seized with fits of delight, twisting, whirling, whistling and leaping as if possessed.

Andante, the rhythm would slow and the overture recede, guiding Juan and I to resume drifting together; two bright stars, locked in magnetic, binary orbit. He held such a diffident charm and sinking into his unwavering gaze, I felt him stranger than all my poor thoughts.

Even when all of us would come to drift and rest together for a time,

Unior could still be seen trying to entice me into attending him. Ignoring this mischief, I'd remain basking contentedly between Juan and Christine. Choney chose the periphery, resting beyond the safety of Unior's bulk, while he continued trying to catch my eye over the sparkling curve of Christine's back. Christine appeared to have taken a shine to me, seeking me out to engage in the pec-pat exchanges she was so fond of, inviting the evolution of trust. Exploring the amber hollows of Christine's dappled gaze, I glimpsed again those double teardrop shaped pupils, so utterly unearthly. Unannounced, she would appear and lead me on forays about the lagoon, while I absorbed further lessons in delphic communication.

Socially, dolphins communicate certain information via whistles, often releasing tiny air bubbles from their blowholes as they vocalize — like a balloon, but with exquisite precision and control. The full function and meaning of these bird-like trills and arpeggios have yet to be deciphered by Homo sapiens (wise though man may be). However, it has been discovered that some dolphins appear to develop their own unique whistles, different in form and tone from others — a signature whistle — a name. As dolphins regularly learn and mimic each other's signature whistles (in effect, announcing themselves and calling their peers by name), it was perhaps not surprising that Christine began to try and teach me hers. Though my repetitions were wobbly and much lower in pitch, the inflection was recognizable and I hope, appreciated.

Keeping their own counsel on these matters, Unior and Choney watched it all with more than a passing and casual interest.

In addition to the four dolphins, the Cuban dolphinarium also held, paddling in continuous futility, a number of sea turtles inside a tiny concrete pool, and in two barbaric iron cages, a lethargic crocodilian and a huge, shaggy South-African sea lion, known as the "Sea Wolf." The dirty, cramped conditions these creatures endured were appalling and daily I walked among them, offering silent compassion to their pitiful suffering. Compared to these poor animals, the dolphins enjoyed a luxurious existence.

Every couple of days, the filthy water in the Sea Wolf's tiny cage was emptied and exchanged for that from the dolphin lagoon. At such time, Umberto and Benicio warned me to remain on the dock and desist from swimming for several hours, until the beast's refuse was carried away by the tide. Predictably, no precautions were taken to keep the dolphins from swimming in the fetid water.

During one such afternoon, I was snoozing on the little dock with Juan drifting in the water beside me. Apparently dissatisfied with our elemental separation, Juan made known his wish for my submersed company. At first he merely stirred before me, mute, brimming gaze bespeaking his request, and though I understood perfectly, being temporarily barred from the dirty water, I was unable to comply. The subtle attempt having failed, Juan started nudging me in an attempt to bestir, softly at first, but then with a rising vigor, which became almost painful, finally causing me to move out of his reach. Stalemate, the two of us regarded one another. Unable to convey the reason for withholding my companionship, I fidgeted. But for his sipping respiration, Juan remained still, keeping his eyes glued to mine.

Calmed, I moved forward, offering a smoothing caress in apology. Juan seemed just about to bask under my touch, when with a sudden surge of acceleration, he shot off into the murky water. Emerging an instant later, he flew into a succession of imposing breaches, slamming down on his side, over and over, creating terrific fountains of sunlit water! At the height of each leap, Juan looked *right* at me, before descending to the thunderous impact! I was simply awestruck, each glance he threw, more laden, more dizzying than the last, holding my astonished stare with his own, bright and mercurial. I was his and he knew it.

Drifting together later, calm and quiescent after the last tourist-bustle of the day, I heard Umberto's faint call, signaling the bus' arrival. As I rose to go, Juan began to pace and keen. Caressing his distress, I wished — *willed* him to understand I would return with the sun. But as I turned away, Juan reared up from the water, his plaintive cries striking me with arrows of regret, blurring my vision with sharp, unexpected tears. It was as if he understood too well that one day I would not return.

Time passed, trying to understand the intricacies of him: His stillness, his seething, his distance, his immediacy, his vital, internal rhythms — their roots, their conductor — silent, strange doctrines. He would lay pliant in my arms, allowing me to wander and wonder with the fingertip's inhalation of minute detail, among droplets of water, archipelagos shivering on his skin. In this closeness, edges blurred. Our reveries sometimes seemed to extend a sylvan net, holding both dolphin and human on-lookers within invisible strands, and the silence pervading sacred moments and holy ground would prevail.

And then the delphic tempo would morph, Juan suddenly circling, pressing against me furiously silken, half-leaping from the water and buzzing with escalating excitement. Sometimes on these mad passes, his fins or flukes would jolt me with a sudden and significant impact, producing an instantaneous subdued secession and mute apology.

More shows, more tourists eager for dolphin-hauling-rides and still

Juan refused to work. Christine eagerly took his place and his food, next to Unior at the smaller dock. Only Benicio's alms kept Juan from starving. "*No work, no fish*," the other trainers would say.

Perhaps it was hunger that put the edge on Juan's behavior one afternoon, when I joined him in the water. Turbulence arose almost immediately, as he slid against me at high speeds, the hard edges of his dorsal and pectoral fins, leaving me bruised. In his riotous whirling, what would normally have been a caress with his tail became a *daunting* contact! Ubiquitous, sinuous and tameless, raking his teeth (painlessly) over my limbs; arching against me and even sweeping me bodily from the water, Juan was a tempest of power and speed! In the face of delphic exuberance, the frailty of the human form is glaring: I knew I could *easily* be smashed to bits — and it was a *very* near thing.

In the middle of the chaos, Unior again chose to try and insinuate himself into our entanglement, but Juan would have none of it. Benicio observed that when the issue was pressed, in all other things Juan gave way to Unior's bulk and seniority — except where I was the subject of contention, when Juan refused to tolerate the bigger dolphin's interference.

Catching my eye, Juan led me to follow him down, along the net. There in the mossy light, he revealed another ragged hole — he remained dedicated to his cause, *still* trying to *escape!* Such a courageous spirit, enduring daily belligerence and starvation, continually rejecting his enslavement, and all the while working in a clandestine fashion on an escape route!

However, I had recently learned that no direct conversation existed between the salt lake beyond the net, and the ocean.* Direct access was blocked by a road, and only a series of tin tunnels beneath this highway connected the smaller body of water to the sea, allowing tides and smaller sea-life into the lake, but firmly blocking the escape of anything as large as a dolphin. So despite Juan's brave efforts, freedom could not be so easily won. Even so, I imagined the lake would allot Juan far more space, filled with natural mangrove-dwelling prey, while removing him from demeaning activities and the hunger of full human dependence.

Diving to examine the hole once more, I wondered why none of them had gone through it yet; the opening certainly looked big enough to admit a dolphin. Scanning for unwanted eyes upon us, I sipped a quick breath, dove, and swam through the yawning portal, heart thundering in my ears. I turned, calling to the four dolphins hovering just on the other side of the

---

*   see map.

festooned barrier, their collective sonar swarming over me like a nest of buzzing hornets. Zipping back and forth, always careful to surface for air on the correct side of the net, so as not to give our fugitive actions away, I continued calling to my companions, demonstrating the unscathed ease of my escape. Though all four dolphins took turns moving right up to the hole, examining it through a storm of excited buzzing — not one of them went through. Remembering dolphins have an infamous phobia of passing through, over or under barriers, this came as little surprise. Still, I hoped that seeds of encouragement had been sown.

However, soon after the show and tourist-hauling, I noticed Benicio readying to enter the water with an aqua-lung, in order to begin a routine check of the net — *Oh No!* Hovering over the cloud of rising bubbles marking the trainer's decent into the depths, tremors of agitation and anticipation ran through me. I didn't know what to do! The dolphins were staying out of the area, perhaps in petulant foresight of the inevitable impending discovery of this latest escape attempt. In some pathetic hope of distraction, I swooped over Benicio's dusky form, shrouded in the dim water, uttering mournful mewings. Though startled, the trainer continued on his errand, and Juan's hole was indeed found and blocked. Realizing this hole-making/patching was an on-going process, I hoped this latest setback wouldn't keep Juan from trying again.

The next morning Juan was by the net, enmeshed in misery, probably contemplating the newly patched hole. Just as he had on that first morning, Juan rose out of the water, almost to his flukes, coughing out painfully discordant utterances, shaking his head at the net, as if to deny its existence and finally in a desperate act of defiance, pulling at it with his teeth. The sight of his suffering was scalding — seeing this being burning beneath the yoke of his captivity.

I went to him and lifted my eyes into his. *Come with me.* Christine, Unior and Choney flanked me, as if awaiting Juan's reply. Somewhat reluctantly, Juan left his post and accepted our invitation into the dance. Our synchronicity brought solace, and with visibility over ten feet, I found the dolphins revealed in breathtaking quick-silvered fluidity, their perfection, innate, resplendent and strange.

We were interrupted by Umberto, requesting I translate something for him ashore. It may be Juan resented this intrusion. Pacing back and forth before me where I stood on shore with the trainer, he made every effort to catch and hold my eye. Struggling to lend Umberto my attention despite the subtle enormity of Juan's distraction, I none the less noticed when Juan quit pacing and dove. I also noticed him resurface, balancing on his slippery back, a decrepit and very sodden boot! Umberto spotted this decidedly odd spectacle a moment later, bellowing and pointing, *"Ai! Mirada — Look!"*As we stepped forward to peer at Juan, parading his prize, the dolphin, with a mischievous twinkle in his eye, let the shoe slip back into the murk — his disruption a success!

Days piled atop one another, rife with raucous music, persistent crowds and endless lines of eager tourists clamoring for dolphin-hauls. One afternoon, after the dusty crowds had died down, I returned to the water to find on the dock, a girl of about ten or so with two long braids, wearing a pink short-suit — Iago's niece. Unnoticed, I settled down, curious to observe the child's conduct. The little girl began by teasing the dolphins, pretending to have a dangling piece of fish in her hand, before yanking it away. It did not take long for Choney, Unior and Christine to evacuate (after all, they had all just eaten, and couldn't be bothered). That just left poor, hungry Juan.

Continuing her irritating and irreverent teasing, the child grabbed at Juan's face, poking at his eyes and sensitive blowhole. I watched Juan's patience wearing thin, his breath and movements betraying increasing annoyance. The girl persisted in her rude endeavors and I saw it coming — Juan bit her — hard enough to let it be known he meant business. Affronted but hardly humbled, the child attempted to strike Juan in retaliation, but he wisely stayed out of reach. Bent on punishing Juan for refusing to be a plaything, she flailed her feet in the water, trying to kick him — and he bit those too. Finally, the message got through and the nasty imp retreated, scolding and shaking her little fist. It was disheartening to see someone so young acting in such an aggressive and disrespectful fashion — but considering the poor examples so abundant in that place, it wasn't that surprising — because it is *impossible* to teach respect while demonstrating disrespect!

Juan was still simmering from the exchange when I joined him in the water. Speaking softly, I soothed him, and in time it all slipped away. We knew the times we touched it: We were within the garden, and it was within us.

The following morning, a vet arrived to check Christine for suspected signs of pregnancy. Teaming up with Iago he attempted to convince the female dolphin to perform her beaching behavior from the show routine (where she would slide right up out of the water onto the big dock), which would enable them to grab and restrain her for examination. Slippery and wary as she was, Iago and his cohort were having no luck with their quarry and had to give up in the end, as Christine continued to view their motives askance and refused to cooperate.

At the other end of the lagoon, Juan lay alone by the net in a pool of asperity, from which I eventually coaxed him. However, it was not long before he was again erupting into turbulence, sliding against me at high velocity and adding bruises to my bruises with the continuous contact of his hard fins and flukes. In fact, he became so rough and boisterous that I had to leave the water and climb up onto the dock — but the moment I rejoined him, he reared out of control, causing me to again scramble from the water. It actually got a little ridiculous, this getting in and out. Our imbroglio was momentarily interrupted by Christine's arrival. Looking a little wild-eyed after the vet-episode, she nonetheless slid forward to share her trust in a pec-pat game with me, appearing to draw some reassurance from the contact.

Juan remained exasperatingly over-forceful, but my leaving the water seemed to provoke enormous distress in him — it was an impossible situation, and though I understood he wanted me to remain, he made it unbearable to stay. Drifting low in the water, Choney watched all. Things were getting out of hand and when I tried to swim away, Juan deftly cut me off, expertly corralling me to prevent my escape. Yet again the dolphin zoomed by, nicking me first with the hard edge of his dorsal fin and then catching me with the edge of his flukes! It was the final straw. Uttering a caustic oath, I gave the water a great WHACK with my swim fins! *Enough!* Bruised and beleaguered, I climbed back onto the dock turning my back upon the doleful attention of my suddenly subdued swain.

Unwilling to admit defeat, Juan began nudging the dock persistently, pressing harder and harder and threatening to sink the precarious little platform with his weight, and tip me right back into the water with him! Rising up to his waist from the water, issuing rebuking quacks, Juan actually attempted to *pull* me bodily back to him, flooding the dock as he did so! I was simply incredulous at the force and insistence of his behavior and decided to retreat from the dock altogether. It was just *too* much.

Whisking up my things I migrated overland to the big dock, ignoring the eruption of Juan's loud protestations as I receded. Forming a parallel feminine escort, Christine and Choney swam sedately alongside me as I made my way along the lagoon's edge to the big dock. There, I was able to rest in blessed quietude for some time before the weight of the tropical heat stirred me. As if aware of my awakening, Christine appeared before me, cruising by with something black draped over her head. *What the...? Hey — my shirt!* I made a grab for it — but that most practiced and pilfering dolphin just zipped away with her purloined prize! *What cheek!*

Having collected my patience and resolve, and thanks to Christine's prank, my sense of humor, I returned to Juan. Before reentering the water, I had to apply some lip balm — so many days of sun and salt had left my lips cracked and abominably painful, just as my swim fins had left my heels raw and bleeding from so much swimming, though it was an insignificant price to pay. Juan still insisted on rocking the dock, but upon rejoining him in the water, I found he was no longer intolerable, and we were able to reconcile the waters between us.

Sitting on a stone, under the starved shade of a dying tree, I watched Choney and Christine disport themselves for chunks of dead, frozen fish. I watched tourists crowding onto the little dock, waving fists of cash, eager to knead and paw the dolphins, like prize plush toys. Despite the heat, a chill crept up on me — the blindness, the hopelessness of it all. No one cared, no one saw the true wonder of these creatures, estranged and stolen, bought and sold by the might of the Dollar. When the sickening scene had dissipated for the day, I slipped into the water, silent and morose. All four dolphins encircled me, Juan pushing forward, eager to engage. But his bulldozing approach was too much for my delicate condition. Something seemed to snap inside, and I just couldn't stop the tears. I felt caught between two worlds. The dolphins were defenseless and their situation seemed so hopeless and unbearable — it broke my heart. Drawn into the underworld below, I dove deep, curving far, just for the feel of the cool water rushing past — to awaken any sensation other than anguish.

Juan awaited my return with amaranthine eyes, evening's rippled clouds reflecting in the water all around us. Though he was tranquil and temperate, I flinched at every movement, remaining close to sorrow's precipice. Unbidden, another wave of sadness broke, spilling more silent tears. Softly, Juan lay his head on my shuddering shoulder. The sky infused the quiet water with cobalt edged in peach and gold. Slowly the sadness ebbed. Juan remained quiescent, pressed close. Though he was much the paler, his eyes mirrored a familiar melancholy. Shivering, I realized I was spent and chilled. Climbing onto the dock, I lay with my head close beside Juan's, silent and still. Carmine streaks unfurled in the sky. The tide was going out, stirring the water into hypnotic ripples. Under this undulating spell, the two of us were lulled, dozing. The other three dolphins, their shining clouded, floated in a line gazing out past the net.

After leaving the dolphins and returning to the sea, I'd swim, or perhaps wade, thigh-deep in the waves, gazing at the sun's sinking splendor. Having rinsed myself of sand and salt, it was then time to retire and transcribe the day's events. Gathering as much detail from my interaction with the dolphins as a disciplined combing of memory allowed was always a long process, requiring several hours.

Only after completing this task would I allow the sweet call of the waves to sway and transform me: Out of the little adobe villa and into the glorious wanton night, with only the geckos to mark my passing. This was my time, a handmaiden of the moon, rising to meet the stars and the night waters. Once in my element, a new creature awoke and called; human words and thoughts were left behind like a worn, papered skin on the sand. Held effortlessly arching on the waves, skin turned to moonlight, the ocean offered warmth and rapture. Adrift in this other world, I felt it keening to my soul, through my dreams, through my blood... Emerging from the moon's brilliant path, shivering on the water, I felt my being: Awake. Aware.

On certain days, Unior seemed to show a marked preference for Christine's company, rather than Choney and observing these switches in companionship, I wondered what unseen exchanges precipitated them. There were so many complex, social details in the dolphins' lives — and so much to learn. On this day, capricious Unior, having now abandoned Christine's company, was to be seen trailing along with Choney all afternoon. One interest they shared was apparent — watching Juan with his amphibious companion. Over in the show area, Christine started a series of loud, tail-slaps, which soon progressed into a string of breaches, and I couldn't help but wonder if Unior's fickle favoritism inspired her. The slap of her body against the water, echoed like gunshots over the lagoon — she was right pissed about something. With so much going on between the dolphins at any given moment, the majority of which I was unaware, there was no way of knowing what kind of bee buzzed in Christine's bonnet.

Yet lessons were always being learned. Now, when tensions began to climb, causing Juan to careen around me, I began to wrestle with him. Lining up my hands on the tip of his rostrum, we would push against one another, testing strengths. Larking about, splashing, falling over each other and laughing, I loved to tickle him, especially in the softest spot under his pec-fins. Despite Juan's vast strength and unceasing energy, becoming even more interactive in the face of his rambunctious moods worked well.

Perhaps bestirred by Juan's coquetry, Choney decided one morning, to emerge from the observational periphery and begin a flirtation of her own. Coming up under him, arching invitingly, pec-fins open wide, she half leapt around him, revealing the shell-pink blush infusing her nether region, a clear banner of her amorous intentions. I very much hoped Juan would take

Choney up on her ardent advances, as the female dolphin could and would provide Juan with the kind of healthy release that only one of his own species could deliver. The two dolphins vanished into the murk for about ten seconds (and the fact is, dolphins don't need much more than that) before resurfacing. Whatever had or hadn't transpired, Choney made no more advances and Juan returned to engage my company once more.

Ironically, it was only on my last day that I arrived to find Juan awaiting me at the dock, rather than brooding by the net. Though Unior rushed up bright eyed to solicit a flurried greeting, the larger dolphin gave way when Juan moved forward, impatient for me to join him in the water, and nudging me to say so. Soon drifting contentedly with a now indolent Juan, luminous in my arms, I mulled over how much we had shared together. Tenderness, sadness, fun and silliness, quiet thoughtful meditation, everything between snoozing and revelry, including argument and reconciliation; a chromatic spectrum — the watermarks of true friendship, at least by human standards.

Juan was inexhaustible in his attentive affection, becoming restless if ever my skin ceased to touch his. Lacking his endurance, I established a "time out" zone just to the side of the dock, where I could rest when need be. Though Juan buzzed and rumbled in stormy complaint of our temporary sundering, he would not cross the invisible line. It seemed he had learned something of my limits, and in more energetic play, his unabashed rollicking was no longer overbearing. A balance had been met.

Splashing — laughter — Splashter! Joyous interuptus. Iago appeared, leading a chattering throng of tourists seeking dolphin-hauls. I fled. Afterwards, Umberto and Benicio requested my assistance with several minor matters. Trotting about on various errands, I heaved a hundred sighs, looking over at the bright water and before I knew it, the end of the day was almost upon me. Having completed adieus among my human amigos, I was at last free to bid my farewells to the dolphins.

Juan waited for me, eyes incandescent. Unior, Choney and Christine floated before the net in a dolesome row, staring out past it; ever a forlorn image. A subdued air pervaded all. Becalmed, Juan and I drifted quietly together until it was time for me to go. Rising from the water, all four dolphins stirred, gathered round, nibbling, clicking and nuzzling beneath my parting caresses. I turned to Juan, wishing there were some way to tell him I would return — but not for a long while.

Lingering; in the dark grottos of his gaze, in the unassailable sumptuousness of his skin, in the depth and strangeness of our impossible kinship...

This can't end
But it will.
(it did, it did)

Dusk coiled itself to strike as I gathered my strength to leave him, fighting against a powerful current. All rivers in this land led to him. Drifting low in the gray water, Juan's eyes, heavy unwavering drops of darkness, held me, heart-rending, mutely beseeching me to remain. Barricading myself against a strangling tide, against the first hints of frost, my sight seemed to mist, shadowed wings coalescing between us, glimpsing a dark path ahead: The fate he and I would tread together, until our parting. Nothing would ever be the same.

CHAPTER EIGHT

ESCAPE VELOCITY

"You were the one who taught me... I never looked at you without seeing the sweetness of the way the world goes together, or without sorrow for its spoiling."
from *The Last Unicorn,* by Peter S. Beagle.

A dolphin bearing crescent scars graced my changeling dreams, waking me to remembrance of the peculiar, pull of his noctilucent gaze. However, my days contained plenty of more corporeal distraction and I returned from Cuba with more than Juan's sapphireine imprint.

I'd discovered that Cuban dolphin capture operations had moved from Varadero, to another area several hundred kilometers down the coast, pillaging new and as yet un-depleted dolphin populations. Germany, Spain, France and Canada (Marineland) all held wild-caught Cuban dolphins in their aquariums and marine parks. Switzerland, Denmark, Argentina, Chile and even the United States were making inquires. With the going rate at about $20,000* US per dolphin (and more than twice that for trained dolphins), Cuba was eager to deliver and had become the active center of international dolphin exportation! I immediately compiled a report on this repellent matter for dissemination among the network of conservation organizations addressing these issues. Simultaneously we participated in an international campaign, deluging Marineland with post cards from thousands of concerned persons, urging the marine park to remove Duke from the warehouse where he still languished, and allow his retirement, if not his rehabilitation, in dignity and natural surroundings.

Always, Juan remained in my thoughts, treading seas of tenderness. Balmy evenings gave way to chilly nights, crisp with the papery aroma of fallen leaves and the promise of frost. Unable to dispel my neritic longings, I returned to Cuba in October, but grave news awaited me.

* This was the 1990s; in 2009, the price may be much higher.

Only a month or two after my last visit in spring, both Christine *and* Choney had given birth, within days of each other — gracing the lagoon with *two* tiny, perfect, healthy baby dolphins. But bleak history had repeated itself and within days, *both* infants had become tangled in the net. Unior had broken some of his teeth trying to tear up the barrier and free them, but tragically, both baby dolphins drowned. I received the story in stony silence. On one level those deaths were so awful, so neglectful, so needless, it left me numbed. On another level, this grim news only added to my resolve. More innocent blood shed — more little lives come and flown — all in the name of profit. It had to *stop*. Benicio had repeatedly advised the dolphinarium's manager to install new netting, his counsel continually falling on deaf ears — and now the worst had happened — again.

However, further tidings followed of a more welcome nature. After over a year of covert contrivance, Juan had at last succeeded in escaping from the lagoon! Unraveling the entire story, I learned that several weeks after the baby dolphins' deaths, Unior, Christine and even Choney had all started fighting with Juan. These attacks grew progressively worse and were probably what pushed Juan to flee the lagoon. That had been three months previously, and Juan had remained in the salt-lake ever since. Had a true avenue to the sea existed beyond the net, Juan and the other dolphins would likely have vanished without a backward glance. It was then I realized Juan couldn't have known — that *true* freedom did not, in fact await him out beyond the lagoon. It must have been a bitter and cruel discovery, when he realized all his persistence and effort had only earned him a larger enclosure instead of oceanic freedom.

Inquiring, I learned that though Unior and Choney regularly went out into the lake, they always returned to the lagoon at meal/show times. Though over a kilometer long, the lake couldn't fully support the appetites of four dolphins, but as long as the others continued to perform, they continued to be fed.

Juan had been the odd one out, the rebel who wouldn't be content or complacent with his lot, refusing the human limits imposed on him. While he'd been glaringly unhappy within the lagoon's confinement, making constant efforts to escape, his smooth skin had not evinced any particular evidence of violence against him. As the lightest scratch shows on a dolphin's skin, it would have been obvious if the others had been attacking him then — they hadn't. Something had changed in the weeks following the infant deaths. Perhaps the stress of those grievous losses magnified latent dissent, or perhaps Juan had somehow upset the status quo in the lagoon and become the target of the other's aggression afterwards. Whatever the case, Juan had finally made a break for his freedom and fled as far as he could go.

Walking along the wharf in the channel I searched across the lake's pensive surface for some sign of his familiar falcate fin. Juan's situation had changed deeply, yet my affection for him endured. How he would react to my presence? Would he remember our rapport? Before our last parting, I had sheltered his vast, silken quiescence in my arms. Doleful cheek resting upon his skin, I had felt it, the great and intimate rhythm of his heart beat.

The solemn thorn of a dolphin's dorsal fin sliced into the mouth of the channel. The moment of truth approached — but the tide was low, and the wharf high — I had to get closer. Floating in the channel and neatly tied to the jetty were several small, brightly painted rowboats. Picking the least precarious looking vessel, I climbed gingerly into it.

Parting the surface with a misty exhalation, the dolphin's gaze met mine. Juan paused, staring. Silently reeling beneath the vertigo of those embered glances, I watched him, hesitant and trepidatious, sliding nearer — how different his rhythms now — taut, alert and cautious. As he drew closer, I saw deep, white tooth-rake-marks scarred his dorsal fin. His body, no longer smooth, had become etched with scrapes and lacerations — clear signs of confrontation with the other dolphins. Tremulous, I held Juan's gaze as he drew closer, attenuating the distance between us, so thick with anticipation. I caught recognition's fiery flicker in his eye. And then, negating the yawning threat of the abyss, Juan slid forward to receive my caress on his cheek. He knew me. I hadn't realized I'd been holding my breath.

It began to rain. Juan waited for me in the dimpled water. The channel's greenish brine was shallow, fluctuating between about five and seven feet with the tides, and its silted floor was strewn with stinging jellyfish. Despite these uninviting conditions, I managed to maneuver — not without some difficulty — to join Juan in the water. I remained by the little boat, holding its flaking edge, so as not to stir the stinging medusas below. Though Juan flowed his lacquered body head to tail repeatedly under my offered hands, he was never still and I found myself missing the undivided indolence we had shared in the past.

I met with Unior, Choney and Christine a while later, at the little dock in the lagoon. Invited into the chilly water, I paused to roll slowly under the dolphins' acoustic shower. For them, as creatures of sound, this was a very important component of our reunion. Acoustically satisfied, the four of us undulated towards the net. No sign of Juan, only the gaping hole his passage had left behind. Unior, Christine and Choney kept close, engaging me within their glimmering presence and distracting me from the absence of the dolphin that was no longer among them.

Failing to find any sign of Juan the following morning, I met the other three dolphins on the dock. Almost immediately Christine and Choney began jostling and tussling (Unior's bulk left him largely immune). As time passed, I realized the two female dolphins were really not getting along, each putting great effort into interfering with anything the other showed interest in. Clearly at times my presence served merely at the level of a social prop. Throughout the week, the rivalry between Christine and Choney grew worse escalating into bashing, biting and eventually fully-fledged chasing, leaping and fighting. I wondered if all this aggression was some sort of displaced backlash after the loss of their infants. In all likelihood it was the glacial tip of a number of complicated social problems being magnified by captive conditions.

Picking my way across the over-grown rubble littering the grounds, I made my way to the channel. All was calm and silent out upon the far, misted reaches of the lake, betraying no rumor of Juan's presence. When at last he appeared, Juan took on a pleased attitude, his incline indicating a growing receptivity towards companionship. I found I loved this new wildness and vigor in him. Immersed, Juan scrutinized me intensely with his buzzing echolocation. His nearness invited soft delineations, and it seemed to me that though our bond had changed, it had not weakened. Plucking a strand of eelgrass and undulating it before Juan's alighted countenance, I released it to him and the game was on! With ever-deft alacrity, the dolphin expertly balanced the filament, first on one fin and then another. When he let the strand slip, it was my cue to attempt a similar display, through a storm of excited buzzing, until I passed it to him once again. Juan's spirits seemed to soar with this amusement, until he was half leaping with exuberance, mouthing my limbs and pressing against me in a cloud of excitement, just as he so often had in the past.

Suddenly, another dolphin blasted into the fray — and then they were off — streaking into the lake, erupting into periodic fits of splashing and leaping in the distance. Thrown off guard, I decided it must have been Choney, seized with a sudden fit of flirtation. After some minutes, the mystery dolphin headed back up through the channel, passing me. It was only at close quarters that I realized — it was *Unior!* The burly dolphin eyed me as he slid past towards the lagoon, but did not pause or offer any comment.

Juan returned only after the bigger male had vanished. Immediately I saw a wound trailing ribbons of blood in the water, where Unior's teeth had ripped into the soft skin of his shoulder. Juan turned to me, mute eyes brimming and unknowable. *Why* had Unior done this? Was it any accident that the aggressor had chosen to intervene *right* when Juan began cozying up to me? I remembered how Unior used to challenge and irritate Juan by injecting his presence into our company — but there had never been anything like *this*!

Subdued, Juan drifted beside me as I mulled over these distressing thoughts. Stirring after a time, he curved himself gently around me, extending an invitation to follow him out into the lake. I hesitated only a moment, his proximity lending me courage to venture out into the mysterious expanse beyond the channel. The lake was colder and clearer than the lagoon, its floor softly mounded and mossy, (rather than silty), with rippling fields of submerged sea grass and translucent, drifting layers of temperature and clarity. Crouching on the bottom below us, the pallid medusas pulsated gently, or occasionally drifted on the current, though not in the concentrations that left me so anxious in the channel. A hush lay on the place.

Moon colored, he orbited, flowering in mythical silence and swimming again at Juan's side, nothing else mattered for the moment. Surfacing synchronously, I followed as he shared his diaphanous world with me.

Returning to the channel after our long, tranquil tour, I realized our passage had unknowingly attracted the attention of a crowd, pointing, yelling, snapping photos, loading into the little boats, paddling and hollering after us, extinguishing our reverie with cretinous clamor. Suddenly Juan and I found ourselves bombarded by people jumping into the water all around us, flailing, thrashing and bellowing! Neither he nor I had any wish to remain, and with an exchanged glance, we agreed to part and fled our separate ways.

Soon afterward, passing the tiny concrete turtle-pools, I noticed one was empty and peering inside I beheld a mammoth sea turtle. Her shell was almost five feet long, encrusted with algae, ridged, pock-marked and chipped; a testament to all she'd seen and endured over a century of existence — to end up like this — stranded ignominiously in a be-slimed concrete pool, to die of heat exhaustion. Not if I could help it. Quickly, I scooped water from the lagoon into my dive mask, returning to pour it over the ancient sea-creature's beleaguered head. The obsidian eyes cracked opened to gaze up at me...fissures swallowing me up, echoing all things strange and wondrous residing in Poseidon's pelagic realm. Could I have borne the weight, I would have carried her to the sea myself, rather than have her continue to endure suffering and degradation for idle human curiosity and amusement. I located Umberto, sipping a coke in the shade, bantering with the ice cream man and his wife. Ever absent minded, he had forgotten to fill up the turtle's pool after "cleaning" it. I reminded him of this unfinished duty, and eventually the poor creature's torments were somewhat lessened.

On a hazy afternoon, the dolphinarium staff gathered for a meeting,

Juan & I in the channel.

escaping the heat beneath the patchily thatched roof of the fish grill restaurant. *Juan* was to be the main topic of discussion and mindful of my keen interest, Umberto made a point of inviting me to join the council. I was somewhat ill at ease with the lack of likely altruism coming to the table on the dolphins' behalf, as Benicio was conspicuously absent, visiting relatives out of town. Listening carefully, I learned that Juan's diet was still supplemented with a daily portion of dead fish — costing the place money, rather than generating it — and because of this, the dolphinarium actually wanted to be rid of him! Churlish Iago suggested they just *shoot* Juan and be done with it. Fortunately the others retained a somewhat more humane view, settling finally on the idea of simply dumping the dolphin back into the sea! Needless to say, this news sent my wheels churning furiously.

I felt it was important to be sure Juan could survive completely independent of human handouts before returning to the ocean, though I knew he had retained his ability to hunt and catch fish as he ranged about the lake. It was also to his advantage that he had been of an independent age when captured and would be released into back into familiar waters.

Contemplating the actuality of Juan returning to his oceanic home and regaining his freedom, my excitement grew until I couldn't be still. I found him, still surrounded and harassed by tourists — there seemed no end to them and their disrespectful grasping and flailing. Yet now I harbored a hope — that this unhappy existence could end and Juan might soon be *truly free!*

Benicio returned late in the afternoon on my final day, and together we discussed Juan's fate. My concern over Juan's partial dependency on human hand-outs eased, as I learned he was given only one third of his necessary daily intake of fish. As Juan remained healthy and vigorous, this indicated he was able to forage for the remainder and hardly appeared hard-pressed to do so. For this reason, Benicio maintained that a long, organized rehabilitation was unnecessary. Additionally, an extended endeavor would beg unwanted official attention, dredging up various tolls, permits and red-tape and without money for bribes, one would encounter non-stop set-backs, like a possible twenty-day quarantine incarceration in a swimming pool for the dolphin! Both of us knew Juan would only lose valuable ground under such conditions. Instead, over the next month, Benicio would slowly reduce Juan's daily ration of fish, until he was completely self subsistent. In one month's time I would return to assist and document as Benicio and a team of divers recaptured Juan in the shallow channel. After obtaining a clean bill of health from the dolphinarium's vet, Juan would be moved twenty minutes down the peninsula to an uninhabited tract of beach, and released in the same area he'd been captured about five years previously. By renting a small boat, we might even manage to follow and film Juan's initial period of liberation. Under the limited circumstances, it was the best we could do. After all the difficulties he'd endured, I felt certain Juan was tenacious and resourceful enough to see it all through to a life of freedom in the wild. All he needed was a little help.

After customary, lingering farewells among Choney, Unior and Christine, I found Juan, drifting in the channel, free for the moment from insolent boaters. He was restless, dipping and swirling below the mirrored water. But he came at last to lay his exquisite face in my hands, allowing me to enter the depth and liquidity of his gaze, while the sun's retreating flicker danced and rippled over the two of us. A last caress farewell, confident our reunion would come quickly and I hoped, under the most uplifting circumstances.

That evening, as the honeyed horizon beckoned toward the sinking sun, several wild dolphins appeared, streaking through the marbled hollows along the shore, riding the waves! That they might be even be Juan's long-lost kin, choosing this moment to re-visit old haunts, seemed a good omen.

CHAPTER NINE

UNDONE

"The educated vandal, without mercy or tolerance; the collecting man, that I once tried to prevent from killing an endangered falcon, who raised his rifle, fired, and laughed as the bird tumbled at my feet…but I, extending my childlike mind into the composite life of the world, bled accordingly."
Loren Eisley, *The Star Thrower.*

As planned, I returned to Cuba the following month, ready to document, observe and assist with Juan's long awaited release. The dolphinarium was almost deserted when I arrived (it being the middle of the hurricane season), and though at least one of the trainers must have been about, I saw not a soul and so, greetings and an immediate update on Juan's proceedings had to wait.

Seeking the dolphin himself, I found the channel empty and experienced a momentary pang of doubt — had he already been released? Just then, the little rowboat in which I sat, began to bob, betraying a submerged arrival. Juan appeared beside the boat, swirling before me in cloudy indefinitude, studying me from beneath the water. Tilting my head, I gazed patiently back, tendrils of honeyed hair spiraling into the water and diffusing into foggy filaments. Through the silence of delphic distillation, my troubled reflection danced on the water. Moving forward, Juan slid the sublime softness of his cheek in my hands, telling me through this tacit sweetness that he knew me. Curving graciously around, he then swept himself, head to tail under my palm, grandly flourishing his flukes in greeting!

I had only just joined him in the gummy brine when Unior, with Choney beside him, appeared in the channel. Juan vanished without a ripple. His actions spoke louder than any words — the timing of his disappearance was no accident. Determined to reclaim his vanished company I headed into the lake myself. Unbidden, Choney and Unior joined me. I did not see Juan.

With subtle tilts and curving postures, the two dolphins encouraged me to accompany them, and finally, with a last longing look out into the lake's misted distance, I followed them into the lagoon through the hole that remained in the net. There, Christine greeted us and with synchronous exhalations, the four of us dove together, twirling and soaring only inches apart in the turbid water. Sonorous as this greeting was, the flickering desire to return to Juan persisted. But when I struck out once more towards the channel, once *again* both Unior and Choney followed me. Christine remained alone in the lagoon, and I wondered in passing, why. There was no trace of Juan and I was certain his continuing absence had everything to do with Unior's presence. Hoping he and Choney would tire of my company and return to the lagoon, I idled around the channel. They did not.

Rolling and submerging with impotent distress I called out, a long, wavering note. Silence. Again, I called; a keen drawn from me almost of its own accord. Suddenly Juan was there, filling my sight with the rainy bloom of his shivering skin. I had called and he had come.

Rising for air, I met the dolphin's dark gaze, breathless. It was only then that I realized the possibility of danger, with Unior still close by. Immediately protective, I encircled Juan, keeping a wary vigilance on Unior's proximity. Caressing Juan's tattered skin, I could see the fighting had continued and some of the wounds were fresh. I had already noted there was hardly a scratch on Unior — telling me what Juan could not about the results of their rivalry.

Appearing to confer a moment, Choney and Unior lined up before Juan and I, hurling a thunderous barrage of buzzing at us. While this sonic-sussing didn't seem aggressive, it was certainly *intense*. The bond between Juan and I had always bore some fascination for Choney and Unior — and at the moment, it did not seem very latent. Taking my cue from Juan, I ignored their sonic scrutiny and followed him out into the lake. Unior and Choney remained with us, our quartet swimming close together, yet divided into obvious couplets. Meandering through the warm shafts of sunlight, the mossy seabed rolled by beneath our rippling shadows. Intent upon their own errands, Unior and Choney soon left us and with their passing, a tremor of tension eased.

The lake hung with a silent mist, as I remembered it; a watery dreamscape set for passions and conflict to unfurl. Traveling once more alongside Juan, I felt the seep of his sea-born strangeness, infusing me, becoming me. Submerged at his side, human thoughts, even human music faded, trailing away, to be replaced with another rhythm, another life, another sort of knowing — but only partially, as if lunar-fed in its ebb and flow. Leaning into the sunlit hollows of Juan's underwater gaze, I sensed the liquid depth of him; I saw myself there, a cousin to strangeness. I couldn't know that the days would come when I would look back and envy myself every glance, every graze against that torn, silken skin. There was a subtle heaviness in Juan, a sadness I hadn't remarked the month before. Then, he'd been taut and ready, but now he seemed strained and weary. Despite the expanded freedom of the lake, his situation was taxing him — and not just because of the fighting.

Hours later, while preparing to leave, I finally located Umberto — eager to hear what was going on. It was evident my questions regarding Juan's release discomfited him, though whether the trainer's reticence was due merely to the language barrier, or something else, I couldn't be certain. In any event, I learned only that Benicio would provide details the following day. Despite the typically light-hearted banter that followed, I returned to my little villa with a gnawing sense of foreboding. Benicio didn't own a telephone, so I was unable to call him and obtain immediate answers — I would just have to wait.

The moon had risen before I'd completed the day's notes, drawing me out onto the balcony. This tiny adobe casa with its clean simple lines was my favorite, sitting right on the shore behind my familiar, gnarled pines. A wild wind had come up, stirring the waves into foaming ferocity and causing the trees to sway and hiss. I could smell the storm's approach. Slipping over the winding roots, I passed those sentinel trees, the same ancient pines that had seen my tender shadow pass as a child, seeking towards my fate and the awakening of a great love. Head held high, I passed into the tumultuous water, the waves rising past my thighs, past my waist, calling, pulling. Facing the wind I raised my arms to the sky, back arched, letting the tempestuous elements throw themselves against my body, their fierceness soothing and familiar. It was tomorrow I feared.

I found Benicio the following morning, and extracted from him the dreaded news. My fears were confirmed — Juan would *not* be released. Apparently it was the head trainer Iago, that I had to thank. The release plan had stood firm, until about two weeks previously, when Iago had approached the manager, insisting that the dolphinarium should retain Juan, for "breeding" purposes. He'd proposed a plan to rein the dolphin in, bring him under control and force him perform for his keep once more. It wouldn't have been difficult for Iago to convince the manager that his plans for Juan would be profitable — it had all come down to money — and thus, all preparations for Juan's release had been halted. Benicio had attempted to contact and warn me that it was all over, but had been unable to get through (I was all too familiar with the cantankerous Cuban telephone system). All our efforts had been futile — and the dolphin, who mattered more to me with every second that raked past, would remain enslaved for life. We had come *so* close…

Dazed and bereft, I drifted past glum puddles, to the wharf, seeking the doomed dolphin where he paced, restless and irritable by the boats in the channel. He was hungry, waiting for his fish. I hadn't realized then, how Iago planned to twist and pervert Juan's behavior, to bend and crush his will. While Juan was being fed, Choney appeared in the channel, alone. With Unior still back in the lagoon, hauling tourists on his dorsal fin, I wondered what sleek, slight Choney was up to, as it became obvious she was waiting for Juan to finish eating.

The moment he'd swallowed the last fish, Juan and Choney went streaking out into the lake, where I saw them leaping and splashing! I imagined they were stealing this opportunity for sexcapades, while Unior was still occupied and unable to interfere. But Unior wasn't kept busy for long and I watched with fascinated and fretful concern, as he barreled down the channel and into the lake after the furtive couple. Shortly afterwards he returned with Choney at his side. There was no sign of Juan. It became almost like clockwork on most days: immediately after the shows, Choney would appear in the channel, to steal away into the lake with Juan, until reclaimed by Unior. Though I assumed Juan and Choney were engaging in some kind of sexual encounter, I realized this wasn't necessarily the case. Observing further details proved impossible from shore. If I wanted to learn the truth of what transpired between those three dolphins out in the lake, I would have to join them there.

Juan was clearly making concerted efforts to avoid Unior. Unfortunately, almost every time I went to the channel seeking him, Unior, usually with Choney, would get there first. So long as I remained, so did they, nosing about, their presence effectively keeping Juan at bay. Eventually I'd return to the lagoon (where Christine still remained alone), only to discover Choney and Unior awaiting me there as well! At first, I was inclined to dismiss my suspicion that I was being purposely followed, assuming the dolphins had better things to do, but as time passed, I began to wonder if this was not so. Everywhere I went — Unior and Choney followed! They did not engage me, or invite me among them, merely remaining my silent shadows, watching — and of course, because of this, I hardly saw Juan.

Brooding in the lagoon one afternoon after several days of this, I decided to try once more, swimming out through the net's hole and on towards the channel. No sign of Juan. Suddenly Unior appeared right before me, gigantic in the swirling murk, moving in a peculiar manner that inspired immediate wariness. Then I realized he was purposefully stirring up clouds of silt and stinging jellyfish right in front of me! Retreating before the ominous, stinging fog, I attempted to circumvent the danger and escape out into the lake, but Unior deftly cut me off, stirring up more jellyfish. Defeated and shaken, I left the water. And still, Unior and Choney persisted in shadowing me everywhere, thereby keeping Juan and I apart. I so much wanted to understand *why*? There were no answers, only a steep weariness in my soul.

Only while they were distracted during shows and training could I gain respite from Unior and Choney's vigilance. Unfortunately, this was also when, at Iago's insistence, Juan was fed, which always saw him at his most irritable humor. While awaiting the now thrice-daily arrival of the fish bucket, Juan often became impatient and unsociable. It pained me to see him this way, especially when there were perfectly good mangrove snapper collecting all around him, hoping for scraps — fish he should be hunting. The independence Juan had worked so long and hard to gain was withering, his rebellious fires smothering right before my eyes. And the awful realization — he *knew* it, and that was why he became so angry when fed in the channel — he *knew* he was slipping, losing ground...

It was on just such an occasion, just as Juan was finishing eating, when I finally rejoined his company in the water. Meeting his impassive gaze, I glimpsed the forecast: A cooling trend, flowing towards indifference. He turned away then, his scarred dorsal fin carving a path out into the lake. Frozen by the flensing glance, I floated, staring at the place where his dorsal fin had sunk in final dismissal, swallowing the sudden burning of tears. I had been utterly unprepared for this icy reception. The water's empty chill eventually bestirred me after an unknown time lost, staring at nothing. Just as I turned to go back, Juan reappeared. Eyes mute and brimming, I regarded him.

Inclining gently towards me, Juan extended an invitation to swim, and still silent, I allowed his slipstream to draw me out into the lake. He seemed distracted and distant, slowly moving ahead and fading into the shrouded water, returning as if suddenly reminded of my absence. Slowly, Juan's attention seemed to be returning from whatever remote shore it had visited. His gaze warmed, replacing the frosty overcast with the ineffable incandescence I so loved. There was no mistaking the familiar intensity gathering in his eyes and through it, we seemed to exchange some current of understanding between us, acknowledging the struggle and suffering. Further still this shared strangeness reached, to a pith of lucid, numinous opalescence, where tenderness knows no form...

But returning to the channel, Juan became noticeably restless, heavy with unhappiness, as if the location taunted him with invisible and confining connotations. Then Unior and Choney appeared, following Juan out into the lake, where he fled.

I'd been wondering about Christine — if she ever left the lagoon or entered the lake. She was hardly a timid dolphin and her remaining in the lagoon seemed odd, so on my last day, I asked Benicio about this. The trainer explained that shortly after Juan's escape from the lagoon, Christine had also gone out into the lake — and refused to return! Repeatedly, Benicio had paddled about in one of the little boats, blowing his whistle and attempting to lure Christine back with fish, but she had refused and remained at large for several days. Then one morning, Christine inexplicably returned to the lagoon and she had not been seen to leave since. Both Benicio and I suspected that Christine had returned only once she had established unequivocally, that no true escape existed from the lake. But why she refused any further visits, I could only wonder.

Due to Unior's vigilance, I'd managed only a few precious moments with Juan, but now, at the end of the day Unior, Choney and Christine lined up at the net, just as they had when no alternative path into the lake existed. Their skin seemed formed from the water around them, reflecting the sky's deepening cyan, their day's silver spent. There they remained and it was not until much later that I stopped to wonder: at the eleventh hour, they had left Juan and I undisturbed.

The sun was deep into its descent, feeding the gathering shadows, when I returned to the channel seeking Juan one the last time. Looking over the water I could not distinguish so much as a ripple. Immersed, I called out once, uncertainly. Coalescing out the evening's ethereal light Juan appeared. Tentatively I reached out to the nimbus of his presence, letting the tender immensity I felt for him flow from my fingertips — and suddenly it was just like old times between us, just like heaven. Side by side, we slipped out into the lake's twilit radiance. Shoulders brushing, we circled, curving and twining through the last slanting sunbeams, turned to liquid ore; every tiny fleck in the water, imbued and illuminated in gold. Dusk crept around us and even the medusas pulsing on the emerald moss below seemed possessed of a ghostly beauty. Long, I contemplated the mystery tided and trembling behind his gaze: Fierce as the unfolding dawn, pure as summers' storms; and so sad…sadder than the angels looking down on our continued folly.

I had missed the bus a long time ago. We came to rest by the boats in the channel, but in the gathering gloom, Juan was becoming restless, feeling his plight; the pull and declivity of the place. I had to go. One last, immortal, despairing caress. He watched me leaving him, as I would one day watch him leaving me, the recriminations of that abandonment, to return again and again.

Juan, left behind.

CHAPTER TEN

EAST OF EDEN

Blood is shed
My Love is red

In the wan blue light, their forms hover, strangely contorted. Upon closer inspection, the filaments of netting can be seen, binding the bodies and extremities of its victims. There are sea birds, their wings bent all wrong, hanging underwater, where they struggled and drowned. A young manta ray, its life almost spent, flaps feebly against the nearly invisible mesh. And then there is a dolphin. She is suspended, her head pointing downward towards the darkness of the deep. Her crescent flukes are wrapped in the netting, hopelessly entangled. Her streamlined form, though shrouded in the deadly strands, remains heartbreakingly beautiful, but her eyes are now devoid of life. She will never take another breath. The ghostly wall of death will kill again.

Our conservation group had joined forces with others to combat the devastating impact of oceanic driftnet fishing, a highly un-sustainable fishing method condemned as the most indiscriminate, irresponsible and destructive fishing practice ever devised.

Drift nets are made of cheap, non-biodegradable thin plastic nylon mesh, strung with floats along the top and weights along the bottom. These nets can be fifty feet deep and up to *forty miles* long and once unleashed, they catch *everything* in their path, as they are released at dusk to drift on the tides, stripping the sea of life until retrieved the following morning. Then there are ghost nets: swaths of this netting torn loose in storms or discarded through negligence and left adrift, continuing to trap and kill marine life — even whales, which become so hampered that they slowly starve or suffocate under the entangled weight. When this issue was brought to my attention, it was estimated that an *appalling 600 miles (1,000km) of* ghost netting was being cut adrift in the North Pacific annually. Drift-netting was the favorite method of several highly industrialized fishing nations, Japan, Taiwan and

South Korea, being the worst offenders, releasing up to *45,000 miles* of drift-netting in the North Pacific *each night* — far more than enough to encircle the entire planet. In the Atlantic and Mediterranean, the US, Italy, Spain and France were operating similarly.

As a result of these irresponsible practices, many thousands of sea birds, sea turtles, sharks and entire schools of non-target fish species are wiped out, in addition to whales, seals and dolphins, as it appears dolphins are unable to detect these thin nylon nets until it is too late. Once entangled in the deadly net, dolphins like so many other sea creatures, drown and die. These nets are used in the full knowledge that they harm non-target marine life, including cetaceans and once hauled aboard, all these other unfortunate victims are simply thrown overboard as waste. Reports estimated some 125,000 marine mammals dying annually in Japanese driftnets in the North Pacific alone — but Taiwanese and Japanese drift-netters had also moved into the South Pacific in large numbers — ironically, while Japan banned large-scale driftnets from its own waters because of their adverse effects.

Thanks largely to efforts by global conservationists, the devastating impact of drift-netting finally started to become more widely recognized. New Zealand reacted by banning both the use and the possession of drift nets in its 200 mile fishing zone, and responding to public pressure, Australia soon followed suit. Canada, South Africa and a number of South Pacific islands also banned drift-netting in their waters. However, the US had initially made a special allowance in its marine mammal protection act, enabling the Japanese to legally kill over five thousand cetaceans in Alaskan waters each year, drift-netting. Only after lengthy court battles, were environmental groups successfully able to repeal this state of affairs.

By the time I'd joined the bandwagon, it was the drift-netting in southern Europe that was the target of growing public outrage as thousands of dolphins died in driftnets on the French Riviera and elsewhere. Our group joined forces with others, continuing to lobby international governments and raise public awareness, while pushing to halt and banish drift-netting practices. These efforts did eventually pay off as the UN mobilized and issued a global moratorium on high seas driftnet fishing, while the European Commission banned all member nations from using nets over a mile and a half long. Of course out upon un-policed international waters, illegal drift-netting continues.

But in addition to the indiscriminate drift net deaths, I was shocked to learn that all over the world dolphins were being killed *deliberately!* In some places the slaughter stems from traditional sustenance practices, which have out-lived their historical purpose. In other areas, the advent of over-intensive industrialized fishing methods has resulted in the inevitable decline of fish species, which some fishermen mistakenly blame on dolphins, killing them as competition for dwindling food supplies.

The full scale of these dolphin deaths is unknown, as so much killing goes on at sea and in remote areas and records are rarely kept. In Sri Lanka and Peru, tens of thousands of dolphins were being deliberately harpooned or caught in coastal gill and trawl nets. In the Arctic waters of Canada, Greenland and Russia, thousands of harbor porpoises, narwhals and belugas were being killed. Many thousands more were being massacred by nets and harpoons in Venezuela, Argentina, Brazil, Panama, Chile, Mexico and along the coasts of Africa, India, China, Thailand, Indonesia, the Philippines and South Pacific islands like the Solomons. France, Spain, Italy, Finland, Sweden, Turkey and Portugal also killing dolphins in their waters, often in fishing nets. Norway and Iceland continued hunting whales despite an international moratorium, while murdering hundreds of dolphins, shooting or harpooning them for dog meat. Even in the Caribbean, on the islands of St. Vincent, St. Lucia and Dominica, dolphins are hunted, harpooned and butchered, their flesh fried in its own fat and eaten as a snack.

Japan has the largest commercial whaling fleet in the world and despite the global moratorium on whale hunting, continues killing them under the spectacularly weak guise of "scientific interest" Japan has earned further international criticism because of its slaughter of *vast* numbers of dolphins — tens of thousands every year.

Blaming dolphins (rather than an increasing human population and industrialized fishing methods) for dwindling fish catches, Japanese fishermen retaliated against the perceived culprits by rounding up groups of dolphins and pilot whales (a species of large, pelagic dolphin) in their boats, driving them into shallow bays and there, massacring them.

Of course these remain merely sad statistics until one sees film of the actual carnage: Amid the clamor of engines and shouting, the hapless dolphins are set upon in the shallows, stabbed and hacked at with axes and cleavers, dragged up onto the beach to be eviscerated, where even with their bellies slit open and limbs hacked off, they can still be seen thrashing and screaming while the sea runs red. Bleeding and mutilated, they writhe in agony, as their families are subjected to the same torture all around them. Their thin, piteous screams rend the air and the scarlet water froths as they struggle and suffer.

These are the most abhorrent and monstrous scenes I have ever witnessed. Film of these atrocities continues to elicit international outcry, but the killing persists, these revolting operations merely becoming more furtive.

Sometimes the dolphins' flesh may be sold and eaten, but they are more likely to be ground up into animal feed or fertilizer. Meanwhile, sinister characters from the captivity industry view these vile bloodbaths merely as opportunities to acquire cheap cetaceans for aquariums and dolphin-swim enterprises (more on this in later chapters).

In the Faeroe Islands of the North Atlantic, the killing of dolphins and small whales has degenerated from traditional sustenance to a brutal blood sport. Much like the Japanese massacres, dolphins and small whales are rounded up and driven into shallow bays where they are stabbed with massive gaff hooks and once impaled, dragged ashore by their torn flesh, where the merciless islanders, including even children, wade out and proceed to stab and hack them to death. As they are savaged, the whales may snap their own spines, as they thresh and writhe in agony. Afterward, the flesh is distributed among the murderers but much of it is wasted. One reason for this is that the bodies of cetaceans, being at the top of the marine food chain, are so heavily contaminated with high levels of mercury and other toxins that it is increasingly dangerous to eat their flesh.

Countries refusing to stop killing whales and dolphins are also often among those making efforts to obstruct conservation efforts. Our group was part of an international outcry against these barbaric practices, pushing for the implementation of international protection for all species of dolphins and smaller cetaceans, which (at present) remains non-existent.

Amid these harrowing, nightmarish issues, some good news seeped through, hailing from the Turks and Caicos Islands in the Caribbean, where recently three dolphins that had spent much of their lives caged in concrete pools at marine parks in England had been rehabilitated and released! Even more encouraging was the tide of changing public opinion, particularly in England, where there had been some thirty dolphinariums dotting the country, with only two remaining, which would soon close down. *That* was progress!

Our group continued pressuring Marineland to allow Duke's rehabilitation or retirement, along with improved conditions for all the other unfortunate animals at the marine park. This work gave me pause and perspective — at least Juan and the other Cubano dolphins still swam in seawater and sunlight.

On New Years Eve, I found myself wandering upon a drifting sea; an ocean of white, rolling snow. The sun was paling in the frozen sky when I crossed the fields and headed towards the woods. In the stillness at the forest's beginning I heard the unexpected and unmistakable laughter of water and led by this trickling song, I discovered a winding stream, only partially overcome by ice. In the failing light, the black water wavered like liquid obsidian. Following the footprints of deer in the snow, I cleared the stream in one leap. A hill lay before me, crowned with a copse of trees and continuing on, I ascended to watch the sun set on the old year. Standing silent among the slender, sleeping trees, my breath rose in frigid clouds to drift before me, my thoughts resting upon a dolphin, with crescent scars along his back — oceans and worlds away.

Revelation stole upon me in the afterglow. The struggle on Juan's behalf was far from over — I still had breath in my body. I would continue, seeking any possible means to create an avenue for his freedom. Somewhere in the woods wolves lifted their voices, kindling the stars; the power of the night filling me with the secret exultation of wild things.

If Juan was ever going to be free, I was going to need help. In light of the recent dolphin rehabilitation and release project, I decided to make my way to the Turks and Caicos Islands, hoping to gather support and assistance for Juan. Somehow.

Peering out through the plane's window as I descended toward the island of Provodenciales, I saw the dappled malachite of the barrier reef, tracing the island's curving coastline. Standing on shore before those waters they were no less astonishing — a pure, perfect aquamarine hue. I made my way to the Island Sea Center, where the rehabilitation project had taken place. The staff were kind and informative and led me on a tour of the grounds, where I was shown the enormous enclosure where the dolphins had resided — some eighty acres of marine reserve. It was within the gorgeous crystalline waters of this secure natural environment that the three dolphins, after decades without sunlight, spent a six-month rehabilitation period. After their release, local sightings continued to come in marking the dolphins' progress, free at last of human constraints. Because they were not radio tracked, the long-term fates of the three dolphins were unknown, but the project marked a positive benchmark.

I presented the staff with the details of Juan's situation in Cuba and my hope for his release. I fielded their many questions as best as I was able, and after some open conferencing, they came to a remarkable decision. If the necessary permits could be obtained from the Cuban and Caicos governments, the Sea Center was willing to host Juan in their sea pen for the duration of his short rehabilitation, with the use of all their facilities and experience! Perfect — if only Juan could be wrested from where he languished. But this was a strong start. In the meantime, I found myself inundated with information: construction and costs for pens, budget estimates for housing, feeding and transport, and ideas for funding and government contacts.

I also learned about a local wild dolphin called JoJo, who for reasons known only to himself, had become a regular visitor to Provo's shores, seeking out human company and amusement. Tourists who tried to grab and touch Jojo were often surprised to find their lack of respect met with a nasty knock, or even a bite to let them know they were being presumptuous. Though JoJo had been declared a National Treasure in the Turks and Caicos Islands, the biggest threat to his welfare predictably sprung from human activity in the form of careless tourists tearing around in speedboats and jet skies and on several occasions Jojo had received life-threatening gashes from propeller blades.

With the new possibilities for Juan reeling through my mind, I roamed night silvered shores, and even drifting into sleep I could still feel the pull and sway of the waves, wondering if my dreams might decipher their murmuring.

I awoke before sunrise on my final morning, wandering to the jetty where I sat dangling my feet in the water. In the sun's rising glow tiny fish flashed, their flow revealing the unseen bond between them, their scales gilt with gold and lapis. I had found support, learned much and felt well armed for the next stage of my quest toward Juan's freedom.

CHAPTER ELEVEN

PELE'S ISLAND

"Civilization ends at the waterline.
Beyond that, we all enter the food chain — and not always right at the top."
Hunter S. Thompson

Her island conceals a heart of turbulent fire; dominated by five soaring volcanic slopes, their summits obscured from my flight's curving altitude by a misted crown of clouds, their feet, plunging into the remote Pacific depths below. Geologically, the largest of Hawaii's dusky necklace of islands is also the youngest, still heaving and expanding with the active volcano of Mauna Loa, its molten core welling up from deep within the earth. Echoes beneath my feet, of flame and violence, thrusting mightily up through the chill ocean abyss and still cooling after five hundred thousand years. Everything surged towards the sky, or tilted towards the sea, mountainous immensity imposing itself upon every vista, though softened by the carpeting of lush vegetation creeping against the stony inclines. These were the voluptuous curves of Pele, the tempestuous Hawaiian goddess of fire and this island was her irrefutable and undisputed domain.

I was headed for a cetacean conference in Kona on behalf of our conservation society. Traveling from the airport toward the coastal conference hotel, I found the entire region appeared overcome with exotic efflorescence. Not just the purposefully planted gardens, but the loose, lawless areas left unattended, flowed and flowered with rambling color — in the dead heart of a North American winter! Already the rich, seeping tropical humidity was healing my flight-chaffed skin. Unknown fragrances, fleeting and succulent, mixed with the waxen plumeria blossoms of the lei around my neck, pleasantly dizzying, as dusk seemed to gather and intensify the novel impressions sifting over me. Overhead, a great tear appeared in the clouds, spilling light over the rough land and into the emerald hollow of my eyes, flooding my senses anew.

Journeying onward, I noticed mounds of stones carefully piled by the roadside and inquiring, I later learned that these cairns held messages within the way they were set — but only for those initiated into their meaning. I had already been warned not to take *any* stones from the island, as all were held sacred as corporeal manifestations of the body of the goddess and such blatant impropriety would provoke Pele's wrath. I would eventually encounter innumerable stories from people, who having chosen to ignore this advice, had afterward become plagued with tragedy and bad luck — until the stones were returned from whence they came. Apparently, packages containing such hastily returned rocks were not at all uncommon in the Hawaiian postal system. The misfortune was always said to end once the goddess was placated with the return of her own.

The sweetness of birdsong filtered into my dreams, dissipating their details and reminding me, with an internal swoop, where I was. Stretching luxuriously, I rose, eager to behold my surroundings in the morning light. From my lofty dais I surveyed a curving inlet of the ocean sparkling faintly in the morning mist, through which I glimpsed the mammoth side of a mountain. This was Hualalai and though at a mere 8,000 feet, the smallest of the big island's three volcanic peaks, from my vantage point, its gargantuan swell filled the landscape. Contemplating its sheer size through the clouds' teasing veils, I found myself thankful that for the time being, Hualalai slept, showing no signs of activity. The air held the lushness of the land and the fresh purity of the sea. I had never inhaled such potent draughts and could easily imagine their sustaining me without need for any other nourishment.

Much of the hotel seemed to have been built as an extension of nature; open to the sky, incorporating rough basalt and tumbling waterfalls — all over-run with rampant verdure, amongst whose colorful blooms many birds freely flitted. This was yet another new experience: modern structure blending with nature in so a harmonious manner, each making allowances for the other to flourish.

Seeking the sea, I followed the scent of spray and the roar of water and discovered not a flat, sandy beach, but ebony lava precipices, frozen in sinuous molten fury where they had poured over the edges of the earth and into the ocean, to jut like black fangs from the frothing white water. I picked a delicate path among the naked stones, to perch upon an outcrop, gazing down, transfixed by the immense lift of oceanic breathing; the seething split as one element pitted itself against the other in a charge of thunder before slipping into a soothing hiss of foam webbing over the dark water.

Though I searched the oceanic horizon, I saw no sign of the whales. They were out there somewhere; Humpbacks singing, courting and birthing in the shelter of the islands' clear, warm waters, through this, their season of love, birth, challenge and song. The prospect of glimpsing any of Hawaii's many cetacean species, in tandem with an international gathering of people come to share a common interest in conservation and discovery had drawn me many thousands of miles from my ice-encrusted home.

The swirling conference hall echoed with people's laughter and conversation in a delightful array of accents. Some I knew in person, some through correspondence or publications and others not at all. There were scientists, activists, artists, mystics, conservationists — an entirely cosmopolitan cross section. The lecture topics covered during the seven-day conference were as diverse as those delivering them: scientific discoveries, observations of interspecies communication and issues of conservation, all duly explored.

Particularly uplifting were two presentations by Japanese businessmen. One fellow had taken his fellow corporates out to meet friendly, curious whales in Baja, and Patagonia. Having filmed these encounters, he was now raising awareness in Japan about the nature of the creatures they continued to slaughter and eat. The other regaled his encounter with a pod of Pilot whales, while swimming near Iki Island.* Finding himself suddenly face to face with one of the sleek, twenty-foot predators, he explained that despite his surprise, he at the same time felt somehow safe. Reaching out hesitantly, he touched the whale, recalling how very soft its skin was. The warmth of his feelings were obvious and his sense of communicative friendship with the whale very moving. Both men continued to share their experiences with associates through informative lectures, describing a harmonious path between cetacean and Japanese, reporting that their message was being well-received. I viewed such efforts as vital in awakening and changing minds — the only hope for ending the continuing carnage in Japan.

After each day's proceedings, I would thread a twilight trail back to the edge of the sea, over dusky lava rocks so sharp, I worried they might slice right through my old canvas tennis shoes. Silently regarding the smooth shifting of the sky reflecting over the water, I watched with undimmed wonder, as the moon gathered her brightness.

Perhaps it was the lunar light that drew them. Reveling in the celestial pearlescence, great winged, humpback whales began to leap and breach, twirling in vigorous fountains of white foam, out upon the ocean. The

---

* A site infamous for the vicious mass-slaughter of dolphins and other small cetaceans by Japanese fishermen.

majesty of the sight held me rapt until the chill of the sea mist crept through my thin sweater.

We set out with only faintest flush streaking dawn's pale cheek. The moon had long since fled, and the rising sun remained hidden behind the immense shadow of Mauna Loa when our little contingent from the conference arrived at the bay. Outlined by the conjoined lava fields of both Hualalai and Mauna Loa, the bay formed an enormous sweeping crescent, girdled with towering cliffs below which, the explorer Captain Cook had finally met his death at the hands of righteously incensed Hawaiians. Curving along the bay, the cliffs tumbled down to a rocky shoreline, sifting into glittering, black lava-sand.

Diving into the cool, sleeping sea and venturing further into steadily deepening water, I paused, knowing it would be unwise to continue out into the unfamiliar bay alone — yet none of my party seemed willing to investigate the deeper waters. Ever enamored with all that lay beneath the ocean, I fell to exploring my submerged surroundings, trusting that a solution would present itself. With my attention so focused below, hardly broken in surfacing for breath, it was a while before I noticed that there were in fact people, floating way out among the waves. Eventually overtaking them, I found familiar faces from the conference, among them one of the Japanese fellows, whose lecture had lent me such hope. All were bobbing in a circle — and rather curiously, playing ball! Welcomed, I joined the game, attempting with an astounding lack of grace, to kick the ball with my swim fins.

This sequence of ungainly hilarity was interrupted when suddenly, exhaling in unison, a row of Spinner dolphins surfaced close beside our group, vanishing as suddenly as they had appeared! I imagined it had been a group of adult male dolphins, sent to scout our group and discover the nature of our little human congregation. Like the others, I soon returned my attention to the ball game.

Then familiar, high, sweet sounds reached me — without thinking, I dove, fading into the blue amid a hazy cloud of Spinners and vanishing from human sight. It was a large group and their collective whistles, buzzing and chirps created a cheerful din. Though this was my first meeting with Spinner dolphins, as more and more of them poured into sight all around, I found an entirely familiar feeling settling over me — *being* among *Them*.

A squadron of eight or nine males, identifiable by the hump of muscular tissue on the undersides of their tale stocks, drew close, sussing me efficiently with a brief sonic barrage. These male Spinners were protectors of the pod, every movement, flawlessly choreographed and synchronized. Satisfied that

I was indeed what I appeared to be — a single, diminutive human female of non-aggressive demeanor — the dolphins led me deeper into the group, and the ranks of females and young were revealed and opened to me.

So-named for their whirling leaps, Hawaiian Spinners are delicate and exquisitely formed dolphins, more slight and slender than the Bottlenose species, with whom most people are accustomed. They wear three distinct bands of color: a dark charcoal cape, soft gray flanks, and pearly pale undersides. Dark rings around their eyes, rimmed as if with kohl, lead gracefully into arched racing lines, sloping down towards each dainty pectoral fin. Their rostrums, like their bodies are long and slender and possessed of more than two hundred tiny pointed teeth for capturing small fish and squid in the deep waters offshore. After a night of diving and hunting in large groups, the Spinners split up into smaller pods and head into various bays and inlets among the islands to spend the daylight hours socializing and resting in safer, shallower water — just as they were all around me.

After so many hours in the sea and among the Cubano Dolphins, slipping into the Spinners' midst was instant and intricate; the roll and curve of breath combined with something more subtle and fleeting becoming the medium and rhythm of our colloquy.

Visibility was over one hundred feet, before hazing into a perfect, crystal blue and I could clearly see about five or six subgroups of dolphins, including the group of nine males, who after their initial appraisal had allowed me to travel peaceably among them. These sub-groups came and went around me, occupying different levels in the water column, which seemed to coincide with their level of activity. The most alert dolphins usually swam closer to the surface, vocalizing, actively caressing ever-changing partners and occasionally leaping into the sunshine. Those that were resting could be seen spread out fin to fin, in an orderly phalanx, slowly skimming the sandy sea floor sixty or seventy feet below, almost completely silent. I was careful not to disturb these resting dolphins and engaged only those that approached me near the surface. When invited with an affable tilt of the body, I mirrored their arcs and twirls, answering the dolphins' bright chirps with my own. Respectfully, I did not pursue the dolphins, allowing the Spinners to come and go around me, though the sounds of their soaring whistles never wholly faded.

Drifting on, the sea floor misted away into endless empty azure, shot with flickering shafts of sunlight. Alone, I noticed tiny iridescent motes of life, suspended in the water, glowing turquoise or gold when sun-struck. Glancing up from these minute wonders, a smoky shape moved out on the cerulean expanse edging my vision, coalescing amid a glitter of silver, into a blue marlin, over ten feet long, from its scimitar tail, to the point of its sword-tipped snout! Faced with the steely predator whose attention I had obviously caught — as it started winding in sinuous curves towards me — I tried to recall everything I knew about marlin — which wasn't much. Usually found in deep, open water, they're among the fastest of fish, powerful and unpredictable. I'd heard tales of sharks, whales and even small boats being attacked and impaled! So, it was unpredictably aggressive, strong, swift, fearless in attacking even a whale — and getting closer every second! Yet even so, I found myself struck by the deadly beauty of the great fish; the mesmerizing glint of flame across its scales — an exquisite pinnacle of predatory grace and strength.

Unable to formulate any other course of action, I began as controlled and casual retreat as possible, praying this wouldn't provoke my pursuer. But the marlin's cautious pace was more rapid than I could ever swim — *it was gaining*! Scanning the surface for any aid, I saw the towering black cliffs above and Cook's pale marble death monument at their dark feet.

Then I spied help — well, something, at any rate. Floating in a shiny inner tube, strayed from some recreational vessel's mooring, a somewhat corpulent fellow lay sunning himself, blissfully ignorant of any drama below. Arrowing straight towards him, I surfaced, gasping, "Swordfish!" Despite his understandable alarm, the man's portly midsection kept him firmly wedged in his inner tube, which at least prevented him from tipping over. "Swordfish! Swordfish!" I splashed, while he gaped at my abrupt appearance. Peering about under the water, I found the marlin had inexplicably vanished. Flooded with relief and met with the flustered fellow's unmistakably flummoxed look, I found it impossible to stifle a giddy and entirely irreverent giggle. Attempting to explain myself only caused his furrowed brows to begin an incredulous retreat towards the prawn-pink pate — clearly he disapproved of this entire *undignified* encounter. Rather than risk any more facial contortions, I offered a final, limpid shrug and throwing an impish grin over my shoulder, dove away.

The dolphins found me once more and surfacing among them in the morning air, I felt my sphere of knowing in simple harmony with theirs. There were now perhaps thirty-five Spinners, some gliding silently along the bottom and others more lively, occasionally offering a spinning leap to the sky before falling back into their element with a splash. Again a group of nine dolphins engaged me and I strongly suspected it was the same male patrol I had met earlier. On an inviting incline, several Spinners trilled, sending out tiny trails of silver bubbles. I trilled back. In response one of them moved closer, the sheen of his sleek shoulder only an arm's length away. Meeting the mystery of his gaze, a familiar feeling ignited: despite all our differences, some understood kinship lay between us. The illuminated plumes of our respiration soon caught the attention of various people about the bay and when I noticed company on its' way, I left the dolphins, unwilling to crowd them.

Alone, suspended in endless blue space, I thought of the Spinner dolphins, of their lives, in a vast, aqueous domain, where all they had were each other. In the yawning abyss of the open ocean, obsidian, or sapphire in the sun, all texture and comfort gleaned from the invisible bonds between them. They must mean *everything* to one another.

Another peripheral flicker scattered my reverie. Once more shadows were converging — not one, but *two* huge marlin, stalking towards me, their striped, finned, dagger-edged forms holding me spell bound with their fierce, scintillating splendor. This time, I was alone. No boats or swimmers, no floating rolly-pollies — nothing — and I was far from shore. I did not experience the clawing of fear — feeling only intensely conscious and alert: a taut violin string before a concerto. My instinctive response to the encroaching danger was born of this state. Arcing deep into the water column, I uttered an urgent, wavering keen of distress.

Somehow, faintly, incredibly — an answer! Again I cried out — and was answered — the Spinners' reply! Swallow-swift our calls flew back and forth, the dolphins pinpointing my exact location. Yet the marlin were almost upon me, so close I could see each scale glinting with lethal brilliance and the deadly intent behind their cold stare.

Moving as one, they streaked into view — nine Spinner dolphins, arching protectively around me. That instant, with a single scything thrust, the marlin vanished, only a few flickering scales gleaming and falling through the water where they had been. Enveloped, I felt myself immediately reassured, knowing these nine. One sleek male slid close along side me. Silently, he told me I was safe and holding his calm gaze, I felt as if tranquility had, with a look, been lent to me. Equilibrium recovered, they slowed, keeping me with them, rising synchronously, our exhalations turning rainbow against the morning sun, mirrored over their curved backs. Held within this grace, the Spinner dolphins escorted me back to earth.

A silent farewell passed between us, the dolphins slipping back into the depths, fading from the shallows, like so many dreams upon waking. Tearing myself from the water, I staggered ashore, suddenly exhausted, only to learn I had been gone for almost *four hours*, causing my human companions much concern! But it was some time before I could push the wondrous tale past my lips.

Group of male Hawaiian Spinner Dolphins.
(photo copyright 2007 Toni Fohoff.)

With the conference drawing to a close, I returned one last time to my familiar promontory, gazing over the sparkling sea, once again privileged to glimpse the whales. They were much closer this time, breaching and crashing against the water, colossal forms dressed in streamers of froth. Even from my shore-bound distance, the might and vigor of the leviathans' displays brandished the booming splendor of a thunderstorm.

A post-conference party was held that evening, at the home of a woman who lived right on the dolphin bay. Talking together, I learned that though she'd been swimming in those waters for years, never once had any marlin appeared. Turtles, whales, sharks, manta rays and of course dolphins — but never marlin. Odd, that. The sun was a perfect, fiery sphere, sinking past streaks of amethyst and scarlet. Mingling with so many marvelous people from all over the world, I was quietly amazed to find that my very bruised faith in humanity had been greatly restored. Despite our far-flung homelands, the sense of community and purpose was warm and palpable.

An informal, eclectic brethren, we met upon the ebonite cliffs at whose feet the ocean slashed and clawed, sending fine spray up hundreds of feet, to mist around us. Those who had not previously fashioned instruments, chose sticks or stones from the natural landscape. The earthen, weather-worn faces of the men who would lead our journey were deeply etched with care and though their eyes held the penetrating sorrow of those who live to see their people decimated and their culture fading, their bearing remained regal. These were members of an Aboriginal Council who had graced the conference with their wisdom and now they waited, to lead a *Chant* down into the volcano.

Ancient ages past, a seething river of lava had carved a winding channel up from the blazing, igneous core of Mauna Loa, from root to tip, the largest mountain on earth, and one of the world's most active volcanoes. Now, a long, reticulating tunnel remained, marking the molten path where dusky stone had once crept, glowing like the sun. Gathered at the cave's darkened portal, veiled among lush, emerald ferns, a mantle of ancestral magic seemed to settle. With prickling pulses we stooped, one by one and entered the threshold of the Underworld. Swathed in stygian blackness my only guide became my hand upon the bowed back of the person in front of me, likewise led by the person before him, wending ever onwards into the darkness. All sight swallowed, other senses engorged. Reaching up from the abyss came the primordial pulse of music: Chanting. Rock. Bone. Wood.

Wildly capering acoustics told me when the tunnel opened into a cavern — our destination. No light, only a primal circle of many voices blending into unceasing song, in the womb of the goddess. I *knew* this Singing —not with my head, nor even my heart, but through my very sinew and fiber — and this sudden, visceral recognition inspired a raw, voluptuous thrill, driving me to answer, like a wolf to its clan, raising my voice into the hidden choir of welcome and gathering. As others continued to emerge into the cave, finding their place amid the rich blackness, I knew not who sat on either side of me clasping my hands, and in the darkness, it did not matter. Here, all were *One*. All praise.

Time fled away, leaving the song to take a life of its own, the music changing and flowing like a tide; slipping effortlessly from instrumentals to vocals, blending both and back. And through it all, the ominous rumbling of titanic, oceanic turbulence, hurling itself against the mountain, setting the very bones of the Earth atremble. From quickening to trance: Dionysian calls, forgotten chants, echoing in the deep places. Millennia falling away… From the dawn of humankind such music has sounded across the ages, trickling down through time in hidden pockets and sacred places. In this, the House of Spirits, secrets are whispered; secrets of a path in life that renews itself rather than leaving a swath of ruin. Elemental songs — knowledge, balance and belonging, remembered and restored; a psalm in Nature's spheres — like the Path we left so long ago.

Slowly, slowly our own time found us again, calling us forth from the darkness in which we sang. Emerging from the palpitating grotto into the spray-laden air, we gazed in wonderment upon the risen moon, a nebulous medallion reflecting upon the sea. Beyond her corona, coruscating galaxies lit the heavens.

I returned to the bay to find the shifting winds had teased up tumultuous waves. Only with perseverance and timing did I slip between the breakers' violently rolling charges. At last admitted past the frothing surf, I perceived the flash and spout of whales further out in the bay. Curiosity and wonder drew me closer, until I realized a small flotilla of kayaks and canoes were also heading straight for them. Refusing to add to the convergence, I instead elected to let the whales be.

Upon discovering a coral reef just beyond the bulk of a rocky out-crop, the whales were temporarily forgotten. It was a place potentially fraught with danger, as the frantic tides ripped over the jagged shoals, obscuring them in foam, but I let the flow of water against my body guide me, keeping me from harm.

By their expectant swirl, I guessed that the reef fish were often fed by swimmers, as they were noticeably fearless, congregating beneath me whenever I remained in any particular area. I found the comings and goings of this submerged metropolis endlessly fascinating. Vivid yellow Tangs rushed to and fro among exotic, striped Moorish Idols; Parrot fish flashed a turquoise even more decadent than the Caribbean variety alongside speckled trunk fish, so awkwardly shaped, they looked like they would sink if ever they ceased fluttering their tiny fins. Brindled with ivory and dark chocolate, a moray eel snaked by, close enough I could make out the tiny projections over its golden eyes. Amid such wonders the world above was forgotten, as if I had never known life as a creature of the land.

Then the whale song began: haunting strains holding me in thrall, pulsing and echoing through the water, resonating in the chambered hollows of my body. August. Ethereal. Sonorous. And then came the fluting trills of the Spinner dolphins; a star-dusting of lyrical notes tinkling over the Humpback's deeper cello and violin. This, I recognized as an invocation; a liquid counterpart to those hymns of earth and fire offered up from the volcano.

I found myself effortlessly undulating amid a large, active group of Spinner dolphins, chattering, whirling into the air and exchanging avid caresses with much apparent ardor. There was an air of gay festivity, with the languor of afternoon sliding towards evening's quickening.

Without warning, a terrible whining roar suddenly rent the water, seeming to come at once from every direction — a speedboat — ripping through the dolphins' midst, scattering their sunny congregation and drowning out the whale song. *Chaos!*

I later learned there were those who did not wish humans and cetaceans to meet in these waters, and charging recklessly about the bay in speedboats was their way of thwarting encounter. Imagining that tearing through schools of socializing dolphins and interrupting courting whales with speedboats is somehow beneficial, betrays dangerously weak thinking. The resulting fright, confusion and interruption from the aggressive assault had been obvious. While able to relate with feelings of protectiveness towards the bay's marine inhabitants, I couldn't condone such rash action, no matter how well intentioned. As a guest in the cetaceans' world, chasing or harassing them was simply *wrong*. I had taken time beforehand, to investigate something of the local Spinner's habits and behavior, and I could recognize dolphins uninterested in investigating human company. Those evincing disinterest in human presence *must* be let alone. Simple.

A last delight in the rolling Pacific, slipping beneath the still pounding surf, through stirring clouds of black sand and into deeper, calmer water. Further out, I glimpsed the glint of a whale mother with her baby, but no echo of the dolphins rang through the sea today. Thinking of them, I again sent out silent thanks for my deliverance. Always the ocean offered ever-changing mysteries — today the water was riddled with pale, minute fluffs, like snowflakes, or dandelion down, suspended, drifting, never falling in an oceanic paperweight world.

Though slush and sleet awaited me among concrete towers, the warmth and vitality I had been given — by the elements, the island, the whales, dolphins and the many people I had met — would remain. Never again would the world seem as vast and impersonal, dotted now with these precious others, struggling in their own corners towards change and hope.

CHAPTER TWELVE

EROSION

As Above
So Below
-Hermetic texts

The spring equinox brought news from Cuba. The golf club which bordered the dolphinarium was buying up the entire area to expand its courses and because of these developments the futures of Christine, Choney, Unior and especially Juan were suddenly thrown into question. The Havana aquarium had expressed interest in taking the four dolphins, but worse still, rumor had it that Marineland was also considering snatching up Christine and Choney to refill its killing tanks.

Would the dolphinarium close down? If so, would Benicio open a new dolphinarium, as he'd often claimed he might? Or would Unior, Choney and Christine be shipped off to an anguished, chlorinated death in Havana — or *worse*, Marineland? What would become of Juan? In the wake of this sudden news, a slew of questions bayed remorselessly for satisfaction. I needed answers — only then would I know how, or even *if*, I might be able to aid the dolphins.

No thorn-like fins or hypnotic ripples disfigured the lagoon's immaculate azure sky. But down on the dock the water erupted in liquid silver as Unior, Christine and Choney poured into my open arms! Though it was unlikely they lamented my absence in the same way I missed them, the warmth of their welcome was unmistakable. As was customary, I rolled in the water amid a cloud of their sonic review, and then we were off, diving and spiraling in perfect synchrony, the water ringing with our calls.

Passing along the net, I discovered Juan's hole had been mended and noticed Unior nosing at the muddy seafloor, where strands of the net's rope had been pulled up around a small opening. Taking a couple of deep breaths, I dove down to scrutinize the aperture, which appeared too small for a dolphin to pass through. Pushing back traitorous worries over becoming ensnared, I was only just able to squeeze through by wriggling against the silty bottom.

Emerging with relief on the far side, I turned to find Choney had unexpectedly chosen to accompany me. Undulating alongside, she trilled her signature whistle, producing a tiny silver stream of bubbles from her blowhole. Entering the channel, we were joined by Unior and, I was surprised to see — Christine. With no indication of Juan in the channel, I continued on with the dolphins into the lake, subtle cues flowing among the four of us punctuated with various chirps and whistles, affirming all was well.

I couldn't help but remark how shallow the lake was. Obviously, the lagoon's environment was far superior to any concrete pool, and the additional space offered in the lake dwarfed that of the lagoon — but even so, there could *never* be any replacement for oceanic freedom.

No tattered dorsal fin or misty plume whispered of Juan's whereabouts, doubtless due at least in part, to my entourage. It was only upon returning to the channel that I glimpsed the tender dome of his head catching the sun alongside one of the moored rowboats. I had found him at last — predictably, begging open-mouthed in the dank channel, before a dull crowd.

Regarding that magnificent being, so reduced and dishonored, sent a terrible, aching weariness through me. Gliding up alongside, I sought Juan's gaze; clouded and despondent. Every drop of vivacity seemed to have been leeched from him, leaving a sullen void. Despite the apparent space and relative freedom available, Juan seemed worse off than ever, the leaden air he exuded, unmistakable. Myriad scars and lacerations marred his listless form — some gashes quite deep and many unmistakably fresh — so the battles with Unior continued. *Why* did Unior seek out violent confrontation with Juan — and what was Choney's part in all of it?

Umberto arrived carrying Juan's bucket of fish, and I hoped that with the edge taken off his hunger, Juan might evince some of his old, able spirit, but after mechanically gulping the contents of the bucket, he merely continued to float vacuously in place. Peering earnestly into his rain-sweet face, attempting to penetrate his overcast mien, Juan stared firmly downwards from beneath heavy lids, before squeezing his eyes closed. I remained at his solemn side and in time he did raise his eyes to mine: a hollow well of sorrow.

Due to food shortages (sadly, an all too common occurrence in Cuba), the dolphinarium's usual supply of mackerel was dwindling rapidly and the bonito (a small oily tuna) used to supplement the dolphins' diets were being chronically rejected. Time and time again, I observed Juan refuse these offerings, ejecting them with a contemptuous shake of his head, leaving the uneaten fish to sink down towards the floor of the channel where mangrove snappers eagerly converged on the free meal. Surrounded by fat, living fish — Juan refused to hunt and feed himself, instead allowing his hunger to taunt him. I couldn't bear it: his pacing and pathetic begging in the face of the gabbling sightseers. He would remain, languishing in the fetid channel, as if invisibly trapped, with no respite from the jeering, teasing tourists. Helplessly disgusted, I would retreat.

After the shabby shows and tourist-hauling, Unior would fly out into the lake, following Choney's earlier path. Almost immediately afterwards, leaping and splashing would erupt far out upon the water.

Longing to discover what transpired, I set out in hopes of some glimpse and at last stumbled upon the dolphins' curious entanglements there. I had found Choney and Juan. The two dolphins were swirling madly about, twisting and raking their teeth against one another in a furious tangle. This sudden scene struck me as quite a bit more inimical than the scenarios I had assumed they shared and every so often a dull thud shuddered through the water, as one of the pair struck the other with great, walloping blows from their powerful flukes. Their activities stirred up clouds of silt and sent jellyfish billowing up, making it necessary for me to keep in continual movement in order to maintain a clear view of the happenings and avoid being stung.

The two would streak off and return, roiling round one another, with cessation just as sudden — the pair coming to swim calmly on either side of me — and an instant later at it again. So strange and wild, these vigorous tempos they followed! Both dolphins' bellies were flushed pink, and whether from exertion or arousal it was clear that Choney was seeking out Juan and he was most certainly obliging. Losing them temporarily in a cloud of silt, I emerged to find Juan now engaged with Christine in a similar fashion — the same sort of rough, possibly sexual dance.

Again engulfed in silt, I emerged to spy surfacing dorsal fins just ahead. Heading towards them, I felt the sussing prickle of echolocation pinpointing my exact location. My surprise deepened further, as all *four* dolphins hove into view, gliding forward and enveloping me amongst themselves. In an expression of immaculate unity the five of us rose, offering misty exhalations to the sun. On my right side, Christine rolled slightly, pec-fins open, inviting caresses. Unior's presence remained warm and unthreatening.

Then came a familiar graze against my shoulder blades. Juan. Lingering, mingling at his side, we drifted on together in sunlit silence, remembering the nectar of nuances; the dialogue of our bond. Approaching the channel, I observed a crowd gathering on the wharf, pointing, shouting and filming. Amongst my sable companions I was at home — those chattering masses were utterly foreign to me.

As if drawn by some grim compulsion, Juan went to drift in his usual melancholic pool by the moored rowboats. I was all too familiar with this immediate and torpid transformation.

Retaining her cheer, Choney had found a discarded paper bag, and was trailing around with it lodged firmly on her pec-fin, chirping in a sunny manner, while Christine and Unior echoed the lithe glyphs she described through the water displaying her prize. Juan floated alone, ignoring their frolic. Approaching him, I peered into his shadowed eyes, trying to understand why he chose to stay alone. The others gathered round, inviting me back towards the lagoon with them, but I chose to remain with him.

On the wharf more people were gathering, some obviously drunk. It wasn't long before these vociferous characters started jumping into the channel, thrashing towards Juan, grasping and groping at him. Umberto appeared with a fish bucket, and seeing him unfazed by the scene unraveling before him, I guessed that this appalling melee wasn't at all unusual! Half of Juan's fish were bonito, which he rejected — all the while dodging the bawling insobriety and repellent harassment with which he was surrounded. It was Benicio's day off and Umberto had made it clear that he wasn't about to intercede. My protestations in defense of the beleaguered dolphin proved wholly ineffectual — I couldn't get through the language barrier or the booze.

The dolphinarium was indeed set to close down at an unspecified date. Rather than see the dolphins shipped away to Havana or elsewhere, it was Benicio's hope that he might find the means to open a new dolphinarium that he proposed to run himself. The next day I accompanied the trainer on a tour of the proposed sight. Camera in hand I listened as he explained his plans for an up-coming to visit Canada to discuss funding for his dolphinarium project. I learned that in exchange for capital, Benicio had offered to assist Marineland in renewing its withering supply of dying captives with yet more wild-caught dolphins from Cuban waters!

Beyond quaint stone walls and wrought-iron gates, lay a lovely, somewhat overgrown little park. Trees, flowers, ornamental ponds — then Benicio showed me the abandoned swimming pool. A scummy concrete enclosure, harboring a frenzy of mosquitoes: a mere thirty by forty-foot rough square and not more than seven feet at its deepest point. -*This*, Benicio proudly announced, was where the dolphins would be kept. I tried to imagine Juan, Unior, Choney and Christine crammed into the tiny pool, less than the depth of their bodies, but was unable to form the image. It was *unthinkable*.

Yet this might well be their fate once the dolphinarium closed down — unless Marineland took them — a still worse scenario. Either way, Benicio intended to lead another capture, dragging more innocents from their ocean communities, to die enclosed in concrete. Impassively recording every detail and snapping composite photos of the horrid pool, I desperately wondered what could be done to prevent further evils befalling the Cubano dolphins and their remaining relatives at sea.

Through it all, another thing galled me: *How* could Benicio involve himself in any of this? How could anyone who claimed to love dolphins, who fought daily for the improvement of their lives, be so impartial and so blind? Carefully broaching the subject, I realized that Benicio suffered not the least moral twinge in his blithe designs. He responded dismissively when I attempted to describe Marineland's grim tanks and drastic death rates, making it clear that this information lacked the strength to shake his convictions — or ambition. He simply refused to embrace any realization or responsibility for the results of his proposed actions. Like so many dolphin trainers, he was a walking contradiction.

The fish shortage continued and though the dolphins largely refused to work due to the lack of acceptable food bribes, throngs of tourists continued to overrun the dolphinarium. Juan remained both restless and inert, but I refused to give up on him, drifting close by in silent vigil. Sullen and evasive, he ignored my hopeful presence, turning his indifferent, battered dorsal fin towards me and a moment later, gliding out into the lake.

Alone, in wounded silence, I journeyed out into the cloudy reaches of the lake, where a familiar resonance found me. I knew it was *him*, felt his halation upon me like a ghostly photograph, like frost forming on a windowpane. As if made from mist, the dolphin appeared, the sight of him more piercing than any riving blade. For circumstance was changing his shape — like waves carving out a cliff, the vice of his life was eroding him. And he knew it.

The following day I again encountered Juan and Choney together out in the lake, actively tussling and spiraling in brazen helixes. Suddenly Choney went shooting off into the haze, pursued by Juan, maneuvering expertly on his back. I never witnessed any actual union, as the dolphins continually vanished into brief clouds of silt, while I kept a keen eye on the jellyfish, which their exertions sent sailing in all directions. When they next appeared, Juan and Choney were quiescent, swimming side by side, seemingly content. Curving around, they slowed to collect me and the three of us continued on together.

Then Unior arrived.

Initially the larger male seemed unperturbed, surveying Choney swimming intimately at Juan's side without visible comment. Despite Unior's evident unconcern, I realized that this was an obvious snub — one that the massive male was unlikely to let slide. Wary as I was, the sudden savagery with which Unior launched himself at Juan sent me reeling.

In an instant, the calm veneer of our company detonated into violent turmoil! Desperately, I tried to deflect the assault, but Unior was too swift. The two males tore around the lake, their ferocious battle broken by mighty leaps and explosions of white froth, while harsh, dissonant buzzing and shrill

Unior (photo: Camilla Singh)

whistles rang through the water. Again and again I saw Unior, all jagged, taurine rage, charging Juan, jaws agape, slamming with jarring impact against his smaller adversary: a massive maelstrom of choler-driven ferocity, snapping and slashing. Their threshing stirred up the sea floor patch by patch, encasing us in opaque, sepia clouds. Irate medusas flew in all directions, and worse still, tiny stinging organisms in the boiling black silt. Retreating from these painful clouds in which the dolphins were immersed, blind and horribly stung I cursed my inability to aid Juan against his powerful foe. Unior was merciless.

Overwrought, issuing impotent cries, I watched as the dolphins twisted and tore at each other, lunging and pivoting powerfully. Even through my horror and distress, their every movement possessed a terrible and fearful beauty. Bleeding and exhausted, Juan would orient, flying towards me, seeking any faint island of shelter in a sea boiling from his adversary's colossal wrath. Throughout the relentless onslaught, I tried to shield Juan from the heaving threat of Unior's circling rancor, placing myself between them. Only too aware of my form's frailty, I knew Unior could easily kill me with even a glancing blow, just as an accidental brush in the fray by either dolphin with the fearsome force they were using would likely prove fatal, but I could not do less.

Uttering defiant cries and shivering with determination, I faced Unior's might. But his strength and speed were too vast; with grim and sustained pressure, he would crash past my guard, even coming right up under Juan when I threw my arms around his torn and lacerated body. Countless times I was inches from being smashed by their thrashing tails, crying helplessly while sickening thumps marked the crushing blows of battle. Only when the stinging clouds descended, inflicting blindness and pain too piercing, would I retreat.

On and on the siege went. Fighting to exhaustion, there were short periods of armistice while Unior recovered his strength. Choney was now keeping close at his side. Ragged and bleeding, Juan would press into my arms in a swoon of fatigue, but respite was short-lived and all too soon it would begin again. Now I understood how Juan had become so terribly scarred.

From the distant wharf, Umberto and Benicio set up a clamor, calling me to attend a trainer's meeting, but I refused to leave Juan until I was certain the fighting had ceased and Unior, with Christine and Choney in tow, had returned to the lagoon. Joining the meeting, I learned that everyone had supposed the dolphins were playing. I was swift to alert them all to the severity of the situation. Somehow, I was not surprised to hear that Christine had bitten a tourist while the battle had raged. However, the trainers' main concern was the continuing difficulty of providing regular shipments of fish for the dolphins, and thereby keeping their cooperation in allowing an eager, paying public to fondle them three times a day.

With Juan's recent tribulations in mind, Benicio prepared an extra portion of fish for the wounded dolphin, dipping into the precious supply of vitamins that I brought for them on every visit. Looking on with some grim satisfaction, I watched Juan gulp his enriched fish, hoping it might lend him the strength he would surely need — but I would have felt far more reassured to see him catching and eating his own.

When Choney reappeared in the channel, Juan immediately sped out into the lake with her — Unior hardly a heartbeat behind. Hurrying to follow, I found the two males just igniting battle, but blowing his whistle and holding aloft a fish bucket Umberto was able to coax Unior and Choney back to the lagoon, for the moment staving off the continuation of conflict. Juan returned to brood by the boats. Was his life so lonely, that a few stolen moments with Choney became worth such bloody contention? Yet he never hesitated in following her, knowing all the while, the wrath that would result. And what of Choney — her actions belied little concern for the effects of her affections. There was so much I didn't understand about their ways. I couldn't have known that in several weeks, Choney would conceive — so for Juan and Unior, there may have been more fueling their battles than mere sexual favors.

I met with grave tidings upon my arrival the next morning. His amber eyes troubled, Umberto explained that the previous evening, while riding home on his bicycle, Benicio had been struck by a car and was now in hospital! While his condition was serious, I was relieved at the trainer's assurances that our friend would certainly survive. I made arrangements to visit Benicio that evening.

Much of the Cuban hospital lay in shadow and in the darkened, drafty halls, people lay unattended on gurneys, flies crawling over their wounds. The lack of light was due to a shortage of light bulbs — and those weren't the only things the hospital was lacking. Simple, vital necessities like bandages and anesthetic were also in short supply, and I saw wounds bound with brown paper towel, because there was nothing else available.

Trailing through the labyrinthine halls, trying to locate Benicio, moans of suffering drifted out of the shadows. At length, I located the correct floor and the doctor responsible for it. The poor fellow, obviously exhausted and under enormous strain, brusquely informed me that there was no one belonging to the name I was seeking, before hurrying away down a dark corridor. I didn't know what to do.

Just then, a soft call came fluting down the hall, and glancing up, I beheld a matronly woman with a kindly face motioning to me from a dimly lit doorway. Moving hesitantly forward, I learned this lady, with long, silver streaked hair was Benicio's mother — I had found him. Pale and wan beneath his tanned skin, he was hardly lucid, which I supposed was for the best, as there was nothing but paper towel and iodine for his fractured skull, broken ribs and wrist. His oozing wounds were not a sight for the faint-hearted. Benicio's condition, though serious, was not diagnosed as critical, and though recovery would be a prolonged process, he would pull through.

I left the eerie place drained but quietly relieved that the trainer was not in mortal danger. More than anything I had seen, I was disturbed by the knowledge that the nearby tourist hospital was fully stocked with everything necessary for the best possible medical care. *That* was where all the supplies were.

Having shrugged off the remaining tourists, all four dolphins emerged from the lake's ghostly fog, enveloping me. So often impassive and unreachable, Juan was now all warmth. Christine and Unior arched head to tail under my chilled hands, offering reminders of my place among them. Spirits rising, I dove, rolling to contemplate their streaming silhouettes above me; diamond formation of memory.

Dipping languidly, our weave loosened and the dolphins began questing through the mossy sea floor ferreting out tiny fish, which they devoured with great relish. Judging by the manner in which Unior and Choney began to play with one of their unfortunate finds, their search was not in earnest. Noticing my curiosity, they brought the tiny battered creature over to me, its eyes glazing.

Swimming at Juan's side, singing with his proximity, we slowed, hanging suspended in the water, gazing at one another. Quietly blossoming, islanded tides of tenderness poured through each winged caress wandering across his torn skin.

In an instant, the limpid image shattered. Choney, who had been showing signs of jealous displeasure, suddenly lunged for Juan's tail, biting him. Rearing up in pain and surprise, Juan's powerful flukes accidentally bashed my thigh — the spell was smashed!

Physically and emotionally stunned, I was unable at first to move my limb, but as the numbness wore off a throbbing pain began. All around me the dolphins had erupted in torrential furor — fighting. It was all too much;

the sudden impact, the violence, the helplessness, the despair — all the pain and uncertainty of the last few days — howling floodtides and no strength for struggle. I hadn't known it was possible to weep underwater. If only the noise and fighting would just *stop!*

Whether or not in response to my distress, the dolphins suddenly ceased their tumult, gathering to surround me, Juan pressing close. Unable to bear the sorrowing sight of them I turned away, shuddering, dragging myself slowly to the lake's far shore and into the weedy shallows. The dolphins followed, scanning me carefully with their sonar, perhaps gauging the depth of the injury, which dwarfed the physical bruising. I didn't care, wanting only to escape their scrutiny. Vaguely it came to me that they were doing odd things, silly things to get my attention, to cheer me. Juan never left my side, and at last I raised my tear-bright eyes to meet his patient gaze.

An instant later, violence again ignited; intensifying, seething, *dreadful!* Through the churning bodies, I glimpsed three dolphins attacking the forth with unbound ferocity. Fatal certitude told me who it was that they threw their fury at. Clouds of silt rolled, now veiling, now revealing the appalling scene as they continued hitting and hurting, allowing their victim no respite. Stricken, powerless, heart bursting — such anguish, I felt reason might leave me. *Please. Please* let it stop.

Sudden cessation. Once more the four dolphins enveloped me, silent, surreal. It began to rain — to *pour*. As one, the dolphins melted away into it. Exhausted and chilled to the marrow, I knew I had to go. Just before I left the water, Juan materialized, regarding me through the rain: a light nudge, over my heart — a wordless statement, before turning and vanishing once more into the gray water.

The morning tide in the lagoon was high and clear from the rain. In that mysterious way of hers, Choney produced from some submerged stash, an enormously long piece of lime-green fabric. Ingeniously draped on her dorsal fin, the bright cloth rippled like a banner, as she proudly paraded it before the rest of us with expert confidence. The chase was on, Unior, Christine and I following her every move, our voices trebling with excitement. When my turn came to take up the bright cloth, I was surprised by how cumbersome it was — the dolphins had made it look effortless — such strength, skill and control!

Later, searching the lake for Juan, I glimpsed him as he flew by with both Unior and Choney close behind, their swiftness immediately abandoning me. I called out uncertainly and moments later, all four dolphins appeared, a little out of breath. Juan took his place beside me and collected among them we undulated onwards. Under the unmistakable intensity of our shared gaze, Juan and I slowed and drew closer.

The other dolphins became immersed in a rough bacchanalia, but Choney was watching Juan and I, again seeming none too pleased. This time I heeded the warning signs, and was ready when I saw her lunge at him, sliding nimbly out of the way. A brief scuffle ensued, though it was unclear if it was fueled by passion or anger. In any event, Unior stayed out of it, for which I was thankful. Except when provoked by Choney's licentious insistence, Juan chose to remain with me, and it appeared Choney wasn't accepting his refusals kindly — but for the time being, he seemed immune to her delphic charms.

There was a marked contrast between Juan's sudden, jagged movements among the other dolphins, and his unfailing gentleness with me. I got the sense that he was tired of so much fighting and biting, tooth raking and tail whacking — and now he sought tenderness. Without reticence, Juan sought my encircling arms, like a garland around him; each caress further dissolving dissension — the cordial for all ailments carried within this intermingling. The forgotten foxfire once again stole into his eyes, infusing me with inflections of Eden, lingering in lotic love.

With twilight the dolphins' Beltane fires burned low and a sweet calm settled over the five of us. Looking into their faces I understood that somehow, despite the oppression, the dissidence, the sorrow, the hunger — somehow, I had a place here, among them. My garbled, warbled attempts at repeating their whistles, my attenuated speed and lack of strength meant nothing in such mellifluous instances. They took me wholly, as I was — our differences impossibly and effortlessly superceded with the grace that marked their every movement. For these immortal, golden moments, drifting through the rich, wavering sunbeams, peace reined and I was *home*.

But as we neared the channel, Juan's mood fell. Leaving us all, he went to brood in his usual spot by the boats in ruinous solitude. The inter-glacial interlude was over, our shared incandescence already a memory. The flame of his gaze diminished. Soon there would be only ashes...

CHAPTER THIRTEEN

A ROAD LESS TRAVELED

"Bring all the shadows into the sun of your eye,
So they will merge in the light of your cheek
My heart's domain is disordered by your distance
Torn with civil strife."
Rumi

Spring's thaw drew the redolence of awakening earth past still melting snow. Despite a persistent impression that time was running out for Juan, necessity dictated I wait for further developments with the Cubano Dolphins' situation. No matter what prayers one offers up to the gods of patience, waiting is often a hard thing.

In May, Benicio came to Canada to pursue negotiations with Marineland and continue recovering from his accident. Visiting with him on several occasions that summer, I was relieved to learn that plans for further dolphin captures had been put on hold and along with it, the trainer's park proposal. By the time the first leaves were turning, the trainer had returned to Cuba, thankfully empty-handed.

Another laden summer tumbled towards fall, and in the forests I wandered beneath ember canopies, inhaling the silent smell of sunlight amid the heavy dampness and riotous colors. Autumn signaled a pleasant return to warm, murmuring libraries, rare book and reference collections, studying and researching in humble glory among the tomes. Page by page, my understanding of dolphins (and many other things besides) continued to expand. But how I missed them.

Word reached me from Cuba in late fall. Both Choney and Christine were again pregnant and due in spring. Benicio had strongly advised delaying the plan to remove the dolphins from the lagoon until after the females had given birth and their infants were at least six months old. Ignoring his advice in the past had already led to the deaths of three infants, and at last it seemed the trainer's opinion carried some leverage.

For many months I'd been trying to raise assistance for Juan and the other Cubano Dolphins through a network of conservation organizations. Though I'd been assured of their interest, these organizations remained reticent in offering tangible aid. Material support failed to manifest and time passed. Finally I realized if I anything further were to happen, it was again my move. I returned to Cuba in mid winter, after a long flight and stopover in Santiago.

It was late when I finally arrived, following the waves' whispers into the night, passing through the trees' tossing, moon-laced shadows. At last submersed and claimed, feeling a familiar sea change, I gazed upon the twinkling stellar multitudes; ciphers of splendor. Far across the quickening waters, lighting snaked and flickered amid seething black clouds.

Abandoning the rumpled sheets to morning's sweet humidity, I headed to the lagoon, arriving so early, I found the place empty. Christine, Unior and Choney all drifted in a solemn row before the net, which now hung in lank strings that clearly could not contain them. This discolored scene produced a barb of uneasiness. Settling in a hush on the dock, I waited — but none of the dolphins appeared to appraise my arrival. In fact, they all seemed to have vanished. Puzzled, I waited and my uneasiness remained.

Submerging, I found the lagoon's water so murky with suspended particles that I could hardly see my hand before my eyes. Attempting to swim in this olivaceous soup, I made another discovery — the brine was *riddled* with jellyfish. Though they had always been common enough in the lake and channel, I had rarely seen them in the lagoon's deeper water. Something was definitely amiss.

The dolphins remained silent and invisible, so I decided to make my way towards the lake, hoping to find Juan, and clearer waters ahead. Just as I entered the narrow, gloomy channel, Unior came looming out of the cloudy water, crossing rapidly and repeatedly in front of me, his rough movements stirring up the silty sea floor and battalions of jellyfish!

Too late, I realized all the little moored boats were gone (sunk in a storm) leaving me with no means of escape from the channel's confined quarters where I now found myself trapped, surrounded by stinging medusas and the unexpectedly aggravated dolphin who was issuing an ominous, aggressive buzzing! Desperately I searched for any means of escape, but the tide was too low to reach the edge of the wharf. Unior's caustic droning seemed to be menacing me from everywhere at once as he tightly circled. I had seen him clash with Juan and knew all too well what he was capable of — I had to get *out!* Somehow, impossibly, I managed first to cling and finally to climb out onto the wharf, scraping myself up nicely in doing so. Still heaving with alarm, be-slimed and bleeding, I looked down at Unior in the channel, still watching me intently.

Why had my actions provoked such agitation? Was there some danger ahead in the murk he was warning me away from, or was I breaking some new established taboo? Perhaps Unior still wished to keep Juan and I apart. I very much wanted to understand what had just happened, but while the dolphin's posture belied watchfulness, rather than anger, his impassive smile offered no answers.

Unior waited until I'd headed back towards the lagoon, before diving to return there himself, arriving even before I did. With him Christine waited, sliding her icicle smooth skin beneath my hands, instantaneously reconciling my hiatus with reciprocal pec-pats and pleased nuzzles. Impatient and Lilith-lined, Choney pushed forward demanding caresses herself. At this haughty intrusion, Christine narrowed her comely eyes, and with a loud, staccato exhalation, departed. In time, this would become a pattern.

As for Unior, he behaved as if *nothing* unusual had occurred, adopting his usual friendly and flirtatious manner and even as I slipped into the water, he grazed up against me coyly. A reminder of the strange wildness of their ways — and the associated risks — which I accepted willingly. Weaving in close along side me, Unior lead me down into the dim recesses. I caught the twinkle of excitement in his eye and keeping pace at his side we curved upward, rushing up now towards the muted sunlight above. Breaking the surface synchronously, Unior's girth exploded up into the light, soaring high over my head in a magnificent arch, before crashing back into the water, where the two of us immediately drew together, surging down once more into the depths to repeat the entire passage again and again! This sequence of frenetic leaps became an often shared ritual, spontaneously bursting into being between us.

Nevertheless, in light of recent occurrences, I decided it might be prudent to *walk* rather than *swim* to the channel to continue my search for Juan. Moments after my apprehensive arrival, on the pier, Juan surfaced right before me, dispensing a witheringly dismissive glance before continuing on past. Hope's sandcastles smothered beneath an indifferent tide.

A moment later I saw what drew the dolphin's attention so singularly. As I watched, Juan glided on through the grimy channel towards the old water bar — a dilapidated, rotting and recently resurrected pontoon, floating on the water's edge, not far from the lagoon's net, serving booze and snacks to passing tourists. Swimming right up to the barge's peeling edge, Juan rose up from the water and began to beg open-mouthed at the tourists for fish. My heart dropped further, as with growing concern, I watched him perform several of his old tricks, begging all the while. *This* was all part of Iago's plan: wearing down Juan's will, demeaning him for the pleasure of paying passersby, reeling him back under control and making the once feral dolphin earn his keep once more.

I was determined to reach the water and without access to the channel, I decided to try entering the lake via the tiny mud flat at the wharf's end. The fetid mire sucked at my legs and too late, I saw that even these shallows were riddled with jellyfish. Unable to turn back, I plunged forward, resolute in my attempt to try and reunite with Juan.

Drifting over the lake's diluvian meadows, silent, plaintive moments drifted past. Feeling a subtle tremor — I turned to find Juan had come, pale and stormy-eyed. His nearness beckoned, but I knew better. The old wounds had healed over, leaving his once smooth skin streaked with pallid scars. Yet the absence of fresh lacerations indicated the battles between he and Unior must have tapered off — and of course both Choney and Christine were now pregnant.

Swirling restlessly before me, Juan turned his face—and I *froze*. The silent, screamless fall of darkened dreams; the visceral constriction felt through a vitreous spine, before the impact rushing up from the blackness below... Juan's left eye had been injured — leaving it squeezed and puckered closed! I couldn't tell if it had been gouged out, or poked in, or stung by a jellyfish or *what*. Realization left me stunned. Devastated.

Ever afterwards, when stress so plagued Juan, he would repeatedly lift his head from the water — slowly arching and twisting in an eerie, weighted manner — the motion reminding me of a horse straining at short reins. This motion, this *"straining at the reins"* seemed to take root from this injury.

Each day swarms of tourists lined up for dolphin-rides, the entirety of their oppressive weight falling squarely on the backs of Unior and Christine. Clamoring and strident, waving fistfuls of cash, they pushed and jostled while Iago relieved each of them of their money. In order to satisfy this demand, Iago often drove the dolphins to haul tourists for over two hours straight, three times a day.

Choney no longer went streaming out into the lake to engage Juan, instead remaining in the lagoon, and the armistice between Unior and his rival continued. But later, traveling along with Choney and Christine, I realized that Unior had left us. There was only one likely place to find him.

Hurrying overland towards the channel, I saw the two males, twisting and splashing, all around them signs of silt and jellyfish stirred by their activities. A glance at the profusion of jellyfish told me it would be pointless to try and enter the shallow channel to help Juan, and so caged and pacing I watched from the wharf, wondering in passing, how the dolphins could endure the stinging brine.

As events unfolded between Unior and Juan I recognized what I was seeing was a sexual component of dominance vying. Twisting almost leisurely around his rival, Unior pushed his head and neck over Juan's back. No harsh aggressive sounds or buzzing were audible above the water, only the odd whistle, nor did I observe any full out chasing, thrashing or whacking. Only the dolphins knew the true undercurrents of their actions. Threat? Malice? Tenderness? Humiliation? At times, both Juan and Unior's behavior seemed to take a more sensual turn, with vast shinning bellies rolling skyward, or pressing together. This puzzling exchange soon progressed into more overt sexual gestures, as the two dolphins demonstrated brazen attention towards each other's genital regions. I was aware that male bottlenose dolphins often use sexual violence as a deciding factor in situational battles of skill and will, yet for the moment there remained an absence of malignant turbulence. In fact they were taking up so much time with careful pec-fin caressing that I had to wonder if there were not some hidden dimension of relationship at work. Perhaps Unior was somehow servicing Juan in lieu of the females, with whom he may have forbidden contact — allowing a certain peace, which would crumble were his authority directly challenged? Certainly I had never seen such slow, drawn out behavior directed by either male at Christine or Choney.

I watched them continue for over an hour, often separating and turning nonchalantly away from one another right in the middle of things. During one of these "breaks," Juan curved over, gazing up at me with his one good eye, where I knelt on the wharf. At this, Unior sped over, cutting between us and leading Juan back into their encounter, twisting and vying in slow-motion. Whatever the obscure substrate beneath their dance, it at least didn't involve bloodshed — unless of course, this was merely a prelude…I couldn't ignore the scars Juan bore or forget the very real and angry force that had made them.

There was another fish shortage at the dolphinarium. How I hated seeing Juan, miserable, hungry and begging. Over in his tiny, filthy iron prison the poor sea wolf circled endlessly and on the floors of their cramped concrete cells, the sea turtles lay sunken and listless. The crocodile had died — and been replaced with a pelican, which unable to fly or swim, could only stand in its own refuse gazing forlornly past the iron bars. A carnival of nightmares.

Hordes of tourists continued crowding for "dolphin-hauls," fueling with their ignorant lust, this great machine of misery. Fleeing the lagoon, I would kneel in a forlorn heap near Juan at the water bar, watching the dolphin begging for scraps, keeping just beyond the grasping painted claws of the tourist-ladies.

No escape
No escape
No escape

Each day Iago brought Juan's daily ration of fish in a bucket to the water bar, where for a nominal fee, it was dolled out in minute portions to tourists so they could tease him into performing various abject, defiling tricks. Just as Iago intended, Juan now spent much of his time begging for shabby scraps from tourists and attracting yet more as he did so. It was past disgusting, but no one seemed to notice or care. I knew Benicio wouldn't approve, but the trainer had been away from the dolphinarium for some time and without him, there was no one to police where, how much or in what manner Juan was fed. At the end of the day, I watched the bar's slovenly custodian dispense the last of the day's tepid leftovers to the eager, open-mouthed dolphin. Hungry as he was, Juan gulped the fish down too fast, choking and spitting them back up, while I looked on, helpless, seized with despair.

Afterwards, Juan drifted over and our eyes met; captured by the dark draught of that fatal absinthe, we suffered side by side, in silence.

Almost fully recovered from his terrible injuries, Benicio returned to the dolphinarium and I immediately questioned him about Juan's wounded eye. However, Benicio proved just as shocked as I'd been, insisting there had been no such injury when he had last seen Juan, three weeks earlier — so it was quite recent. As for how it had happened, it was only too easy to imagine some inebriated oaf with a pointed stick… I'd never know the truth.

From the trainer I at last learned it had been decided that rather than deliver Choney, Christine, Unior and Juan to the concrete tanks of Marineland, Havana or Benicio's sordid park-pool, all four dolphins were to be moved to another salt lagoon further down the peninsula. Several months previously, the dolphinarium had been preparing to close down, just as I had been warned, but without Benicio's experienced assistance, the divers had been unable to net the clever dolphins and so they'd remained where they were. As things stood, the big move would wait until some unspecified time after Choney and Christine gave birth in May or June.

In answer to my questions about the profusion of jellyfish, Benicio explained that the lagoon and lake had become polluted with pesticide run-off from the neighboring golf course and this toxic over spill had upset the biological balance — resulting in a jellyfish over-population.

In the lagoon, with Juan begging only yards away at the water bar, I decided to brave Unior's possible displeasure, pushing past the decrepit net and through the blind murk, which provoked much buzzing inspection from the other dolphins. Drawing near to Juan, he greeted me, inclining his mercurial form under my gentle hands. Though his injured eye remained a wrenching loss, the lingering gaze we still shared nourished threads of hope.

But then, with climbing anxiety I watched as Choney, who had been pacing the perimeter of the net watching, nudged past it and came over to join us — closely followed by Unior. Knowing the explosive potential of these particular three dolphins, I tensed.

However, Juan appeared to ignore Choney and Unior entirely. With sovereign poise, he lead me away from the rank water bar and out toward the channel. Unior and Choney followed alongside us and it soon became apparent they were inviting me out to the lake with them. As much as I longed to linger with Juan in that expanse, my misgivings at running the channel's stinging gauntlet in confined quarters with two male dolphins that might at any moment explode into battle were too strong to ignore, and reluctantly I turned away. Rather than leaving me behind, Juan chose to remain, making clear his wish to continue our companionship. Glancing up, I noticed the tangerine and ebony flutter of a monarch butterfly hovering over our heads — a winged symbol of freedom. I wished I could lead Juan away from this squalor, to where the ocean's pure, clean waters could wash the stink of the place off him.

The following morning I found a wearied Juan with deep, angry-red rake-marks all across his head — Unior's attacks had resumed! Keening softly over his lacerated skin, I gazed past the dilapidated net at a faint dolphin-sparkle in the lagoon. Choney's forays beyond the net the previous day bore an obvious correlation to Juan's raw wounds.

While I understood that in wild communities, aggression has a part to play in the maintenance of dolphin social order, wild dolphins enjoy the freedom of large ranges, which allows individuals the option to disperse from unsolicited conflict — or to seek assistance. Despite the seeming size of the lake, Juan could only flee so far, and could hope for no effectual aid from

Juan showing his injured eye.

friends or family — and before me lay the heart-rending results.

Over in the lagoon, Christine launched herself into a series of breaches, slamming herself against the water's surface with noticeable zeal, and finishing off her display with several chuffing breaths and a tail slap. Perhaps she was protesting her hunger — the fish shortage continued. However, in the absence of any acceptable food bribes, the dolphins had turned the tables on Iago's usual *"No work – no fish"* rule, adopting a *"No fish – no work"* policy of their own, forcing the dolphinarium to cancel the rest of the shows and "swims" for the day.

I arrived to a bizarre sight the next morning — the normally olive brine of the lagoon having turned an unnatural shade of turquoise. Umberto blithely explained that this was due to the loads of chlorine that had been dumped into the water, to combat the jellyfish plague. My jaw dropped. *Chlorine!*

The effects of this chemical pollutant were immediately evident in the eerie pale water. Death. All the fish were dead, floating at the surface, or lying on the bottom, the glitter gone from their scales. All the crabs, the shrimp, the anemones, sponges and coral — dead or dying. All the delicate, jewel-like water plants — dead, collapsed and grey. And as I traveled around the lagoon, I saw it was the same everywhere — everything dead or dying. The delicate blooming diversity I had once known now resembled the surface of the moon, cracked, crumbled and lifeless. I never saw a single dead jellyfish though. The water by the barge was also littered with bloated fish corpses, but the dolphins appeared unaffected.

Pomegranate sweet, Juan twined close, until I felt the faintest tug of hope amid our bleak surroundings. He rolled to collect my caresses over his niveous chest and belly, where I saw bloody rake marks, ripping beneath his sensitive pec-fins. Earlier I'd noticed Unior had similar injuries — they had certainly done a number on each other. While Unior remained reluctantly hauling tourists for the last few remnants of fish, Choney surfaced beside Juan, where he and I were resting quietly together. Choney became fitful, nudging and buzzing at Juan's genital region. Juan remained unresponsive. I caught Choney's eye over Juan's scarred back and as our gazes held a moment, I wondered how Choney perceived me: A rival, a friend, an amusement or an annoyance? Perhaps she took me by mood and moment.

Only when Juan returned to the water bar to beg did Choney and I sail back over the net into the lagoon. Passing over the rotting ropes, I saw they were covered with tiny crabs, frantically trying to climb up out of the poisoned water; all of us caught within a house of horrors made real. Slowly, the lagoon was returning to its usual green, as the chlorine was carried out to sea on a poisoned tide.

Farewells were unexpectedly attenuated. While speaking with Umberto regarding the seriousness of the chlorine's effects, the trainer mentioned in his absent-minded way, a strikingly important "detail": Six *newly captured* dolphins were being held near a boat marina at the end of the peninsula, for acclimatization before shipment over-seas!

Wasting no time, I tore back to my room, grabbed my camera and immediately hailed a taxi for the long ride to the marina. It was farther than I had been led to expect and took me into a completely unfamiliar area of tangled jungle scrub and abandoned, overgrown buildings. Ill at ease, I steadied myself to document the situation and gather as much information as possible. With Cuba as one of the top exporters of dolphins into the world market, it was terribly important to find out who was responsible for their capture, where they were bound for (maybe Germany, Spain, or even Marineland?), and what, if anything could be done to rescue them. If only I had found out *sooner*! As it was, the shadows were already long when the taxi pulled up to the seedy, run down marina. The place seemed pretty much deserted except for a dejected looking parrot hunched in an iron cage and some shady looking dockhands slouching in the shadows. With no one else in sight, I summoned my courage, suppressed my better judgment, and approached the skulkers with my broken Spanish, asking where the dolphins were and if I could see them.

My halting questions provoked a staccato discussion between the men, but no response directed at me. The curious taxi driver, who was still hanging around to see what was going on, volunteered translation in stilted English: permission to take out one of the boats would have to be obtained in order to bring me to the dolphins. *Ah.* I waited, determined to ignore the leers protruding from the stretching shadows, wondering when or *if* anyone intended to take me to the dolphins at all. The sun had been swallowed up behind the tangled mangroves leaving the gloaming to tighten its talons around me, when one of the dubious dockhands appeared: a hulking skulker, wiping grimy hands on his soiled shirt and motioning towards a rickety motor boat. Warily, I stepped into the precarious, wooden vessel, suddenly conscious of the man's size — small boat, big creep.

Motoring down the mangrove-lined channel, the ruffian began an almost immediate groping advance, his foul breath and prickling jowls slavering against my neck. Ire awakened, I refused his roving meat hooks, *insisting* he take me *straight* to the dolphins! Glowering, he guided the boat on into the threatening gloom. After what seemed like ages, we arrived at a tiny mangrove islet, where a pen was strung between poles driven into the sandy bottom. In the last light I could see that the pen was divided into three sections, each containing two dolphins — three males and three females, my scowling companion revealed with a guttural grunt.

Watching the dolphins nervously surfacing as the boat drew alongside the pen, I took in every possible detail, noting all six were small and unmarked. I could see them furiously scanning the boat from beneath the darkening water between brief breaths. It was too dark to take photos. This realization, combined with the lewd groping I was *still* fending off, made me *furious.* Again I repelled the man's lecherous weight. Fortunately my disgust and determination outweighed my alarm and I was successful in repulsing his crude rape attempt. Perhaps knowing I could escape into the water if necessary, gave me courage. Though he initially refused to start the boat, my stridently rising voice and increasing wrath eventually won out and I found myself returned to shore, fuming and be-slimed, but unscathed. Thankfully I'd had the sense to prevail upon the taxi driver to return for me and I found him waiting as agreed.

All through the night, I could think only of those six young dolphins I had seen. Newly caught, they remained wild creatures — and if the net were cut, they would likely flee straight to freedom. But once the psychological warping and conditioning of training sets in, dolphins often hesitate at the sudden appearance of an escape avenue. Under the circumstances, cutting the net would have been impossible and my flight departed early the following morning. I would have to seek immediate help through one of the European or American protection organizations. There were names known to me, of people who might hop a flight to cut a net, and save a dolphin. There was still hope for them and I had a lot of work to do.

CHAPTER FOURTEEN

CORROSION & FAILURE

"I, I had a swing when my salt was my own,
I'd my teeth bared for battle, til love lost made me dull."
Lisa Hannigan, *Teeth*

Immediately upon my return, I compiled a report for dissemination to organizations on both sides of the Atlantic, describing the situation facing those six newly captured dolphins in Cuba. Despite the eventual expenditure of much time, money and energy with follow-up faxes and phone calls, a month passed and *still* employable assistance failed to manifest. While the capture, export, import and treatment of all and any dolphins was technically of grave concern to a number of protection organizations, the plight of these unheard-of Cuban captives inexplicably failed to inspire any useful action or investigation, which was *terribly* frustrating.

Individuals whom I knew would have unequivocally flown straight to Cuba to cut the captives' nets proved unreachable, in distant countries, attending to other situations of similar magnitude. Time was ticking by and it appeared no one could or would help, so that just left me — but I wasn't sure what to do. I decided to return to Cuba (bringing vitamins and medicine for Juan and the others), determined to discover any further information concerning the plight of the six captives. At the very least, I had to try and learn where they were bound for. I wasn't ready to give up on them.

New management had taken over the dolphinarium and all about the grounds things were being knocked down and put up — pretty much the same as usual. Though the hapless sea turtles and sea wolf remained, I was told that at least the poor pelican had been released. At Benicio's insistence in anticipation of the approaching dolphin births, the lagoon's net had been re-strung, with finer double netting, to prevent further infant fatalities.

• Lyrics from the album *Sea Sew*, 2008.

116

Slipping into the water, Unior (as ever, unfazed by my sudden reappearance) immediately collected me, for an enthusiastic round of our synchronistic dive-leaping sequence. Flying to break the surface at the massive dolphin's side, I watched him smash out of the water and go rocketing ten feet up into the air over my head. After four or five rounds, I was exhausted — oh for a dolphin's tail and Olympian endurance!

Impatient to reunite with Juan, I found him begging amid the daily ruckus at the rotting water bar. Unsure of my reception, I hesitantly drew closer. I could see his injured eye remained squeezed shut — a loss I remained almost unable to comprehend. It was a grim and familiar scene: Juan begging pathetically, open-mouthed among discordant, grasping tourists. Every movement betrayed his obvious misery, inducing a sudden wrenching stab of pity.

Suddenly Juan turned, erupting with aggressive buzzing, arching his body and slapping his tail forcefully on the water. Uncertain, I hovered, torn between retreating and trying to persevere. Along with the furious pitch of his buzzing, thundering like a speedboat engine, the dolphin's violent roiling began to escalate. I froze with disbelief — *never* had any of them reacted to me like this!

At that instant, Unior came barreling past from somewhere behind me, instantly engaging Juan in full-out battle! As the two powerful males leapt and thrashed against one another, the frightening drone of their rancor resonated throughout my painfully tensed body. Dazed and shaken, I kept wondering if Juan's aggression had been aimed at me — or at Unior? Had Unior just saved me from pulverization, or were Juan and Unior just carrying on their usual hostilities? There was no way of knowing the truth, and at that moment, not knowing was difficult to bear.

Though Choney and Christine were firmly pregnant, Juan and Unior continued to fight — this was *not* some seasonal breeding scuffle — this was *war* — but *why*? Obscured in the deep, cloudy water, Juan and Unior continued their fearsome animosity. With their terrible sounds echoing all around me, I returned to the lagoon. The tension must have been contagious, because suddenly Choney and Christine began to squabble, twisting and snapping at one another's flukes, creating their own harsh symphony. Dissidence everywhere!

Unior's return settled matters quickly. Having just come from thrashing poor Juan, he now flaunted noticeably flirtatious spirits, dallying with Christine, the two of them whetting their pec-fins together, undulating almost belly to belly. With her head thrown back, squirming with delight, Christine became the very picture of joyous abandon. Passing by the net, I paused to gaze with forlorn concern out at Juan, who had rejoined the teasing tourists at the water bar to beg. Alone.

The dolphinariums' meager supplies of vitamins and disinfectant had dwindled and Benicio was most thankful for the supply I brought. Accompanying the trainer to the channel, I watched him feed Juan — away from Iago, Unior and the pollutant noise and incessant grasping at the water barge. I could see Juan's new wounds, some still bleeding freely, but his preoccupation with eating gave me an opportunity to apply some medicated salve to his eye. It did not look swollen or infected, just closed. Despite downing the contents of an entire bucket of fish, Juan headed straight back to the water bar after his meal — to continue begging, though he was full and had no need. I could almost feel the repulsive texture of this addiction, fueling the mad fires beginning in him.

Another battle broke out between the males the following morning. Unior and I had just commenced our dive-leaping sequence, when I noticed Juan surfacing just on the other side of the net, arching his body aggressively, clashing his powerful flukes on the water and issuing an angry, rumbling buzz. It appeared he was calling his rival to duel, and Unior accepted the challenge. Facing each other through the mesh, head to head, arching, buzzing and snapping — they actually fought right *through* the net. Twice Juan leapt with such vehemence he almost sailed right over it! Soon afterwards, both of them went streaking out into the lake. Struggling with internal knots over the violence, I hurried to the wharf to see what was happening. Peering across the lake, I observed only the occasional fin breaking the surface — no leaping or thrashing. I wanted to arrow out there and impossibly shelter Juan from Unior's wrath, but my courage failed. And it wasn't Unior I was afraid of. It was Juan.

We were hit with a tremendous storm the next day and in deciding to forgo my daily trek to the dolphinarium, I felt a certain relief. Drained, weary and encumbered with melancholy, hope seemed hard to come by. Stepping out into the wildly billowing wind, I released my sorrow, my worry and my heartache into the fierce weather until it was impossibly exchanged for exhilaration. The Sea bought ablution and renewal, until I became just another Nereid, sporting amongst the foam-flecked waves.

In the calm after the storm I found Unior and Choney in high spirits, engaging in lots of pink-bellied sex play. But dolphins play by rules as fluid as the element they inhabit, and soon afterwards, it became Christine whom Unior was wooing. Now the odd one out, Choney occupied a subordinate position, trailing behind the other two. Unwilling to endure such insult,

Choney protested this arrangement and a moment later some mild squabbling and splashing erupted, which ended with Unior and Christine chasing Choney away. However, Unior soon endeavored to make amends, drawing suavely alongside Choney, and after having caressed her with a great deal of ardor and finesse, they finally swam off together, belly to satin belly.

Unior even took time out of his busy schedule to swim alongside me, inviting sumptuous caresses and regarding me with dulcet, half-lidded eyes. Hanging in the water, as we gazed intently at one another, I could almost hear the wheels turning behind that unfathomable stare of his. His meditations concluded on whatever unknowable note, Unior, with an almost sardonic flourish, presented me with a small yellow leaf. This gesture couldn't help but remind me of a similar gift bestowed, what seemed like ages ago. I still had the little yellow leaf Juan had given me one day, long ago. Before the scars.

Every day the dolphinarium was overrun with tourists. Some, after eating ice cream, gawking at the poor sea turtles and the caged sea wolf, watched the sham dolphin show and left — just something else to do on their list of holiday activities. However, many came specifically to "swim with the dolphins." In a profit-driven frenzy, Iago worked Unior and Christine beyond exhaustion and into aggression almost daily. This meant that in addition to snapping at Iago in pure exasperation — as no matter how hard they worked, he still refused to feed them their full portions of fish — the dolphins often took out their considerable frustrations on unsuspecting tourists, paddling in the water with them. Already there had been more injuries, bruises, bites and scary near misses than I could count. Benicio knew it was only a matter of time before someone *really* got hurt, and when he worked with the dolphins and saw tension climbing, he would simply halt the proceedings. Iago, under no such compassionate obligation, worked well into the danger zone to collect more money — and that, in the end was what counted to the new manager: Iago made more money, so Iago was put in charge of the dolphin-swims. Danger to tourists, like cruelty to the dolphins, didn't matter and wasn't taken into account.

Sometimes, when unable to face the crowds, the slave driving, the blindness and the futility, I would take the dust strewn path over to the water bar, seeking Juan and enduring a different kind of despair. Kneeling softly down before the begging, open-mouthed dolphin, I would wait. Wait to catch his one good eye. Wait for the hope of recognition. Wait to share solace. But worn and wan, Juan continued to beg, gaze cast firmly downward, with no interest or recognition of his old friend.

Juan had broken the rules, refused to perform or haul tourists, and with much persistence, made good his escape. But the lake had no access to the sea, only a larger prison. And now, shackled by Iago's diabolical will, Juan was slowly being broken; dragged back under the harness of captivity. And he knew. He *knew*, and before me his hope and his will withered. All that mattered now was food. And so he would not meet my eyes.

Returning to the lagoon, I drifted alone by the net, quietly aching over Juan and his deteriorating situation. I never saw it coming. I felt the clammy jelly against my neck — and after a strange, breathless delay, the fiery pain. Instinctively pushing the medusa away from my face, it stung my arm as well — a sting that would leave a scar for weeks. Swimming was for the moment out of the question. I could only hang in the water, enduring wave after burning wave of pain. In the dark water, becoming very still, I felt myself turn inward, almost exploring the pain, and slowly, it became sort of more an itch, and then only an awareness of sensation.

Wholly unexpected, Juan appeared before me, floating just on the other side of the net, scanning me softly. He remained quiet and close, until the wretches at the water bar began hammering on a submerged pipe, rudely recalling him to beg for scraps. Why had he come? Had he sensed my distress? Bored? Curious? Lonely? Not long afterwards, while straining for a glimpse of him from the wharf, he came gliding slowly into the channel from the lake, his entrance making hardly a ripple in the water's green glass. Spying human presence, Juan rushed up, begging open mouthed — but then he stopped, closing his gaping jaws and lifting his inscrutable gaze to mine. Did he know me at last?

For some time Benicio had been pushing for the dolphinarium staff to instate an introductory briefing prior to the so-called "dolphin swims" and it was arranged to give it an experimental try. Most of the waiting tourists came to sit in the dappled shade to ask questions, learn about dolphin basics and more importantly, absorb Benicio's thinly veiled warning about the risks of sharing the water with these powerful, moody creatures. As if to demonstrate this potential violent streak, Juan and Unior flailed and thrashed in the nearby channel all throughout the session.

Watching Juan gulp his breakfast the next morning, I saw him suddenly duck under the water and speed out into the lake — pursued by Unior. With the tide high and clear, I decided to venture into the lake myself, in an attempt to follow. Undulating alone across the lake's misted pasture, I heard and felt the prickling suss, when Juan and Unior oriented on me. Side by side, the two dolphins soared into view. Not knowing what to expect, I remained silent and still. Without a sound, they collected me among them and we continued on together. In the clearer water I could see how much larger Unior was. Both dolphins carried a lot of raw rake-marks from heedless and ferocious contact with one another's teeth.

Nothing happened immediately. At first Unior swam at my side — and then Juan. After several minutes, they paused, both dolphins regarding me in the stillness, Unior, ominous as an imperceptibly darkening thundercloud. I felt caught between crosscurrents; balancing between a dual radius of tension and wordless, discarnate threat. On some silent accord the three of us continued on once more. I was not lulled by any seeming serenity. We were all waiting for something to happen.

From the wharf, irritable Iago appeared, blowing his whistle and calling Unior to haul more tourists. Unior paused, as if considering, and then with a quietly derisive breath, he made his decision to remain, dismissing Iago and his fool whistle. The three of us continued on, but something had changed, because now Juan swam firmly at my side and Unior a space away. All the while, Juan — so often silent — repeated a certain shrill whistle.

With sudden taurine vigor, Unior lunged at Juan and in an instant they were seething amid battle, right below me! As their powerful tails lashed out, jellyfish flew in all directions and the water thrummed with their savage rancor and stomach-caving thumps every time one of them scored a shattering blow. With furious fervor they churned the water, all snapping jaws and raking teeth. I wanted to rush to Juan's aid, to somehow stop their fighting — but some sense warned me not even to try. The two feuding dolphins appeared oblivious to me and though I tried to keep out of the fray, there were some very near misses. Meanwhile the numerous, billowing jellyfish were becoming a greater threat than the dolphins!

Then Iago returned, blowing his whistle and waving fish buckets from the wharf. This time Unior heeded the call and returned to the lagoon. But Iago didn't leave, he had plans for Juan. He wanted Juan to remain by the horrible water bar entertaining tourists between rum drinks, and had gone so far as to petition netting Juan off from the lake, to further rein him in. Every time he tossed a fish to Juan, the villain blew a piercing blast on his whistle — a domineering training procedure. Despite his persistent hunger, Juan was obviously reluctant to cooperate with Iago, even in eating, and the moment the fish was gone, he sped out into the lake and away from his oppressor.

Instead of leaving the water — which I admit, may have been the wiser decision — something drew me to follow Juan into the lake: A core-born hope that I might *somehow* get through to him.

The pale green mists parted and Juan appeared silently. No guarantee of safety, no promises, just the shiver of a shared past. I felt the arcane intimacy of his gaze as he curved inquisitively around me. Wavelets stirred by a rising wind had sent the jellyfish down to crouch on the seabed. Side by side Juan and I traveled, spending the next hour or so together. Cruising along, we paused occasionally as one or the other descended to the mossy lake bed to inspect something; a sea cucumber or perhaps some half buried, rusted refuse.

Though it was a relief to share Juan's company far from the distraction and disgust of the water bar, tourists and fish buckets, it was *not* like old times. Despite our slow pace and synchronized breaths, I could not release my wariness. Something shimmered between Juan and I like a heat haze — a warped wrath, waiting to erupt in him. Yet always, my heart went out to him and the conditions he endured. Continuing on, I felt Juan's gaze growing heavier upon me and turning towards this intensity, I realized he was displaying an obvious erection, something which had never happened before. There were several possible reasons for such a demonstration, none of which I wished any part in. At a loss for the least stirring response, I decided to ignore him, continuing onwards and soon Juan settled down.

Our journey slowed and the two of us hung in the water, side by side, shoulders brushing. Earnestly I tried to peer into his good eye, but Juan remained staring firmly downwards, windows boarded, sealing him alone with the scourge of his loneliness and anger.

Severing my searching gaze, Juan jerked into sudden movement, slowly starting to circle me in a most worrisome manner — however I'd just realized I had even bigger problems. Increasingly I was becoming distracted by a burning sensation on my face and lips. Sun and salt had taken their usual toll, but this was the stinging of tiny jellyfish larvae stirred from the silt. The Cubans call it *"carribe"* and get out of the water when it manifests!

I had to escape the water, but now Juan was surfacing rapidly, creating small pressure waves as he circled around me. Perhaps because of Unior, he had so long associated companionship with aggression that the two were in some muddied manner becoming synonymous for him. Having gleaned the distinct impression that attempting to part with Juan's company was going to present me with a slew of dangerous difficulties, I tried to meander along an indirect path back towards the channel. But the crescendoing force with which the dolphin was moving around me made avoiding rough contact with his tail and dorsal fin increasingly difficult.

It became obvious that he was trying to corral me away from the channel and lead me back into the lake and when I appeared unresponsive to his directives, Juan started arching his body in an aggressive manner, issuing an ominous, low growling. I had almost reached the medusa-strewn mudflat where I could wade from the water. But certain now of my intention to leave, Juan's ire rose, and still waist deep in water, I remained completely at his mercy. I felt terrible shame, leaving him, but I knew it would be foolish to remain. Still I paused, regarding him, trying silently, vainly, to convey the compassion and caring I still so keenly contained. Turning a little on his side, Juan regarded me coldly a moment before arching to *slam* his tail down on the water right beside me — the message like a slap in the face, leaving me unharmed but shaken.

Feeling like a jerk and a coward, I slogged through the stinging mud and out of the water, the burning of his betrayal worse than the *carribe*. Turning his tattered dorsal fin to me, Juan departed back into the lake. He reappeared not long afterward, drawn by the sound of my rinsing muck from my swim fins on the wharf. Surveying my actions Juan stared at me (accusingly, I thought), and waited, perhaps hoping I might rejoin him in the water. I so wanted to offer him the renewal of companionship and friendship, to somehow help lighten his life's terrible load, but I could not. When I failed to rejoin him, he turned away. What a mess.

Show time: Despite Christine's pregnancy, Iago continued demanding she perform the high jump through the hula hoop. With her tremendous round belly and precious cargo within, Christine was clearly just too encumbered to make the jump. Though obviously straining, she continued to fail, eliciting a sustained stream of miserable threats and ugly abuse from Iago. After this, Iago brought his foul attention back to bear upon Juan. A fierce revulsion arose within me, watching Iago feeding Juan, dangling pieces of fish over the dolphin's head, trying to lead him up and down the channel while intermittently blowing his annoying whistle.

At last Iago left. Juan remained, but it was almost time for me to leave. I didn't know when I would be back or what state I might find poor Juan in upon my return. I longed to join him in the water but just *couldn't* dismiss a persistent unease. Sitting on the wharf undecidedly, with my swim fins dangling in the water, Juan drifted before me, watching and waiting. Wariness clung to me like the fetid smell of dead fish and decomposing pond water that permeated the dolphinarium on still days. A faint sense of lingering horror pervaded the air, like those first fuzzy moments after awakening from a nightmare where dolphins were being brutally massacred. And still Juan waited — and I could offer no shelter.

With Benicio's help, I'd made arrangements to meet with the trainer responsible for the six captured dolphins I had discovered. They'd been removed to a more remote location, and though initially rather guarded, this trainer had finally agreed to take me to where they were being held. His name was Augustos and he was from Spain, where he worked as a dolphin trainer — and that was where those dolphins were bound for, in several short weeks.

Strolling casually around various and particular questions, I learned where the dolphins had been captured, almost four months previously. As I had surmised, all the dolphins were young, between four and six years old. Soon after I'd discovered them, a tropical storm had almost destroyed the ramshackle pen and the dolphins had nearly escaped, however, Augustos had discovered the disintegrating barrier and prevented them from fleeing to freedom. Since then, the dolphins had been moved to another hidden location, down at the very end of the peninsula to continue their "acclimatization" before being shipped to Spain.

After the trainer had carefully rationed and prepared the dolphins' fish, I joined him in his little Boston Whaler, motoring out to the area where they were being held. The new enclosure partially encompassed a tiny mangrove islet to allow access via land if need be and the submerged portion was triple

Site of Cuban Captives.

netted to prevent any escape. In the clear, pale water, it was easy to observe the dolphins stirring at our approach.

As we pulled in alongside the net, I made another discovery. Only weeks before, there had been *six* dolphins — now only *four* remained! When I inquired what had become of them, Augustos became evasive, muttering something about pneumonia. Less than four months and *already* two of those young dolphins were *dead*. More innocent lives claimed by the captivity industry. If only people realized the reality — the **true** costs, hidden by this deadly business!

With much misguided care, the trainer proceeded to dispense the morning meal to each dolphin through a storm of submerged whistling, audible even above the water. I was pleased to observe only the odd eye break the surface to peer at us, understanding that generally, the more dolphins keep their head above the water, the more acclimatized to humans and handouts they have become. Curious to assess the dolphins' progress and reaction to an unfamiliar person at close quarters, Augustos asked if I'd consent to enter the water with them for a short while. I was curious myself and wanted to get an idea of their physical condition and so I agreed.

At first, the four dolphins circled me quickly, keeping close to the edge of the enclosure as a unified group, whistling and echolocating continuously. Recognizing this alarmed response I decided to try and calm their fright with vocal contact. Quickly isolating three different whistles being repeated, I began by trying to mirror these sounds. Soon slowing their startled circling, the four dolphins started responding to my attempts. It was time to put to use some of what Christine, Juan, Choney and Unior had taught me: the nuance and rhythm of tilt and breath, putting the young captives further at ease, while continuing to elicit their answering chorus. Relaxing and slowing further, the four young dolphins broke their tight formation, the same-sexes pairing off into two separate units, revealing clearly how small they were —just the way the captive industry wants them. *These were children.*

The four youngsters became quite bold, keeping their wide dark eyes on mine and wiggling to within inches while sonically investigating me with quietly intense detail. Diving down, I dragged one of my hands in the sand. Immediately, one of the males dove alongside me, mirroring my action, and thus making a basic acknowledgment of communication. Sensing their heightening curiosity, I went to the middle of the pen and just floated quietly, allowing each dolphin to come right up, sussing with sonar and peering intently at me. Their faces were soft and sweet and heartbreakingly *young*, and their eyes still held hope.

Augustos busied himself checking the net for holes, because the dolphins made regular attempts to defeat the barrier and escape. Once he had completed this activity, it was time to depart. Offering them my gaze one last time, I left the tremulous foursome, desperate to somehow help them, before it was too late. Otherwise, I knew those four beautiful beings would die behind concrete barriers, never to see home or loved ones again.

That evening, in the thickening dusk, I paced against frantic rescue scenarios, where I made my way to the end of the peninsula, "borrowed" a small boat, and (despite a lack of experience navigating water craft of any kind) slithered to the dolphins' pen in the dark (through a black labyrinth of mangroves) to dismantle the pen (without any tools or light) and set them free. But this was Cuba, and small vessels were kept under lock and key and *very* closely guarded, especially after sundown. I'd never get away with it and with so many Cubans regularly attempting exodus from the peninsula, it wasn't hard to imagine the coast guard shooting first and asking questions later.

I was afraid and without experience or support — and so I failed them.

Returning, I redoubled my efforts, desperately trying to raise interest and help for those four remaining Cuban Captives. Eventual attempts were made to hedge the dolphins' importation into Spain on technical grounds, but nothing came of it.

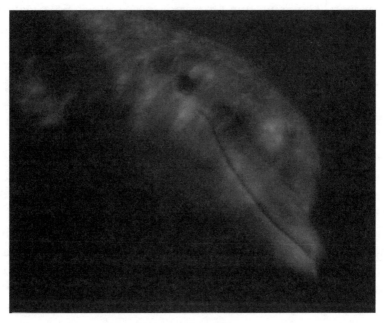

Young male captive.

It was years before I discovered the final fates of those four dolphins. From Cuba they were shipped to a Spanish dolphinarium in Cadaques, which after four or five years closed down. They were then exported across the Atlantic, to another dolphinarium in Costa Rica and there, hardly upon the first bloom of adulthood at around ten years of age, *all four dolphins died.* Forgotten casualties of the captivity industry.

But I remember.

Greed combined with ignorance fuels this disgraceful slave trade. We cannot replace that which is stolen. It *must* stop.

CHAPTER FIFTEEN

LAST DANCE

"There is no excellent beauty that hath not some strangeness in the proportion."
Francis Bacon

The dolphin conservation work continued. During a peaceful protest at the local marine park, I found myself unexpectedly thrust into a threatening encounter with the millionaire who owned the marine attraction. I had leaflets to distribute to people, on *public* property, which brought to readers' attention some little known facts about the captive industry and the effects of captivity on dolphins, requesting that folks take a good look around and ask themselves what kind of message they were really coming away with.

The rest of our company had gathered a little farther down the road, waving signs and cheering as supportive passersby beeped their horns. As obliging cars slowed to turn into the park's parking lot, I, standing on the sidewalk, smiling, dressed in tidy shorts and a dolphin T-shirt, offered the occupants flyers, which most visitors cheerfully accepted.

Then, without warning, the park owner came tearing out of the parking lot behind the wheel of a large, dirty, pick-up. Hanging out the window, screaming septic obscenities, he whipped out a baseball bat, swerved right at me and took a rabid swing at my head! Not an instant too soon, I leapt back from the side walk, scrambling out of the screeching apparition's way, convinced I was about to be ridden down and clubbed to death like a baby seal! I am told the park's owner has since assaulted other protesters, which somehow isn't surprising.

At last, towards autumn's inception, one of the European conservation organizations finally sent someone down to Cuba to meet with me and appraise the situation there. It was too late for the four captives I had discovered, but while the European representative collected information about Cuban dolphin captures and exports, he would also inspect poor Juan's situation first hand, and it was my hope this might encourage aid for the dolphin.

Returning to Cuba, my first concern, apart from Juan's ever-deteriorating condition, was the fate of Choney and Christine's new infants, born only days apart, four months previously. Thanks to Benicio's intervention with the net, both infants had survived. As I initially beheld those two tiny, flawless dolphins surfacing alongside their sleek mothers, I felt such a burst of tender affection — that for a moment I forgot the kind of life they had been born into.

Despite being new mothers Christine and Choney, were still forced to perform in the tedious show, throughout which both continually ducked out to anxiously check on their little ones, leaping and tussling together merrily. I wished I could have been present when they had been born, emerging tail-first, after almost a year's gestation; wish I'd seen them rise to the surface for their first gasping breaths. For the next year they would subsist almost solely on their mothers' exceptionally rich milk. Afterward, while learning to take solid food, they would likely continue nursing for three years or more, enjoying a relatively carefree life — until they were made dependent on human sources for nourishment, or separated from their mothers by some calculating human urge.

Choney and her baby (Sebastian)

From the dock, Choney, Christine and Unior engulfed me in their sensuous slip and slide, greeting me with much caressing, pec patting and chortling commentary. At less than two feet, the water's visibility was terrible, but this was somewhat overcome by keeping tightly knit as we traveled together, reaffirming bonds in sunny reunion. Both Choney and Christine paraded their effervescent infants before me, while I looked on in warm wonder.

A celebratory air prevailed as we flew together, twirling and swirling with much enthusiastic sing-songing — what a gorgeous racket! Catching my eye in this pleasantly churning chaos, Unior and I plummeted into the dim depths to begin our dive-leap game — his mighty pewter bulk erupting from the water beside me, surging upwards like an incredible bean stalk and flying ten feet into the air over my head! Unusually, instead of our game ending with my exhaustion, I lost the huge dolphin in the murk. *Rats — where had he got to?*

Suddenly, loud, chainsaw-like buzzing erupted somewhere close by. In the blind water, there was no way of telling what was going on, so I retreated to the edge of the dock, searching and listening for some clue, but everything had gone quiet. Venturing forth a moment later, Unior suddenly launched out of the gloom, again emitting aggressive thunder, spiraling in rapid circles around me in a ubiquitous and frightening assault! Whipping by out of the opaque water, he first grazed my swim fins and then on his next charge, my wrist, creating an instant bruise with the force of his passage. Alarmed, I retreated back to the edge of the dock and once more everything fell quiet. *What the hell was going on?* Had I unknowingly committed some grave offense? As far as I understood, we had, at Unior's invitation, merely begun our old game — why the sudden aggression?

Deciding to quit the lagoon and its unfathomable and moody occupants, I headed for the water bar. The rotting pontoon remained afloat, though only just, still harboring its usual nest of sodden fatuity.

I found Juan there, tilting and swaying in an eerie manner, as if straining at invisible reins. Spying my arrival, he raced over, begging pathetically, his familiar face a mess of deep scratches from persistent battles with Unior. For the safety of the baby dolphins, Benicio had become vigilant about keeping the net free of holes and for the time being, Unior didn't seem to be pressing the issue, though he and Juan inexplicably persisted in fighting right *through* the net.

Still blindly begging, it was obvious Juan failed to recognize me. Brushing away this unintentional injury, I knelt down before the drab, smelly water. I carried no bribes of dead fish, nor the will to use such repulsive leverage, offering only the simple solace of friendship. Mechanically, Juan rose up from the water to touch his rostrum to my face in an ever-popular trained parody of a "kiss" but I refused this gesture moving out of his reach. Perhaps mulling over this unusual response — my failure to squeal delightedly and bestow a gobbet of dead fish — Juan drifted quiet and low.

Finally, he lifted his gaze to mine, producing a familiar palpitation as our eyes held. His injured eye remained squeezed shut, but looking deep into the other, past the scratches and scars, past that strange double pupil…was like peering at someone trapped at the bottom of a deep well.

At times one would never guess that the lagoon contained five dolphins. Minutes would march past without so much as a ripple or a fin revealed. This was one of those misty mornings of stillness, until my soft step set the little dock awobble. An instant later, the water boiled with silvery shapes as Unior, Christine and Choney, with their infants entwined, rolled in slippery welcome, beckoning me to join them.

Unior, in a wooing mood, curved to reveal the irresistible snowy vastness of his smooth underside for caressing, gliding along with eyes half lidded. Christine and Choney no longer showed signs of squabbling, now engrossed in attending to their glimmering charges, which was a relief.

In the middle of this lovely choral interlude, Juan burst into a sudden series of stupendous leaps and breaches just past the net! Another enraged challenge against Unior, surrounded by females and progeny? Whatever the case, Unior appeared to be ignoring his rival, continuing his affections, swimming smoothly at my side, pec-fins open invitingly, eyes closed in seemingly serene enjoyment. Invested with a sudden doubt, I paused in my affections, wondering — could this luxurious display be something *specifically choreographed* for Juan's unhappy benefit? Was flirtatious Unior, wallowing ostentatiously among "his" females, just trying to rub salt on Juan's wounds, as it were? Did dolphins, as supremely complex social creatures, understand and use such nasty nuances? Was *that* the reason behind Juan's sudden roiling racket?

Almost as if privy to my rising reservations, Unior's mood completely reversed, and in another instant angry dissonance arose in the dark water, as the imposing male began jaggedly circling me! As quickly as possible, I made my way to relative sanctuary at the dock's edge, shaken, but still puzzling over what exactly brought on these contrasting changes in the Unior's behavior. Glancing beyond the net, I could see Juan, bobbing above the water, watching what transpired. *Was there some connection?*

Unior reappeared, approaching me by the dock, still buzzing loudly, the thick, vibrating sound easily audible above the water. Yet now his stance conveyed not aggression, but rather… intensity. *What was he trying to tell me?* Contemplating his eternal smile and inscrutable gaze offered no keys to the mysteries surrounding me.

Abruptly, the noise doubled — another dolphin had joined Unior in front of me, obscured in the murky water. Responding to Unior's insistent, softened buzzing, I gently tapped a single finger on the pitted tip of his rostrum. Slowly leaning out of the mist, the other dolphin resolved, lining up her rostrum with Unior's. I looked — and doubted my eyes — it was *Choney*. With her pearlescent infant at her side, this most diffident dolphin now hovered an inch from my finger tip! And then, easing forward, Choney bridged that tiny and tremendous chasm that had always lain between us, waiting quietly for over *four years* for the flowering of her trust: underwater *contact* — a colossal moment, both of us quivering with excitement. Not to be left out Christine then appeared, her little one glued to her curving side, swooping between Choney and I, diverting my hand to run the length of her robust, flowing form.

I rejoined Juan later, via the rusting water bar where he surfaced before me, jaws open in the automatic begging, which so many tourists mistook for "flipper's gay smile of greeting". Again I gently rebuffed his blind begging and my quiet persistence was eventually rewarded with eye contact. Juan's difficult proximity beckoned to be soothed, but it was clear he did not wish to be touched — and how could I blame him — bashed up, grasped, groped, teased and tortured day after day?

Then the idea arose to try slipping my feet into the water, which I did. Regarding me with his liquid eye a moment, Juan slid forward, gliding head to tail under my arched insteps, and appearing to find the sensation favorable, repeated the gesture several times. How long it had been since he'd felt a familiar, gentle touch? Trying to imagine the existence he endured, I could not repress a bleak shudder. But for the moment Juan was seeking contact rather than food. Rising rosily, almost gaily from the water before me, he invited caresses across the bone-pale delight of his gleaming chest, belly and sides, sweeping in sinuous curves, squirming with pleasure. Seeing him interact so enthusiastically in the place of his usual mechanical begging, I felt the slow ascent of an almost forgotten joy.

But over on the other side of the net, a tumultuous churning suddenly erupted — Unior, leaping and surfacing in furious challenge to his rival. Juan responded, bolting to the net, leaving a wake of white water, surfacing adamantly opposite Unior. *What* fueled their animosity? And was it coincidence that Unior's challenge had come right when Juan began to evince pleasure at companionship? Curious to over hear the tone of their confrontation, I took a chance, slipping into the water to eavesdrop, but Juan immediately detected my entry into his element, and leaving Unior, he approached, pausing a few feet away to scan my presence. Unable to predict how he might react, I hovered nervously beside the water bar's rotting bulk.

Apparently amenable to my company, Juan slid forward, curving solicitously about me, inviting parched caresses and once assured of my undivided attention, he fixed me with a strong look before zooming back to the net, where he rejoined more roiling activity opposite Unior. Moments later, he came streaking energetically back to me, requesting further caresses. All of which rather gave the appearance of showing off, flaunting his female companionship before Unior — but of this it was impossible to be certain.

Later I rejoined the others, Unior and Christine rolling warmly under each hand to sandwich me between them. No longer evasive, Choney, with her wee one in tow joined in, weaving sensuously amongst us, and I remained amazed by her bold extension of trust and touch. The evolution of delight continued, as both mothers allowed their tiny infants to swim right alongside me as we traveled! As dolphin mothers are often notoriously protective of their new infants, these gestures indicated an increasing level of trust.

But as we passed by the net, I saw Juan there, pressed against the mesh, watching all of us together. Immediately I broke away from the group and went up to him, peering through the murky water and wishing fervently, for the umpteenth time, for the power to grant his freedom. All of them. When the others returned, chattering and whistling for me to rejoin their midst, Juan turned and left. Alone and outcast.

I turned to regard Unior, steadily returning my gaze, aware of the wheels turning in his head, measuring and weighing the situation. Thinking of his weird mood swings, and their possible connection to his cutting rivalry with Juan, I knew that as enchanting as Unior could be when he tried, I had to keep my wits about me.

Again, almost as if responding to my thoughts, Unior became restless — and vanished. I made for the dock — just as the sudden, sharp, organ rattling buzzing began somewhere in the turbid water. But Unior expertly cut off my escape, streaking from the gloomy water at frightening speed and on his next mad pass he grazed my elbow, bruising it. *Any* contact with him at those speeds was dangerous!

I reached the safety of the dock. Well aware of the dolphins' exquisite physical control, I knew the bruising was no accident — but again, *why?*

Unior easily could have smashed me to bits, or missed me completely, but instead, he chose to strike me a glancing blow. *What did it all mean?*

My concerned musings were interrupted by Benicio's arrival at the dock. A moment later a now cordial Unior surfaced beside me in the water, and fixing me with a squinting eye, promptly spewed out a decidedly odd string of opaque-inflectioned sounds. All trace of agitation had melted. Head cocked, I stared quizzically at him, completely at a loss. With a decisive and deliberate gesture, Unior swept up a floating leaf and with it jutting from the tip of his battered rostrum, presented it to me.

"He gave to you a gift!" blurted an incredulous Benicio. Indeed he had. Again.

I awoke still swimming, still shimmering amid the dream: tumbling with Juan, free from any over-cast, awash in our combined sunlight.

Patience gathered Juan's oneiric gaze into my own, when I found him that morning, and I saw the teardrop pupils widen, as recognition flashed through the nebulous depths like a fiery fish. An impossible fissure had opened in the grim barricade constricting him, unearthing his tarnished resplendence from a ruin of despair. Turning on his tender side, Juan regarded me softly, pec-fins outstretched in invitation, and swept into his incomparable presence, I submersed.

Suspended in the dark water, he stole into my gaze; dissolving against his indelible opalescence, beneath a swooning blue sky. His familiar foxfire had rekindled, imbued, as the night with stars. Mingling in memory's bittersweet marrow, I traced the scarred paths over his silken skin, unfurling relief cartography from the limpid mists, encompassing every translucent moment of shared pain and perfection. Arms wound round his sleek girth, cheek resting against his sumptuous skin, exquisitely entwined, he began to glide, flowing and rippling with the redolence of silk, carrying me off into a numinous light — morning's dream reincarnated — leaving every other thing in this world to fade into shadow and nonentity. Timeless, we echoed, we rippled; our shared imprint ephemeral, yet absolute. Because it was, it always will be, forever.

Curving and recumbent, with implicit strength, Juan began to pick up speed, my presence as slight as a festoon of seaweed around him. Unable to remove my eyes from the compelling overflow of his, we finally slowed. A circle completed, our last dance stilled.

With a sudden glint of impish glee, Juan began tickling me, poking between ribs with diabolical accuracy — and then we were falling over each other in the water, splashing in the light and life of laughter, together. Aboard

Last Dance.

the water bar, people were drenched by sweeping waves of water from his tail as we continued to roll and wrestle.

Only later did I learn that throughout this entire enrapture with Juan, Unior had been pacing and leaping at the net. The roiling activity of Juan's rival only permeated my sensibilities when my melodious companion suddenly leapt up, rushing over to engage Unior in a flurry of churning foam. Beneath the water, the horrible heat of inimical buzzing battle ignited.

Drawn by the spectacle, more and more tourists were piling onto the water bar, their noisome presence becoming difficult to ignore. The spell that had held Juan and I aloft and alight for an immortal instant was over.

Huge thunderclouds were rolling in. Out upon the ocean it began to rain and when its cascading curtain closed over us, Juan vanished. And I wondered, when I was gone, who would lead him from that grey place he goes to?

My last morning, collected and encompassed among the dolphins. So much had changed, with the two baby dolphins careening inquisitively through our midst and Choney no longer shy. The downpour had left the lagoon's water a littler clearer and watching Choney displaying a strand of eelgrass proudly draped over her head, I wondered if her little one would inherit her passion for parading temporary curiosities.

After a while Choney awarded herself a little break from motherhood, leaving Unior and I to baby-sit while she amused herself elsewhere. It was quite a sight, the massive, scarred Unior, with a tiny, flawless baby gliding alongside him. They appeared entirely relaxed and comfortable together and more then once I saw the saucy little one glue its miniature rostrum to Unior's bulbous melon, while buzzing persistently. *What was this?* Was the little one investigating the production of Unior's echolocation, or perhaps just pestering him? I suspected the latter.

Rejoined by Choney, Christine and her infant, a grand bout of caressing commenced, throughout all of which, the two baby dolphins issued a hardly ceasing duet of wobbly whistles. Within this festive nest of caressing, bonds always grew and strengthened, perhaps obliquely leaking into the next generation. Diving steeply, I turned to view them all, swirling over my head, shadowed against the sun…all, but one.

During the show, my attention was stolen by the antics of the two baby dolphins and their unwearied, impish radiance. Observing them playing, falling over one another, trying to balance sticks on their heads — their pure, fresh beauty had me smitten with the species all over again.

But after the show, the brightness dimmed, watching from the bigger dock as the smaller one was swamped with tourists. Now that Christine had better things to attend to, it had fallen to poor Unior alone, to haul each and every one of those people on his back. Between inane circles, he begged, open-mouthed for each limp scrap of food, while tourists rubbed and fondled him. The silent horror of this degraded spectacle could never dim.

Choney glided by, pausing as she caught my troubled gaze. Very slowly and very deliberately she came up and with weighty calm, nudged the bottom of my foot — a silent statement — as if she somehow understood.

With an ironic ache, I found that only on my last day — when again I must betray and abandon him — Juan was actually awaiting me, gaze alert and luminously lifted, entreating me with an immediate lilt and sway to quit the distance between us and join him in the water. Immersed, we curved along together, side by side, relishing the shared balm of companionship. I wanted to remember the exact serene sensation of his welcoming skin pressed against mine, to absorb these fleeing moments so I might cup the embers when hope dwindled.

Straying close by the net, restless agitation seemed to reach invisibly out, clutching at the dolphin with palsied, discordant fingers. Prevailing past this chill tremor, we came to drift instead by the water bar, which wasn't much of an improvement.

Side by side, drifting in private pluvial contemplation, Juan and I watched the sun's last warmth being swallowed by ravenous clouds. It seemed as if some speaking passed between us, stealing along my conscious periphery on levels I could barely sense. I wanted to remain and dispel the weighted despair that threatened to consume him, but I could not. The dirty green ripples of an ebbing tide were slowly carrying him away from me, a subdued, grey mound drifting low in the water.

For once, the water bar was devoid of its usual unsavory clientèle; only one fellow reclined there, unobtrusively strumming a guitar and like us, watching the sky. Born of elemental inspiration and mirroring some veiled portent in the billowing clouds, exquisite Spanish music tumbled like rain drops from the player's fingers.

This was good-bye. This was the mercurial song of the sky, which is never still; the song of my leaving him alone with his desperation. Again.

CHAPTER SIXTEEN

WHERE THE WILD THINGS ARE

"Tell me what you love, and I will tell you who you are."
Arsene Houssaye

I was heading for a ship rendezvous — at last seeking the wild spotted dolphins inhabiting the balmy, shallow seas of the Bahamas islands; those interminable aquamarine waters lying along the latitudes of lassitude, legendary for their clarity (and so very different from the stifling mangrove murk of the Cuban lagoon). These wild dolphins were also among those increasingly rare populations that, for the time being, endured little human-induced adversity.

Here, wild dolphins could be observed, surrounded by the chosen members of their society, engaging in natural daily rituals, rather than those almost constantly marred by human manipulations. Amid the heavy impingements of captive life, time and patience were slowly revealing the Cubano Dolphins to me, as both intricate individuals and dynamic members within their human-imposed social group. Comparatively, the complexities unfolding among this wild dolphin tribe were astronomical. Researchers had been studying these Bahamian spotted dolphins since the early 1980s and found that at almost any given moment so much was going on socially, that recordings of dolphin interactions could take weeks or months to analyze.

Setting out across the ebony swells of the Gulf Stream, our sixty-five foot boat rocked as if moonstruck. We were traveling towards the rolling dunes of an inundated desert; the surviving remnants of an ancient, submerged landmass, of which the Bahamas are only the protruding tips.

Much of the following day was spent plowing through gorgeous aqua hillocks, keeping a lookout for dolphins amid the jousting waves. The sky remained overcast and windy, but my delight in the magnificent swell continued. Those who took less kindly to the ocean's treatment found their afternoon punctuated by bouts of retching over the railings — or "feeding the fish," as one crew member so affectionately referred to it.

I'd been on the roof-deck, gazing adoringly over the aquarelle ocean when they first appeared, flying over the churning water towards us. I found the boat's bow, just as a pair of dolphins did, weaving with swift facility and unbridled grace below me. Sighing with the sweet ache of this flowering vision, I watched several more dolphins join the initial couple, gently jockeying for a peak position on the ship's invisible pressure wave. As the thrumming vessel slowed, I readied for submersion, gazing with crescendoing pulse toward the rippling shadows waiting down below. Undulating into the vivid water, the dolphins' flickering forms continually caught the eye, shimmering close, flashing puckish grins, obsidian glances brimming with fleeting, cognitive curiosity. However, my wonder at their surreal shining was soon overshadowed.

Twelve passengers and several crew members suddenly filled the sea with flapping flippers and flailing limbs — and too late, I realized that conditions were *far* too crowded. When the human quotient out numbers that of the dolphins, a melee ensues — and with our ratio at some fifteen humans to five or so dolphins, things stood firmly skewed. To be graced with the presence of dolphins, free from repressive human thrall, was undeniably moving, but the confusing cocktail of desultory bodies surrounding me was hardly conducive to the kind of communion I sought.

Rather than attempting to insert myself into the fray, I lounged at ease beneath the swell, content to contemplate dolphins darting amongst the human throng. To an informed eye there was much to be discerned and I made ample use of the opportunity afforded by the bright water.

For the first three years of life or so, spotted dolphins remain largely *spotless*, rather resembling, with their burnished silver skin, slender, smaller bottlenose dolphins. By three or four years of age, juveniles begin collecting their spots, first on their ventral side and then later as young adults, dorsally, until as fully-fledged adults aged fifteen or so, they become so peppered with speckles that they begin fusing together. This sort of natural color-coding made it relatively easy to gage the general age of the dolphins I saw and hint at their social groupings.

Groups of spotted dolphins often divided into nursery pods, containing several mothers (affiliated through blood or bonding), and their sprightly young; bands of socializing juveniles, largely independent (though sometimes supervised by adults), and coalitions of heavily spotted mature adults without young, who appeared more solemn and serious.

I recognized the dolphins that had chosen to linger among us, as two mottled adults, possibly the mothers of the two unspotted baby dolphins with them, plus an additional, speckled juvenile who might have been an older sibling. At one point a party of large, heavily spotted adult dolphins swam past in the blue distance, choosing to remain in deeper water, engrossed in private, un-guessable exchanges amongst themselves.

I couldn't help but marvel at the transportive effects induced by resplendent proximity to these effervescent wild creatures. But under the circumstances intimate rapport seemed nearly impossible to cultivate, so I had to content myself with observing dolphins bestowing avid (envied) caresses upon one another, soaring in lustrous and celebrated symmetry and winding rapidly among the floating human flock, whistling excitedly. They appeared perfectly confident, coming right up to within inches to peer at us, despite the muddle of bobbing bodies and the ruckus from an underwater scooter.

When invited with an affable tilt into their dance, I joined a speckled youth swimming belly up beneath me, streaming and spiraling down towards the sandy sea floor, ardently reminded of stolen moments among the Cubano Dolphins when the leaden mantle of their oppressive enslavement was thrown off in brief and piercing pangs of joy. At last, one by one, the dolphins slipped away into the boundless turquoise periphery until their giddy singsong faded.

One morning, un-remarked by anyone else, several bottlenose dolphins came to surf on the bow, allowing me to bask in their fluid presence as they skillfully surfed on the bow, clearly demonstrating their more robust form, in contrast to the more slender spotted dolphins. Moving above them with the wind over the water, I could almost feel the surge of the invisible pressure waves below…the delicious quicksilver pace and precision of it! *This* — this sweet fleeing must surely be among the simple joys missed most by captives.

We traveled on, still tipping drunkenly over the swell. Gazing dazedly at a rainbow in the stormy distance, a sudden elation struck me — and I just *knew* they were on their way. Moments later, dolphins appeared, vaulting over the unruly waters! After many fruitless starts and stops throughout the day, only seven or eight people bothered to swim, and this immensely improved the encounter's quality. Though a certain amount of milling activity remained, the mood of this meeting was of a noticeably more interactive sort.

A band of approximately ten to fifteen dolphins had found us, which seemed to include several mottled adults with young and a freckled gang of juveniles. Submersed, I found this group rather jovial, demonstrating telltale delight in spinning circles of high-spirited hilarity around one swimmer after another, which appeared to be one of their favorite pass times. Those who could dive down deeper, towards the bottom, would find themselves enveloped in a cloud of jubilant dolphins!

One of the youngsters came to collect me and meeting the impish glint in his eye, I felt a flash of accord between us. In perfect time we spiraled grandly down through the crystalline water, before rising to surface boisterously together — a moment of pure flow — freely given and freely accepted. Continuing along, our glances linked with mutual curiosity, I unexpectedly felt something nudging at my shoulder and realized with astonishment that this dolphin was actually caressing me with his little pec-fin — initiating *contact*! As much as I would have liked to return this gesture, I decided to keep my hands to myself — out of respect — rather than risk startling him. Better to err on the side of caution rather than breach a fragile trust.

Amid a tempest of loquacious chirping, another youngster leapt zestfully from the water before streaking off to dizzy human swimmers in mad circles. Perhaps deciding things were getting a little carried away, the older dolphin attending this little ball of energy attempted to corral the agile youth, who made every effort to evade discipline, swimming saucily on her back!

Dusk soon claimed the dolphins and though we remained merry ships passing in the night, witnessing the unclouded quality of their lives, I felt a vast contentment. These wild dolphins engaged our company only when they chose, and this sat at the *vital* core of the entire experience. This *freedom of choice* was the key element and it lent each encounter, no matter how brief, a true grace — so different from the profane charade of swimming with unwilling captives.

I spent most nights on the roof-deck under the stars, lulled by the ocean's soothing gait, until celestial vistas faded into dreaming. But the next day dawned to a moody, fluctuating sky with no sign of cessation in the restless waters. Our first submergence revealed two distinct dolphin pairs, winding leisurely throughout the group, evincing the droll interest of window shoppers or the passing patron of wax museums and curio shops. Later, checking in the ship's dolphin photo-ID book, I recognized their distinctive dorsal fins, and suddenly an otherwise relatively nondescript encounter acquired additional depth. One pair comprised an adult male dubbed Stubby, escorting a young female just reaching sexual maturity, named Caicos. Both of these dolphins were known to be curious towards swimmers, as was Knowles, Caicos' female friend, also swimming along with an unidentified male escort of her own. Two girlfriends taking an afternoon stroll with their consorts and pausing to view the human figures frogging about. I savored these insights, knowing I could happily spend a lifetime deciphering dolphin details.

One day several of the passengers decided they wanted to swim nude, convinced this would attract the dolphins and aid in some kind of super-transcendental-melding (rather than for the pure sensuality of the skinny dip). I remained without comment. To creatures which routinely peer right through each other's skin, the absence or presence of a bit of nylon was unlikely to matter, any more than its pattern or the color of the skin beneath. Essentially one is always naked among dolphins — as no words, clothes or outward expression can mask one's very pulse and respiration, of which they are always aware. Choosing to ignore this, these persons experienced repeated disappointment, as several groups of dolphins came to flirt with the bow, but after enjoying the free ride, chose not to remain among the naked humans depositing themselves into the drink.

Later in the afternoon, a large mixed pod found us and while many dolphins appeared and vanished about the blurred edges of vision, a core group of about six or so young adults stayed to visit. Three approached, inviting me with synchronous tilts of their bodies to undulate among them. They carried a certain cadence, tacitly encircling me with it, creating a porous space between us — Threshold.

But then, sensing a slight quiver from the dolphin closest beside me, I threw a glance behind — to see a horde of human swimmers, thrashing furiously towards us! Wanting *no* affiliation with of *that* sort of business, I dove, peeling away to watch the dolphins disperse back into the general cocktail. Eleven people were still simply too many in the water at one time, and I just couldn't imagine needing this experience bad enough to crowd or chase the dolphins to get it.

Moments later, glancing up from the cute, whirling distraction of a circling youngster's nodding squeaks — I was horrified to see a woman flailing towards a pair of dolphins, carelessly knocking other swimmers out of her way in her eagerness to get closer. Watching this person, with arms desperately out-stretched, grasping and clawing at the nearest dolphin's dorsal fin, made me feel <u>ill</u>. Reacting to this clutching affront, the dolphins made an immediate exit from the scene. Protocol had been breached — and everyone else's experience cheapened. And unfortunately, it wasn't the only instance of such offensive and inelegant behavior I would observe.

The crew had duly admonished all passengers, firmly insisting upon a hands-off situation. However, it appeared the golden rule of *"Look, don't touch!"* hadn't got through to everyone. Always, any physical contact had to be left to the dolphins' discretion. As guests in their ocean home, chasing and grabbing represented disrespectful and aggressive conduct. After so many years spent as an impotent witness to the daily groping that the Cubano Dolphins unwillingly endured at human hands, I realized this issue was particularly sensitive, but this did *not* excuse the atrocious behavior I witnessed.

During another immersion, an adult spotted dolphin with a companion at his side, appeared to glide alongside me, inviting accompaniment. Nebulous gaze never leaving mine, this dolphin narrowed the distance between us from about two feet, to two inches, bringing my face so close to the marvelous skin, I could see the fine texture along his back. These dermal ridges (almost like fingerprint swirls), are thought to reduce drag as water flows over a dolphin's body, while providing information regarding speed, pressure, temperature and depth.

Retaining intimate proximity as we traveled, I could clearly see this dolphin looking back at me and wondered if this were an invitation, or perhaps, a test. I would never know. Spying our presence, a nearby swimmer made a sudden grab for the companion-dolphin's dorsal fin. Immediately, the pair zipped forward and away, my brief escort throwing an unfathomable look over his shining shoulder. *Again,* this intrusive, arrogant assault!

I stopped then, watching the rest of the swimmers pedaling frantically after the remaining dolphins, fading into the distant blue fog. Letting the feelings of disgust and displeasure dissipate, I shifted my attention (not without some effort), to wonder at the clouds of moon-jellyfish, drifting in luminous profusion throughout the water, grateful they were not a stinging variety. Hovering amid the pulsing, specter-like jellies, I felt their company preferable to a pack of thrashing, grasping humans with no respect for wild things.

While I acknowledged that with their superior swimming skills, the dolphins might well look upon grasping, boorish humans with something akin to amused pity or even snickering glee, I remained firmly affronted at my species' behavior.

Back aboard the boat, listening to the other passengers' talk, I realized that despite being told otherwise by captain and crew, there were some who fully expected to be able to pet these wild dolphins like any bridled pony — and even presupposed being pulled around on a dorsal fin ride!

These were clear signs of the "Flipper Myth" at work, and proof of the damaging effects derived from the ever-popular, cartoonized image of captive dolphins grinning happily while toting around squealing tourists.

Ingrained with false images of dolphins, people fail to understand that these are powerful, wild, willful creatures with minds of their own. Captive dolphin attractions embody a domineering and disrespectful attitude, cultivating distorted relationships between humans and cetaceans, which in turn, breeds a kind of contempt — an irreverent arrogance. In the wild, our human role was that of benign observers, and if invited, courteous participants in these dolphins' lives. But obviously some people had been blinded to the magnitude of the gift, the *privilege* — every time any wild dolphin *chooses* of its own free will, to approach humans with friendly curiosity — and that they are under no obligation to fulfill *any* human demands.

After dark, an ocean that during the day was often crystalline became almost opaque with millions of minute, wiggling organisms. This living soup was part of the deep scattering layer — marine life of all kinds, comprised of tiny zoo-plankton, squid, shrimp, marine larvae and far stranger creatures, which normally reside in the depths, far from any ray of light. With the coming of night, dense layers of these primordial creepies rise up through the dark waters, likewise drawing those that feed upon them.

Night was an active foraging time for the spotted dolphins. Though equipped with excellent night vision for hunting in the dim reaches, their echolocation provided a distinct sensory advantage as they pursued squid and flying fish, two of their favorite foods.

Different dolphin species feed on diverse prey in varied habitats including sea grass beds, mud flats, sand banks, lagoons, bays, coral reefs, deep offshore waters and mangrove estuaries. Highly opportunistic predators, dolphins employ many different and creative techniques to capture a variety of prey including mullet, mackerel, sprats, sardines, eels, shrimp, squid and other invertebrates. For captive dolphins, learning to eat limp, dead fish might be akin to us having to eat road kill, but reduced from monarchs to beggars, captives can rarely afford to be choosers.

I slipped into the night waters, among the clouds of minute and unidentifiable beasties. The blackness pooling just beyond the submerged circle of light gave me pause. *Anything* could be prowling out there in the darkness. Dolphins have few natural predators besides large sharks, and though dolphins have been seen harassing potentially lethal sharks, it is certain they do kill and eat dolphins, especially those who are young and inexperienced. Peering into the gloom, I saw some kind of long, pale eel wriggle by. Fascinating as this submerged night world and its strange denizens were, I returned to the boat, eager to rinse the abundant sea-life out of my bathing suit and turn in for another night sleeping under the stars.

On the last day, several groups of dolphins appeared to ride our bow, but somehow sensing they would not stay, I remained on board. Each time, they vanished before most passengers had hit the water. It was later in the afternoon before we encountered a group, which some intuition told me might stay. Entering the water, I surveyed a nursery pod comprised of three pairs of adult mother dolphins, all accompanied by unspotted young. With only about five or six people swimming, this encounter enjoyed a more sedate pace.

Almost immediately, I noticed that one heavily dappled female had an extremely tiny infant at her side with a series of vertical lines on its body — "fetal folds" — from being curled within its mother's womb. Looking closely, I discerned the mother's underside exhibited signs of swelling from the recent birth, and I realized this tiny baby couldn't be more than a day or two old and might easily have come into the world only hours previously! Despite its newness, the miniature dolphin kept a somewhat wobbly pace at its mother's side, bobbing like a cork to the surface to breathe as she did. Newborn dolphins have to be able to swim almost immediately, as separation at such tender age would result in death. Like all dolphin infants, this one made messy, irregular whistles, which with practice, would gradually become more refined.

Mother spotted dolphin and new born infant.

As I looked on, another pair descended to the soft sandy bottom, rolling and rubbing, sending fine pale clouds up around them. Rising effortlessly together for breath mother and child again descended to poke about in the sand, searching out tiny flounder and wrasse upon which to snack, their echolocation clicks clearly audible as they scoured the sea floor for their buried prey. With a little assistance from the attending adult, I saw the baby dolphin collect a tiny fish and swallow it down.

At the surface, another youngster, swimming with his belly to the sky, slapped his little tail on the surface, before diving to join his mother to nurse from her underside. The suckling was brief, as the mother with a contraction of mammary muscles, squirted a rich cloud of milk right into the baby's mouth. With a fat content of 20-40%, dolphins grow quickly on their mother's rich milk. Within a few months this young dolphin would also begin learning the intricacies of detecting and devouring prey from its mother while making lengthening forays to play and socialize with other youngsters, beginning its incorporation into dolphin society at an early age. Within three to five years, the mother would in all likelihood be ready to give birth again and the young dolphin, just developing his first spots would be ready to join a rollicking group of juveniles, continuing his education among these peers.

I watched two of the adults caressing the tiny newborn lovingly — a warm welcome into a sensual culture, based on mutual support and cooperation rather than exploitation. Not that I harbored any illusions of wild dolphin life being some utterly peaceful utopia, but a grace and dignity prevails there, which captives are cruelly stripped of. The wild dolphins' lives are their own.

As the three pairs drew together to continue on their unknowable journey, I could see them still caressing one another, before descending to the sea floor to inspect what appeared to be an alarmed stingray. Returning to the surface after their brief inquiry, the tiny newborn suddenly lurched forward in a burst of speed, matched pace for pace by its mother, trying to corral her precocious little one. With synchronous breaths and much caressing, the mother dolphin calmed her excitable infant and they followed the other two pairs, slowly vanishing into the gloaming.

For me, the mother's introduction of her newborn among human kind was not only a gift, but also a ray of hope; the unfolding continuation of rapport between two species. Still, I wasn't entirely convinced mine was worthy of the honor.

CHAPTER SEVENTEEN

LAUGHTER & FORGETTING

"Come away, O human child!
To the water and the wild
With a faery, hand in hand
For the world is more full of weeping than you can understand."
William Butler Yeats, *The Stolen Child*

In memory's halls that winter slumps as one of particularly dreary and bitter polar chill. Despite the rallied efforts of the animal welfare community, the unfortunate dolphin *Duke* continued to waste away in a cement prison cell among his ailing brothers behind Marineland's barred gates. No miracle manifested foreseeable help for Juan either and without word from Cuba my apprehension grew, hardly unfounded worries clawing diligently at me —anything might have happened to the dolphins. Finally, goaded by the unending grapple with doubt's many, monstrous tentacles, I planned my escape from the frozen core of winter and booked a flight. At least the ocean's replenishing essence could be anticipated without apprehension.

Exchanging placid and amicable greetings with Umberto, Benicio and my other friends at the dolphinarium, I realized with relief, that the trainers carried no glaringly awful news.

At last standing before the glinting water, I saw a sudden flash of silvered grace; mother and child, leaping in perfect symmetry from the sky's rippled reflection. Surfacing in fond and eager unison before me, Unior, Christine and Choney, with their little ones in tow, bloomed from the water. Through the familiar and slippery gusto of our greetings, I glimpsed the growth of the two baby dolphins, just under nine months old and already well over four feet long! No longer tiny infants, I began to refer to the precocious pair as young ones. Choney's saucy son had been christened *Sebastian*, and Christine's somewhat more sedate daughter, *Bia*.

In sharp contrast to those pellucid Bahamian waters, visibility in the silty lagoon was next to nil. Still, the dolphins' familiar, misty faces stayed close as we surged along, seeming to illuminate the murk in ways sunlight alone could not. After our initial swirling greetings, punctuated with much buzzing scrutiny and excited, simmering whistles from young Bia and Sebastian, the nursery group soon returned to the activity they'd been engaged in prior to my arrival. Moving as a unit, the dolphins slowly circled the perimeter of the lagoon, surfacing for occasional breaths *en masse* — resting on the go — much in the manner of wild dolphins. I called it *snooze-cruising.*

Wild or captive, dolphins don't experience sleep in the typically terrestrial mammalian sense. Being *conscious* breathers, if dolphins fell fully asleep, they'd cease breathing and suffocate. Instead, they seem to nip quick naps, swimming slowly, often in formation with one or both eyes closed, silent except for the occasional click or whistle. At such times, rather than relying on active echolocation, dolphins seem to use passive listening to sense any unfriendly approach.

After about ten more minutes of silent snooze-cruising, the prickle of searching ultra-sonics alerted me to an unseen approach. Using a particular,

Traveling with Christine & Bia

familiar buzz, the dolphins could both pinpoint my location and alert me to their imminent arrival, seeming to use frequencies when "addressing me" that I could easily hear or feel, and fully expecting me to respond accordingly. I suspected they regularly used their echolocation simultaneously for purposes both expressive and exploratory. All five dolphins materialized from the murk, Unior and Christine immediately flanking me to offer and solicit jovial pec-pats and caresses. As always, this glorious proximity elicited a familiar rush of wonder and gratitude, that I should somehow have a place of welcome among them.

Choney appeared, coming to hover before me, mirroring my submerged, vertical stance, issuing the particular soft buzzing, which I recognized as her prelude to contact. As I proffered the desired fingertip, she emitted a wide band of sound, narrowing to a point on the moment of touch, punctuating the meeting of rostrum and fingertip. This became an established rite of response, often followed by a pec-pat session, the evolution of these simple signals creating a familiar, mutual understanding. Though the other dolphins sometimes preceded particularly focused or intense contact with similar rituals of sound, it became a calling card of Choney's. Hovering quiescently, the others observed intently, as our greeting unfolded.

And then, with a delightful flick of delphic rhythm, *allegro* — our pace quickened, twining and coiling together in the billowing jade clouds below. Wedded with their knowing glances, I knew just how to move — oh, I had missed this dance, attuned in their midst, arching, curving, twisting, flying weightless through misted shafts of sunlight and rising clouds of silvered bubbles. Any excuse seemed enough to send Bia and Sebastian into mad, chortling, fits of unruly exuberance, and my addition into the group was no exception. The renewed vitality they injected into our family was marvelously self-evident. Winding down from this excitement, the two mothers soon collected their little ones and resumed snooze-cruising. Passing by me at the edge of the dock during their circuit, I detected only the barest wisps of echolocation issuing from them — even the ever-piping young ones seeming silent.

I took this opportunity for some quiet reflection. I had recently read *Dancing with Whales*, a treatise on the importance of *rhythmic* communication in Nature, by biologist Dr. Peter Beamish, highlighting an avenue of communicative insight to ponder with the dolphins. The scientist's basic theory proposes that a kind of communication can occur between animals (even between different species, as long as they are able to perceive one another's signals), by establishing a common rhythm — by *synchronizing* their behavior. This behavioral synchronization — any behavior, even a hoot to a stomp — could effectively encode a message, indicating the willingness to continue a communicative exchange. Following synchronization, a second set of signals in this rhythmic communication, might be *mimicry* — acknowledging mutual perception and a basic, mutually shared rhythm. These simple steps could establish a venue for what Beamish terms *Rhythm Based Communication*. In a nutshell, he found that under certain conditions, *when* an animal does something, can be of even more importance than *what* it does. Rhythmic signals are easily combined within components of behavior normally engaged in — a blink, breathing, breaching, tail slapping, in whales for example — imbuing certain actions with a rhythmic component, or code to their meaning. Beamish found that huge creatures like whales adopt slower rhythmic signals, while smaller creatures like birds seem to use much faster ones, making them difficult for human senses to distinguish. Nature's Morse code.

I was already somewhat aware of this aspect of communication used between the dolphins and also with me. In my own terminology, I referred to it as that integral, almost Dionysian rhythm, intrinsic to all things delphic. Though the dolphins' rhythms were often as swift as they were subtly intricate, I was learning to perceive increasing depth in our wordless, fluid exchanges. Beamish states that at best, human recognition of *Rhythm Based Communication* seems largely subconscious, except through feelings. I could certainly relate; among the dolphins my intuition proved just as valuable a tool as previous experience, alert observation, and active erudition, in guiding my responses.

Unior appeared to engage me, and bearing this rhythmic facet of communication in mind, his every movement and breath, held the possibility of deeper meaning. Rich subtleties dwelt in eye contact, the merest incline of the head, the exact timing of an exhalation, or the least flourish. Often I had the distinct feeling my reactions were being closely gauged and that Unior was trying to teach me something. With his gaze so full of recondite conveyance, his every gesture — nudging my hand or nodding his head — seemed intensely *deliberate*. Trying to quantify the process as it was happening, could spoil everything, so I usually just let things flow and asked questions later.

However, right about when Unior cozied up to me, Juan suddenly exploded into a stunning series of crashing, dramatic leaps and boastful breaches, just past the dilapidated net, positively *throwing* himself around! I felt an acute significance in the *precise* timing of Juan's strident eruption, one that should not be dismissed. While drawing premature conclusions would be unlikely to shed useful illumination on the matter, I was unable to shake the troubling feeling that my presence, combined with Unior's had somehow sparked off Juan's display.

Appearing unperturbed by his rival's outrageous behavior, Unior began a shameless flirtation, curving up against me, eyes heavy lidded and raising his pec-fins invitingly beckoning caresses over the pale silk of his underside. As was so often the case when one of them was onto something good, the other dolphins appeared, crowding close and issuing an insistent clamor for similar treatment. Rather than pick favorites and choose how to divide my attention, I descended instead into a slow spiral, inviting all to dance.

All the while Juan *still* continued his vigorous plunging — at last bringing Umberto hurrying over — worried that Unior had passed the net and a massive fight had caused the unusually prolonged and emphatic roiling! Of course Unior had remained with me the entire time — thus confirming that Juan's behavior was indeed markedly strange and persistent, and strengthening my suspicions that it somehow related to Unior and I.

Unior began trying to lure me pointedly away from the dock with him, but the jolting ferocity of his past mood swings made me wary and well aware of my vulnerability, I didn't care to stray far. But then our eyes met in the dim water, acknowledging the spontaneous initiation of our dive-leap sequence, throughout which Unior kept up a mad whistling concerto. After several rounds keeping Unior's tremendous pace, I stilled to catch my breath, noticing as I did so, that Juan *still* continued his troubling and tumultuous thrashings!

Suddenly I realized both Juan and Unior had vanished below the water. A moment later, the harsh aggravated buzzing commenced, resonating in my lungs from powerful sonic beams aimed directly at me! Having carefully maintained my proximity to the dock, I now pressed against it, wondering from which direction the massive dolphin's surging assault would issue. Whipping out of the ominous water, Unior knocked my swim fins as he barreled past. *BUZZ, BUZZ, BUZZ!* Pivoting powerfully, he leapt towards me again, *careening* by over and over, repeatedly nicking me as he volleyed past. Suitably unnerved, I climbed from the water to watch him, *still* continuing his rapid passes below me. Why did he persist even once I'd left the water? Surfacing, Unior's sharp stare pulled magnetically at mine as he began a series chuffing breaths — or sneeze-breathing, as I referred to it — resounding, violent exhalations, often indicating exertion or displeasure. After his performance, it could have been either. Still eyeing me, Unior blurted out a number of odd, raspberry-like sounds. What did it all mean?

Beyond the net, Juan was still vaulting and plunging with tenacious vehemence. What unwitting part could I be playing in both male dolphins' weird behavior? Were they exchanging sonic insults or challenges, while Unior flaunted the acquisition of another female companion before the solitary outcast? Did my tandem exertions with Unior hold connotations for the dolphins of which I was unaware? All I knew for certain was that their agitated behavior was *not* random. Strangely, Unior's aggression though clearly connected to me, seemed almost impersonal, with no remaining trace of it minutes later. I knew dolphins were more than capable of holding a grudge, but this was something else and when the need for the behavior became irrelevant, it ceased.

I went seeking Juan soon afterward, while Unior was occupied with hauling tourists for his breakfast. I wished the fetid water bar would just collapse and sink, as it always seemed about to do. Kneeling with leaden pall at the pontoon's sodden edge, I fought advancing dread at facing the tattered, treasured creature, so very central to my efforts. I knew I could hope for no improvement in his failing state and it was a hard thing to be helpless before — yet all my prolonged and passionate efforts had failed to summon deliverance.

Juan was still surfacing by the net, not far from a large hole that was easily big enough to admit him. I learned later with some surprise that despite the barrier's increasing dilapidation, Unior and Juan were now seen to engage one another only rarely in direct physical confrontation. Leaving the festooned barrier, Juan started an eerie, slow, almost autistic rocking, "straining at the reins" this repetitive, stress-related behavior sprung from years of torment and imprisonment. Watching Juan pulling uselessly at the short lead life had lent him, evoked a bleak and savage sorrow — familiar to anyone who has ever found themselves helpless before the suffering of a stricken and ailing loved one.

Jerking into a sudden series of irritated head slaps, Juan made his way to his begging spot at the water bar, where I waited in grievous, barbed silence. His injured eye remained squeezed shut. White battle scars carved his powerful body, and there were jagged pieces torn right out of his dorsal fin by Unior's jaws. In only a few short years, he seemed to have aged so much, burying the undimmed, morning-eyed creature that had once so eloquently, so irrevocably encircled me.

Followed by several eager tourists and carrying a plastic bucket of fish, Iago arrived just as Juan did. Quickly withdrawing from this unsavory company, I saw Juan reward the graspings of the exclaiming tourists with a warning snap. Then I did a double take — Iago had Juan performing the full repertoire of obscene and tiresome tricks — all of them. It felt like the final blow. Iago's plan to reel the dolphin under his grinding heel had succeeded. Juan was undone — fully enslaved — only now, isolated and injured. Only a fraction of Juan's food was dispensed with the morning's vulgarities, the remainder to be sold to tourists throughout the day to keep him endlessly begging. It was this arduous, unending and utterly destitute existence that had left Juan in a sort of blind, automatic torpor.

As expected, he refused all eye contact and my soft-spoken appeals had no visible effect. Head tilted in pained patience, sea wrack hair falling in my eyes and trailing into the water, I regarded him, remembering the quiet communion we had so often shared through the years. Perhaps, somewhere within Juan's chaotic insides, this familiar pose pulled some thread of recognition, for he looked up at me then. The somber twilight of his gaze illuminated only a remote rift between us, where once a garden had bloomed in tender color — now eclipsed into ash.

Ceasing his supplication, Juan closed his gaping jaws and just stared at me. Breathless, I balanced. Would I get through? Would he allow warmth into his world? With a sudden, harsh chuffing exhalation, Juan turned away, as if to say, *"SCREW IT!"* before vanishing beneath the water's dismal shroud. When he reappeared, he was again begging blindly, refusing all eye contact. And why should he let me in, I thought bitterly — when time after time I must inevitably abandon him in hell.

Weary and troubled, I returned to the lagoon, where Christine awaited me with a replenishing invitation to swim. Meeting her dark, chocolaty gaze — I felt awash with gratitude at my companion's sweet timing. Surging along I caressed her midnight flank, as Christine curved gently beside me, administering the tactile and remedial compress of friendship. Surfacing together, my arm sliding over her broad back, I felt the palpable comfort in the easy familiarity between us. Perhaps this sonorous scene touched Unior's sensibilities, for he soon abandoned hauling tourists to join us. Caressing his chalky cheek and meeting his offered pec-fin by way of greeting, the three of us aligned and continue traveling. Choney soon slid gracefully among us, rolling head to tail under my offered hand in sociable salutation, graciously flourishing her flukes.

Quartet assembled, with attendant satellite youngsters, our blithe wanderings had just begun, when the nearby dock began teetering crazily beneath Iago's heavy step. Towering above our gaily trifling troop, the scowling trainer fairly spat: *demanding* I vacate the water *immediately* because *paying* tourists were waiting for their dolphin rides and my presence was unforgivably distracting Unior. Leaving my companions I climbed reluctantly from the water to commence recording the day's observations from the other dock. A reality check: a reminder that the dolphins' lives were *not* their own and that it was greed and ignorance that dictated and controlled their fate.

Some minutes later, I glanced up from my meditative scribbling to find Sebastian, Choney's young son, peering curiously at me from beneath the water. In an attempt to amuse and interact, I plunked a foot into the brine, wiggling and splashing it around. With innocent and ogling wonder, Sebastian twisted this way and that, following my movements with such wide-eyed astonishment that I had to laugh. My delight doubled as he was joined by little Bia, both of them faultlessly attentive, as I skittered my submerged foot about like a frightened fish. When Choney joined the goggling pair, their comical, triplicate concentration sent my laughter overflowing.

This merriment seemed to carry into the afternoon and during the second show, Choney left off her absurd clowning to go breaching about the lagoon. Though Choney was eventually lured back to the fake theatrics with fish, Sebastian, under no such impetus to hush and behave, rallied Bia by his silvered side, and together the dynamic duo breached and leapt in fantastic miniature right in front of the audience, utterly confounding all of Iago's irritable efforts. Oh yes, they lightened things around the place! Impervious to both the young ones' dear antics and the audience's uproarious laughter, Iago swelled with ill temper. But there were repercussions.

The glowering trainer stole upon me while I was readying to depart for the day. I smelt his rum-sodden breath even before his ornery, guttural voice came hissing into my ear, *commanding* me to abstain from swimming with the dolphins and *purposely* causing them to disobey him. Iago had made this complaint before, insisting the dolphins often refused to work when I was around. Whether this was true or not — who could blame them for distaining the pleasure of Iago's abrasive, heavy-handed company? Nonetheless, I would have to tread carefully. Iago was trouble.

Keeping that charming exchange in mind, I made for the water bar instead of the dolphinarium's main entrance the following morning, forcing myself to face the nightmare of Juan's painfully eroding condition. Treading yet-tender notes inside me, the dolphin appeared. Drifting close by, he started to nudge a loose piece of wood nailed to the edge of the barge with a disturbing and repetitive rhythm. Judging by the raw area on his chin, I guessed this neurotic little ritual had become a part of Juan's daily pattern. Pausing in his disfiguring repetition, Juan glanced up at me a moment. *This smile is not who I am.*

I know, love. I know.

He turned away then, uttering a dismissive snort and moving out towards the channel, head slapping and "straining at the reins" the entire way. Everything in his rhythm and manner revealed him to be increasingly damaged and short-tempered.

Making a somewhat tentative appearance at the dolphinarium later on, I found the trainers exhibiting expanding frustration with Sebastian and Bia's distracting larks — which clearly had nothing to do with my presence. While Unior hauled grinning tourists among blowing whistles and fish buckets, the youngsters had taken to appearing in the midst of things, curving enticingly alongside Unior and luring him off to romp with them — and given the choice, who wouldn't choose their luminescent companionship?

Benicio joined me on shore, having decided to call it quits for the moment. With evident concern, he warned me that Iago had raised a big stink with the new manager, complaining about the dolphins' refusal to work whenever I was around, and demanding I be barred entirely from keeping their company! Benicio felt certain the whole thing would blow over in a day or two, but advised me to restrict my company to Juan at the water bar until the dust Iago had kicked up settled.

Reluctantly I retraced the parched path back towards the derelict barge, following my heart's ache to Juan. At least the filthy pontoon was emptied for the moment, of tourists. Fitful, haggard and humorless, Juan was there, still mechanically scraping his chin on that loose piece of wood. Hoping to disrupt this detrimental behavior and concerned at his injury, I removed the scrap of wood, but it did no good and Juan persisted vacuously pressing the spot where it had been. The monstrosity of his leering past and the interminable bleakness of his future seemed to have left him a hollow shell.

Yet after a time he glided over and slipping into his lingering gaze, a whisper arose: *Not yet.* Through the tear-stained silence, I glimpsed a tiny flame, shrouded behind pained, stained glass, but burning still. I wanted to beat on the barriers hemming him; smash the garish glass — make it all go away; the taunting and teasing, the fighting, the madness, the loneliness — everything this captive life had cursed him with. Unable to restrain an affiliative gesture, I lowered my feet tentatively into the water.

Juan moved closer, a maelstrom of powerful feelings seeming to swirl within him. His only contact with others included Iago's harsh demeaning commands, the daily grind of teasing tourists and his hostile exchanges with Unior. While there might conceivably be the odd kind word or gesture directed toward him, it had to be rare — *terribly rare.* For such a profoundly social creature, the dragging days of this hostile, isolated life had to be deeply scarring, causing a bitter and resentful reaction to all that approached him. And yet, beyond the clash and turbulence within him, I sensed there remained some trace of hope.

A single, curious tourist appeared and finding the inevitable questions about the dolphin earnest, I offered what answers I could. Unbeknownst to me, Juan had marked the turn of my attention, drifting closer and closer, watching and waiting. As my distraction continued with the conversation over my shoulder, he moved forward and very gently pressed my semi-submerged knee with his rostrum. Eyes widening with realization, I turned back to meet his expectant gaze; clear and unclouded — he was requesting *contact* — not fish. There *was* still hope.

Afterwards, having deemed it prudent to avoid the dolphinarium for the day, due to Iago's meddling complaints, I delivered myself instead into the Sea. Restless as the waters, I lost myself beneath their muted, myriad splendor, under galloping, sunless clouds with only the spangled fishes for company. Only with nightfall did the moonless sky clear until the stars rang out. My thoughts lingered with a scarred dolphin, mulling pensively at the heavy ages that seemed to have fallen between us; memories, sifting and reverberating — my turbulent, misplaced star.

Returning to the dolphinarium I discovered Benicio had managed to mollify the management, reaching a tolerable agreement: So long as no paying tourists were in the water, I was free to rejoin the dolphins. The difficulty remained in coming to terms with the fact that men like Iago had power over dolphins' lives. I wondered how the tourists would like to find themselves suddenly delivered into the hands of someone like Iago — to have *him* decide when, or even *if* they should eat, how hard and how long they must work and whether or not their children should be taken from them and sold.

Choney and Sebastian's welcome arrival at the dock served to distract me from these impassioned contemplations. Their puerile grace dispelled dark thoughts, disintegrating human words and leaving me empty and clean. Head tilted quizzically to one side, I watched the pair's apparent fascination with my be-finned foot, trailing in the water. They were soon joined by Bia and Christine — all four dolphins, bodies curved like question marks, staring at my finny limb. Then Unior appeared, joining their scrutiny. *What* was *so* interesting about my swim fin? Bright eyes and frozen smiles were my only response. *Buncha weirdoes!*

Still chuckling at their idiosyncrasies, I soon melted into the water amongst them. Unior, Christine and Choney came to drift in the show area, resting and watching while the gleeful youngsters collected me amongst them, squeaking and spiraling! Once the rambunctious little dolphins had tired me out with their shrilling and spinning, I joined the three adults floating quiescently, while tireless Sebastian and Bia continued to romp around us. The six of us soon began to travel and passing along the net, I paused to peer through a large hole. It took me a moment to realize that only two feet away, Juan hung in the water, only the dome of his forehead breaking the surface — but before I could reach out or utter a sound, he sank and vanished. My wistful calls followed him, but only silence answered.

I couldn't know all the reasons and rules that kept Juan at bay, separating him from communal comfort and the refreshing presence of the youngsters. I wondered how my understanding of the dolphins' social nuances might improve if only the lagoon's waters were clearer — so often I drew blanks in the foggy murk. Yet I would not deny them that last refuge: with so many eyes and so much noise, the ability to escape it all by diving away into the privacy of the turbid water was an unequivocal blessing. Peering through the tattered net, searching for some sign of Juan's whereabouts, my wavering calls elicited no detectable response.

Swimming together in close formation, all five dolphins swept past, uttering, sharp, warning cries — but I didn't care to leave off my attempts at calling to Juan — until Unior turned back and began literally *yelling* at me! Cowed at incurring the huge dolphin's buzzing retribution, I allowed him to collect me and lead me away from the net, finding myself unceremoniously deposited by the dock. Fixing me with a parting fish-eye, confirming my disfavor, Unior then departed. It seemed I had been given the boot. Fair enough.

Recalcitrant, I returned to the water bar, sagging beneath a rowdy load of tourists. There had been another fish shortage and Juan's rations were the first to be cut. Yet I realized he rarely seemed to go out into the lake anymore. Perhaps its empty reaches only served to emphasize the loneliness.

Amazingly, Juan met my flinching gaze, and encouraged, I slipped my feet into the water, alert for signs of his displeasure. Drifting forward, sculling his pectoral fins, he nudged my feet roughly before suddenly lunging forward, jaws open in threat, spinning and rolling right below my feet, buzzing loudly, his rostrum's axis pointing directly at them. I immediately withdrew from the water, realizing that under the current wretched circumstances, any further efforts I made would only add to Juan's frustrations.

Had Juan slipped into sadness, as it once seemed he might, he would probably have succumbed to sickness, as so many captives did, and died. But his listlessness was being replaced with a caustic ire and if nothing else, these vigorous fires were sustaining him. But all semblance of the being I had once known, seemed to be drowning in a corrosive sea of suffering. Temporarily leaving off his restless head-slaps and "straining at the reins," Juan returned to pin my pained gaze with his own. The moment between us spun out longer and longer, until at last it snapped, and he went rushing into the channel, bursting into a series of passionate breaches.

The following afternoon, collected amongst all five dolphins, I could see both Bia and Sebastian, swimming sweetly with their heads pressed against their mammas' warm bellies, in a typical baby-travel position. Adopting a slowed pace, they allowed me to travel among them, falling strangely silent. Then it dawned on me — I had been invited into the middle of their *snooze-cruise* formation.

Eventually we came to dally in the show area where throngs of tourists were gathering for the afternoon shows, surrounding us with rouged, sun burnt faces, staring — unseeing. Hollering obnoxiously and blowing self-importantly on his whistle, Iago appeared, his raucous, blustering entrance causing the dolphins to begin groggily milling around. Iago was after Unior, demanding his presence at the small dock, to haul an expectant crowd. Looking distinctly undecided, Unior drifted towards the dock, eyeing the mess of excited, babbling humans. Eventually, with evident reluctance, he submitted and with blasé resignation, started hauling them one by one on his dorsal fin.

I retired to the other unused dock to keep out of Iago's way and record the day's observations. Christine and Choney cruised by with their glossy children at their sides, inquiring into my activities. I'd assumed my frantic scribblings would be of little interest, but the uncanny weight of so many eyes fixed firmly upon my person proved otherwise. Meeting their collective, expectant gaze, I felt suddenly certain what they were waiting for, and plunking a foot in the water, I began skittering it around like a frightened fish. Sebastian's quivering interest surpassed even the others', as he toggled this way and that, ejecting hilariously squeaks and quacks. Becoming bolder, he inched closer to my wriggling toes until almost touching them with the tip of his rostrum, still spewing a stream of wobbly whistles. Squelching giggles, I continued my whimsical pantomime, now using my hand, undulating and arching it from the water, like a leaping dolphin. Apparently entranced, Sebastian encouraged these gestures with his shrilling, warbling delight, until we were forced to part by the start of the show.

We met again the following morning, little Sebastian ready to pick up right where we'd left off. While I sang him a merry greeting and tried to photograph his silliness, the little fellow squirmed and wobbled, blurting out more ridiculous sounds. Quieting, he came to hover less than an inch from my proffered hand. Hesitating a moment Sebastian then brushed my fingertips with his rostrum — *first contact!*

Increasingly curious, Sebastian peeked at me above the water; his fresh beauty, like inhaling lilac blossoms. Contemplating this familiar radiance, I speculated — Juan might indeed be Sebastian's father. Choney and Juan had persistently pursued regular rendezvous despite Unior's powerful wrath throughout the time when Choney would have conceived, but unless blood work was done, the true identity of Sebastian's father would remain a mystery.

While Unior stoically hauled the last of the morning tourists Choney appeared, her deep, thoughtful gaze drawing me into a slow and very deliberate pec-pat exchange, while ever-curious Sebastian looked on. The three of us drew closer together and then Choney started nudging my hand with her rostrum, encouraging Sebastian to do the same — introducing her son to the mysteries of interspecies contact. After much squeaking and squirming, he followed his mother's example, offering me an excitable little nudge — *Hello!* Later on, a somewhat envious Benicio reported that Christine and Choney had not previously allowed anyone to get so close to the baby dolphins.

Sweet Sebastian

Seeming satisfied for the moment with her son's progress, Choney returned her attention to cultivating another prolonged pec-patting session with me. However, having encouraged Sebastian's boldness, he now had no intention of being left out, repeatedly sliding between the two of us whistling and beeping insistently.

Once Unior had completed his arduous task and the tourists were temporarily satiated, I joined the dolphins, slipping beneath the water, to be met with their soft scanning. I responded to their gentle intonations, touching their rostrum tips, acknowledging our greeting ritual. Unior made it known he was in a tactile mood, rolling to invite sumptuous caresses over his sleek and powerful form, reminding me of just how huge he was — unable to reach my arms all the way round him. Looking up, I saw Choney, with Sebastian at her side, watching all.

With an air of deliberate concentration, Choney started scanning me up and down with shivering sonic scrutiny. Watching closely, Sebastian began copying her — it appeared Choney was giving her young son some kind of sonic lesson!

My last day, and Unior was again hauling an endless line of soggy tourists while I watched, hating what I saw. I was in a rainy mood, reflecting the sky's overcast, just like the dolphins' skin. Seeking an undisturbed spot on the wharf, I settled down to write. Kneeling there, I felt a faint shudder, and glancing up — there was Juan, his dark gaze resting on mine. Stirring restlessly in the water, Juan's movements revealed an inner turmoil that never seemed to abate. But no matter how estranged, he would always remain incomparably beautiful. I found him again soon afterwards, at the water bar, but we had company.

While their rowdy parents downed rum and cokes, several children clutching fetid fish-bits in their grimy hands, taunted and teased Juan. Growing bored Juan soon dove from sight. Immediately, the kids began clamoring peevishly, demanding the dolphin reappear, but for the moment, Juan was on his own time. When he did show himself again, they threw the gobs of fish in his face, screeching, *"Do something!"* Juan merely begged, open-mouthed. Angry because flipper wouldn't flip, one of the bunch lashed out at Juan, trying to kick him! Such deplorable behavior in children so young disgusted and distressed me deeply. Unconcerned, Juan scooped up a shred of fish and went off, tossing it jauntily up, before diving dismissively with his tail high in the air.

Feeling cheated that 'flipper' was not acting like the subservient and jolly pet he was supposed to be, the querulous kiddies continued whining. The vigor of Juan's mood remained and when the noise finally roused one of the soused daddies to come and see what the problem with the dolphin was, Juan was ready for trouble.

Commanding Juan to jump had no effect. Nettled, and trying to cover up his lack of Neptunian authority, the man grabbed Juan's rostrum, wagging his finger in the dolphin's face and calling him a "naughty flippy!"In response Juan reared up from the water, snapping fiercely — but the message just wasn't getting through. The harassment continued, and the next time, Juan drew blood. Sporting a foolish and unbelieving look on his face, the man seemed completely dumbfounded — another victim of the "Flipper Myth."

Thoroughly disgusted, I returned to the lagoon, slipping into the water and staring, submerged, out into the green haze. Poor Juan, surrounded by nit-witted cretins. Unior appeared, offering his pec-fin to my palm and then sweeping head to tail under my hand before vanishing. How had he known just when I needed that?

Just before the final show, all five dolphins collected me amongst them, undulating sonorously through a few straying sunbeams. Then, while the adults lounged in the show area, Sebastian, Bia and I rollicked, enjoying the pirouetting pace young dolphins tend towards. Thoroughly exhausted and blowing like a whale, I finally halted to rest. Slowing, Sebastian swam up alongside me and meeting his glimmering ebony eyes it occurred to me that through our games and play, we were foraging bonds of friendship. It began to rain and as the light faded the dolphins melted away into the water and fell into their snooze-cruise formation.

After the brief downpour, I retired to the channel to write. The water was like green glass when Juan appeared, skimming along the bottom, rubbing himself against the sea moss. Away from the water bar and teasing tourists, Juan's movements held more grace and less tension. I wondered what would happen if I dared join him in the water — unwise with no escape available. Juan waited, regarding me through the haunting silence now strung between us. Mine belied powerful passion — there would be rage and tears at the sorrow and injustice — or there would be silence — what lay behind Juan's, I could only guess.

I was certain that if only he could be freed from this horrible place, breaking the draining patterns that devoured his days, then he could be healed and released, sane and strong. But in all the world there seemed to be no help for us and repeated failure had left me emptied and exhausted.

CHAPTER EIGHTEEN

THE RITE OF SPRING

"Men stumble over the truth from time to time,
but most pick themselves up and hurry off as if nothing happened."
Winston Churchill

Almost imperceptibly, spring began to push winter's inclement and uncivil door ajar. With the first soft-spoken sighs of vernal air, came a longing to leave behind the polluted, jarring din of distended urban sprawl. After more than twenty years amid the unmitigated concrete of a major metropolis, I made my move to a relatively small town, owning the scholarly benefit of one of the country's top universities — and the less scholarly, but equally beneficial presence of several close friends.

Magnificent and stately trees lent streets ample and affable shade, rising grandly amid the eclectic Victorian architecture. Relieved of the rumble of streetcars and highways, I ambled among stone churches and the dappled cool of riverside paths with their sun-flecked glades; over bridges, quaintly covered or elegantly arched, reminiscent of an easy and established Old World grace. On the grounds of the university campus, tree-lined boulevards and ivy-encrusted edifices beckoned similarly.

Everywhere sprawling gardens revealed bright green shoots burning from the ground and fuzzy buds bursting from the trees. Led by the inherent charm of my surroundings, I prowled often, investigating inviting arcades and lane ways, just to uncover further appealing vistas. Once, I stole past a crumbling stone wall, half-hidden among lilac and lily of the valley, to find my curiosity rewarded with the discovery of a cherry tree orchard in full bloom. Beyond, stood a venerable manor, the solemn windows, empty and darkened. I felt as if I had just entered the beginning of a C.S. Lewis story. Unremarked, I knelt upon the brilliant new grass, gazing enraptured at the delicate arabesque of the blossom-laden bower above me. Every succulent breeze stirred the arbors' arching, laden limbs, spilling fluttering clouds of pearlescent petals to moth-kiss my face and catch like snowflakes in my hair. Surrounded with their living hue and fragrance, inhaling the blossoms' rosy-pale splendor…transportive, exquisite — like *Their* skin. Amazing how one love drifts into another.

I remained unwilling to admit defeat on Juan's behalf and though his condition was declining, I felt certain that removing him from the demeaning squalor at the Cuban dolphinarium was the key to his restoration and recovery. More than anything, I knew Juan needed *change*: the grinding routine, centered on his begging for scraps at the vile water bar had to be broken. Extricating him from jeering crowds, domineering tricks and Unior's antagonistic proximity, would raise his morale and wake him from the stupor of despair and rancor swelling in him.

Living in a natural environment had lent Juan many advantages, especially working use of his echolocation — ensured by the cloudy waters he inhabited. Juan also maintained some ability to forage — apparent during prolonged fish shortages, when he remained healthy and vigorous, showing no signs of weight loss. Juan's initial refusal to perform, his escape from the lagoon and bid for a better life, despite Iago's and Unior's separate, but equally depreciating efforts, were all indications of his strength, independence and resourcefulness and I was *certain* all these factors could contribute towards a quick and successful rehabilitation.

But thanks to Iago's efforts, Juan's presence at the Cuban dolphinarium was no longer considered superfluous, making it unlikely they'd consider just "giving" him away, as it once seemed they might. The pittance Juan's unhappy presence earned at the water bar kept him in chains, because any income in a poor country, no matter how minuscule, was unlikely to be thrown away. If I really wanted Juan out of there, it began to look like I was going to have to make a bid on him. However, this reared the yellowed tusks of a rather gruesome ethical quandary. If lots of people started going around buying captive dolphins in order to liberate them, it would set a precedent, eventually adding lucrative incentive to the barbaric slave-mongering — and thereby perpetuating the very thing we struggled to eradicate! Also, in most cases, a captive that was bought and freed would likely be replaced — by capturing more wild dolphins. Though it was highly unlikely the Cuban dolphinarium would replace Juan, were they to give him up, it remained a miserable position to find myself in. Yet leaving Juan to rot was simply *not* an option. He was infinitely too precious to be relegated to some merely unfortunate statistic. Impossibly, unregrettably, through some hallowed, recondite egress, Juan had become kin — and while any chance of deliverance remained, I would labor towards his emancipation.

But, *if* custody of the dolphin could somehow be obtained, *where* would he go? At the time, there was a facility in the Florida Keys in the process of rehabilitating several dolphins, but the political logistics of getting a *Cuban* dolphin into an *American* sanctuary were not promising. Some sort of temporary site would need to be set up in a secure location. An ideal rehabilitation would be quick, inexpensive, well documented, and release Juan back into his original home waters to find the remainders of his people. Familiarity with his surroundings could only improve his chances of survival. Finally, he would need a clean bill of health from a marine mammal veterinarian.

So I began contacting individuals and organizations that might offer aid me in creating a temporary rehabilitation site and obtaining, transporting, rehabilitating and releasing Juan. With the initial response encouraging, I commenced the Herculean task of trying to lift my design from the ground, but my inexperienced wings remained uncertain and awkward.

Over the course of the summer, I initiated contact with various Cuban governmental agencies to learn about permits, fees and negotiation procedures. Getting through the substandard, temperamental Cuban phone system remained frustratingly difficult and the Internet was completely unheard of in Cuba at that time, which left me with good old snail mail — and in typical Cuban fashion, it would take months to receive replies.

Assuming the experience would prove useful when Juan's day came, I decided to accept an invitation to spend some time working at the rehabilitation facility in the Florida Keys. So, in late August I traversed the familiar drive from Miami, down the Florida Keys to the dolphin rehabilitation sanctuary. I had been to the site before. During my first visit to the Keys several years earlier, our party had paused at a lagoon behind an otherwise unremarkable motel, where a lone dolphin had been kept for over twenty years. A scrawled sign beside the stagnant water proclaimed this poor, companionless creature — dubbed *Sugar* — a pet. Drifting vacuously on the lagoon's oily surface, Sugar carried an unmistakably dejected air, stirring only to push pathetically at several plastic toys — the only consolation for her privation. During thrice daily feedings Sugar was roused enough to execute some half-hearted tricks for slack-jawed bystanders and was otherwise left to her own meager devices. Naturally her keepers maintained their "pet" was as happy as could be and suffered no ill effects from her prolonged solitary confinement. Four years later, little seemed to have changed for poor Sugar, still blindly pushing the same pitiful plastic toys around her motor oil-fouled pond.

Sugar's "owners" remained nonchalant about harboring her blatant travesty, while simultaneously boasting America's first official dolphin rehabilitation sanctuary on their property. Prolonged lack of stimulation and companionship had likely left Sugar a social and psychological cripple — yet the culpability of her ugly and shameful situation, right alongside that of the rehabilitants' lent the whole situation a strangely variegated cast.

In another lagoon adjacent to that containing the unfortunate Sugar, three female dolphins were preparing for release. Though less than a quarter of the size, the Florida rehabilitation lagoon very much reminded me of the Cuban lagoon, sporting the same murky mangrove-edged waters and, I remarked with a decided lack of delight — the same species of jellyfish. Freed from shows and training regimens, the dolphins seemed to spend the majority of their time engaged in recreational social romping. Part of the *un-training* process involved weaning the dolphins away from their patterns of captive dependency by minimizing human interference and interaction, encouraging them to ignore human presence and extinguish begging behaviors, while brushing up on their hunting skills. Each day local children brought live fish for the dolphins to practice chasing after their slippery prey.

I slept in a trailer beside the dolphin lagoon and often awoke in the night to hear them splashing and surfacing in the moonlight. Mornings over the bay were glorious and almost cool, before the day's oppressive heat fell. I spent part of each day observing and noting the dolphins' behavior, assisting with the preparation of their meals, answering the general public's questions and meeting with the sanctuary staff to discuss daily developments.

Time cantered by and soon my assignment was over and I bade farewell and good luck to both the dolphins and the sanctuary staff.

CHAPTER NINETEEN

AN INTERLUDE WITH ILLUMINATIONS

"A state of Grace no human can grant or replace."

Leaving the dolphin sanctuary, I made my way to West Palm Beach to visit an old friend and quite unexpectedly, found myself invited along on a sailing expedition to the Bahamas seeking the very same wild spotted dolphins I'd met the previous year. An unforeseen return to the liquid land of my heart's desire!

The morning remained misty in the harbor until we set out across the Gulf Stream in our thirty-five foot vessel. Our captain was on intimate terms with this tribe of wild spotted dolphins and remembering my previous visit, I sensed that among this small, sensitive crew, a more intimate interspecies connection might coalesce. Flying over a smoothly undulating sea of blue glass, I gazed rapt, into the oceanic depths sweeping past below, inhaling the vibrant, living sapphire hue. Journeying onwards this piercing lapis gave way, imperceptibly at first, to the rending aqua spectrum that signaled the shallow sandbanks, which our thalassic quarry frequented.

The first dolphins found us, sheering the seas and vaulting with gazelle-grace towards the bow. Weaving just beneath me was a vivacious nursery pod of freckled mothers with their spotless young. Looking thus upon them, fleeing so far from shore, I felt the veil of a half-life on land lifted, leaving me ringing with un-wearied elation.

Submerging among them, a dappled young dolphin immediately collected me, sailing along with confident confluence. This was a calm, quiet meeting; a smooth stirring of species. With the number of dolphins exceeding the human content in the water, there was no swirling cocktail of bodies. Instead, each person in our party, temporarily adopted by a dolphin, undulated undisturbed, just as I did alongside my own companion.

Only inches away, this wild, free being peered with earnest interest into my eyes, nodding jovially and occasionally turning on his side towards me, a gesture I mirrored in turn. Changing tactics, the dolphin glided forwards to float just ahead, crescent flukes hovering under my nose, keeping watch over his glimmering shoulder. I wondered if this deliberate positioning wasn't a little experiment — to see if I might be tempted to reach out. When it became evident I wasn't taking the bait, my comely companion slipped back alongside me once again, seeming satisfied. After a simple and sublime twenty minutes or so, the dolphin pod faded gracefully into the blue and swinging back aboard we sailed on.

Soon afterward, some ten to fifteen Spotteds found us, streaking to the bow and rolling through our wake. A youngster among them demonstrated some astonishing leaps, tearing gasps of admiration from all of us on board. Plowing through majestic watercolor clouds reflecting on the sea, I leaned pendent over the bow, as close as I could get, soaking up their presence, suffused in sensation as they danced before me. Every breath, every heartbeat, a reminder of the ripeness, the possibility held within each moment, invisible.

Watching a delicate baby dolphin spinning in sweet curves before its mother, I knew without any doubt where I wanted to be… Again immersed, a pair directed me towards a patch of seaweed and as I watched the mother dolphin, with unmistakably fluid and practiced alacrity, took it up first on her pec-fin, before catching it expertly on her dainty flukes. This gesture reminded me of Choney, with her fondness for parading around with such momentary prizes. Glancing up, I saw the rest of the group engaged in similar activities with the other dolphins.

I took up a strand of floating seaweed, which immediately caught the interest of the youngster who slid up alongside me, displaying her own strand, draped jauntily over a pec-fin. Exchanging a knowing look with the little dolphin, we swooped downwards, synchronously dropping our seaweed strands while curving round to collect the others'. Intent upon this game, I glanced up — too late — to see another young dolphin also heading for the same seaweed scrap. Arriving simultaneously, it was the little dolphin, who demurred, turning away — which provoked a sharp tail slap of disapproval from a nearby adult! Oops — as a human guest, deflecting a youngster away from a plaything did indeed appear rude.

My unintentional faux pas was quickly forgiven, as two other dolphins collected me between them. Spiraling in a triple helix, they dressed my pirouetting form with volute accord, piping excitedly. Another pair arched down to the bottom where they commenced rooting through the pearly sand in an effort to flush out some tasty morsel hidden there.

More dolphins arrived on the scene and between swimming engagements I caught glimpses of their behavior among themselves: A speckled male, chasing after a companion, trying to nip his flukes — no aggressive expletives, just a pectinate display and a couple of half-hearted tail swipes. I knew that to fully interpret the meaning of such interactions would require an understanding of the relationship and history between the dolphins because they were *contextual*, depending on the past nuances of friendships and rivalry between the individuals involved.

Back aboard, scudding towards the sunset, I felt myself awash in the afterglow, the vibrancy of it all. This euphoria did not fade with the coming of night, nor as I drifted into dreams rocked by the tender waves beneath a billion burning stars.

I dreamed of them in the night waters: Moon shadows, slipping over undulating sand and into the deep places.

The next day found a dynamic vista of rumbling umber clouds laced with

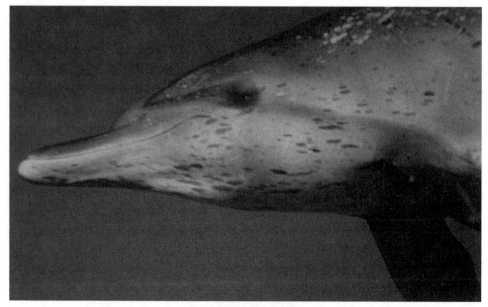

Wild spotted dolphin

sun-misted veils releasing faintly chromatic prisms, traversing the sky's azure — all reflected in shifting splendor on the sea.

Socializing actively among themselves, a group of about seven speckled juveniles hove onto the scene. Though they would have left their mothers at what, by human standards would be considered rather tender ages (somewhere between three and five), I could tell by their degree of speckling that these dolphins were coming upon adulthood, at perhaps twelve or thirteen. Typically, they were engaging enthusiastically in roughhousing and sex-play (favorite pass-times for young adults everywhere), and thereby honing the social skills they would rely on for the rest of their lives. In leaving the experience and protection of their mothers, young dolphins' survival skills were put to the test, both in seeking prey and evading predators. Foraging strong bonds between members of their peer groups was essential — as these could mean the difference between life and death. Though some might well live to be up to fifty years old, without companions to aid in foraging and detecting danger, the chances of a young dolphin's survival would be greatly diminished. I imagined it must be both a difficult and exciting period of life for them, though the sight of one with a healed shark bite scar on its side, was a reminder that inexperience combined with irrepressible curiosity could be fatal.

Sailing onwards we encountered a grand melee of some thirty to forty dolphins, comprised of both Spotteds and Bottlenose. The spotted dolphins seemed to encompass all ages, but most impressive were the organized groups of heavily mottled adults, surfacing synchronously amid the much larger and mightily scarred bottlenose dolphins. The dolphins' rapid and decisive movements suggested something unusual and intense was stirring. Though their velocity prevented us from entering the water for first hand observation, I was determined to glean everything possible from the deck as the boat kept apace. Surfacing militantly, the dolphin pairs and trios quickened further, indicating impending aggression. Turbulence and dissention ruptured moments later, the dolphins' sudden jagged movements sheering walls of water and churning foam!

Research suggests that degrees of social aggression in dolphins may be somewhat species-related. Bottlenose dolphins tend to boast many more tooth-rake marks — evidence of clash and confrontation between them, whereas the Spotted and Spinner dolphins seem to possess a generally less turbulent culture. Before us, the brawny Bottlenose continued their vehement threshing, executing impressive cohesion in a succession of prodigious leaps! In all likelihood, they were using these powerful, synchronized displays to intimidate the more diminutive Spotteds.

Despite the delight of some of the others on board at the breath-taking spectacle, I felt a rising concern over what was to me, clearly not a gentle or celebratory meeting between species. I was aware that these electrifying aerobatics were a likely indicator of some rather involved conflict concealed beneath the water and that the most escalated contention observed in the lives of these spotted dolphins involved the Bottlenose species. Apparently, elder Spotteds were known to monitor such dissidence, interfering to prevent the progression of acute violence. Peering doubtfully into the darkening water I saw a large older Spotted race by, eyes wide, while pivoting dorsal fins ripped through the furious water.

Suddenly, I saw a tiny baby bottlenose dolphin roughly and repeatedly buffeted from the water by a huge adult! What was this? Clearly it was not any spotted dolphin brutalizing the infant, whose blunt rostrum positively identified it as Bottlenose. But why would an adult Bottlenose batter a baby of its' own species, amid a conflict with the Spotteds? Our captain entered the water to try and report something of the dolphins' doings, but the swift and vigorous nature of their continuing feud made this impossible.

With the on-set of night, the dolphins were lost in the gathering dusk, leaving me to wonder what complexities transpired beneath the darkening swells. The event served as a reminder; that these were wild folk with wild ways, as yet little understood by humankind.

The majority of the dolphins we encountered the following day seemed to be resting, keeping a slow and sedate pace rather than engaging us. Hardly surprising — if these were the same dolphins — they might well remain wearied from the tremendous clash we had witnessed the previous day. Out of respect we let the Spotteds be, opting instead to dive on a nearby shipwreck.

First to inspect our arrival came glinting barracuda, their coldly appraising eyes reminding me uncomfortably of the marlin in Hawaii. Such thoughts were quickly abandoned as I descended towards the jeweled kingdom below. Dour grouper and candy-striped squirrel fish crouched furtively beneath coral overhangs, while angelfish fluttered overhead flaunting rare peacock and topaz hues. On the sea floor, a stingray muffled itself in the sands, while bold schools of jacks and yellowtail dazzled in flurries of silver and citrine. A school of electric blue chromis appeared, throwing the sun off their shivering azure sides. Their cascade ended abruptly as it had begun, leaving me dazed at their exquisite, glittering display.

Drifting to graze the surface for breath before returning below, I wondered anew at the abundance of sea life attracted to the ship's skeleton. Faintly, the singsong of dolphin whistles reached me on the gently shifting current. Back aboard, the lookout announced that there had been a couple of bottlenose dolphins poking about on the far side of the wreck, choosing to keep out of sight.

Setting forth through dawn's luminescence, I sensed the fragrant promise and possibility of the day before me. How keenly this life called — the nourishing nimbus of the tropical latitudes and keeping the company of wild dolphins.

About a mile off shore, a flock of feeding gulls and frigate birds swirled and dove. Thus alerted to the possibility of dolphins feeding below, we quietly drew closer. Across the calm water the telltale exhalations and thorn-like fins of dolphins dipping beneath the birds could be distinguished. As they were in all likelihood just finishing off a meal, it was decided to halt the boat several hundred meters away, and keep an eye on the dolphins as they completed their breakfasting. Joining the captain in the cool blue water for a swim by the boat, a single, large spotted dolphin appeared, circling round us in perfunctory surveillance, before returning to its companions; a scout sent to investigate our presence.

Returning from our leisurely soak in the sea, we began to sail slowly toward the dolphins, careful to skirt around the area of their feeding activity. This was an inquisitive pass, to see if any might engage us, signaling their willingness to play after mealtime. Marvelously, three dolphins were immediately drawn to the bow, where as always, I leaned sighing over the water.

Weaving flawless glissandos before me, one of them turned on his speckled side to glance up. As our eyes met, I felt moving within me something akin to a mild electric current; an entity unto itself, quite apart from the elation of beholding these exquisite creatures enjoying their element. It happens now and again; the eyes of two creatures from different worlds meet, and somehow there is the feeling of recognition and affinity. A very real exchange, defying all dissection — *someone* looking back at me, into me — and realizing a mutual *connection*!

Having finished up with their repast, many more dolphins were finding their way to the boat. Bursting from the rippling waters, a pair of youngsters came skipping over the sea like polished stones. There were heavily patterned elders, mottled adults, speckled juveniles and burnished babies of various sizes, including a yearling with a remora fish stuck on its side. *A pest or a pet?* I wondered.

As the captain skillfully navigated the turquoise seas, the dolphins chose to amuse themselves either flirting at the bow, or surfing in the wake of our passage. Unable to tear my eyes away from the vision of eloquence they so embodied, I began noting some of the distinguishing scratches and markings of the different dolphins twining below me.

If only I could stay and share their daily lives, come to know each of these dolphins as individuals, and to learn the particulars of their relationships, as I had begun to among the Cubano Dolphins. These fleeting glimpses left me longing ardently to know more — to somehow find myself invited along as an honorary member of the wild dolphins' fluid groups and participate in the unfolding of mutual discovery.

The ocean remained immaculate, reflecting a gloriously flowering sky. It was all too beautiful, these resplendent colors glimmering between heaven and the fluorite waters...combined with the coronal presence of the dolphins — drawn past all commentary and into pure delight of being. Every detail I drank evoked further raptures until there was nothing to do but surrender to the ultimate ecstasy offered in the moment. Theirs was a consummate, mercurial grace; dolphins flying before me, leaning this way and that, seeming to bow and nod to each other; fluid, artless, effortless, the flickering hue of hematite and hydrophane — curving and caressing one another — before peeling off the bow and soaring like swallows, unencumbered into aqueousness.

It was a sort of suffering to know such elemental perfection through only the meek senses — unable to enfold it somehow more fully — leaving a powerful longing to somehow taste this flowing opalescence with senses I did not have and could not name. For me, this became a timeless, heavenly journey, with sun-sequined ripples echoing out from the bow and just below, the dolphins; lithe, lyrate, lilting — this flowing, their natural state.

A state of Grace no human can grant or replace.

There was one, who turning upon his taut, pluvial side to gaze up at me, again stirred sensation — as if there were something charged, though ephemeral between us; an expectant air. His amaranthine eyes were on mine; the incorporeal caress of his sun-shot glance causing a shiver of impossible recognition. The sun was at its zenith and the sea invitingly warm as I phased into it among them.

Enveloped by silken speckles, everything else pales... There was one, peppered in sunlight, who captured my gaze with his, inviting interminable sunlit realms, awakening that same swelling elation I had felt from the bow.

Was he the same one? An internal quickening told me it must be. As if in answer, his misted moonstone skin brushed feather-fine against mine, shivering in diluvial delight. Again, moth soft, his shoulder against mine. I hesitated at this invitation, unbelieving, heart racing, but those incandescent eyes erased all doubt, erased everything, but the promise held there.

Softly, softly, succumbing to this tacit collusion, as if to touch a floating bubble, afraid to break the spell…impossible aqueous metallurgy, sumptuous, sublime, whispering silken against my fingertips; both of us held in exquisite initial sensation. Certain of his assent, my touch lingered, delicately tracing his sleek side. Another dolphin slid against us; sensuously enwreathed — these others reminding me of Choney, Unior and Christine — because here was all the sweetness I had ever known with Juan — *with none of the sadness.*

Slipping beneath me with the curving grace of a wave, my consort offered his niveous underside, a faint blush infusing his porcelain pallor, while every flower I had ever seen unfurled orchestrally within me. With powerful strokes of his crescent flukes he swept me onwards within his slipstream and swimming in this shared sweetness, I know what I am — see I have always known. The others had slipped away, only my consort and one other remained. One last lingering look; oneiric, unspoken colloquy…and they too faded away into the jeweled water.

For a timeless moment I remained silent and submerged, the halation immortalized in memory — before bursting to the surface, into the sunlight with laughter!

Back aboard the boat, a celebratory air prevailed and traveling onwards, the dolphins were drawn once more to swerve in the wake or soar at the bow. Draped in exhausted elation over the prow, I contemplated several dolphins rippling in ophidian arabesque just below. One of these, turning on his gleaming side, gazed obliquely up at me, and again, I found myself brimming with an unnamable affinity. Was it he? Certainty, impossible as snow set afire told me it was so. In celestial silence I sang out my echoing thanks.

One of the crew had brought a large, inflatable rubber manta ray, which after a fatiguing group effort was finally inflated and tied with a long lead behind the vessel. While the others took turns riding the manta surrounded by rollicking dolphins, I chose to remain at the bow, seeking insight and taking careful note of any distinguishing markings on those who came to glide and dance beneath me. Both species were in high spirits, and every time the dolphins surfaced or leaped beside the manta's rider, the shouts and laughter made me smile, despite my concentration. It *was* quite a sight: hilariously bouncing riders astride a giant red rubber manta ray, whooping with glee and surrounded by rows of tumbling dolphins disporting among the waves!

Meanwhile, a picture was coming into focus for me: attending us was a mixed group of roughly fifteen or so dolphins, comprised of three large adults, darkened with many layers of spots and speckles, perhaps acting as protectors for the four pairs of mothers and young traveling with them. And then there were three or four speckled young adults, just on the outskirts of maturity without infants at their sides — probably all young males. This was the subgroup that had enveloped me and one among them was *he*.

Taking our cue from the dolphins, we settled down for lunch, watching as they knifed through the water only meters away, plunging, leaping and rolling after ballyhoo. Drifting with the hunting dolphins into deeper waters, the ocean took on a siliceous ultramarine hue and soon it was time again to swim! Arching to meet the five humans in the water were some six or seven dolphins. Immediately, a speckled pair glided towards me.

Held in their incomparable gaze, I knew them — as they knew me. The two dolphins flanked me, drawing me tenderly between them, curving towards me like wings, proffering lotus-like undersides. Encircled, immortal, absolute; pouring myself in one long, cool draught, into their eyes, this dialogue between us inscribing my essence, liquid, like them. Sealed, with a final inhalation. It was not until after the pair had flown, and my silent extollations somewhat subsided — that the *impact* — the singularity of the situation struck. Yet nothing could have been more natural; so many times mingling and entwined among the Cubano Dolphins, I had never questioned my company. Yet these were wild dolphins. I had been blessed, and I knew it.

Back aboard, the captain observed the pair who had held me among them were known as "Horseshoe" and "White Spot," two young, inseparable males, close in adolescent age, around eleven or twelve years old, much as I had surmised. Strangely, the year before, during my previous visit among these dolphins, I had chosen a single photograph, from the dozens available — a perfect portrait of White Spot, with Horseshoe* gazing sagely over his shoulder.

Deeper waters soon drew the dolphins and with the gathering seabirds, it became apparent that another meal must be at hand, hidden beneath the waves. Leaving these dolphins with whom we had passed the day to enjoy

* Also known as "Black Spot."

their victuals, we journeyed on — I with many a backward glance and private sigh. A rolling front of dark clouds was approaching from the west and with it a wild, sharp wind.

Soon afterward we encountered a last pod of dolphins, and indulged in a final late afternoon swim. Six heavily spotted adults moved through our group, carrying with them a sedate *presence*. After the trilling and fifing of the younger ones, these larger dolphins seemed more solemn, their unfathomable ebony eyes sweeping us with venerable appraisal, before proceeding past with pelagic lordliness. From the deck, we saw they were headed towards the other dolphins, still feasting in the distant deep water.

Roiling sepia clouds had overtaken the last of the sky's blue — it was time to return. Riding the enormous black swells, I reveled as the ocean revealed a glimpse of her might and power, so different from the glassy calm we'd rode in on. Shafts of light escaped the dark veils overhead in a slithering sun-dance over the water, creating a memorable sunset.

Unlooked for, I had found a great refueling of the spirit: Hope and courage, revived, refreshed and renewed. *Reilluminated.*

CHAPTER TWENTY

SUNDERED

'Say a prayer for my release, when every hope in the world is asleep.'
lyrics, David Sylvian, "Before the Bullfight"*

Leaving behind the vivacity of the wild dolphins, I returned to face my formidable task. *Still* awaiting replies from Cuban ministries, I began developing a rehabilitation proposal, a budget outline and assembling a task team for the project, should it suddenly spring to life. Though I was still seeking a proper rehabilitation site, I did manage to secure the services of a marine mammal vet to oversee basic husbandry for Juan. Possibilities surfaced and submerged like dorsal fins in proverbially muddy waters — and still, I awaited replies to my inquiries from Cuba.

Time wore on, the last of summer's triumphant vaunt fading into autumn's pudic flush. A visit to the dolphins was overdue (it had been over six months), and in order to make the most of the trip, I arranged to meet with my marine mammal vet in Cuba. Fluent in Spanish, the vet agreed to check Juan's general condition, travel to Havana to inquire into the progress of my requests, and if the correct authorities could be located, negotiate for Juan's acquisition and removal.

Upon my cautious arrival I immediately noticed the lagoon's net had almost completely disintegrated and no longer constituted any real sort of barrier. Locating Benicio, I learned that all the dolphins now regularly left the lagoon and that they taken to begging at the water bar, snagging a portion of Juan's meager fish supply — which of course had led to trouble.

Waiting on the empty dock, I watched the water, listening to the faint, familiar rasping of butterfly wings scraping against my innards. Unior was the first to appear. One look — and he *knew* me — evincing only a sort of droll pleasure rather than any indication of surprise. Meeting the blunt, scar-

*from the album *Gone to Earth* (reproduced by permission of Opium Arts Ltd).

etched pectoral fin he offered against my palm, the two of us indulged in our greeting ritual of pec-patting and then, from his pale head to his notched tail, the enormous dolphin slid under my hands and vanished into the gloomy water.

A moment passed in silence. Then another. Suddenly five dolphins coalesced before me — Unior had brought them all! I opened my arms to their mercurial satin surge, gloriously engulfed and willingly lured among them into the cloudy water where they continued excitedly buzzing and burbling, filling my vision with their glimmering faces.

Visibility quit at about three foggy feet, but their proximity allowed me to remark how much Bia and Sebastian had grown. All five dolphins, large and small, lined up, scanning me thoroughly up and down with mysterious, mandatory sonic showers — and then the six of us were off, nudging, caressing, reaffirming and weaving amongst each other in sunny reunion. This particularly bountiful and affectionate reception lasted more than twenty minutes, at which point we were interrupted by Benicio, calling me back to discuss further developments in the dolphins' situation. Still in the throes of our initial greetings, the dolphins set themselves to distraction, continually enticing my attention away from conversation with the trainer.

No contest really. Rolling slowly to offer the sumptuous shining plain of his chest for caressing, Unior settled the matter. But judging by his persistent nudging — he was up to something and even as I speculated about his curious behavior, the redoubtable dolphin hooked his battered rostrum into my unsuspecting palm, and with expert confidence *pulled* me away from the dock with him, taking me completely by surprise! Steadied by Unior's even, delving eye, I offered no resistance as he swept me away with him, skimming along the surface, before gently descending beneath the water.

Sebastian appeared, darting around us and transforming Unior's gentle abduction into a dance. Suddenly mindful of Unior's past mood swings, I disengaged myself, turning back towards the dock, but the mighty and mellow dolphin inevitably and unhurriedly cut me off, directing my attention towards his smooth flanks, suggesting further caresses instead. Fortunately, Unior failed to manifest any sign of his previously disturbing attitudes and it was tempting to correlate his continuing docility with Juan's failure to react with any protest or violence, as he had in the past.

Benicio and I continued conversing later in the day and I learned that ownership of the dolphinarium and its unwilling inhabitants had recently been transferred to a Cuban entertainment company. Despite the trainer's earnest advice, the dolphinarium's manager still insisted on retaining Juan, though Benicio thought it might be possible to bypass his strident objections by negotiating directly with the Cuban company. Benicio advised my Spanish-speaking vet on how best to tackle the situation. Without the company's consent, no amount of planning or permits would do Juan any good. With any luck, direct negotiations would lead us through the bureaucratic maze somewhat faster than a lame tortoise trudging through tar.

Benicio also had other news. Plans to close down the dolphinarium had been finalized, as the present location was indeed going to become part of a resort's golf course. As things stood, all six dolphins were scheduled to be moved to another similar, but smaller lagoon farther down the peninsula, sometime in the next six months. Perhaps, with the correct timing, an offer to take problematic Juan off the dolphinarium's hands would stack the unsteady odds in his favor and his freedom would at last be granted.

In answer to my inquiries, I also learned that though the other dolphins regularly wandered beyond the lagoon's confines, Juan and Unior were rarely seen to fight. In fact, Benicio adamantly maintained that it was dainty little *Choney* who was now Juan's biggest adversary! *Choney?* — how could that be? This, I would have to see.

Surfacing with natural elegance before the dock, Christine pinned me with an unusually intense stare, before firmly nudging my shoulder in inexplicable acknowledgment, and then vanishing. She reappeared moments later among the others and collected, we all headed towards the dilapidated net together. Reaching the stringy, slimy barrier, the dolphins sailed untroubled over it, instantly swallowed by the murk. Wavering, I failed to follow. There was more than just jellyfish to take into consideration; Juan's powerful and temperamental presence moved somewhere ahead, and a knot in my belly whispered, *caution.*

Sebastian and Bia reappeared, whistling encouragingly and criss-crossing forth and back over the net, demonstrating the ease with which the barrier could be passed — but of course it wasn't the barrier, but what lay beyond it that daunted me. Perhaps comprehending my hesitation, Unior appeared from the turbid fog to gather me gently alongside his suddenly reassuring bulk. Swimming slowly in his comforting shadow, I finally crossed over the net — but more than a little stung: Once, I had sheltered Juan from Unior's violence — and now it was Unior safeguarding me from the possibility of Juan's vitriolic tempest. Though I acknowledged change as life's only constant, this failed to ease the ironic abrasion.

Choney joined us on a slow tour past the water bar and eventually we all came curving round back over the net, undulating along, until a peculiar buzz from Choney brought us to a halt. Hanging vertically in the water, mirroring her stance, I faced Choney, who steadied her slender form and issued a soft buzz, narrowing the sound band until the tip of her rostrum met my proffered fingertip. Continuing our established initiatory protocol, Choney invited a long and enthusiastic bout of pec-patting, in the middle of which, an excitedly piping Sebastian appeared, eager to somehow insert himself in the exchange. Her vivid, sagacious gaze pressed to mine, Choney issued a fine-tuned sonic spray, scanning me carefully up and down with minute movements of her domed head. Though I was familiar with this behavior, I wondered anew at its specific function.

Having failed to catch our quieting, Sebastian continued to nudge and pester his mother, cutting between us and making a continuous, fifing racket. Turning toward her turbulent offspring, Choney fixed him with a baleful look and with measured weight, poked her son heavily in the chest with her rostrum, as if admonishing him with a *'Just you settle down there, big guy.'* This gesture failed to dissuade young Sebastian from his rampant ways and the moment his mother returned her attention back to me, the insouciant imp dove down and nipped her tail flukes! Jolting out of the water in surprise, Choney set out in hot pursuit, her sassy progeny having already (wisely) fled the scene.

Choney turned up again soon afterwards — in a most unexpected spot. Heavily, hesitantly, I'd gone seeking Juan at the moldering water bar — and instead found Choney *and* nippy Sebastian hanging around clearly keeping an eye out for scraps. Juan appeared only after the pair had returned to the lagoon. Fresh, bloodied rake marks still oozing from slashes across his forehead indicated recent confrontation!

In vain silence I fought the hope — that he might look up and with a nebulous internal flicker, realize the arrival of a tender companion. Jaws gaping in blind supplication, Juan gave no sign of recognition. Estranged and farouche, he paced beyond any remnant of remembered warmth. His presence was piercing, and struggling against futile floodtides, I told myself it didn't matter; my private pathos was of no consequence — that only his freedom was important — but I was bereft. Juan had withdrawn to some remote shore, leaving only his shut body close to me, devoid. Like Orpheus into the underworld, he had gone where I could not follow.

Don't look back — but I do; at the rending a heart may sustain. Unremarked, unloved, unremembered, I slipped away.

This early in the season the dolphinarium was only partially inundated with crowds, yet always a persistent knot of people waited for dolphin-hauls after the shows. By the following month, when the tourist season was in full swing, the place would again be overrun. The dolphinarium had raised its prices from two dollars per "swim" to twenty, signaling an ominous raise in the dolphins' monetary value, which did *not* bode well.

Show time. An insistent and precious pest, Sebastian allowed his mother little respite during the thrice-daily vulgarities, leaning and rolling jauntily over her back while she strained to earn her meager meal — unaware that soon, he too would be trapped by his hunger and made to toil endlessly for each morsel.

Meanwhile Christine, bored with catching the ball for the zillionth time, abandoned the bright trifle to float slowly away with the tide. Eyes bulging with amazing distemper, Iago bellowed nastily, ordering her to fetch it. The crowd waited. Christine seemed to be taking great amusement in this opportunity to frustrate the bawling trainer — making a move as if to retrieve the ball — and then with cheeky disdain, turning away at the last moment. Iago's enraged cursing failed to bring results and the situation continued to devolve, with Bia and Sebastian engaging the ball, tossing it gaily hither and thither, until finally Umberto managed to scoop it up from the smaller dock. But instead of carrying it over to Iago, Umberto made the mistake of trying to throw it. The distance was simply too great — and the ball landed back in the water once again, where all the dolphins pounced gleefully upon it. The ball was soon forgotten, and the dolphins all went off for a romp together, breaching and splashing with much apparent levity — and effectively dismissing Iago, the audience and show business — *hoorah!*

My later diligent note-jotting was happily interrupted by Sebastian's unexpected arrival at the larger dock. Sprightly, sapient eyes fixed on mine, Sebastian edged close and with buzzing precision, located a straying tendril of hair floating in the water. Delicately capturing the strand in his jaws, he tugged — appearing most pleased with the cry of surprise this elicited! Thinking of the way we used to play when he and Bia were a little younger and a lot smaller, I plunked a foot in the water, skittering it about in a frightened, fishy sort of way. Emitting burbles and hiccups of excited concentration, Sebastian followed every movement, just as he used to. His earnest attitudes had lost none of their hilarity and my sides soon ached from laughter. Pausing to cock a comely eye upwards to see what all the guffawing was about, Sebastian's quizzical look only encouraged my merriment.

Immersed, Sebastian curved against me and with an impish glint, subjected my hair to further persistent tugging, before diving to nibble my swim fins. Swirling and spiraling, Sebastian and I soon discovered to our mutual delight, that we could pec-pat on the go. Having ascertained this,

Writing notes on the big dock.

we amused ourselves practicing this tricky maneuver for some time. Together he and I were forging and cementing *relationship* — play being the medium through which a mutual weaving of trust occurred. Far from facile, *this* was the stuff that would last between us while I was away for months and months. Looking deep into each other's eyes, *Being to Being* — became the forum where everything that mattered happened. Suddenly almost solemn, Sebastian moved forward and softly touched his rostrum to my forehead.

Soon afterward, I watched as Choney cruised by, catching Unior's eye with a curving, flirtatious glance. An instant later, both vanished in a flurry of splashing. Moments later the pair glided by below the silent screen of the water's green glass, Unior's rostrum firmly glued to Choney's nether region. In response to this persistence, Choney whacked her consort smartly over the face with her flukes — Unior's supremely unfazed appearance eliciting a small, privately appreciative chuckle.

A little while later Unior appeared to collect me for a swim. But Sebastian tried to push the two of us apart, making strident squelching sounds of petulant protest. Pausing, Unior turned to face the defiant youngster. With dauntingly deliberate gravity, he tapped the youngster in the chest with his blunt and scarred rostrum, fixing Sebastian with a look that implied a rapidly thinning humor at youth's impatience and impropriety. Cowed at last, the little fellow quieted right down. *Wise idea.*

Blaring music announced the show, hastening my immediate retreat from the lagoon. Eager to record my recent exchanges, I retreated to the channel, sitting with one leg tucked under and the other foot just brushing the drab water. An unexpected exhalation lifted my gaze. Surfacing close by Juan approached, jaws agape in entreaty, his amnesia or perhaps indifference to my presence, scaldingly obvious. Emptied and impotent, I could only stare at him fending off memories and ruin.

Scything closer, Juan lined his scarred bulk up inches from my foot, as if *daring* me to reach out. Oh, and I longed to push past the mutable peril, to entreat friendship's tender resurrection, but I *knew* that any attempt at contact would ignite in him only displeasure and vexation and so, despite the visceral call, I made no move towards him. Unable to bear the rending sight of him, I bowed my head and tried to write; tried to ignore the crushed lilies of our past.

Feeling the over affections of the sun, I returned to the dock to apply a dab of sunscreen. Shading my eyes against the clinquant water, I saw Juan, now begging at the water bar, dive and vanish — an instant before Choney's arrival. There was no mistaking it — he left when she came. But *why?*

With Choney having vacated the lagoon, Christine soon reappeared at the dock to visit. For such a slip of a dolphin, Choney's presence (or absence) certainly had a noticeable effect on those around her.

Christine often seemed to reside on the outskirts of the core group (Choney, Unior and Sebastian) and though she wasn't an obvious outcast like poor Juan, I had to wonder if her aloof absence was entirely voluntary. I suspected that Choney, having established herself as Unior's firm favorite, was somehow responsible for excluding Christine from the group and wondered if it was this, which contributed to Christine's often muted and melancholy air. Without other friends or family to turn to for support and comfort (other than little Bia), Christine remained largely confined to the outskirts of her makeshift society and because of this, I was eager to reciprocate whenever Christine approached me.

Holding aloft a curved pec-fin, Christine fixed me with her interminable chocolate gaze, initiating a deft bout of pec-patting. Not wishing to miss the opportunity, I joined Christine and Bia in the water. Wobbling along between us, Bia repeated a particular, adamant whistle. Her demeanor showed no signs of distress and I wondered if perhaps she was practicing and sharing her signature whistle — her dolphin name?

I found Juan late in the day, drifting alone in the channel, a desolate grey lump on the water. Because the miscreants inhabiting the water bar dolled out fish indiscriminately to any dolphin that appeared, Juan was being underfed and had acquired yet more rake-marks from challenging this unwanted arrangement. Yet there remained an upside to his situation. Since this cut in his handouts, Benicio reported regularly observing Juan fishing in the channel and lake — successfully, it would seem — as he showed no evidence of weight loss, despite his tribulations. This squalid situation was actually forcing Juan to hone his hunting abilities, increasing his independence.

While I brooded, the dolphin glided over, alert for signs of food, even seeming to squint out of his injured eye at me. Unconcerned with the emotional floods surging above him, Juan amused himself with a strand of seaweed, tossing it carelessly into the air. Abandoning this brief jollity, he focused once more on my presence, again coming to rest with his rostrum inches from my feet. But he did not choose to bridge the parched and desolate plains still separating us. Exhaling, he slid out into the lake, sailing smoothly along underwater, the milky pallor of his belly turned toward the sun.

Night: wading in restless nostalgia, tenderly tracing the familiar pale curve of coast, with *Him* always on my mind, still trapped in dark circles, somewhere in black water. I looked up to the stars, fearful of the future and the stars whispered to me: *Be not afraid*

The next morning Choney, Unior and I exchanged greetings, while an indignant and immediately meddlesome Sebastian nudged and squawked at us, seized with a fit of jealousy. Buzzing emphatically, the impudent imp tossed an open-mouthed threat at his mother. This time he earned the *full* attention of both adult dolphins and collecting the protesting youngster between them, Unior and Choney led him over into the show area. There followed some obscure exchange, which resulted in their parking Sebastian by the edge of the dock and despite his lusty and discordant objections, leaving him firmly behind as they continued on together. It was almost as if he'd been made to "sit in the corner" and judging from his strident, squalling complaints, he felt it a thoroughly unfair decision — *what a racket!* Once his protestations had deteriorated into displeased raspberries, I approached. In a fit of residual petulance, Sebastian gaped his little jaws at me in peevish threat. Demonstrating my lack of trepidation towards his pearly teeth, I agreeably stuffed my arm into his open mouth, effectually deflating his tantrum.

Incorrigible and hardly contrite, Sebastian continued his efforts when Unior and Choney returned, but Unior was just too massive to push out of the way. Still, a shoving match ensued, punctuated with much ridiculous squeaking and honking. Despite the vast size difference between the two dolphins, such was Sebastian's zeal, that there were moments when one might almost have thought they were evenly matched. Drifting side by side, Choney and I watched the two silly males chase each other round and round, sounding like a bunch of angry geese in a room full of wet balloons. Jaunty and coy, Unior sailed by right by us, recumbent and sporting a full erection, followed a moment later by Sebastian, brandishing his own miniature version. Choney and I exchanged a look. Men.

After the hauling, the show and the rest of the morning mess, I retired to the dock, scribbling diligently. Overhead, a flight of impossibly enormous iridescent dragonflies hovered, sporadically darting hither and thither over the gently coruscating water, beneath which, Bia and Sebastian soon lured me to soar among them. Each time I angled towards the surface for breath, the two little dolphins would surge just ahead of me, bursting into the air and leaping over my head, twittering and twirling! Their swift, unfettered resplendence reminded me keenly of many similarly shared bouts of play among the young wild spotted dolphins.

As long as they subsisted primarily on milk (consuming fish only as a snack), Bia and Sebastian could afford to remain untroubled, but all too soon they would be weaned. Ensnared by hunger, they would find themselves shackled to an inescapable wheel of misery and ceaseless degradation at the hands of endless, grasping crowds. But not yet.

We dallied together for some time before I noticed that Unior, Choney and Christine were all away over at the water bar and I realized — I was *babysitting*! Though at their age and in this setting, my over-seeing was hardly critical, I remained privately pleased at the implied compliment of trust.

After the youngsters had been gathered back to their mothers' gleaming sides, I left the lagoon, circumnavigating my trepidatious way to the water bar to discover how Juan fared. He was there, stolen and shadowed, worn and wounded, ragged and tattered, but to my eyes, soul-stoppingly beautiful.

His sightless begging was interrupted by the appearance of Christine, who immediately began vying determinedly with Juan at the frayed edge of the shabby pontoon for scraps. Bia was there too, keeping well back, watching the two adult dolphins strenuously shoving at one another, uttering harsh cries. Suddenly, amid further flailing and splashing, they were off, one chasing the other! I found Christine and Juan clashed regularly over fish scraps at the water bar, while oblivious tourists happily dangled fish shreds over the dolphins' heads, exclaiming how *cute* they were as they strove in earnest and ungentle contention to ease their hunger. These scuffles

Juan & Christine vying for scraps.

always seemed to conclude with Christine beating a retreat and Juan returning unchallenged.

Soon afterward, Choney surfaced by the water bar, whereupon Juan swallowed a last scrap and immediately made himself scarce, diving out of sight — giving every indication that *she* was the one he didn't care to challenge. Choney couldn't possibly threaten Juan in any physically significant way, so I was left to imagine the existence of an implied threat, most likely from Unior, or perhaps their combined efforts — *something* that inspired Juan to evacuate the area with all haste.

Back on the dock in the lagoon, I commenced recording the day's observations, while fending off unwanted attention from mosquitoes. Choney appeared, with Sebastian in tow and as soon as she and I began our greetings, little Sebastian bent his efforts towards removing his mother, rudely and roughly shoving her! But this time our rash, uncivil puck had bitten off more than he could chew. A sudden flurry of splashing ensued, terminating with Choney's dignified return — with a very *chastened* Sebastian at her side.

As almost any mother mammal can relate, discipline is of utmost importance for a young social creature. In wild dolphin society, complying with strict group cohesion is sometimes essential, not only in coordinating hunting, but also in dealing with the approach of danger — say a large shark. The undisciplined action of a sassy young dolphin veering away from the group could end up in attack, injury and even death. Choney was firmly instructing her rebellious little son, just as her own mother had doubtless dealt with her, making it clear when to quit fooling around and accept the direction of an elder and protector.

However, the irrepressible Sebastian still had plenty of sass left in him, only now *I* had become his target. At first he only tugged insistently at my hair, but then he hatched a new ploy — *pinching.* Using just the tip of his rostrum, he got the taut skin just above my elbow — *ouch* — *little bugger!* Immensely pleased with himself, Sebastian then nudged my ribs, belly, knees, and shoulders, squirming, buzzing and leaping, with excitement, until he suddenly — *zing* — zoomed away! *That child...*The following day, I discovered that wee sassy Sebastian had acquired brand new rake marks, slashing across his forehead — evidence that serious discipline had indeed been dispensed.

However, there were times of confluence among the five dolphins, during which I felt keenly a powerful cohesion settling — that magic present only when our entire group traveled along, as if all of a single purpose and mind.

Roaming at length among them, an unusually clear tide allowed ample opportunity to survey the minute inflections of social dynamics and the interplay of personality politics from my place within the group.

Within the social entity our group formed, I knew that for whatever reasons, Choney was without doubt, the Queen Bee. All other evidence aside, the tooth-rake marks resulting from disputes rarely fell on her. As for raw power, Unior was definitely King. But, I wondered, when push came to shove, whether it was Choney's will or Unior's that prevailed. I suspected Choney possessed immense powers of persuasion, which she used ruthlessly to harness Unior's might and obtain his constant, willing companionship. With this arrangement, Unior became the unspoken brawn buttressing Choney's wishes. Despite his fearsome rivalry with Juan, Unior's usual personality appeared to lean towards indolence and with Bia and Sebastian he manifested as a doting, tolerant figure.

Because of the limitations captivity imposed, natural dolphin social groupings were an impossibility. Within the confines of the lagoon Choney and Unior appeared to have drawn together to form a male/female alliance — something almost unheard of in the analogues of wild dolphin behavior, (aside from fleeting courtship and adolescent play). Unified, Choney and Unior had become stronger than any other single dolphin. The advantages of this arrangement were obvious — a desirable, fertile female companion for Unior and for Choney, the protection and muscle to enforce her willful wishes.

I wondered how and why Choney had come to own Unior's affections rather than Christine. In the past, Christine had sometimes challenged Choney and there had been times when Unior paired up with Christine, effectually leaving Choney out. Temperamental Christine was no timid dolphin, being the most likely to threaten and bite tourists when pushed past her limits by Iago, but despite Christine's larger size and taurine personality, her place in the group seemed firmly beneath Choney, with little love lost between the two. And it seemed to me that she suffered for it. Within the fluid expanse of wild dolphin society she might very well be found enjoying day to day associations among courting males, aunts, sisters, sons and daughters, transforming a seemingly reclusive Christine into a regular socialite. But within human confines, she had little choice.

Then there was Juan the outcast. Though Unior was obviously older and more powerful, Juan had fought his rival every step of the way. Initial turbulence seemed to have spiked over who would possess Choney's affections and sire her offspring. For the time being, with the *issue* technically settled, it appeared Unior and Juan no longer clashed with the violence and regularity they once had.

Following Choney, Unior, Christine and Juan, I recognized my own amphibious place within the group, deferring without complaint to the adult dolphins' wishes, whenever they were made apparent. In time, as Bia and Sebastian grew in girth and wisdom, this deference would extend to them as well. In the meantime, I took it upon myself to watch over them and let them know if they were getting too rambunctious.

Perhaps because of the lofty status his mother enjoyed, little Sebastian was always pushing his boundaries, even to the point of challenging Choney and Unior. Though they were generally very tolerant of his willful ways, it was clear Choney didn't hesitate to met out discipline when necessary. It was also clear that Sebastian had learned not to test Christine's limits — having likely become acquainted with her temper early on in life. Through all of this, I couldn't help but gaze towards the future — when a growing Sebastian must inevitably become a serious challenge to Unior...

And then, there was sweet Bia who seemed to spend a lot of time coasting along in baby position, beneath her mamma. Among wild dolphins, acceptance and survival of the young could be influenced by the status or abilities of the mother. Socially unskilled or unsupported mothers might not enjoy effective protection and resources for their offspring. However, having made the best of her situation, Bia had foraged a friendship with Sebastian, her only playmate and didn't seem as secular as Christine.

In time, the group dispersed, Sebastian, Bia and Choney remaining close by. An unerringly dear nuisance, Sebastian nudged and pestered me for attention, while I added a few last minute observations into my cantankerous recorder on the dock. Rising up half his length from the water, practically into my lap, Sebastian certainly knew how to draw attention to himself: *Yikes — no wet dolphins on the tape recorder!*

I slipped back into the water and quieting, Sebastian scanned me softly up and down, just as his mother had taught him, before gently running his ivory jaws over my arm. For her part, Choney closely studied our interactions, showing absolutely no interest in involving herself, or collecting Sebastian to move off. Ever since Juan and I had first entwined in tender conversation, Choney had displayed a continuing and keen interest in my most intimate interspecies interactions. *I was being studied.*

Though her mother appeared to have gone elsewhere, Bia had remained with us and now began a subdued buzzing, offering her own little pec-fins to initiate contact and play. When I reciprocated, Sebastian became predictably jealous and agitated. Choney solved his shrilling by issuing a mild, bubble-buzzing threat at Bia who promptly scooted away, leaving Sebastian to his quarry.

Soon afterwards, thrashing erupted close by the water bar. Trying to determine who was responsible for the ruckus through the milling dorsal fins, I distinguished Juan and Unior — and there, begging by the sagging pontoon, quite unmolested, was Choney. Moving back into the channel, the two males separated, Juan, with freshly bloodied rake marks on his dorsal fin, vigorously tail slapping, in obvious displeasure. So much for diplomatic encounters. The two males continued to move about the channel, remaining several lengths apart and without fail, Unior remained positioned between Juan and the water bar, effectively blocking him from returning to where Choney still lingered hoping for handouts. Suddenly with decisive exhalations, Unior and Juan engaged, frothing and splashing. Surfacing separately, Unior cruised over to look up at me. Though his notched smile was unreadable, his movements and body posture announced him relaxed and confident — everything under control — while Juan's movements were jagged with frustration.

I strongly suspected that this had everything to do with Choney — only now for different reasons. With the net having disintegrated, Choney had discovered another, somewhat random food source — Juan's fish at the water bar — and with the demands of her growing son and the stinginess of her rations, she likely wanted unimpeded access to this food source whenever she wished. It was this situation that so clearly outlined her alliance with Unior. Directly challenging Juan herself would be futile, so Choney utilized a very effective resource at her disposal — *Unior* — more than able (and willing) to challenge Juan, directly and physically. How much force Unior now used seemed to directly correlate with how gracefully Juan backed off from Choney's presence at the water bar. This had probably been the arrangement for several months, so that now Choney's arrival at the water bar carried an immediate, implied threat: *'Keep out of my path, or Unior will settle you!'* Depending on how hungry Juan was on any given day, he might or might not push the issue, doing things the hard or the easy way. He certainly didn't sit back and allow Christine to bully him — but Christine didn't seem to have enlisted Unior's cooperation on the matter.

Despite my continually protective anguish regarding Juan's circumstances, I had to remind myself that this harsh situation was likely forcing Juan to hunt and feed himself more often and that could only work to his advantage.

Then my vet arrived, carrying the dreaded news. With Benicio's quiet assistance, he'd been able to meet with the dolphinarium's owners to discuss the possible acquisition of Juan. Initially they had seemed interested in the idea — until consulting with the dolphinarium's manager, who remained emphatic about retaining Juan. *More dolphins, more money — less dolphins, less money*, was the managers stoic bottom line — and so our negotiations had failed, leaving me with a flat, crushing refusal. I thanked the vet for his time and effort. Numb and suddenly chilled in the fading tropical heat, I sought solitude on the wharf.

Kneeling amid hope's scorched remains, twisting limp flowers in my cold hands like mad Ophelia, I glanced up, as Juan surfaced with a sibilant exhalation. Approaching me where I knelt, he lifted his amaranthine gaze to mine for the searing breadth of a breath: Utter tenderness, utter despair — looking at him. Undone. *Sundered* — and *still*, the Love. And I know I shall never be rid of my tenderness for him. Yet, all was lost, leaving me staring dead-eyed, through absent tears spent a long time ago; the heart can break in so many places.

Oblivious to any requiem, Juan slid smoothly beneath the mangroves along the channel's far side. Sluing back and forth, a fish leapt before his swinging head and an instant later, he raised his triumphant jaws, holding the gleaming silver-scaled prize! Juan's spirit remained strong and vigorous — *he* had *not* succumbed to sadness, despite an endless winter of discontent. And looking at him I knew I must also somehow find the strength to keep fighting...but I just couldn't see how.

I wanted to wrench apart the killing chains; raze this miserable maze in which we suffered and struggled. Scream these murdered truths, until our secrets can be told.

CHAPTER TWENTY- ONE

FAIT ACCOMPLI

"Some are born to sweet delight,
Some are born to endless night."
William Blake, *Auguries of Innocence*

Fading beneath winter's raw, crushing weight as the months crept by with the grinding stealth of glaciers; emptied and defeated, staring over the edge of despair. No help, no hope, everything burned to ash...dark night of the soul.

Cold ashes form the richest bed for new beginnings and in time, every winter must give way. Spring, heralded by trickling icicles and the shrieking of crows, also brought concussive news from Cuba — an urgent message from Benicio:

After over eight years at the dolphinarium, all six dolphins — including Juan — had been netted and moved to another lagoon further down the peninsula. Since the recent move, Juan appeared to have completely shaken off his stupor, becoming at once independent and terribly aggressive. At last relieved from the oppressive ritual of the wretched water bar and its teasing tourists, Juan had ceased all begging behavior and was refusing all offerings of dead fish! The now feral Juan hunted the new lagoon's teeming fish population, apparently able to feed himself sufficiently because this new lagoon had *direct*, replenishing communication with the sea. But Juan's self-sufficiency wasn't the problem. Along with this new independence, Juan had begun attacking the other dolphins, particularly Unior and Christine, choosing the moments when they were most distracted and encumbered — hauling tourists! In fact, Benicio reported Juan had now started turning his enmity upon the tourists themselves and people were getting bashed up almost daily. Benicio was dreadfully afraid *serious* injuries would be impossible to prevent, as Juan's violence escalated. The manager didn't give a toss, brushing off the trainer's repeated warnings and thinking myopically only of the money the other dolphins continued to bring piling in. Benicio was distraught: if something happened, *Juan* would likely pay — with his life, and despite the serious repercussions, the trainer was considering cutting the net if no higher authority intervened to prevent disaster and harm.

I immediately sent Benicio a telegram, urgently advising him to ignore strict protocol and bypass the dolphinarium's manager to contact the dolphinarium owners *directly*, explaining the imminent danger and adamantly advise that Juan be released — rather than shot, or sent to another aquarium. Any businessman would recognize the volatile situation and its connection to bad press and potential profit loss (sadly, the most persuasive arguments to secure Juan's freedom). If Juan was self-sufficient and refusing human handouts — he was pretty much ready to go.

Amid this chaotic news, hope seemed to rise from its own spent cinders. But though I had entreated Benicio to contact me the moment he had any response or any change occurred in the situation, spring turned to summer without any further word from Cuba.

I burned to arrow straight to Juan's side, but my pitifully depleted funds remained tensed for a final emergency flight, and I was unwilling to squander them in a premature, futile visit, where I could accomplish little. Leaves began to turn; the balmy days, edged in evenings with hints of frost. I awoke one late September morning still amid the dream's undimmed echo. Hazed sunlight and the damp, muted musk of fallen leaves surrounded me — but I had just risen from the depths of the midnight Sea:

Above, the moon rippled, etched in silver. From the deep shadows, indelible lines coalesced: Lucent skin, amaranthine eyes, spilling indigo secrets. I wanted to reach out and touch his star-lit luminescence, trace the scarred, silken paths over his skin one last time. We spoke in oneiric silence, tremulous with remembered wounds. *Can't you see I tried?*

Acknowledged, through this long loneliness. One final, numinous caress, lighter than the shadows against his skin; his dark eyes burning on mine, nacreous foxfire recovered. Bow your head and join the deep.

Set me as a seal upon thy heart...
For many waters cannot quench love
Nor floods drown it[*]

---

[*]Song of Songs, 8:6 & 8:7.

The dream remained with me, stayed close, whispering down memory's velvet halls, lucid, like the tear-taste of the dark water. Curiously, this insistence left me strangely tranquil. It would be some time before I realized its portent and timing.

I was invited to attend a conference in Seattle, where conservationists from around the globe were gathering to address the issue of cetaceans in captivity, including the Cuban-capture connection. During the conference, I was able to connect with a colleague who was shortly scheduled to go on an investigative trip to Cuba. After filling him in on Juan and the Cubano Dolphins' situation, he agreed to meet with Benicio, report on the dolphins' current condition and if possible, assist the trainer in persuading Juan's owners to release him before they had a serious injury-related law suit on their hands. It was worth a shot.

At the close of the conference, I joined some of the attendees on a whale-watching voyage. Though Seattle was surrounded by the sea, I had been unable to catch the ocean's smell, finding only the familiar urban fragrance of rain-wet concrete and the occasional hint of mossy woodlands. The journey took us through a full spectrum of weather; heading out of Seattle braised in dark drizzle, to find ourselves engulfed in thickly shifting banks of fog from which we finally emerged blinking into a blue sky. The chill waters rolled by, offering up a shivering wind — recovering the lost marine scent in full. Despite the cold, I remained on the boat's bow for most of the journey, inhaling vast, rugged vistas of tall evergreens and steep, tumbling shorelines. Deer browsed in sun-flecked clearings, eagles wheeled overhead and ravens argued hoarsely among the pines, while sleek seals peered up from the rocky surf with cautious curiosity. The somehow mnemonic, pneumatic majesty of the Pacific Northwest resonated in my senses, lingering like a perfect note.

None of the Orca families for which the region was famous crossed our path, though we did pass several Minke whales, quietly feeding. Then delight came calling, as several Dall's porpoises came shearing the waves to visit the ship's bow! Surfing with rapid skill, the rounded little porpoises, resembling yin-yang symbols (both in shape and coloring) kicked up impressive spumes of spray each time they surfaced. Their jubilee was instantly contagious, decking the bows with laughter.

Turning back, we passed once more through a veil of mist. Our muted passage caused a harbor seal, resting upon a buoy to glance up and as its liquid gaze seemed to find mine, the dream of Juan in black water came pouring back. Suddenly shivering with unknown portent, I held the seal's obsidian stare until the mists separated us.

Once home I compiled a brief background report on the Cubano Dolphins to send along with my colleague for his imminent trip. He expected to return during the first week of the New Year and promised to update me immediately on the situation.

I waited, not knowing what to expect, almost afraid to find out what had transpired during months of silence. I paced. I dreaded. I waited. The call came and with it the news, and my knees seemed to turn to water and I was tripping over the conversation, trying to separate the torrent over the receiver, stupidly repeating the words, because if I didn't say them out loud and hear them sung back to me, I wouldn't believe them:

JUAN is FREE!!!!

So many years, of waiting and working...
Every dandelion tuft riding lackadaisical breezes, sent with the same silent prayer:
Let him go Free
Every whisper to the stars watching over distant shores; every moon-secret conversation:
Let him go Free
Every sympathetic droplet, running down rainy windowpanes:
Let him go Free
Every sudden flight of birds overhead; every sigh, slipping nightly into sleep:
Let him go Free

The pacing panther, pushed through the bars, fled to the ripe jungle; the corral torn down, the mustangs racing against an open sky; the air again filled with a thousand wondering wings! My soul's deepest wish, come impossibly true:

JUAN IS FREE!

CHAPTER TWENTY-TWO

THE ART OF UNCERTAINTY

"So does man, in the deep interior of his mind occasionally
clamber up into sunlit meadows
where his world is changed and where in the case of some few, for such is the way
of evolution, there is no return to lower earth."
Loren Eisley — *The Star Thrower*

I had to go, to see the truth of it with my own eyes, to learn the details of Juan's passage to freedom. Speeding along down the familiar Varadero peninsula towards the new lagoon, I passed the old place, where bulldozers were leveling the russet earth and filling the water with rubble, transforming the area into a tidy golf course. Leaning out the taxi's window, I viewed the proceedings with a difficult alloy of emotions. So much had happened in that haunted, hallowed place. Soon tourists would be teeing off and no trace would remain. All that had transpired there would remain buried — unless one day their story was told. One day.

The setting of the new place was more compact, the new lagoon, over three times the size of the other — but minus the expanse of the salt lake. Besides the dolphins themselves, no other caged animals remained — the poor sea turtles and the pelican had thankfully been released. The Sea Wolf had not been so fortunate, shipped off to the Havana aquarium to live out the rest of his life behind bars.

After greeting Benicio, I demanded Juan's story *in full*. The last I'd heard from the trainer, Juan's aggression was roaring out of control, leaving Benicio desperate to release the dolphin from the confines against which he rebelled. As I'd advised, Benicio wrote an urgent letter to the dolphinarium owners, stressing the danger of the situation. This had been in spring, and the trainer had no response for four months. Now I found out why. As protocol demanded, Benicio had passed the letter to the dolphinarium's *manager*, who should have delivered it directly to the company's executives. Worried the situation might somehow reflect poorly upon him, the manager had instead withheld the message, feigning perplexity at the company's failure to respond. Meanwhile Juan's rancor continued to escalate, posing a daily danger to unsuspecting tourists, which appeared to leave no creases in the manager's conscience.

Finally, when things had apparently gone several decibels beyond unbearable, the truth about Benicio's letter emerged — that it had never been delivered at all! *At last,* late in September, the letter was sent — as it should have been — four months earlier — recommending Juan be released from the situation that was causing him such rage and putting the dolphinarium's paying customers at risk. The *very same day* it was delivered, the company responded, giving the dolphinarium an *immediate* go ahead to proceed with Juan's release! Simply shooting a troublesome and aggressive dolphin, or shipping him to another aquarium might easily have been the prescribed solution — but thanks to Benicio, that had not happened.

It took days to net Juan in the spacious lagoon, but at last everything was ready and Juan was loaded onto an air mattress on the back of a flatbed truck and taken down the peninsula to an unpopulated beach and there, released into the warm turquoise waters where he'd originally been captured, almost ten years previously.

The nightmare of torment was over. Juan had his life back. Curiously, this occurred in late September — about the time I was visited by that strangely lucid, liquid dream…I wished I could have been there to witness his release; seen him surfacing unencumbered through the waves. It had been a rush job and the infamously cantankerous phone lines had prevented Benicio connecting in his single attempt to contact me. But all that really mattered was this miracle that had at last rewarded our long, Sisyphean struggles.

All Juan had really needed was *change* — away from the old place, especially his addiction to scraps at the wretched water bar. The move to the new location had sparked a great vigor in him, along with an apparent desire to free himself of human involvement. Refusing all handouts, Juan had become an avid hunter, fishing competently in the well-stocked lagoon. His hunting skill indicated his sonar abilities were in fine working order and having been blessed with natural surroundings, rather than concrete and chlorine, his ties to the sea remained strong. In the end, Juan had rehabilitated himself and it was his own sustained vehemence that actually instigated his release. Having been returned into an area familiar to him, I knew Juan had a good fighting chance to make it as a wild dolphin.

Juan had been released in the morning, but that very night, he *reappeared* back at the dolphinarium lagoon net. It seemed he'd had no trouble circumnavigating around the tip of the peninsula and threading his way back to the new lagoon. Discovering Juan's arrival, all the other dolphins had gathered at the net — and it was this that had caught the attention of the dolphinarium night guard. It seemed Juan had returned for one final parliament with those who had shared his captivity for nearly a decade. *What I wouldn't have given, to have overheard that exchange!*

With the morning light, Juan still lingered beyond the net, which Benicio arrived to see with his own disbelieving eyes. As the sun rose higher and human activity stirred, Juan was seen making his way out to sea, surfing on the bows of boats, reclaiming this privilege so favored by wild dolphins and forever forbidden to captives.

The story's conclusion came several months later (shortly before my own belated arrival). Benicio had been sailing with a group of friends visiting from Montreal, and in celebration of Juan's release, they decided to sail around the reefs and islets beyond the peninsula's tip — where the area's remaining wild dolphins were known to frequent — in hopes of spotting him.

They did indeed come upon wild bottlenose dolphins there, traveling and foraging in small, sprawling groups, and among them, Benicio distinguished Juan's *unmistakably* tattered dorsal fin and shark-scarred back! At such close range there could be no doubt about the positive identification of the dolphin, whose blatant markings were so familiar to the trainer's experienced eye. Benicio described Juan as looking robust and healthy and best of all, he was keeping company with other wild dolphins and like them, neither solicited or avoided the boat, or human attention. The trainer remained long enough to determine that to all appearances, Juan was in good health and without injury before leaving him to his own life.

That Juan had made it through the first three months of wild living meant his chances of survival would only improve with time, as the first months of readjustment had to be the most difficult. Against all ominously stacked odds, my dearest wish *had* come true — Juan was not only *free*, but alive and healthy, again among his people where he belonged. Back in the wild, life would at times be hard work; to eat, to avoid predators, weather storms and to gain acceptance into social groups. But the choices were his to make; he was a *free being* again — no longer the asset of some money-grubbing company or tawdry amusement for tourists. After an immeasurably long journey, Juan was at last back in the balance and master of his own destiny.

I had hoped to rent a boat myself and go seeking Juan among the wild dolphins, but in Cuba, boats were not easy to come by and rental fees were steep, as most pleasure craft were rather large and meant for tour groups to split costs on fishing or scuba diving trips. With deep regret, I realized that in my present financial situation, it just wasn't going to be feasible. I would have dearly loved to catch even a glimpse of Juan, coursing through the turquoise water with the sun pouring off his back; and perhaps to catch his eye, even for only a moment — without any bars between us. Even contemplating the restoration of his wild rhythms I felt a fierce peace.

An immense weight had been removed, one so profound that it would take years to perceive fully. But this was a private victory, because while the battle had been won — the war certainly had not. The other Cubano Dolphins did not enjoy Juan's liberty and remained prisoners — along with so many others around the world. And so the fight continues — so long as their species suffers because of mine.

Unlike the previous place, this lagoon was more private, as most of the water's perimeter was ringed with dense mangroves and estuary scrub. Though the water teemed with fish, I was relieved to discover that jellyfish were scarce. At the lagoon's near end a large moored platform floated where Christine and Choney still performed and a little further down, a smaller platform, where the ever-lucrative tourist-hauling was conducted. The prices had again been raised — again upping the dolphins' monetary value. Iago was away on extended sick leave and Benicio had been promoted to head trainer. Christine and Choney were again pregnant and expecting in three or four months, and though such news should have been celebratory, knowing yet more lives would be born into slavery was hardly uplifting. Of course I missed Juan, but it went without saying that I'd instantly part with all the dolphins if it would compel their freedom.

It had been over a year since I'd seen them — a year so full of changes. I knelt before the dark water, waiting. It was Unior who first surfaced to investigate my presence. As our eyes met, he became still, slowly bringing his familiar squinting face close, his gaze mutely gripping mine. *He knew me.* Suddenly jubilant, the huge dolphin held out first one and then the other worn pectoral fin to initiate a jolly session of greeting-pec-pats. Sebastian arrived in the middle of it and began almost immediately trying to insert his own smaller fin into the game, as if I'd hardly been gone a day. By the time Bia surfaced among us, things had calmed and I was able to remark how big she and Sebastian had grown. Easing into the water, I discovered it was much chillier than in the old place. Moving at a thawingly brisk pace, I kept close to the warmth of Unior's presence as he led me into the show area, while Sebastian continued cutting between us.

Someone was waiting for me — Choney. Hanging vertically in the water, her sleekness slightly rounded in pregnancy, she scanned me sagely up and down, as I chirped and wobbled in greeting. Completing our ritual greeting, Choney collected me to travel alongside her, my face just by her unblemished dorsal fin. I responded sunnily to her whistles with my own trills, our bodies swaying together conversationally as we swam.

Last to appear and complete my delight was Christine, who showed no hesitancy, greeting me with enthusiastic caresses and pec-pats. Unfortunately, this reception was cut short, interrupted by the resumption of a training session. With a stiff north wind chilling the air, more than the water, I opted to remain submersed at the side of the little dock, watching while Christine was cajoled into various silly tricks. Bia was there too,

Learning the ropes (Photo credit: Camilla Singh)

learning the same ropes that bound her mother. Both she and Sebastian were now eating fish and having become reliant on humans for nourishment, were becoming susceptible to human manipulation, signaling the untimely death of childhood innocence and the relative freedom they had previously enjoyed.

One social feature from old place still remained in effect, dividing Choney, Unior and Sebastian into one clique and Christine and Bia into the other, though the youngsters seemed to switch at wish, their social rules appearing more forgiving and fluid. I noticed Christine carried some new scars, which Benicio affirmed were from hashing things out with Choney (yet again) in the new place. Predictably, Choney remained Queen Bee, probably because she retained her alliance with Unior.

Other changes became apparent over the course of my visit, one of which was the dolphins' obvious lack of interest in working for their food. It appeared this lagoon's abundance of fish made it easier for the dolphins to supplement their diets and the adults were seen hunting regularly in the company of their young. I very much hoped Bia and Sebastian were learning survival skills from their parents, along with a certain concept of independence.

However, the dolphinarium's manager (the same feculent fellow who had thwarted efforts to release Juan for so long), wanted another net put up, separating the dolphins into two groups, in order get them to play less, work more and earn him more money and prestige.

Having to sit by and watch the dolphins begging for their bread, while being demeaned and groped by strangers remained disheartening. However once the daily vulgarities were over, Choney and Unior would often take me to the far end of the lagoon, as far away from the sordid routine of human presence as possible. Swept up amongst their serenity, we would synchronously glide and surface, conversing with a fluid sway, so difficult to convey through words. At Choney's behest, we'd hover before one another just below the surface, eye to eye. These silent moments were ripe — with relationship and the experiences shared over years of growth, hardship, and change. The trust and affection cultivated through our shared past had produced this affinity. Unior almost invariably escorted us and for his part, seemed inordinately mild and even-tempered, appearing to have little reason to act otherwise since Juan's release.

After just such an interlude, Sebastian met us at the far-end by the net. It was a lovely area, with an abundance of tiny aquatic inhabitants dwelling amid miniature hamlets of sponge and coral. Swimming skillfully beneath me, Sebastian extended his pec-fins, patting them against my palms, rediscovering our pec-pat on the go. While this reciprocal social exchange was common enough between dolphins, it was not as simple as it looked and I was quite pleased with the proficiency we eventually achieved. After this, Bia and Sebastian revealed to me a shadowy, cave-like space beneath the mangroves, running all along the lagoon's edge. In this secret, shaded place the dolphins liked to hunt the many fishes hiding among the labyrinthine roots.

Traveling amongst Choney and Unior, with Bia and Sebastian winding around us — Christine's obvious absence bothered me. Because she was so often solitary, every moment with Christine was precious, so when she appeared one afternoon at the dock with an invitation to swim, I was eager to comply. Issuing the familiar, narrowing buzz, Christine arched boldly head to tail under my hands, flourishing her crescent flukes. Nudging me confidently, she curved round and our eyes met in an eternal liquid moment, infused with the distillation of our friendship. It was all there and it was mutual, with no need to second guess. We began to swim together, little Bia now at her mother's smooth side. Christine had always been a robust dolphin (at least compared to slender Choney) and with her rounded belly, her size had become even more pronounced. Silently, I conveyed my private reverence for her renewed motherhood and the unborn within her. As if in response, she rolled, gliding along and proudly displaying her tremendous speckled belly to the sun with a spirited wiggle.

One moment I was swimming along with Christine and Bia — and the next, emerging from a patch of cloudy water — with Choney, Sebastian and Unior. And as was so often the case, Choney's arrival had signaled Christine's departure. Choney and Sebastian moved on after a time, but Unior remained, his eyes resting warmly on mine. Again, that feeling of deep camaraderie. Still gazing sagely, Unior nudged me gently, once over my heart and once on my forehead, in silent, wordless acknowledgment.

Catching my eye with the glint in his, we spiraled into the darker depths, twisting slowly around one another, feeling the flow of water over skin and the expulsive sip of breath. Curving around, Unior offered the pale expanse of his silken underside for caressing and in a fit of fondness, I attempted to encircle his vastness in my arms — he, so enormous I could never reach all the way round him. Sebastian appeared cutting noisily between us and nudging my elbows and shoulders insistently, but Unior's presence carried a focused intensity, not nearly so obvious in the younger dolphins.

Continuing on, our trio cruised toward the net, where I spotted a yellow leaf floating on the surface, which I presented to Unior as a gift — just as he himself had gifted me in the past. Unior accepted the leaf, taking it delicately with the tip of his pitted rostrum. We swam on a little and then Unior paused, studying the seabed beneath us a moment, before descending. Still holding the leaf in his jaws, Unior stood on his head, nosing into the mucky sea bed, before righting himself and continuing along — *still* holding the leaf. A moment later, he was at it again with an air of extremely focused and deliberate concentration. Fascinated, Sebastian and I watched as Unior carefully buried the leaf deep in the muddy sea floor and after surveying his work, moved off. I could only guess what it all meant, though it did appear as if my gift held some special (if obscure) significance to him.

The sun was fainting serenely and in the dying light the water seemed to become chillier. Peering through the net I paused, gazing out into the unknown, towards oceanic freedom and the path that Juan had traveled towards a new life... I was jolted from my reverie by a sudden, concentrated cloud of buzzing and turning, I found all five dolphins lined up before me. The eerily intense volume of their focused attention left me feeling suddenly shy, and I fled away from the spotlight of their combined acoustic interest.

Then, from the bridge above (from which the net blocking the lagoon's exit was strung) I heard someone calling down. Looking up, I realized a man waiting for the bus had lost his sombrero, which a mischievous gust of wind had sent the sailing down onto the water, where Sebastian was curiously nudging it. I retrieved the hat, restoring it to its owner, who had clambered down the steep bank, uttering a rapid, cheerful and largely unintelligible thanks.

Later the following day, Sebastian and I again met at the far end, cruising along the seafloor side by side in the dim water, away from all eyes — this privacy a rare pleasure. Sebastian's argot picked up along with our pace, as we began surfacing boisterously, curving about each other. Soon afterwards, while taking a regretfully necessary breather from these enthused acrobatics, a familiar resonation signaled approach. Up from the misted water Choney, Unior and Sebastian all materialized, lined in a neat row, staring expectantly at me. Greeting all with caresses, I realized a quandary had coalesced: Sebastian clearly expected us to resume our games — and Choney naturally expected me to accompany her.

I was at a loss for the proper reaction. While I would have liked to continue playing with Sebastian, ignoring Choney's request (and her seniority within the group) was simply *not* a good idea. Unsure, I remained where I was, glancing nervously from one dolphin to the other, aware all the while that the clock of patience was ticking. As it happened, it was at each other that the dolphins' tempers flared — Sebastian at his mother, buzzing sharply and threatening her with gaping jaws. Choney left. Though it had only been rather rude posturing, I felt guiltily responsible. Sebastian collected his prize, but swimming alongside him I couldn't shake the fact that it really wasn't much like Choney to just turn tail and let someone else's wishes cross hers.

Suddenly a great flailing and thrashing erupted! Ah — *Choney*. Apparently she'd appealed to Unior to teach Sebastian some respect! Uninvolved herself, Choney glided up, cool and calm, appearing completely unconcerned with the two thrashing, splashing males behind her. Unchallenged, she collected me at her side and the two of us began to swim. Choney had got her way again.

Just ahead of us, Sebastian began a series of loud breaches, slamming his body hard against the water with rebellious force, concluding this strenuous display of displeasure with numerous, derisive chuffing breaths. Perhaps seeking amorous reward for his intervention, Unior nudged up to Choney and the two moved off side by side, following the perimeter of the lagoon. Behind them a little ways, Christine and Bia surfaced, traveling together and trailing after them, still in bad graces, came Sebastian, tail slapping in continuing irritation.

Unior must have really got his goat, because rather than settling down, Sebastian started to breach again, perhaps in further protest or to assuage his injured pride. Each time he leapt, his eyes met mine, redoubling my guilt — he wouldn't have got into trouble if it hadn't been for my indecision. Soon after this display, he approached me, quietly intense. A pec-pat exchange seemed enough to clear the air, after which we began to swim together, brushing lightly as we traveled.

Bia joined us and I welcomed her arrival with squeaking delight — Sebastian however, didn't appear eager to share my now divided attention. Buzzing vehemently, he pushed between Bia and I, interrupting our greeting pec-pat session and lunging at her open-mouthed! At this unexpectedly fierce display, shy Bia fled. Arching authoritatively, Sebastian pressed his silken flank powerfully against mine. Under my steady gaze and assuasive caresses, he calmed and catching a familiar, puckish glint in his eye, we simultaneously began practicing our pec-patting on the go. Maneuvering together in close proximity, Sebastian was clearly concentrating on keeping his movements to scale, taking great care with his powerful flukes while perfecting our social gesture. Arching against the surface for breath, Sebastian offered an artful caress with the tip of his tail, and then began to circle me rapidly — until with a sudden burst of speed, he suddenly shot away into the water!

The last day dawned oddly misty, after a restless and unusually cool, foggy night. At the dolphinarium, Benicio approached with a lined countenance and a glance told me he carried grim news. Seeming shaken, the trainer reported a distressing discovery. Further down the peninsula, not far from where Juan had been released, a dead dolphin had washed up on the beach.

Saber thrust between the ribs — reeling, breath torn away... I had to see for myself — I had to know — or I would never have peace. At the time, the quickest way to arrive at that stretch of coast, still inaccessible by roads, was on poor dusty, tired Cuban horses. Having no apple to exchange for the ride, I instead massaged the stooping, drooping neck of my horse, through a mane stiff with neglect. Riding through scrub and sand, I followed Benicio for about twenty-five minutes in near silence, emerging eventually onto an empty, wrack-strewn beach. A bleak wind was blowing from the north, pushing the faded, sighing waves high onto the shore; above, low, leaden clouds scuttled furtively across the sky.

Gazing down the strand, I saw the melancholy curve of a dolphin, lying on its side in the sand. We drew closer, my heartbeat rising to thunder. The dolphin, a large male, had obviously been dead for days, lying frozen where the sea had abandoned him. The once smooth skin was encrusted with sand, peeling and flaking away, the jaws open in death's grimace, disclosing ivory teeth.

*It can't be. Our story **can't** end this way.*

Dismounting, eyes roaming cautiously over the fallen, dusky form, I sought the familiar scars and tattered dorsal fin — but this dolphin's dorsal was intact — and peering closer, I saw that the teeth were worn almost smooth, marking this as an older individual. Despite the acquisition of so many scars from battling with Unior, Juan wasn't an old dolphin, his teeth, still curved and sharp. *It wasn't him.*

Standing quietly over the fallen form, gazing into the sunken eye, I wondered how this dolphin had lost his life. Benicio said that dolphins only washed ashore in this area during the stormy winter months, when oceanic conditions were colder and rougher. Unable to discover any outward signs of the dolphin's demise, I could only hope it had been a natural and peaceful death and not a result of human activity. After a respectful, windswept silence for the creature's passing, I remounted, following the trainer back towards the lagoon, feeling relieved, but more than a little saddened.

A parched sun had burned away the muted cloud cover, but already the shadows were extending their spines — it was almost time to leave. I had only just slipped below the water among them, when from the bridge, Benicio began hollering at me to get out of the water, or risk missing the bus, which would leave me stranded out in the middle of nowhere. Peering back under, the dolphins hovered before me in the mote-filled water, waiting for me to take my rightful place among them. Sebastian arched invitingly under my hands. *Bus schmush!*

But Benicio continued hollering — and I had to go. I called out a final time, voice wavering and rich with regret, then scrambled from the water, clumsy in my swim fins, cutting myself on the slimy rocks exposed by the low tide. Disheveled, dripping and bleeding, I left the dolphins and got onto the damnable bus. But the abrupt indignity of my departure and the incurred injuries did little to tarnish the priceless significance They and I shared. With a brontosaurian bellow, the bus dove off, while sunlight rode the waters, filling shadowed hollows with fleeting brilliance.

CHAPTER TWENTY-THREE

LIMITED EDITIONS

"If you look too closely, everything breaks your heart."
Ben Okri, *The Famished Road*

Encouraged by ridiculously cheap summer air fairs, I returned to Cuba, hoping to attend the births of Choney and Christine's new infants, but arriving I discovered with a minor pang of regret, that both had already delivered (again within hours of one another), just thirty days earlier. Both tiny newborns were alive and healthy, popping up like corks, as they surfaced alongside their smoothly rolling mamas. Both were female, Choney's daughter informally christened *Li* and Christine's, *Bi*. They were simply radiant and just like two peas in a pod, the only distinguishing feature between them, a beauty mark on Bi's lower jaw (similar to that on her older sister, Bia). Gazing softly upon the newest editions — I couldn't ignore the bleak truth: that these little ones had been born into lives of slavery from which death would be the only likely release.

In an effort to force the dolphins to perform, the ever-irritating manager had insisted on separating them and now, a thick net divided Bia and Sebastian from their mothers, Unior and two new siblings. Ties of blood and bonding are integral to the fabric of dolphin life, but as slaves, the Cubano Dolphins were helpless to prevent this cruel severance.

In wild dolphin society, the arrival of a new infant often coincides with the older sibling joining a rollicking juvenile social group, but wild dolphins remain free to seek the affection and comfort of their mothers' company at any time. Older siblings also take on frequent roles as teachers and babysitters — but how could Bia properly learn the nuances of motherhood if she were unable to participate as Christine raised her new sibling? Though Bia and Sebastian were still acoustically privy to what went on in the murky waters across the net, this forced loss of closeness and support had to be devastating. Additionally, Bia and Sebastian were forbidden the rich social

Little Li & Bi

challenge, adventure and camaraderie of a varied juvenile peer group that dolphins their age would naturally be engaged with. Though they still had each other, these circumstances accented the grim and severe texture of their captive lives.

Detecting my step upon the dock, Unior curved across the water to where I waited. As he drew near, our eyes met and he *knew* me. After touching his battered pec-fin to my offered palm and basking in a brief caress, Unior swooped sensuously head to tail beneath my hands and dove, returning a moment later, leading both mother dolphins with their bonny infants in tow. Choney immediately rose up, her eyes clasping mine, insistently inviting me below.

Thankfully, the lagoon's brine was noticeably warmer in summer months. Awash in the dolphins' soaring arpeggios, I responded jubilantly! Boldly paving the way for the others, Unior arched confidently against me: Incomparable, the Samarkand silk of their skin; the unassailable smoothness of slipping into their company.

Moving forward, Choney emitted the narrowing buzz of ritual greeting, while her tiny infant looked on with wide-eyed with curiosity. Next Christine came forward, less formal and more confident in her approach, but neither mother could afford to stay still for long, as their vibrant little ones impelled almost constant motion and vigilance.

Under no such obligation, Unior chose to remain and with a nodding glance, we aligned, gliding along, exchanging languid caresses as we passed through quiet waters. Adjusting his position, Unior brought his scarred, moon-mellow, squinting face close to mine. *Hello eye.* Matching his steady gaze, I felt myself sinking into the breathlessness of his powerful presence. Placing his rostrum over my heart, Unior buzzed quietly. Choney and little Li reappeared, gathering close to watch. Moving his head minutely, Unior continued his fine-tuned issuance — what *was* he up to? Then I realized — he'd got hold of my halter-top tie and was experimentally tugging on it. With a sportive glint in his eye, the enormous dolphin drew me gently along a bit, laughing. Buzzing softly, Unior began deliberately nudging specific points on my torso, but without access to any acoustic translation, I remained unable to guess the reasons or results of his sonic endeavor.

Afterwards at the smaller dock, Sebastian appeared, eyes widening as he drew close, making several undecided passes before moving tentatively forward to initiate contact. I slipped into the turbid water only once I was certain Sebastian had recognized and accepted me, diving into a cloudy shower of intensely questing echolocation issuing from both he and Bia. Satisfied, the two young dolphins whisked me up between them and our trio set off. Initially the pair were a little skittish, whistling back and forth to each other for reassurance.

I could only imagine the toll that untimely separation from their mothers had taken on their confidence, yet with humor and patience, our trusted familiarity reawakened and flowered. Conversing through our synchronous sway, we traded minute, flowing signals, spiraling towards the dim depths and bursting to the bright surface for breath. With an expectant, narrowing buzz, Sebastian initiated the ritual request for contact, learned from his mother. Proffering the expected fingertip, Sebastian met it with his rostrum on the point of the sound he was producing, before joyously launching into an animated pec-pat session. Bia stayed nearby, observing closely and adding her excited vocalizations to the exchange. The three of us resumed our vivacious dance, which finally ended with my exhaustion. (*Fie on thee, O abjectly inferior human constitution!*)

Throughout the futile capering of each show, Christine and Choney ate gingerly and distractedly, trying to keep their infants collected. I'd rejoin them once all signs of trainers and buckets were gone. Invited beneath the clouded water, all six of us would travel together, after completing our ritual greetings. The dolphins shifted as we swam, exchanging little nudges and caresses, which were extended also to me. This was a reminder of the level of acceptance I was honored with, as these sorts of contact are almost never accidental because dolphins wield such precise control and awareness over their bodies, making even the least or lightest touch a gift of conscious allowance.

Happily I noted that for the time being, Choney and Christine seemed to have put their differences on the back burner, forming a cooperative nursery sub-pod with their infants. Far from showing concern at their little ones' proximity while we traveled, Choney and Christine actually appeared to be purposefully demonstrating interspecies familiarity, *specifically* for their bambinas' benefit. Often I'd find myself installed in the "dorsal baby travel position" with my face close beside mother dolphin's dorsal fin, while the infants adopted the "ventral baby position" below, head pressed to mamma's navel, peeping curiously out from beneath. Choney in particular became quite fond of collecting my company and three of us often traveled as a sub-pod all our own. Every so often she would halt our journeys, hanging suspended before me, carefully scanning me up and down in detailed sonic scrutiny, while little Li looked on, absorbing these obscure acoustic lessons just as Sebastian once had.

Christine and Choney continued taking turns sandwiching their infants between their maternal sides and my delighted presence and on one swim, bright-eyed little Li, carefully held out a miniature pec-fin to me, mirroring this gesture so-often shared with the adults. I could hardly believe my eyes and tentatively, I held my palm a little out from my body and then came the softest touch — *contact!*

Surrounded and swimming among the dolphins seemed my natural place — yet the whine of regret pulled — Bia and Sebastian remained trapped behind the net, leaving our family incomplete. This was underscored as our group passed along the net and a sudden, adamant fifing announced Bia and Sebastian, flanking us on the far side of the barrier. Though the other dolphins soon moved on, the banished pair's urgent calls pulled me to a halt. Side by side, Bia and Sebastian faced me through the mesh, peering earnestly through the gloomy barrier.

My immediate empathy for their situation inexplicably became the medium for an unconventional colloquy. Understanding passed between us with a liquid eloquence, but trying later to translate this shared exchange was like trying to carry water in a colander. All of it was a dance; a richly emotional rhythm consciously playing itself out. Keeping time within our mutual rhythm, our trio began pacing the net, eyes locked, echoing calls flitting back and forth. Pausing to face each other, the desire escalated — to somehow quit the impasse, escape the barrier's confines and align together, unfettered.

The net was simply *wrong* — a jarring note of discord in the scheme of things. Bia and Sebastian's brimming eyes silently beseeched, their every pace and cry sang distress. Gripping the slimy ropes I stared at them — trapped. Hovering hesitantly, eyes wide, Sebastian then held out the sweet curve of a pec-fin to me, requesting the simple reassurance of contact. At this, a tender and all too familiar sadness burst within me. With decisive exhalations, we turned suddenly as one, thrusting back the way we'd come along the net, blindly pacing the unnatural divide. Even our trapped tension and distress somehow held a living grace, though the intensity of our rolling forms told me this tension must soon snap.

A moment later, the other dolphins appeared from the fog, sweeping me off into their midst and away from the net. Moving away among them, I felt keenly the internal contortions — of attempting to let my distress slip away, without forgetting it. It was Unior who calmed me with the gravity of his gaze: He is big, and has weathered many storms; he is my friend — and I know I am well. Nudging under my elbow, Christine reiterated this, and turmoil temporarily suspended, I became again, merely myself of the moment, tumbling with them, through mossy sunlit waters.

Soon I rejoined Bia and Sebastian properly, where the pair immediately swept me up between them, allied and unimpeded in our companionship; our calls sweet now, like birds waking to sunlight after a night of rain.

The blaring of the show parted us, but both Bia and Sebastian remained before me where I reluctantly stood on shore, gazing at them. Leaning persuasively on the water, Sebastian released a stream of wistful, canary-like sounds, but despite his melodious invitation, human rules held me landlocked until the gathering tourists who paid to paw them were gone.

On my last morning, while the dolphins leaped through hoops and dragged about ham-fisted tourists, I enjoyed a privilege forever denied to them: visiting a coral reef. Undulating among its colorful, terraces and whimsical, fantastically painted residents, I descended twenty-five feet, where I discovered a coral cavern. Entering the anemone encrusted grotto, pale streamers of sunlight wandered through a fissure in its roof, through which I allowed myself to drift slowly upwards, grazing the ocean's mirrored ceiling for breath. *This*, in all its dappled, resplendence, was where Sebastian, Bia and the others should have been.

Clouds were gathering in the north, when I left that jeweled kingdom and returned once more to the Cubano Dolphins. This late in the afternoon, the nursery pod was drifting into snooze-cruise mode, quietly readying to begin a submersed traversal of the lagoon's perimeter, but before we parted,

Choney collected me calmly into her secret stare and it seemed we spoke on some unknowable level, as I sometimes dreamed we did, in translucent wordlessness.

Afterward, I joined Bia and Sebastian for a final swim and we began a triplicate spiral in the murk, rolling just above the muddy sea bed. There in the half-light, I was aware of our communing through the rapid, subtle slide of movement and breath. Yet I sensed an additional dimension, drifting like a peripheral fragrance, teetering to trigger in memory's membrane the remaining richness of an all but forgotten sequence.

With them, I was caught up in a great and singular sympathy: Sky, water, trees, wind — sunlight itself, a living, pulsing, laughing, crooning presence. Every grain of sand, the tiniest lizard or crab, the sequined phosphorescence of star-spattered night waters, the swell of a wave, the curve of a cloud, or a dolphin's fin...*everything* speaking. Reverberating, *becoming* the very waters in which I swam, this knowing surfaced in my mind, just as I did, between those two dolphins. In keeping with this great ineffable rhythm, in moving with these tides, irrespective of physical proximity, I would move only *closer* to them. I surfaced from the water, seething with a fierce joy, unsure if I'd emerge from the next moment intact; like facing a lightning storm in the sea.

I realized everyone had gone home and I wondered in passing how long I'd been submerged in revelation. Only the night guard and his dusty old dog remained. Thunder was growling close by. A storm was almost upon us, I could smell the rain, and sense the great rhythm within it. *Yes, time to go.* Though I might waver, I was learning; learning to *listen* and then to move in time with life's inscrutable pulse.

I began to swim, to curve in a wide arc over the water's surface. Beneath, the dolphins flanked me as I picked up speed, all of us swept along in an immense, rushing tidal surge. Their calls surrounded me and as I drew close to the dock, churning the surface to foam, I made that my farewell. The rain began and as the storm descended, I left that place.

CHAPTER TWENTY-FOUR

THIN ICE ON THE TROPIC OF CANCER

"...we circle well worn grooves of water on a single note.
Music lost forever from the others' heart, which turns my own to stone.
There is a plastic toy. There is no hope.
We sink to the limits of this pool until the whistle blows.
There is a man and our mind knows
we will die here."
Carol Ann Duffy, *The Dolphins*[*]

The taxi pulled up to the dolphinarium's gate, leaving a muddy wake. In conjunction with a full moon and vernal tide, the entire place had flooded — every year ocean tides rising higher. I stepped out into the calf-deep water, thinking if the sea rose much more, the dolphins might be able to just swim to freedom. And so I prayed for rain.

Though the detestable dolphin show was over for the morning, the first acrimonious round of tourist-hauling had yet even to begin. The sickening spectacle would drag on for up to two hours and until then, I would have to keep out of the water — or risk blame for any of the dolphins' distractions or misbehavior. Nevertheless, I stole onto the dock for a furtive greeting, kneeling among the abhorred fish buckets.

Peering down into the sepia water, past the sinuous silhouette of my own breathless expectation, an indistinct paleness flickered in the depths. Rising to coalesce, our eyes met and held across the thalassic plane rippling between us — *Choney.* After a moment of keen appraisal, she surfaced and with the practiced confidence of a conductor collecting orchestral attention, she held up a pec-fin to initiate our ritual greeting. A moment later, Unior, Christine,

* from Standing Female Nude (1985).

Bi and Li all rose from the water, streaming forwards, rolling like rain into my parched, desert arms, unable to embrace the entirety of their wildflower wonder! Confounded by the array of pec-fins immediately out-stretched in offering, Choney set herself to clearing front and center for herself — and typically, nobody argued. Despite the warmth and enthusiasm of this welcome and Choney's insistent nudging invitation to join her in the water, I was constrained to remain landlocked. I had to be brief, and with the fish buckets still around, the dolphins would be impatient for the remainder of their meal. I hated to be associated, even indirectly with training or bribes of food, so, after a final flurry of caresses and distracted pec-pats, I hurried back to shore to wait until the human mess had evaporated.

Once the grounds had more or less emptied, I settled on the smaller dock seeking Bia and Sebastian. Instead, sliding up from the murk came Unior — *what was he doing over here?* Must have made himself a hole somewhere in the net. Basking unabashedly, Unior welcomed my caresses until Bia appeared, sliding confidently forward to solicit greetings of her own. Both dolphins hovered patiently as I submersed amid their familiar buzzing. This done, Bia curved forward, delicately caressing my side with her tail, and the three of us set off, calling excitedly back and forth.

Yet this reunion was clouded by a splintering note of obvious absence — *where was Sebastian?* His failure to appear was very uncharacteristic and concerned me. I wondered if Unior's presence, might be keeping the younger male at bay.

My musings scattered as I spied his unmistakable, sickle-shaped dorsal fin and innocuous dimpled dome out in the lagoon. It was so entirely unlike the rambunctious and gregarious youngster to be drifting alone, away from the action. Hoping to cheer his solitude I closed the distance, but when I'd halved the space between us, Sebastian suddenly dove and vanished. *Oh.* Crestfallen, I turned away, not wishing to intrude.

Glancing back, I saw Sebastian had reappeared in the same spot, his presence and solitude plucking at me. Twisting impotently in the water, I keened, voicing my distress at the distance between us. With my call quavering through the water, Sebastian began to arch and shift in place, issuing a haunting reply. *He heard me.* Continuing his swaying deliberation, Sebastian began to move towards me, hesitant and wary. Empathy swelled in my heart for his youth, his aloneness and his enclosed fate. Awash in this overflow, I held out my hand to his diffidence as he slowly dissolved the uncertain distance between us. Then all hesitation seemed to melt and he flowed into my arms, resting the supple silver of his cheek against my shoulder. I held him then, like a lost child, like a dear friend returned from long peril, lending him presence and strength. He turned the tender intricacy of his eyes to mine, all we'd shared shimmering between us; the friendship true, the solace real.

With a conversant and impish glint, he held up a pec-fin, but just as I moved to meet it with my palm, Unior appeared from the murk, sliding between us. Placing his blunt and battered rostrum firmly between Sebastian and I, Unior issued a distinct, beeping refrain, whose message was clear: "No! No! *No!*"

Refusing dissuasion, Sebastian arched with deft defiance past Unior and beneath my halted hand. I knew all too well that defying Unior could incur great risk, but as timing would have it, the blaring show was about to begin and heeding this, the older male turned and vanished into the gloom, sparing brash Sebastian possible repercussion. Scanning the surface, I watched as Unior emerged a moment later on the far side of the net, amid welcome from Choney, Christine and the young ones.

Sebastian's spirits seemed to rise accordingly with the larger male's departure and I watched as he arced towards Bia, now carrying a certain confidence. The two greeted each other affectionately, but Bia did not remain with us, refusing our invitation to swim and instead going to float torpidly in the shallows.

Leaning on his mirrored side, Sebastian regarded me warmly and then with a graceful thrust, swept me away with him out into the lagoon. It was lovely while it lasted, but all too soon, the light of revelry faded and I found myself deposited in the shallows, where Sebastian joined Bia in her miserable, lethargic stupor. Though they were less than five years of age, growing up within captivity's confines was leaving Bia and Sebastian with very adult blues. Beneath their frozen smiles, the chaffing wounds were already apparent: Boredom. Melancholy. Despondency. Ennui. Despite the relative spaciousness of the lagoon and their proximity to the other dolphins, living as slaves failed — as it must — to sustain their oceanic hearts. As wild dolphins, Bia and Sebastian would have been traveling amid a convivial crowd, socializing intensely: tussling, loving, hunting and learning in a vast coral sea. As captives, they languished.

Over the next week I realized that Bia's budding femininity did indeed seem to be commanding increasing interest from Unior — her father (another looming problem captivity incurred) — and while he kept her company, Sebastian was often forced to the sidelines. Though it would be several more years until Bia entered into adult sexuality, I knew these tensions were only going to escalate and as Sebastian grew older, it seemed that like Juan before him, he must become an outcast or invite Unior's aggression.

Over in the show area Bi and Li cruised side by side and as their transient gaze fell upon mine, they paused before me in the sky-rippled water. The flashing weight of their combined stare whispered recognition and their puerile grace beckoned, proving too much to ignore. A moment later on the dock, the two little dolphins surfaced amid a cloud of extravagant fifing — they positively sparkled! Amid an adorable, ceaseless, squeaking, sunny riot, they offered up their small pec-fins in greeting, constantly tussling and interrupting one another. Li surfaced gaily with a rounded yellow leaf held in her jaws, pressing it into my hands.

Tickling first one and then the other with the coveted fragment of foliage, I tossed it over the water, sending the gleaming youngsters hilariously half-leaping over their own shining shoulders after it. Recumbent cheek leaning upon adoring shoulder, I watched entranced, while Li and Bi vied and roughhoused until one of them returned triumphant with the temporary trinket, blissfully unaware of the unavoidable sorrows that must one day find them.

Then Choney arrived, and having decided the little ones had engulfed enough of my attention, shooed Li and Bi away. Silently she regarded me, her marvelous dark gaze pooling into my own, before prepensely initiating a long and intense bout of pec-patting. I was well aware, with those arcane eyes of hers resting so heavily upon me, that I was being very closely studied. Our greeting complete, Choney rose from the water and with a familiar and impatient nudge to the wrist, urged me to submerge.

Slipping into the water I was met with an immense racket, as the squirming youngsters lined up alongside Choney, regal and subdued, barraging me with an impressive acoustic inquiry. Scanning summation completed, Choney collected me alongside her svelte flank, my palm skating dreamily over her misted back. Together we began to cruise along, with Bi and Li doing double-time all around us. The pair of youngsters often seemed to operate as a single unit, whirling together in rapid synchrony — which made traveling with them a little like being in the eye of a cyclone; serenity in a type of tempest.

Ever inquisitive, Li and Bi headed for the show area, to parade before ponderously wading tourists. Every so often, Choney sank a little into the water column, sending out scrutinizing sprays of ultrasonics — to keep tabs on what they were up to from across the lagoon. Soon bored with the repetitive whistles and banal clapping continually directed at them from their unimaginative audience, Li and Bi returned, sliding in sensuous greeting under Choney's chin.

Little Li began to chirp and nudge her mother, who obligingly sank down a little, allowing her daughter to nurse. Perhaps feeling a little peckish herself, Choney led us to the muddy shallows behind the dock where she and the youngsters gleefully set about stirring up the squashy sea floor, rooting and foraging for tiny fishes concealed in the muck. The water was quite chilly and thanks to the dolphins' efforts, becoming muddier by the second, and along with the stirred silt came the tiny stinging *carribe* organisms. While I was pleased to observe Choney impressing some ability to forage on the younger generation, the muddy, cold, stinging water was *not* to my liking. Head ringing from their shrill calls, I decided to leave them to it.

Trekking along the lagoon's sandy shore towards Bia and Sebastian, I paused, noticing Christine. She was floating alone, one forlorn pec-fin draped over the rope attaching the big dock to shore. As Bi and Li grew older, it seemed there was less need for nursery time and so, less need for Choney and Christine to associate. Vacant and dejected, Christine's despondency was the direct result of captivity's unnatural weight, settling heavily — *crushingly* upon its victim.

Looking earnestly up at me as I approached their shallows, Bia and Sebastian trilled. Stepping into deeper water, they came sliding alongside, caressing me with pec-fins and flukes and settling me firmly between them, our trio began to pick up speed. On some unspoken cue Bia and Sebastian carefully nudged their sleek dorsal fins into my hands, moving faster still, skimming along just under the water's surface. This unexpected action provoked immediate internal protest — *I don't like dorsal fin rides* — *a forced, strictly tourist thing*. But Bia and Sebastian were in complete control and when I released them, they immediately moved with firm solicitousness, to cosset me between them once more. Together the three of us slipped smoothly beneath the mangroves and into deep shadow, streaming along until we had traveled way out into the lagoon, where the water was glassy green rather than opaquely olive.

Only later did it occur to me that earlier in the day, despite bribes of fish and affection, Bia and Sebastian had both *refused* to pull tourists around on their dorsal fins, and yet in the spirit of camaraderie, they had of their own accord engaged in that very activity with me. *Choice makes all the difference.*

Daily, Iago was nurturing Bi and Li's growing interest in dead fish. I hated seeing the trainer feeding the little ones (or luring them over to the dark side, as I privately referred to it); it was like watching a pusher hooking little children on heroin, while condoning crowds cheered.

After the annoying and ever-tedious show routine was over and the tourists were sated and gone, Choney appeared, and balancing along the enigmatically edged depth of her onyx-eyed stare, I contemplated those black, inverted-tear-drop pupils. Her steady gaze needed no translation: *time to swim*. The moment broke as Bi and Li burst amongst us, rolling and sparkling like ocean waves into my arms, stealing caresses from each other while holding out audacious, encouraging pec-fins. Their resplendence overflowed around me, helpless but to reflect and offer it back to them.

Unappreciative of their tactless entry, Choney shoved and nipped the two youngsters aside amid a volley of silly squeaking. Unwilling to choose between Choney's quiet intensity and the rosy little ones — both of whom had brought yellow leaves, which they brandished hopefully — the matter was pleasantly decided, as Unior surfaced suddenly into the midst of our divided throng, cresting a wave of his own making, his bulk immediately displacing *all* the smaller dolphins as he eased forward like a continent adrift.

I slipped into the water and Choney took charge once more. Regarding each other intently, I felt the parlance of her gaze. Slowly, strangely, solemnly, Choney rose straight up vertically from the mirrored water; *the lady of the lake*. Submerging, she drew very close, eye to eye. *Inscrutable*. There was often something almost Zen about my journeys with Choney. Gliding at her glossy side, through a tenebrous seascape, she paused every so often, scanning me softly up and down, sometimes nudging my hands, arms, or hips purposefully. Through this acoustic activity remained obscure, the subdued intensity of Choney's vivid stare gave me renewed cause to wonder what nimble contemplations surged beneath her seamless exterior.

Bi and Li avidly observed the ease and affection with which Choney and I interacted, and it became clear they were entertaining similar ideas. Hovering before my shyly proffered fingertip, Bi buzzed in a soft prelude to contact, wiggling with nervous excitement, before sliding forward and bridging the gap — *contact!* Li was next, the delicate tip of her rostrum wavering until, with a certain leap of faith, she too made *contact*. Full pleased with her bravery, little Li then extended her tender pec-fin, for a short bout of patting.

Increasingly confident, Bi and Li raced and chased, orbiting like stray comets through the fog around us, supremely distracting, boldly shouldering and bumping all the rest of us and each other, their sustained clamor and wayward antics eventually provoking an open-mouthed buzzing head toss of annoyance from Choney. Continuing their sass, they placed their little rostrums on different parts of Choney's sleek form, buzzing loudly. Sometimes Choney ignored this impudent behavior and other times she became demonstrably annoyed by this rude sonic badgering.

Unior intervened, filling my vista with his scar-pale vastness, nudging softly against me, eyes half-lidded, pec-fins open invitingly, offering his alabaster underside, settling in my arms, seeming to swoon — and enticing me from Li and Bi's frantic, childish pace — causing them to redouble their efforts, squeaking madly! So long did mild, massive Unior remain limp and malleable in my arms, evincing neither movement nor breath that I became alarmed, wondering if he hadn't somehow expired with bliss. When at last he stirred to exhale I realized he was merely basking at contented length in the lavish attention.

Choney curved against me soliciting similar treatment, offering the rare vanilla of her own underside while Bi and Li tangled amongst us all, transforming the afternoon into one continuous caress. Twining within the pith of my pod, with their misty faces on all sides, the prevailing mood, like the sky overhead, was sunny. Choney was balancing a leaf on her head.

But over in the show area Christine was drifting *alone*...I had remarked how often Bi kept our company (while Christine, of course, did not), and I wondered why little Bi seemed to spend so much time away from her mother. Perhaps therein lay some of the underlying reason for Christine's growing despondency. Glancing up a moment later, I caught a glimpse of her passing silently by, phantasmal in the misted distance. For an instant, her dark, unfathomable eye rested on me, before being swallowed into the murk. I so longed to reach out in some way and make my support and concern known to Christine, but she was gone.

With a jolting barrage of artillery, the pre-show bluster began blaring over the loudspeakers and feeling a sudden melancholy fatigue, I left the water.

El Nino brought intense storms to our coast. After a nightlong downpour, I arrived to find the dolphinarium quite flooded and the lagoon's bath, the opaque color of coffee, double cream. The dolphins appeared briskly animated, surfacing boisterously in the rain-chilled water. Once submerged, I clearly heard their unceasing streams of echolocation, as they navigated through the almost zero visibility below, peeping only occasionally above the surface. They were *hunting* — their keen acoustic senses lending them a distinct advantage over the fish in the murky lagoon, and they appeared to be exploiting the opportunity with relish and gusto. Benicio later confirmed my suspicions, reporting that none of the dolphins showed much interest in performing, having sated themselves well.

The following morning, the water had water cleared marginally, to a gloomy two-foot visibility. Settling on the larger dock, I waited to see what the day would bring. In greeting Choney, I sensed an almost muted quality about her, difficult to describe. Submersed and swimming at her side, Choney's distant demeanor became more subtly pronounced, as if she were distracted by the mutable passage and topography of inner landscapes. Bi and Li were as hyperactive as ever, but when Li interrupted her mother by offering me a bold pec-fin, Choney showed no sign of irritation and after absently sliding head to tail under my hand, just drifted off into the watery fog. It was all very unlike her and I wondered if the powerful weather currents of El Nino were affecting the dolphins' moods.

Later, I noticed Bi and Li playing with a rather anomalous and grotesque looking item, batting at it with their flukes and tossing it unceremoniously from the water. What from a distance looked like a cross between a battered umbrella and squashed snapping turtle, turned out to be what Benicio referred to as a *pesca diablo,* a squat, blackened, rather toadish bottom dwelling fish. Over the next several days, I would find no less than four of these weird, bloated creatures washed up dead on the lagoon's shore and worried that this might indicate something poisonous on the tide, reported my finds to Benicio. Unperturbed, the trainer assured me it was merely the torrents of fresh rain water desalinating the lagoon that were killing these fish and nothing to worry about — easy for him to say.

With Bia and Sebastian I frequently found myself caught amid their tumultuous, sibling-like rivalries. It wasn't difficult to imagine why they were irritable, especially Sebastian — so often cut off from his only remaining companion by Unior. Pacing the same souring space day after day, their natural instincts to roam, explore, challenge, hunt, flirt and play were continually thwarted. Attempting to assuage both dolphins, I discovered (not for the first time) that not having eyes on either side of one's head makes it difficult to divide one's attention effectively.

For reasons unknown, it appeared Unior and Bia weren't getting along. Repeatedly Unior pressed his blunt rostrum to Bia's underside, buzzing loudly, while she gave every indication that (for the moment) she found his advances, unpalatable, expressing her displeasure by releasing clouds of bubbles and decidedly sour expletives. A noisy, splashing, squawking quarrel erupted between the pair and in a flurry of frenzied whistling and frothy water, they were gone. I saw them race by once, Unior's rostrum *still* glued to his unwilling consort's underside.

When they reappeared, Bia was still agitated. Several times she placed her rostrum on Unior's broad back, buzzing loudly and even attempting to push him down. The adults used such gestures to discipline the youngsters and conversely, the younger dolphins could be seen using it to irritate adults (just as Bia was so beautifully illustrating). Yet Unior appeared immune to Bia's efforts — which only served to annoy her further. In fact, his blasé attitude seemed to be sending her into perfect temper tantrums, further nursing her foul mood.

Eventually, the four of us assembled and headed along the net towards the far side of the lagoon, where another noisy, splashing commotion erupted. Looking down, I was quite surprised to see Sebastian poking his head through the hole in the net below! *What was this? Was he about to cross over?*

The buzzing noise increased and unsure what might erupt at any moment from the milky murk, I steadied myself with one hand on the net. Already a bit on edge, a sudden pinching on my fingers made me jump! There, peeking mischievously through the festooned lattice, were Bi and Li — the diminutive, pinching perpetrators revealed! Their trickery discovered, the youngsters moved on in search of other sport.

Below me, the staccato ruckus continued — the reasons for which, along with Sebastian's partial penetration of the hole, remained obscure. There were definitely some strange currents on the water.

Towards the end of the day, I joined Christine where she was resting in the show area. Drifting together, heads almost touching we became still, but for the punctuation of our quiet breaths. We were roused by the clattering chatter of gathering tourists, Christine lifted her cheek from the pillow of the water's surface and meeting her tacit gaze, we dove in perfect collusion, undulating away from the growing human racket. In the turbid depths, Choney, Unior and the youngsters joined us and twining together, the pods' peace and coherence met a deep satisfaction rising in me. But surfacing, my glance was drawn to where Bia and Sebastian paced us, just past the net, barred from this familial comfort.

A raucous bawling from Iago (as ever, evincing all the frothing charm of an irate baboon) jolted my troubled thoughts. Apparently a couple of tourists had turned up, and in a frenzy to pocket some coin before any other trainers appeared, Iago had been blasting away on his fool whistle, signaling Bia and Sebastian to return to the dock. But the dolphins, engrossed in pacing along net failed to respond to the trainer's rude signals, until I was once again, landlocked. Quietly leaking resentment, I looked on as Iago bullied Bia and Sebastian into "making nice" with the tourists.

Afterwards, tourists waded around in the sandy shallows, trying to touch Bia and Sebastian who kept themselves carefully just beyond the forest of outstretched fingers. After hours of repetitive, inane capering, arduous hauling, shouting and whistle blasting (which marked the majority of the dolphins' interactions with humankind), Bia and Sebastian were often short tempered with each other, as the abrasive drudgery of this unending daily routine took its toll. Now, instead of traveling out into the lagoon to engage in conciliatory bouts of caressing, the pair often simply ended up wallowing insipidly in the shallows by shore, slavishly awaiting the arrival of the next fish bucket. These unhealthy habits were leaching the life and light out of them. The bright fluidity of Bia and Sebastian's attenuated youth had all but flown — and they had *this* to look forward to for the cheapened remainder of their lives — satiating endless, lusting lines of humans, hungry for the beauty and grace (or just the banal novelty) of their presence, until every last sparkle was rapaciously sucked out of them. In exchange:

Dead fish.

Dead life.

Dead fish. Dead life. (Photo credit: Camilla Singh)

The dolphinarium's manager appeared, leading a grand tour of dour, self-important suits around. Opting to give this unwieldy, preening parade a wide berth (until they'd retreated from the sun's glare to sip drinks in an air-conditioned office), Benicio and I chatted in the shade of several leaning palms. With good natured rue, he remarked how sometimes, when one of the dolphins was particularly annoyed with a trainer, they might go and catch a fish, return to the dock and then, after making sure the offending human party had noted the prize, gulp it down! Out of respect for my trainer friend, I muted my mirth.

The trap was sprung as I was preparing to leave for the day. Scuttling from his chilled cubby hole, the manager called me over. I'd known something was brewing; several times previously, he'd approached me muttering, but had hastily scurried away before voicing anything coherent. I knew what this was really all about. Having discovered just how much money people were willing to pay to "swim with the dolphins" it plainly galled him that he wasn't making a single cent or somehow *profiting* from my presence. Fastening his beady, greedy lecherous eyes upon me, he demanded to be told how many days I had remaining until my departure.

"*Two,*" I told him.

Swelling pompously and appearing to weightily consider this information (fat fingers clasped behind his back, rocking on his ridiculous little feet), he airily announced that I would be allowed to visit for only *one* of those two days – "*unless...*" A sly leer crept onto his pinched face. I couldn't hide my revulsion and he was quick to remind me that allowing me access to the dolphins *at all* was an *enormous* favor on his part — and by his way of reckoning, he was right. But no way of reckoning could change the hideousness of our situation — with such a person holding power over the dolphins' lives. *One* day remaining, it would be. I was running out of time, my allowance hanging by a thread.

Christine met me at the damp dock on my final morning, lingering, until after a long moment of silent deliberation, the awaited invitation came — a shining pec-fin held aloft. Christine's lonesome ways pained me and this opportunity for interaction allowed some measure of satisfaction. Through the relative clarity of the water, I saw when Unior, Choney, Li and Bi appeared beneath Christine, rising slowly. At their collective arrival, she issued a snorting exhalation and moved off.

Choney, obviously in a *particularly* determined mood, took no sauciness from Li and Bi, nipping and shoving the pair aside the moment they showed signs of interrupting with their leaf-sweet games. Fixed by her adamant stare, I obediently submersed, meeting Choney's expectant Cheshire smile amid the familiar tug of her resonant tuning.

Sailing along, my entire focus remained on my gleaming underwater companions and the weaving of our invisible tapestry, but somehow in the blind brine, it became Unior, rather than Choney at whose side I traveled. With gentle equanimity, Unior slowly began to sweep me along with him — but Choney reappeared, hovering right before us, and fixing me with a straight look, she lightly rapped my wrist with her rostrum, uttering a scolding, staccato trebling, as if to say, *"Enough larking about! Pay attention!"* until I again aligned myself docilely at her dainty side.

Just then, Christine pulled up like a bus, unceremoniously initiating me into a bout of pec-patting. With another insistent, disapproving buzz at this interruption, Choney cut lithely between Christine and I, causing the previously peaceful air to feel suddenly strained. Characteristically Christine departed, and reluctantly, I replaced my hand on Choney's side, continuing on with her. Swimming just below us, Unior seemed to be studying our every gesture and caress with obvious interest.

Choney trilled out her signature whistle and then paused courteously, awaiting my sorry, imitative response. Meeting her bright gaze I continued our exchange of discrepant notes. The longer I spent among them, the more expressive their utterances became.

Then little Li started swirling insistently beneath her mother's chin, repeating a slightly distressed and wobbly whistle — she was hungry and wanted to nurse. For all her brash noise, she was young yet. Maternal duty completed, we continued on, Li and Bi bumping about, Unior slipping over to my right side (Choney invariably taking my left) and happily sandwiched, we traveled on.

Unexpectedly, Christine rejoined us — and *stayed*! Shifting his position, Unior descended below me again, allowing Christine to have the spot on my right, tucking Bi neatly beneath her ample, speckled belly. With much delight, I bestowed tender, remedial caresses over Christine's broad, shinning back. Then, in a burst of unprecedented friendliness, Choney and Christine began pec-patting! I couldn't remember the last time I'd seen such a friendly exchange between those two.

Peace prevailed, and I felt the deep honor of their acceptance and affection — all six of us weaving and soaring in perfect accord; our whole so impossibly greater than the sum of its components.

In the misty water the dolphins faded in and out with spectral proficiency. Goodbyes, as we understand them in our human way, do not seem to exist among dolphin kind. Our eyes clasped one last time, reminding me of the liquidity of time, and we parted.

I joined Sebastian and Bia, moping in the shallows, awaiting the fish buckets. Pressing close, Sebastian led me to the lagoon's far side, slipping beneath the mangrove umbra.With my arm slung affectionately over his gleaming back, we arched among the rippling amber sunbeams striping the deep shadows. The beauty was breathtaking, made more so by the affectionate presence of my quicksilver companion. Drawn down into the dim reaches, Sebastian and I spiraled slowly, before rising towards the light to respire. But it had to end — with the inevitable return toward the shallows, where Bia still floated.

An abrupt, obnoxious din announced the start of the show and I realized how chilled I'd become. The racket roused Bia and Sebastian and caressing them lingeringly, I took in their laden, lyrical, surpassing persons, finally leaving the water with utmost reluctance.

There were people everywhere, but Sebastian and Bia picked me out, becoming very still, their vivid gaze passionately holding mine, reminding me how deep our quiet waters flowed. They paced, calling out piercingly, but I remained held to the ground — just like them. And I knew my difficult, redolent days among them were terminally numbered.

CHAPTER TWENTY-FIVE

SHADOW OF DISSOLUTION

"Love knows not its own depth till the hour of its separation."
Kahlil Gibran

Torrents of morning rain had cleared in the face of a chilly northern front, which stubbornly remained the length of my stay (replacing my scintillating aquamarine strand with a dull and somber turquoise). It had been six months since my last visit and again, the overflow from a lunar tide had flooded the dolphinarium (an occurrence becoming more common), leaving visibility in the swollen, particle-suffused lagoon less than a dolphin-length.

The day's first bout of tourist-hauling had yet to begin, but rather than wait, I stole down onto the smaller dock (the larger one about ready to sink beneath its load of vociferous visitors) for a fleeting greeting. I'd already learned from Benicio that despite his repeatedly patching holes in the net, a determined Unior wasted no time in tearing new openings for himself, apparently having no intention of relinquishing his claims on Bia! And of course, with no other choice of companionship, Sebastian often remained alone.

As I lay down upon the damp little dock, chin resting on heaped hands, sunlight escaped the racing clouds overhead, and turning my face to receive this smiling warmth, I sighed to be back — again caught in the contrast of butterfly rapture and scalding vitriol. When I turned from the sky, moon-eyed Sebastian was there before me. Steadily he and I regarded each other and in the spilling stillness, I wondered at this love — this impossible, incredible, enormous love for him held in me. Hands swimming over his satin skin, I perceived a network of new scars carving his body — *Unior*. As Sebastian grew towards adulthood, his presence drew increasingly dangerous repercussions from the older male.

Glancing up, I discovered both Unior and Bia close by, observing Sebastian and I, and then, all three dolphins came rolling thunderously into my delighted, deluged embrace! Impatient to unfold our full reunion, Sebastian tugged at my hair, while Bia poked her rostrum into my palm, pulling me bodily into the water — urging me to submerse and swim. But human rules bound us both. With temptation so strong and so much at stake, I regretfully decided to retreat, rather than risk reproach within minutes of arrival.

After the morning show and tourist photo-ops, Choney, Li, Christine and Bi, all lined up in a low, dolorous row along the net — a sight all too familiar. As Bi and Li grew older, succumbing to dependence upon their human captors for sustenance (rather than carefree meals of milk from their mothers), they inevitably slowed into sorrow. Though born barred from the true sea, surely the conversation of currents stirring from beyond the far net whispered to them. Fifty million years of oceanic wandering can not be quenched from the blood, nor suppressed from the soul in a generation. As Bi and Li's childhood was stolen away, the narrow bounds of their confinement would continue to chafe, just as the squalor of their impoverished surroundings would eventually suck their liquid spirits dry.

Hoping to remain unnoticed, I stole onto the big dock, where Christine rose first, rolling without hesitation under my offered hands. Bi and Li were not far behind, making up for what they lacked in size, with enthusiasm, followed closely by Choney. Faced again with a collective invitation to join them below the water — I caught the meaningful nod from Benicio across the lagoon, indicating the batch of tourists readying for dolphin-hauls — and so, despite the dolphins' welcome and the miracle of their beautiful beckoning, I could not follow.

Prices had been raised again, signaling a *fatal* increase in the dolphins' monetary value. Small wonder the lack of financial gain so irritated the greedy manager's sensibilities when I kept company with the dolphins. The hourglass had almost run out and I could do nothing.

With these thoughts running and ranting in my mind, I watched Sebastian drifting alone before the tourists wading in the shallows, keeping carefully out of reach. He was turned away from me, the mirrored dome of his head, interrupted briefly and periodically by the grotto of his exhalation. When he turned his exquisite face to look up at me, our eyes met like an electrical current. Nodding rhythmically now, spiritedly tossing his head, Sebastian drew closer — one nudge, then another. And then he pushed his smooth face into my hands, before curving to absorb a soothing caress along the length of him. At this, alert Bia and Unior both moved eagerly forward as well, but Unior's forward surge caused Sebastian to fade back. Seeing the dolphins crowding round, a cluster of tourists came wading eagerly forward, grasping towards the silver shapes, causing both the dolphins and I to retreat.

The tourist-hauling commenced. Some people had come from opulent hotels as part of a package day-tour: for them, "*swimming with the dolphins*" was just another "neat" activity on their itinerary, listed next to the lobster lunch. But many people came *specifically* seeking the thrill of getting close to dolphins, squealing in glee to be pushed and pulled around the lagoon — for the price of a dead fish — and freedom's ruin. Many people returned again and again, year after year, undaunted by the rising prices — the dolphins so beautiful, so alluring, so like being in love; unaware that hunger forced the dolphins to endure this unwanted human contact; unaware that it was *their* blind infatuation feeding the cycle of suffering.

Some people might not care. Some, rather that recognize their responsibility in the evil equation, would still refuse to see — insisting loudly that the sea circus world of smiling-happy-make-believe was the only real one. But many, I was sure, would react with deep, deep *horror*, if only they realized the *truth* — the searing, appalling truth. But as long as people remain indifferent or ignorant, as long as they remain wiling to pay, dolphins will suffer for their pleasure. Only when an outraged majority have *realized* the truth — only when the money flow stops — will these places will go extinct. And then we will look back on these wretched prisons with shuddering shame.

Time crawled in the dust beneath the glaring sun, and still I remained tethered. Eyes skyward, I watched with fascination, a cloud of gigantic jeweled dragonflies hovering over the water, thankfully setting about the task of reducing the over eager mosquito population.

Finally, the last tourists cleared away. Unior, Choney, Christine, Bi and Li all rose up before me on the dock. Smiling at the mischief of their mouths I slipped into the water, drawn gratefully down amongst them. After familiar buzzing inquiry and greeting rituals, I aligned at Choney's side in the expected travel position. All six of us then set out *en concert*, always a rare and prized occurrence. Enwreathed, I was aware of myself as a valid component in the group's ever-shifting alchemy. Taking note of our positioning, it seemed (as it so often did) that Choney was the sun of our traveling solar system, all others radiating outward from her in our variously ordained orbits.

When the pace began to quicken, our formation tightened. I would have quickly been left behind, had not Choney pressed her sleek side close, sweeping me along in her invisible slipstream. Concentrating on the minute manner of my positioning enabled me to facilitate the favor granted. When at last we slowed and I surfaced to breathe among them, I found we had curved *far*, circumnavigating much of the latter part of the lagoon.

Clearly itching to renew our friendship, Bi and Li came inching close, angling their flanks towards me and peeping over their shoulders for response. Offering my hand, I allowed *them* to bridge the gap between us and though shy and shivery at first, the two imps were soon operating at full jaunt, bold and bossy as ever!

Continuing along the net, our carefree play was interrupted by the unmistakable buzzing calls of Bia and Sebastian through the barrier. Pausing, I peered through the ropes, encrusted with waving sea life, barely able to make out their faces on the other side — it was time to go to them.

The waiting pair greeted me enthusiastically and gliding with them into deeper water, they looped loosely beneath my arms. Our trio restored, caressing and careening along, I felt a surge of gratitude for Bia and Sebastian's friendship — to run to the same drum. They whisked me along between them, our pace quickening out to where the water was colder and clearer, where we began to dive-dance, their mercurial forms breathtaking — and I, a third musketeer, rather than a third wheel.

Slowing between their curved, glimmering backs, they led me to Unior's latest hole in the net, located near the far side of the lagoon, some seven or eight feet down. As the three of us hovered before the frayed portal, peering through, I detected the sonic monitoring pulses of the other dolphins somewhere in the murky distance beyond.

I found Christine later at the big dock, and meeting her darkened gaze, I saw the desolation there. Poor Christine — so often unwelcome by Choney, ignored by Unior, cut off from her eldest surviving daughter, while her youngest seemed to prefer other company — so I took every opportunity to offer my affection and companionship, as more than any of the others, she seemed most to need it. Murmuring softly, I soothed her sable skin as Christine closed her eyes, basking delicately in the quiet glow of affection. Drawing back a little, she regarded me and seeping past the melancholy that lay so heavily over her, I knew, *somehow*, that she understood and acknowledged the unconditional kindness which surrounded and held her. *She knew.* In silence, the two of us drew close until our foreheads rested together in a sacred moment of communion; humble mending in a life filled with dreary days.

Each such shared exchange became a unique aquarelle, painted upon an onion skin of memory. Moment by moment, hour by hour, day by day and year by year, these painted tissue pages of shared instance, created the rich fabric and texture of my ever-evolving relationships with the dolphins. An exchange never stood on its own, but rather, rested atop an entire mnemonic library of uniquely inscribed, entwined moments: Our shared history; our friendship; our fellowship; our family.

I noticed Choney close by, studying this interspecies interlude — keen as ever to observe. After Christine had taken her leave, Choney came forward, and her potent gaze lay at velvety length upon my own, as if she were searching for the incorporeal source of the tender emotion she'd glimpsed. Nudging my wrist, she invited me into the water.

However, the beetle-browed manager had not yet granted "permission" to join the dolphins in the water that afternoon — the latest requirement to swamp my visits. I was very tempted to break the arbitrary rules, but I dreaded provoking a peevish withdrawal of my last remaining remnants of time with the dolphins. Though I reined in rude rebuttal at the existing authority, the situation remained nightmarish, and the manager remained a constantly lurking menace — the ticking of the clock was never stilled.

Traveling later along the net with Bia and Sebastian, we passed Unior's hole, and saw him there with his head stuck through it, looking out at Bi and

Communing with Christine

Li on the other side. Bia and Sebastian's immediate sonic scrutiny of the situation set the water abuzz. When Unior pulled his head back, brave Bi, then stuck her little head through and burly Unior showed no signs of dissuading her on this. When Bi withdrew, Sebastian then stuck his head through, with Bia close beside him. All the while the excited whistling and buzzing noise continued. *What was all this about?* I had wondered if any of the other dolphins ever used the holes to visit each other, to which Benicio replied that Unior was the only dolphin observed crossing the net.

Sipping a breath at the surface, I found Choney there too — and I realized that *her* wishes might easily be central to all the animated discussion and activity below — or perhaps this time she was merely a curious spectator. Resting my hand on the lattice, Choney moved close, buzz-nudging my fingers and then holding up a pec-fin to me. *Damn the barrier!*

Down again in the murk, all the dolphins except Christine appeared to have gathered on both sides of the hole (though with the water's poor visibility, she might well be concealed nearby). Drawn to the aperture, I considered crossing through myself, and soon did.

Bi and Li found me, spilling liquid diamonds from their thorn-crowned backs, curving to offer their pretty flanks and pec-fins, whistling encouragingly. However, it appeared bossy Bi resented Li's cute interruptions, and with obvious annoyance, Bi tried to shoulder her half-sister aside. Amid discordant squalling, neither saucy imp would back down. In an attempt to restore peace I placed a quieting hand on each little dolphin, keeping a tenuous balance, until one of them moved forward requesting a tail massage, breaking symmetry. Immediately the other copied this gesture and the squabbling resumed.

Generally among dolphins, social jockeying (of one sort or another) is the norm and a staggering abundance of tactics are used in these perpetual and complex social maneuverings. Bi was again growing aggressive, buzzing sharply and throwing gaping threats at her half-sister, who momentarily spooked. But clever Li returned almost immediately with her *mother*, causing an immediate shift of formation!

Choney received me in our familiar traveling position, while Bi and Li continuing their vying, albeit, somewhat surreptitiously. But upon spying these distracting activities, Choney sent an open-mouthed buzzing threat at both youngsters, and temporarily cowed, they peeled off together, vanishing into the murk. Moments later, they were back, demonstrating the suppleness and persistence of youth.

I wondered why Choney's ire fell on Bi and Li rather than me. Was it because they were the perpetrators of the distraction, or perhaps because of my clearly limited awareness of their social fluidities? But, at least in this instance, I *did* know better — I, like the youngsters, had been quietly testing Choney's limits. Traveling on, Bi and Li eyed each other and me, wondering if they dared make any further attempts. They dared — and though they tried to keep their pec-patting subtle — of course Choney saw. Apparently in no mood for such impudence, Choney again gaped her toothsome jaws at the pair, letting loose a tremendous jaw-clap! *Yike!* Bi and Li scattered and my straying hand flew to my side. There would be no more monkey business — Choney was the boss!

But Bi and Li soon returned — now accompanied by Christine. Bolstered perhaps by the company of her mother, I was amazed to see little Bi now threatening Choney, vehemently gaping *her* little jaws! *Threatening Choney? Not a wise idea.* Perhaps Choney regarded the smaller dolphin's brassy belligerence as (for the moment) beneath her notice — or perhaps Choney had other reasons for curbing her temper — but for whatever reason, she appeared uninspired to respond.

In the past it had been an extremely rare thing for Choney and Christine to peaceably keep company together, yet this was clearly on the increase — they were even pec-patting together again. In retrospect, it is perhaps, not so strange. With Unior's focus and attention shifting more and more towards Bia, Choney's champion was often absent from her slender side. I speculated that perhaps with Unior's growing absence, Choney realized that it might be best if she made some diplomatic effort with Christine, rather than rile the larger female's displeasure without any implicit back up. I also wondered if that might be why she refrained from disciplining impudent Bi?

Soon afterwards, the hole in the net *again* became the center of attention and activity. Now it was Christine's turn to stick *her* head through the hole, with Unior, Sebastian and Bia hovering parallel on the other side. While I wondered what might happen next, Christine withdrew and then Unior put his head through, a continual steam of buzzing and whistling still issuing from the others. With one squinty eye cocked upwards at Choney and I, he pulled back a moment, centered himself — and zipped right through! Coming up below me, Unior slid slowly head to tail under my offered palm, in greeting.

Just then, a sharp, growling din erupted. It certainly wasn't coming from Unior — *what was going on?* Glancing down, I saw Choney now with her head through the hole and right before her, almost blocking her, was Sebastian. Both dolphins were gaping their jaws in threat and releasing fine trails of bubbles with their irate dissonance, as they squared of with blatant aggression, head to head! I could hardly believe my eyes — *Choney and Sebastian?* What cause did mother and son have to display *such* hostility at each other?

Rising to the surface for breath, I met Choney doing the same. Her eyes were bright and alert, but betrayed no reason for such an aggravated exchange with her own son. Yet below the sharp buzzing resumed, as Choney and Sebastian continued to face off through the hole, airing their grievance with wildly gaping, snapping jaws! Though Bia remained at Sebastian's side, this clearly wasn't *her* battle: she did not posture aggressively and none of the angry buzzing seemed to belong to her, and when Sebastian rose for air, Bia remained before Choney, with no noise, or readable reaction. This grievance seemed *very* specific. Clearly this hostile exchange seemed to relate somehow to the boundary of the barrier, but *what* was the cause of their contention? No answers.

Eventually Choney and the youngsters went on their way and Unior crossed back over to Bia. Checking to make sure Iago was not around, keeping a narrowed and disapproving eye on my whereabouts, I decided to cross over myself, but as I did so, I snagged a little on a frayed loose end of the netting—a *dangerous* thing, eight feet below the water, with curious and fractious young dolphins zipping around! So I set about tying up those loose, frayed ends as well as I was able — all through a renewed storm of buzzing inspection from the re-gathered dolphins, who seemed to view my endeavor with unlimited interest. With the errand completed, I drifted back, watching as the dolphins moved forward to inspect my work. Then, to demonstrate the portal's improvement, I zipped through it, turned and returned.

Feeling most pleased with my accomplishment, I surfaced — to find myself nose to nose with Unior. For an instant, I worried that my adjustments to the hole might have invited his displeasure; I hoped Unior understood my finger fumbling efforts were intended to help. These doubts were dismissed as he slowly rolled his goliath form to invite caresses. I realized how different Unior's skin felt from the other dolphins': harder, smoother and more muscular. It made sense, I supposed, that the young and females would be softer. Having so immense and powerful a creature hanging pliable in one's arms can be an almost overwhelming experience — but when it came down to it, it was the implicit *trust* of a still wild heart that made me reel with wonder and gratitude.

By wiggling and rotating them, Unior called particular attention to his scarred pec-fins, but he did not wish to pec-pat. I was at a loss — *what did he want?* Concentrating carefully, Unior laid both his pectoral fins against my hands and then I thought maybe I understood and lightly took hold. *That* was it, and in this manner, belly to belly, he began to carry me along with him, I no more an encumbrance than a festoon of kelp. Dolphins are powerful creatures — but still, Unior's might was extraordinary. Allowing me a sip from the surface, Unior then softly descended into the water, cradling me along until finally twisting to rise for breath.

He was immediately replaced by Bia and Sebastian, who had remained our avid shadows, restoring our trio and cosseting me among themselves once more before streaming out into the lagoon. Peering over Bia's back, I saw Unior pacing us. Catching my glance, Unior suddenly cut towards me, filling my vision, gently, inevitably, unarguably, abducting me away from the smaller (and less-experienced) dolphins — social thrust and parry.

Our two groups merged, all of us weaving amongst each other. Suddenly, without perceptible warning, Unior and Sebastian *detonated* into turbulence! Whatever had transpired had been so swift and subtle, I'd missed the exchange completely. The two males went tearing around the lagoon at a *tremendous* pace, at one point veering tornado-like right past me. What had sparked such anger?

When they next appeared, all three dolphins were together, Bia between the two males, petting pec-fins with both, making peace, it seemed. With the on-going, increasing tensions between Unior and Sebastian over Bia, and the recent contention over the matter of the hole, the air was obviously charged, perhaps so much so, that the least thing could send tempers blasting.

We ended up peaceably in the shallows, caressing in a mellow manner. Idly watching the clapping, hooting crowds gathering for the last show of the day, I again felt myself far more at home among the dolphins, but this affinity couldn't prevent our parting when the inevitable static blaring began over the loudspeakers, spelling the end of our time together. After all, none of this delicate magic mattered to their captors.

Toward the end of the day, after the final show and hauling, I reconvened with sassy Li and Bi, the puckish pair still endlessly interrupting and foiling each other's attempts at pec-patting. Choney's arrival replaced their hectic piping with the gossamer hush of communion — until the youngsters came nuzzling pertly back into our midst, tumbling, twirling and chortling in a mirthful dance, as they flashed in liquid silver beneath the dim water.

Christine joined us and I felt deeply gratified at finding her increasingly social. All five of us aligned together, cruising past the lingering tourists, before diving to more private waters. The youngsters quieted and Bi nursed. It was just about time for me to depart. Without the noise and bluster that usually accompanied the little dolphins' doings, Li and I regarded one another. It was a rare moment of deep connection with the busy youngster and in the quiet, I felt the subtle fragrance of our flowering friendship.

With a flourish, Choney and Christine collected a final caress, gathered and tucked their daughters beneath them, readying to snooze-cruise, and

Choney, Unior, Christine & I.

then we parted ways. I caught a last glimpse of little Li streaming along in the dark water, holding a yellow leaf tight in her jaws.

The water grew quiet, faithfully reflecting the restless sky overhead. A phalanx of dark clouds were gobbling up the day's brightness. If there were other signs heralding the finality of our parting, I did not see them.

Passing through the hole, Unior found me. Cloud-pale, he eased forward, nudging me in silent statement over my heart, before leading me with him through layers of color, clarity and temperature, into the dim reaches to swirl as two partners in a gracious dance. In the dim water, Unior appeared to glimmer and fade with ghostly facility. Recognizing the glint in his eye, I followed his lead and together, we both shot up to the surface and burst from the water, Unior falling back with an enormous splash! Again, we surged upwards, Unior thrusting himself high into the air — some several hundred pounds of silver muscle flying over my head and crashing into the water beside me! Slower now, we descended, he outlined in the last, fleeing watery rays of light, flowing in dying gold. And then he was gone.

Bia and Sebastian materialized from the misted water, collecting me between them. Tenderly caressing their burnished sides and exchanging glances, they swept me up, flowing into the mangrove shadows where I watched both dolphins lazily pursuing several unwary mangrove snapper.

Theirs was a fellowship I'd not have traded for anything — anything except their freedom. I would have gladly agreed never to set eyes upon any of them again, if only they could return to where they belonged — there's *never* been any question of that.

It was almost time for me to go, yet I hesitated. Hovering before me in the water, Sebastian drew closer until our faces were almost touching. I returned the sea-strangeness of his gaze, the moments spinning out, engaging the cartography of our colloquy in bas-relief. Time to go, yet Sebastian remained, asking with his eyes that I *stay* — reminding me at that a moment, very much of Juan — resurrecting familiar arrows of regret. Oh, I wanted to stay and stay and stay, but Benicio's insistent calls pulled me from the water; pulled me from Sebastian's supplicant gaze, drifting low in the last sun-stain.

I was sorely tempted to shrug off propriety and remain, but catching the scowl of the of the dour-faced night guard, I realized this was not an option. The darkening sky was now completely overcome with clouds, leaving the water wan and somber. Leaden in the grim water, Bia and Sebastian drifted in the shallows their enigmatic gaze pulling heavily at me. Shivering, I perceived an uncharacteristic distance, as if a strange rift had opened its lonely, fog-strewn shores between us — a reminder that one way or another, our paths must soon be forced apart. I stood, trying to shake off the cling of an ominous and unwanted feeling.

I did not understand and so I wrenched myself away, hurrying past dolphinarium's irritable night custodian. I hated to leave the dolphins on such a deeply discordant note, but immediately comforted myself — tomorrow all would surely be set right during our final morning, before I had to catch my afternoon flight.

But on this account, I was *wrong*. That night it stormed fiercely, and the muddy remains of this deluge foiled all efforts to return to the dolphins the following day. Roads were washed out and the already sporadic buses were experiencing more than their usual daily difficulties. Time was too short and Nature had spoken.

If only I had known what lay ahead.

If only I had known — I would have fought my way through jungle, flood and blood — would have abandoned my flight and flown instead straight to them — flown to them and clung tight.

CHAPTER TWENTY-SIX

REQUIEM

"They that love beyond the world cannot be separated by it…
Death is but a crossing of worlds, as friends do the Seas.
They live in one another still."
William Penn, *Some Fruits of Solitude*

The unprecedented growth in popularity of "swimming with dolphins" leaves the remaining Cubano Dolphins pulling in terribly huge sums of money. To the greedy and ruthless businessmen who rule their lives, the dolphins are merely lucrative assets. I can no longer rejoin the Dolphins without paying a fee to their "owners" who consider them *property*, rather than *persons*. Because I refuse to support the system that robs the dolphins of their freedom and will to live, I am barred from them forever.

The only remaining way to try and help them has been to tell the truth of their story, in the hope that this needless cycle of suffering can somehow end. So I began to write.

But even as I wrote, terrible things happened. As of 2008, *at least eight* dolphins have already met tragic deaths at the Cuban dolphinarium.

Among them, *Bia* and *Sebastian*.

I have no words to express the loss of Sebastian and Bia, whom I have known since they were tiny sparkling infants. I have shared so much with them, I cannot convey the magnitude of their loss; it is almost beyond comprehension. I cannot breathe, thinking of it.

They have paid for human pleasure with their lives. Our companionship was among the things I treasured most in this world. I loved them like my own children, better than my own blood. But they are gone. It seems impossible that our eyes will never again meet in the morning light; that our trio will never again entwine amid muted waters to rise as one for breath. All the promise their lives should have held, the sweet light of their tender spirits, snuffed out. The world is darker for their deaths and we — *all of us* — have blood on our hands from their premature passing — because it could have been prevented. They should never have been born trapped behind human barriers.

For all they've given,
For all they've shared,
For all they've shown me

This is their story, and the unequivocal truth, which no fabricated human lies can erase: We are *wrong* to steal and subvert their freedom, to inflict the suffering we do, to bring death to these precious creatures for our pleasure and profit. It does not matter what your scientific credentials, how exalted your governmental position, or how long or satisfying your employment within the captivity industry: *Nothing* can excuse the suffering they endure because of our willful greed, our irresponsible ignorance and — perhaps worst of all — our gravely misplaced affection.

Because of changes in staff and ownership at the dolphinarium, I no longer have direct news from Cuba. I do not know for certain how many more of the dolphins there have died. I cannot express how profoundly hard this not knowing is. In this internet age, I gather what news I can. Videos of all manner of amusements and atrocities are posted online. Searching for information about the remainder of my dolphin companions, I have discovered that for the time being (2008). Unior, Christine and Choney are still there: Still hauling smiling, laughing, oblivious tourists around on their dorsal fins; still begging piteously for each morsel of fish, while blind strangers rub and paw them.

It is not a small crime or a harmless indulgence. What the remaining Cubano Dolphins continue to endure is the stuff of nightmares made real. How many more, like Juan, must endure madness and sorrow? How many more, just like Sebastian and Bia, must die young, behind nets, fences, walls and bars to feed our fancy? How many more, like Unior, Choney and Christine, must endure unhappy lives of despair and drudgery? *Death* is the only likely release from a life of enslavement for the remaining members of my dolphin family, and for so many others like them around the world. How many more innocents must die, before we realize — and put an end to this? This cruelty and oppression will not cease until the flow of money from tourists stops.

So, here is their truth and my plea:

Let us put an end to this abomination and suffering. Let us endeavor to make amends and undo the terrible harm we inflict. It is too late for Bia and

Sebastian, but for so many others, there is still hope, if we can only choose to support compassion, life and freedom.

They shall hunger no more, neither thirst any more; neither shall the sun light on them, nor any heat. For the Lamb which is in the midst of the throne shall feed them, and shall lead them unto living fountains of water: and God shall wipe away all tears from their eyes.
The Order for the Burial of a Child; Revelation, 7:16–17

Sebastian.

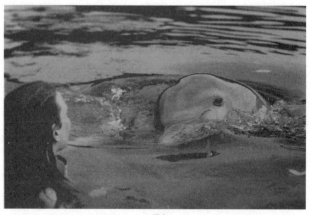

Bia

CHAPTER TWENTY-SEVEN

DECONSTRUCTING THE VELVET CAGE

He that leadeth into captivity shall go into captivity
Revelation: 13:10.

As unhappy as the lives of the Cubano Dolphins are, compared to the conditions endured by many captive cetaceans, they are living in luxury (which is scant comfort). Controversy over keeping dolphins in captivity has increased greatly over the past few decades. In some areas marine parks and attractions are closing down and captures are being outlawed, while in others, dolphins are increasingly sought after as sources of entertainment, recreation — and profit.

Controlled and Inherently Detrimental Conditions

In the US, regulations state that captive dolphin enclosures need only be 30 X 30 X 6 feet deep[1] (less than an adult body length) to meet current standards — this, for creatures that average daily movements of 33-89 km or more,[2] can dive hundreds of meters, reach speeds of over 35 km/ph and are infamous for their love of surfing. Thus, it is perhaps unsurprising that cetaceans commonly develop aberrant, stereotypical stress-related behaviors in captivity. As they endlessly circle or aimlessly float in their under-sized, concrete pools or pens, their dorsal fins may become pathetically flaccid and flop over. *No* tank or man-made enclosure can properly allow for cetaceans' natural proclivity to roam, or replicate their real, varying oceanic habitat.

Ridiculous tricks, bubbly, charismatic trainers and blaring music are used to distract audiences from contemplating stark, barren enclosures. Unimaginable boredom, cramped, stressful spaces, chlorinated, synthetic salt water, noisy crowds, nutritionally inferior dead frozen fish, and in the worst cases, lack of fresh air and sunlight, all contribute to the impoverished lives and life spans of captive cetaceans. Larger pens or concrete pools only *seem* spacious to *us* — but to the cetaceans they enclose, they are still as cramped as living in a closet. How big a room would *you* need, to spend the rest of your life in?

No human-arranged social grouping can mimic the fluid complexities of dolphin society, or especially the extended, lifelong family ties of orca whales. Unnaturally separating mothers and young, despite the integral importance of close bonding and social learning, is a common practice in captivity,[3] one that upon examination seems inexcusably inhumane. In captivity's closed quarters, aggressions magnify and a primitive pecking order arises, but cornered in a confined pool, dolphins can only swim round and round, causing violence to escalate. With no escape, and subject to continual stress, weaker dolphins are sometimes hounded into illness or death by companions.[4] US Federal Marine Mammal Inventory Reports* hint at the numbers of untimely deaths, including those involving other captive cetaceans, listing things like: *'trauma by male dolphin'* and *'killed by another animal.'*[5]

Additionally, some trainers admit to withholding food to coerce dolphins into performing — starving them until they comply. In some places, this is the standard method to force captive cetaceans to cooperate. *Every* aspect of the dolphins' lives is controlled by their jailers: when, how much or even *if* there will be food, light, water, space, companionship, life, death — *everything*. Their right to choose has been stolen. Captivity severely compromises cetaceans' lives, and when one "Flipper" or "Shamu" dies, another takes his or her place and name — and the show goes on.

Petting Pools = Purgatory

Among the most detrimental and ironically most popular of captive cetacean displays are "petting pools" — small concrete enclosures where the public can touch and even feed cetaceans. A study undertaken to examine the effects of petting pools on captive dolphins found that during the main tourist season, Sea World visitors have uninterrupted access to petting pool dolphins for up to twelve hours per day with no escape or respite available to the dolphins. At the busiest times, several hundred visitors crowd around the pool's edge, frequently splashing water and banging on the sides of the pool

---

* All US facilities holding marine mammals are supposed to report inventories of births, deaths and transfers.

using their hands, coins and other objects. Very real risks to the dolphins were identified from ingestion of contaminated and inappropriate food items (dirty, decomposing fish, chips, popcorn and even beer) and ingestion of foreign objects (coins, sunglasses, cigarettes etc.), which could cause intestinal injury or even death. Dolphins that are more aggressive in petting pools may suffer from obesity, while those that are more submissive endure injury and bullying. In these gross daily melees, human visitors have also been observed being butted and bitten, demonstrating that petting pools place the welfare of human visitors at risk, as well as the dolphins'.[6]

Petting pools, like other marine attractions that encourage the public to interact with captive dolphins, subject people to mixed messages, the adverse effects of which may radiate far a field. Following the misleading and inappropriate examples set in marine parks, naïve boaters may attempt to feed, pet or chase *wild dolphins* — which constitutes harassment in the US[7] and can lead to people or dolphins sustaining damage. Trevor Spradlin an agent with the US National Marine Fisheries Service (NMFS) is among those who express concern over this problem: *'There is a growing concern that feeding pools, swim programs and other types of interactive experiences with marine mammals in captive display facilities may perpetuate the problem of the public feeding and harassment of marine mammals in the wild.'*[8]

Public venues, particularly theme parks are indisputably noisy places. Dolphins are highly sensitive, *acoustic* creatures and confined in bare, concrete pools as pumps drone monotonously, auditory echoes may become excruciating. Additional noise is produced by music played over loud speakers, staff talking into microphones, screaming kids, loud music, cheering crowds, fireworks etc.[9] Daily bombarding acoustically sensitive creatures with a constant, inescapable assault of human noise, constitutes unacceptable cruelty.[10] Concrete tanks — especially petting pools, are completely inappropriate conditions for cetaceans.

But — comes the inevitable argument — petting pools allow people to feed, touch and see real dolphins right up close — something they might never be able to do otherwise. My simple retort is: *So what?*

The lives and deaths of these poor dolphins are subjugated *shamefully* for our leisure and pleasure. Charmed by close contact people return again and again — willfully ignoring the harsh reality of the squalid, impoverished existence captive dolphins endure for our weekend delight. People's glowing testimonials, extolling their supposed "dolphin friends" cannot erase the suffering endured by these sensitive, far-ranging oceanic creatures. The petting pool reality is noisy, chlorinated, crowded concrete enclosures, instead of a vast pelagic realm, and a life of begging for limp dead fish, instead of the hunter's dignity to chase and choose from an array of fresh prey. In the synthetic seawater dolphins' eyes can be burned shut due to the high chlorine content — chemicals used to combat germs from the eager grasping, grubby hands of all their admirers.

Masters of the ocean realm — enslaved, stripped of all dignity, liberty and *choice*, feeding from your hand — it's sickening. *This* is the dolphins' reality — and most people don't have a clue. We are so accustomed to our established human role — *always taking* — just because we can. When people pause for a moment of reflection — and take a *critical* look around — the terrible, indisputable truth is plainly revealed.

Scientists, government agencies and conservationists are among those evincing increasing concern over the kinds of psychological and physiological harm that result from keeping cetaceans in captivity.[11] In the face of growing public discontent and scientific questioning of the supposedly infallible necessity of keeping such intelligent and far ranging wild creatures like cetaceans captive, the marine park industry has honed its PR lines accordingly, insisting their facilities are crucial to conservation efforts, scientific research and public education — all of which, they claim, translate into beneficial results for cetaceans.

A closer inspection reveals that these claims ring largely hollow. Criticisms the industry cannot refute are ignored and glossed over, while concepts like ethical consideration are derisively dismissed. Let us never forget that most captive display attractions, whatever slick PR lines they may offer, exist first and foremost to make their shareholders and executives a healthy profit. Keeping cetaceans captive is a *business* that trades in living, feeling, thinking creatures; compassion, suffering and ethical considerations do not figure in their bottom lines. To the captivity industry, dolphins are mere commodities to be caught, bought, collected, sold and when they die, replaced.

Fallacy #1: Education

The simple desire to see exotic animals (or peoples) once seemed enough to justify their domination and confinement. In modern society, purveyors have learned to cover blatant exploitation with pretensions of education, conservation and science — yet it remains exploitation just the same. In the US, the commercial display of cetaceans is legally required to "educate" the public. With this in mind, it comes as little surprise that captive facilities must loudly declare they do just this.

In fact, there is little objective evidence demonstrating the educational value of keeping marine mammals captive.[12] Dr. Toni Frohoff, an expert on human-dolphin interactions in captivity and the wild writes: '*I am not aware of any peer-reviewed research that demonstrates the educational value of dolphin-swims, or captive dolphins in general to the public. If anything, I have come to believe that a false and potentially harmful message is imparted to the public by displaying wild animals, especially marine mammals in captivity.*'[13]

Richard O'Barry, former industry trainer of the famous "Flipper" dolphins, turned long-time and dedicated cetacean advocate, writes: '*When I see a captive dolphin perform, I see a hungry dolphin desperately doing what he must in order to live. I also see people cheering and children clapping their hands and laughing about it.*'[14] As O'Barry points out, while millions of people continue flocking to marine parks to watch dolphins jump through hoops, ignorantly cheering the revolting spectacle — millions of dolphins continue to die from human fishing practices — unaware that it is *exactly* the same combination of greed and ignorance perpetuating both of these reprehensible and harmful practices.

Ripped from their natural environment, social groupings and behavior, captive cetaceans are instead forced to perform silly tricks in such a sterile and removed context, that they can hardly be said to resemble or represent their true selves or species. Normal representations of behavior, lifespan, foraging, traveling, socializing or habitat are quite simply impossible in a captive enclosure — instead there's ball-balancing, hoop jumping, triple-flips and continual, pathetic open-mouthed begging. The spectacle of dolphins or whales taking orders from smiling trainers in exchange for dead fish, or carrying grinning humans around on their backs, offers *nothing* of use or value to either humans or cetaceans. This alone is enough to cast grave doubts on the "educational value" of captive cetacean displays.

Marine biologist Giovanni Bearzi comments: '*...seeing a dolphin in a pool gives little idea of the connection between the animal — or any organism — and its natural habitat, not to mention the right of an animal to live in its own natural setting. The bond that ties an animal to its environment is not something that should be overlooked, and a dolphin out of the sea and out of its complex, fluid society can hardly represent its species.*'[15]

The Alliance of Marine Mammal Parks and Aquariums (AMMPA) assures the public that tourists attending its member marine parks leave with a new respect for the animals and interest in conservation,[16] yet it is impossible to teach respect while demonstrating disrespect. With the emphasis at marine attractions on performance and entertainment, kids would seem more likely to leave marine parks harboring dreams of becoming dolphin trainers themselves, rather than conservationists. Despite industry rhetoric, mere exposure to live captive animals does *not* instantly translate into positive action or heightened ecological awareness.[17] Rather than fostering *real* learning or caring, marine parks do the opposite — promoting public blindness towards circumstances that are cruel, demeaning and rife with suffering, and thus they perpetuate a dangerously dissociated human attitude towards those who are left voiceless in our world.

AMMPA also states that excellent relationships develop between trainers and animals, based on mutual respect and trust.[18] In captivity the relationship is invariably based on dominance and submission. Humans are the ones who drag dolphins kicking and screaming from their families; humans incarcerate them in concrete pools; humans decide when, how much or if there will be food — *humans are calling the shots*. The dolphins have *no choice*. This is *not* a relationship based on mutual respect or trust — it is an intentional deception.

Behaviors that in wild cetaceans often signal aggressive intent, such as tail slapping or jaw gaping are incorrectly portrayed as playful clowning. Over the years I have witnessed many tourists bitten by captive dolphins because they had been similarly misinformed by the "Flipper Myth" and were unable to identify these warning signs.

Shamu kisses a little girl on the cheek — and the crowd sighs at the magical moment... *No* — this is the ocean's apex predator[19] being made to resemble a mighty grizzly about as much as Yogi Bear. To portray orcas as cute sea-pandas, playfully splashing crowds and kissing kiddies is a dangerous untruth. These formidable creatures should be treated with the *respect* they are due — *they are hunters, not beggars*. What audiences are presented with at marine attractions are not actual animals, but carefully crafted corporate *images*.

Having originally conducted captive research, before switching permanently to studying wild whales, Dr. Alexandra Morton, a top expert on orca behavior, expresses concern at the way marine parks have made orcas into cuddly, cartoon-like characters: *'Considered obedient, cute, tongue-wagging performers, tame enough for petting [and] the children I observed were learning that it was a human right to enslave, harm and ridicule another creature just for fun. In a single generation the human memory of orcas as dangerous predators had faded away — and with it the respect that predators command.'* Morton points out that those who support keeping cetaceans captive often use "educational value" as one of the strongest arguments in favor of it — however, as a scientist who saw first hand the children being taught, she had to disagree: *'Some kids taunted the whales and pitched popcorn at their blowholes. When the orcas failed to heed their commands to jump, the kids called them stupid... What exactly were these children learning?'*[20]

I have myself seen exactly the same kinds of coarse disrespect directed at the Cubano Dolphins by children (and adults) at the dolphinarium, year after year — especially when the dolphins failed to respond with bright and immediate cheer to human commands. The captive industry typically presents dolphins as firmly and happily under the control of the human species, eagerly awaiting our beck and call. This does *not* teach people anything useful — but it *does* contribute to tremendous harm. Captive facilities both feed off and *encourage* public ignorance.

Many marine parks and aquariums proudly tote themselves as bastions of positive education, crowing about the millions of school children passing through their gates — but millions of people are learning the *wrong* kinds of things from these places. We learn that "habitat" is not unspoiled wilderness, but concrete and glass enclosures. We learn that dolphins and whales exist for our pleasure and entertainment. We learn that while we come and go, *their* freedom doesn't matter.

Kept carefully hidden from the public is the reality that captive institutions destroy the lives of those they cage; they destroy our understanding of who and what animals and habitats really are and they destroy the potential for *real*, mutual relationships to flourish, not only with those held captive, but also with those still wild. Author Derrick Jensen observes that such exploitation is an empty substitute for *real* relationship, but in captivity, the very notion of what constitutes a relationship is distorted into something based on dominance and submission, closing off any possibility for real — *willing* — intimacy and understanding between species. Captive encounters in no way compare to a meeting in the wild, where both participants can come and go by choice — which of course makes all the difference in the world.[21]

Instead we are left with shells — husks of wild animals in parodies of natural habitat, cut off from the interdependent web of life, in a fantasy creation where the illusion of freedom is provided. Ultimately, these captive attractions produce a terrible gulf: reinforcing the absurd (and lonely) illusion that humans are separate from and superior to all other animals. Lulled by all the glitz and glamour, people are led away from their own instinctual feelings of revulsion at what is so obviously wrong; led away from empathy for the suffering of others and instead led to trust "the experts."[22] However, many trainers, curators, directors and proponents that work within the captivity industry have little or no in-depth experience with the social lives, natural behavior, and therefore real requirements of wild, free-ranging cetaceans, and in this respect, may be as ignorant as any tourist.

Richard O'Barry points out that the problem is bigger than the particular issues surrounding any single captive dolphin — or hundred — or thousand dolphins — the problem also encompasses the millions upon millions of adults and *children*, who are *misled* by the messages inferred from such heavily distorted environments. Seeing millions upon millions of people, *especially* children flocking to sea circuses (or any circus) to cheer animal degradation and suffering *should* be cause for great worry. We need to get out of the ignorant, archaic mindset of having nature caged at our feet. It is wrong to teach our children this way, just as it is wrong to demean and ridicule dolphins and whales by turning them into beggars and circus clowns.[23]

Marine parks *desensitize* people to the plight of the dolphins right under their noses: that it isn't immediately obvious to *everyone* that there is something *deeply wrong* with these places — *proves* the detrimental results of the deception! Skeptics take one look at a dolphin or whale in a pool and *immediately* recognize the disturbing scene. One teacher who had taken her class of youngsters to a marine park wrote: '*For students who have developed admiration and compassion for whales, seeing them confined to a tank or performing tricks to entertain a crowd often leaves such children with feelings of deep sorrow. An aquarium show cannot be transformed into a sound educational experience simply by interspersing natural history trivia among the back flips...*'[24]

There is no healthy or useful educational value in seeing dolphins perform tawdry, repetitive circus tricks in concrete pools — theme parks are simply not places to learn about nature or conservation. Cetaceans doing inane tricks for dead fish cannot teach us about conservation or compassion — you *cannot* teach respect by demonstrating such *profound disrespect*.

Fallacy #2: Captivity Breeds Conservation

In response to such cutting criticism, marine parks often quote attendance figures — as if visitors become educated and environmentally active, simply by walking through turnstiles and purchasing tickets.[25] Many captive display facilities are increasingly promoting themselves as conservation centers, but in most cases such claims are at best, highly misleading. A 1999 study of aquaria belonging to the American Association of Zoos and Aquariums (AZA) found that *less than one tenth of one percent* of the facilities' operating budgets went towards conservation-related projects![26] Insisting that keeping cetaceans in captivity somehow promotes conservation is just more hollow industry PR to allay any pangs of conscience the public may suffer.

Marine parks often argue that they are involved in something positive by sheltering cetaceans from the rigors of the wild, as if the natural state were an evil to be avoided and captivity preferable. This implies wild animals need to be protected from the very surroundings that sustain them. Such a distorted and harmful misrepresentation of the natural environment fails to encourage people to respect, care for or protect it.[27] This is not conservation.

Derrick Jensen writes that those '...*who believe "nature" is cruel and animals are "entirely focused on the fight for survival" have spent too much time with capitalists and not enough time with wild animals. They are just plain wrong and guilty of the worst sort of projection.*' He continues on that this projection of cruelty upon the natural world reveals far more about the psyches of those who claim it, than it does about physical reality.[28]

Dr. Naomi Rose, working for the Humane Society of the United States (HSUS) on marine mammal protection issues has this to say on the matter: '*I see no evidence that the millions of people who visit marine parks every year are any better educated about conservation, or any more aware of environmental issues, than those who do not visit them. I certainly see no evidence that they are **doing** more for conservation...marine parks' insistence that the ocean is dangerous for wild dolphins, full of predators, pollution and parasites, creates a disincentive for people to protect it. If the wild is so inhospitable, surely dolphins are safer and happier in tanks! This is hardly an effective conservation message.*' Speaking from experience, Dr. Rose says she knows it is not necessary to experience a living animal up close to be inspired to protect it.[29]

The industry's typical line is that cetaceans need to be kept captive so people can see and touch real live animals, because this is vital to learning about conservation — which is of course nonsense. Proof that suggests otherwise is easy to find:

- No Humpback whales are held captive in concrete pools or pens so that an eager public can touch or peer at them up close, yet they are appreciated and protected — by people who will never even see one.
- Conversely, though tigers and rhinos have been displayed in zoos and circuses for many years, both are on the brink of *extinction!* Zoos and circuses did not galvanize public outcry over the killing of elephants for their ivory — rather, concerned environmental organizations rallied to make people aware.
- The UK has held no captive dolphins since 1993 — over fifteen years —and yet awareness and desire to protect cetaceans remains very strong in that country. Clearly the British public does not need

dolphinariums in order to foster care and protection for dolphins, and there is no reason to think North Americans or anyone else should be any different.

Obviously, people can be educated and inspired to support conservation in healthier ways.

Many marine parks claim their facilities educate the public about conservation threats facing cetaceans — naturally excluding themselves. Yet, far from enhancing wild populations, many dolphinariums, marine parks, swim-programs and aquariums *deplete* populations of wild cetaceans through continued captures. This is *not* conservation — rather, it is crafted rhetoric so paying customers can feel better about what they're buying into — an empty, calculated rote to promote better business.

Conservation — Or Cold-Blooded Killing?

It has been pointed out that if the captive industry were *truly* concerned about conserving dolphins in the wild, they would be dedicated to determining the effects of their captures on those left behind and to improving disruptive and stressful capture techniques. They would also willingly submit to strict national and international regulations — yet they do none of these things.[30] Marineland in Niagara Falls Canada, holds a number of beluga whales, yet visitors are not made aware of the high numbers of belugas that are killed in the Canadian arctic every year due to shamefully outdated laws.[31] To do so might invite unwanted scrutiny into the marine park's own controversial captures and practices.

In fact, a closer look reveals that far from *protecting* cetaceans, elements of the captivity industry happily works hand in hand with those who viciously murder dolphins — irrefutably proving that the real motive is *profit*.

In several areas of Japan where dolphins (rather than an increasing human population, pollution and industrialized fishing methods) are blamed for dwindling fish catches, fishermen retaliate by rounding up groups of dolphins and other small cetaceans and driving them into shallow bays, where they are brutally massacred.[32]

Despite claims of conservation interest, marine parks and aquariums failed to make the public aware of these horrific events, or take any action to stem this terrible cruelty. In the bloody carnage marine parks merely saw opportunity — to obtain exotic cetaceans at reduced cost. Aquariums and swim-with attractions began placing advance orders for specific species, sizes, ages and sexes. After being rounded up by the fishermen and penned in bays, those dolphins matching order quotas are selected and shipped to dolphinariums — while the rest are murdered with long knives and spears.[33]

Each dolphin sold to buyers from the captive industry fetches the dolphin-hunters *thousands* of dollars, rather than the comparatively meager amounts they would get for selling dolphins as meat or fertilizer. And of course the enormous payoff from selling dolphins into captivity is strong incentive for poor fishermen to perpetuate the captures and killing![34]

These reprehensible operations were shrouded in a secrecy perpetuated by the captivity industry and those profiting from the sale and slaughter of dolphins. US law conveniently ignored it all until film footage taken in 1993 made this impossible. Only then was it discovered that (among others) the Miami Seaquarium, the US Navy and Sea World, America's most popular marine park conglomerate, were involved in this despicable business — legitimizing and subsidizing the mass murder of cetaceans![35] Far from demonstrating any true conservation ethic, this cold-blooded wheeling and dealing reveals a revolting lack of concern for cetacean welfare in favor of a purely profit-driven agenda. Marine park money *creates and fuels* incentive to perpetuate the capture, killing and selling of cetaceans, and each person walking through the gates of facilities holding cetaceans captured in this way unknowingly supports the direct and indirect killing of dolphins and whales.

As international outcry and attention narrows one avenue, the captive industry merely turns elsewhere to find new areas to exploit, where poor fishermen are more than eager to capture and kill dolphins for industry dollars. Meanwhile, *real* conservationists try to encourage alternatives to such dolphin hunts to generate income for poor fishing communities, like the development of responsible wild dolphin and whale watching tours.[36]

Representatives of the captive industry have also actively lobbied to *prevent* the adoption of global measures to regulate the hunting of dolphins and other small cetaceans — hunts which kill many thousands each year. If implemented, such regulations could interfere with or curtail the industry's ability to continue capturing wild cetaceans, and because of such obstructive actions, dolphins currently receive no global protection, leaving them vulnerable to exploitation of all kinds.[37] Rather than promoting *true*, life-saving conservation — the captivity industry has repeatedly and actively sought to weaken laws which protect cetaceans, to better exploit them to their own advantage.

Continuing down the list of excuses, marine parks and aquariums often proclaim the value of captive breeding — as if it were a positive or useful thing. Bottlenose dolphins are not endangered (any more than most things living on this planet, including you). The true reason for breeding cetaceans in captivity is to produce, at no additional expense, the next generation of dolphins and whales to be used for entertainment and profit.

Marine park industry officials are almost universally averse to the idea of releasing captive-born cetaceans back into the wild. However, if captive breeding were actually part of a conservation strategy, then the industry would *foster* research on the rehabilitation and reintroduction of captive cetaceans, rather than adamantly opposing it. At present no captive facilities are engaged in breeding the most critically endangered cetacean species.[38] Trying to keep any of these fading species for captive breeding would only likely hasten the demise of their dwindling numbers (the result of habitat destruction, pollution and entanglements in fishing nets). Efforts to save the most highly endangered cetaceans would be better placed by protecting their natural ecosystems.[39]

Marine parks like to tell the public that because cetaceans are breeding in their tanks — they must be happy. One would do well to consider the fact that among human beings, children are born even amid the most miserable and adverse conditions. The industry also often implies that if a dolphin is born in captivity rather than captured from the wild, that the arguments leveled against captivity no longer apply. The misfortune of being born into a life of oppression and slavery does not exempt someone from deserving freedom and liberty.

Strandings

In certain instances, live dolphins strand and need temporary care before being returned to the sea. A few marine parks and aquariums fund rescue and aid for stranded marine mammals, and use this to help justify their existence. However, strandings of live cetaceans are quite rare, comprising less than one percent of marine mammal strandings, and of these, less than five percent are estimated to survive rehabilitation.[40] However, it has been noted that the PR benefits of such endeavors are likely well worth the investment. Additionally, exotic or desirable species may be retained for display — at little cost and with little government oversight.[41]

In the US there are some very good stranding-rehabilitation facilities that do not involve the public display of cetaceans and in the UK, rescues of stranded cetaceans are conducted by dedicated organizations — without any need for performing captives. Contrary to what the captivity industry likes to imply, live cetacean displays are simply *not* required in order to garner support for causes which help them. It's ridiculous to insist that helping cetaceans simultaneously necessitates keeping them captive — the good work of hundreds of non-profit conservation, welfare and protection organizations around the globe disproves this a thousand times over. The primary drive behind *real* conservation is *care*, while the primary drive behind the captivity industry is *profit*.

Critical scrutiny reveals these flimsy claims of "education" and "conservation" as efforts to dupe the paying public into feeling reasonably justified about participating in activities that are increasingly controversial and ethically suspect.

Fallacy #3: (Superfluous) Science

Scientific research is also sometimes cited as a necessity for keeping cetaceans captive. Recent, objective scientific review of these claims reveals that much *current* research performed on captive dolphins has very limited value. Behavioral research must inevitably be skewed, as cetaceans are *unable* to demonstrate natural behavior in captive conditions, while increasing numbers of wild studies are reaping far superior results through techniques that no longer require captive animals.[42] The increasing sophistication of long- and short-term studies involving free-ranging animals and the greater relevance of data from these studies further throw the justification for research on captive cetaceans into serious doubt.[43]

Research on cetacean visual, auditory and echolocation systems has largely been conducted by the US Navy,[44] driven by controversial military interests. Even captive research experiments on fishing net detection and avoidance may have limited value, as both marine conditions and ambient noise levels differ dramatically in concrete pools and the absence and distraction of other cetaceans, marine life and natural weather conditions may seriously skew valid results. Studies conducted on *wild* harbor porpoises demonstrate such work is feasible and contributes more accurate and useful data to the serious problems of cetacean net entanglement.[45]

A recent study concluded that disease research on captive dolphins cannot be usefully applied in the wild, as the artificial environment and diet of captives alters their blood chemistry. Reproductive, behavioral and dietary information gathered from captives likewise can have little bearing or accuracy if applied to free-ranging cetaceans, as the artificial lives of captives, and the pressures they respond to, are so profoundly distorted.[46] Much veterinary, anatomical, physiological, pathological and reproductive research is self-serving — utilized by the industry in dealing with its inventory of captives and translating into very little practical use for wild populations.[47] At the 2003 Society for Marine Mammalogy's biennial conference, 469 studies dealing with aspects of cetacean biology were presented. Only four percent of these studies were the result of work with captive animals and of these, more than a third were conducted through scientific institutions that are not open to the public. There were no abstracts submitted by the larger marine parks (such as Sea World).[48]

When cetacean experts receive funding from the captive industry, there is always the danger that studies guided or funded by such institutions may tailor their findings in a way which supports a pro-captivity position. Findings that disagree with industry agendas are often dismissed or ignored and facts that might stir criticism are omitted; rationalizations are supplied, harsh facts are softened, and profits are protected.

There are some who believe that *anything* can be sanctified in the name of "Science" — as if it were some great occidental god, demanding unquestioning faith; a god in whose illustrious name horrific atrocities and suffering are justified and absolved. Yet the quest for scientific discovery must not be allowed to pave over or erase all moral consideration. To court science without ethics or heart is to court the demise of our very humanity.

Cetaceans got by just fine for fifty million years without anybody *needing* to hold them in tanks and study them. The best conservation gesture our overly aggressive species can make is to leave them where they belong and have evolved to live.

High Captive Mortality

Sea World proudly states that it provides the best veterinary care available for its animals. Naturally — businesses always take action to protect their investments. Yet despite such corporate loving care, many captive cetaceans still routinely fail to live as long as their counterparts in the wild, as demonstrated by the industry continually stealing more dolphins from wild populations to replace those dying in their tanks, pools and pens. Veterinary care for cetaceans remains relatively primitive and many captive cetaceans die before problems can be diagnosed or treated.[49]

In the supposed "safety" of concrete pools, with reliable meals, no predators, no fishing nets and no storms, many cetaceans *still* fail to live appropriate life spans. "State of the art" veterinary care and medical techniques have not spared captives from various parasites, ingesting toxins and even entanglement in nets.[50] These deaths aren't considered failures by the industry, but as routine operating expenses.

Studies have revealed that the annual survival rates and life expectancies from *free-ranging* dolphins (and orcas) were *persistently higher* than those of captives.[51] In captivity, dolphins that struggle into their twenties tend to be considered "old" by the industry. However, cetacean scientists are finding that wild bottlenose dolphins can live into their *forties* and even *fifties*.[52] Definitive data on the average life span of wild dolphins requires a study to follow an entire population from birth to death and the forty or so years scientists have been studying free-ranging bottlenose dolphins simply hasn't been long enough to do this. For such long-lived species, on-going, long-term wild monitoring studies are crucial to determine the species' true life span. The longer we observe them, the longer we find wild dolphins live; the bar keeps getting pushed back, further delineating the discrepancy between wild and captive life spans.

Dr. Naomi Rose of HSUS states: *'At least 50% of calves* born in captivity die soon after birth. When a captive-born calf dies, a marine park spokesperson will often say that high infant mortality is normal − and so it is − in the wild. But what causes high infant mortality in captivity? What kills captive adult bottlenose dolphins (and other cetacean species) before they reach their maximum potential life span? ...Proponents of captivity cannot have it both ways: captivity cannot both protect dolphins from the 'rigors and hazards' of the wild and yet be excused from being unable to improve on the species' natural survivorship. Something about captivity clearly harms these ocean creatures.'*[53] The industry is hypocritical in its reasoning, on one hand, claiming tanks are so much safer than life in the wild − and on the other, despite decades of veterinary care, repeatedly failing to improve survivorship. Cetaceans in captivity still die young on a regular basis with little or no warning. Dr. Rose offers a likely explanation for many captive deaths: that they result from persistent levels of stress through unnatural confinement and social groupings. Stress in mammals can lead to immune-system suppression and increased susceptibility to infection and disease.[54]

The life spans of captive orca whales are an even more glaring disgrace. A US study determined that orcas survive an average of only thirteen years from the date of their capture,[55] yet long term-studies of wild orca whales have led researchers to determine that males can live up to fifty or sixty years and females can live up to eighty or even ninety.[56] The Center for Whale Research, which carries out annual censuses of Puget Sound orcas, reported

---

* A common term for infant cetaceans.

in 1994 that nearly sixty-five percent of the population were over *forty-five* years of age. Needless to say, it is extremely rare to find Marine Mammal Inventory Reports which attribute "old age" as the cause of death in marine parks.[57] The industry's history is even worse with other cetacean species like pilot whales, who may live up to fifty years in the wild but in captivity have been found to have a life-expectancy of a mere 4.2 years.[58]

Many statistics on captive cetacean longevity, survivorship and mortality have been collected from US Marine Mammal Inventory Reports. However it should be noted that as grim as this information is, the MMIR may reflect inaccurately *biased* data because the information it contains is provided by the *facilities themselves* and increasing criticism over the captivity controversy provides a strong incentive to misreport. Staff at marine parks and swim-facilities have allegedly been fired for refusing to repress incriminating evidence. One way the industry has tried to subdue negative statistics is by refusing to report cetaceans that died during or within three days of capture (when mortality is highest)[59] and those that die stillborn or within the first few days, weeks or months of birth (again, when mortality is high). Such important omissions artificially inflate statistics on the survivorship of captive cetaceans. Other marine mammal scientists have pointed out that *all* sources of mortality should be included when making comparisons with free-ranging animals.[60]

Whatever excuses, explanations or inaccuracies marine park spokes persons may offer, statistics reveal an *obvious,* unnaturally high cetacean mortality rate in captivity. Despite this poor track record, it is likely that US facilities represent better husbandry and higher survival rates than other countries that lack formalized standards and regulations for keeping cetaceans captive.

The Real Issue

Even if all captive conditions were superb and illness and premature deaths were unheard of, when one looks at the *quality* of incarcerated life, there can really be *no* comparison between liberty in the ocean and a life behind bars. *Longevity* and *liberty* are two *very* different things! A recent scientific study for the International Marine Mammal Association, comparing the survival rates of captive and free-ranging cetaceans, concluded: '*Survival rates merely provide a measure of an animal's life-span, but not a measure of its "quality of life"...It is reasonable to suggest that humans would choose freedom over confinement, given the choice and we have no reason to suspect that wild animals would choose any differently.*'[61]

Capture

In the make-believe world of marine parks and swim-with attractions, no mention is made to the public of how many dolphins and whales were forcibly stolen away from their communities in the ocean, in order to stock their tanks, pens and pools. Certain persons that once worked in the dolphin-capturing business have come forward to expose the truth behind this secretive and violent procedure, which the industry is so eager to suppress. Film footage shows families of dolphins being mercilessly chased down in roaring speedboats and surrounded by nets. In the resulting terror and confusion, dolphins may be injured or even killed, as they charge and tangle in the nets, trying to escape. Dolphin "wranglers" leap into the water and wrestle their chosen quarry into stretchers before hoisting them onto waiting boats. Young, unmarked females (who may still be swimming at their mothers' sides) are usually preferred. Struggling and screaming in abject terror, they are wrenched from the water and all they've ever known, never to see friends, family or home again.

All methods of capturing cetaceans are invasive, stressful and potentially lethal.[62] It is hardly surprising that so many dolphins die of shock before or shortly after they reach the concrete pools or pens for which they are destined. A study by US government researchers discovered that bottlenose dolphin mortality rates increased *six-fold* after capture (and took thirty-five to forty-five days to return to normal). The death rate similarly spikes when dolphins are transported between facilities.[63] According to US Marine Mammal Inventory Reports, between forty and fifty percent of the dolphins currently held in US marine parks were wild-caught and the US captive dolphin population is still not self-sustaining.[64]

Cuba in particular continues to be a major supplier of dolphins on the international market, many of which are used to furnish swim-programs. Once trained, such dolphins can fetch in thousands of dollars a day at Caribbean swim-parks where dolphins are in effect mauled to death by tourists all day. It is largely North American and European tourists responsible for this trade in sentient, suffering beings — people who willingly pay a premium both at home and abroad, to force their company on dolphins — and it is they who are *responsible* for the ever-increasing number of tourist destinations holding dolphins captive.

Dr. Guillermo Lopez, formerly chief veterinarian at the Havana Aquarium has overseen the capture of over fifty dolphins, sold to attractions in Europe, Canada and Latin America and has witnessed at least five dolphins die in his nets during captures — including a baby. Necropsy showed the infant had died from a heart attack — *sheer terror* had killed it. Another dolphin lost an eye as it was hauled into the boat. Dr. Lopez now speaks out against captivity.[65] Deaths during capture are a grim part of the business and orca catchers have admitted to disposing of the bodies of whales drowned in their nets by wrapping their bodies in chains, slitting their bellies open, filling them with rocks and trying to sink them in order to avoid controversial criticism.[66]

When the famous oceanographic explorer Jacques Cousteau and his team first captured wild dolphins to study in the early 1970s, they noted how traumatized these creatures were upon being removed from the water. In an acute state of shock, the dolphins trembled and shook, uttering piercing cries. Cousteau wrote: '*It appeared that the dolphin could not accept the fact that he had been stopped, seized; that he had lost his freedom. ...We learned, that the event of capture is an enormous shock to a dolphin, both physically and psychologically.*'[67] Over and over Cousteau and his team watched in despair, as dolphin after dolphin died, in their tanks. Eventually it was decided that dolphins should be studied only at sea — where they belong, rather than sacrificing numerous innocents to satisfy human curiosity. With unusual compassion and astuteness for his time, Cousteau wrote: '*It is our opinion that present studies of intelligence and the sounds of dolphins are violated by the conditions in which they are carried out. Captivity represents a dramatic handicap. The shock experienced by these sensitive animals at the trauma of capture, disturbs them profoundly. ...Captivity, no matter how well intentioned, is no life for a dolphin.*'[68]

In studying the intricate social bonds comprising dolphin society, scientists are realizing that removing individual cetaceans from wild populations can have a substantial negative impact on the survival of the remaining group members.[69] Dr. Naomi Rose of HSUS reports: '*Little effort, if any, has been made by cetacean capture operators to learn what effects removing juveniles may have on the families and social groups left behind. ... A study from 1995...strongly indicat[es] that the capture process and subsequent adjustment to captivity is traumatic and harmful. Having watched videos of captures, this does not surprise me — the violent process involves nets, ropes, loud noise, extraordinarily rough handling, occasionally the death of companions and of course the abrupt removal from all that is familiar.*'[70] Cetacean biologist Dr. Toni Frohoff warns that because of dolphins' complex, interdependent social ties, the process of harassing an entire group to remove *even one* specific individual can result in physiological stress, injury or death of other dolphins, creating substantially damaging effects about which we know little.[71]

Regarding the capture of cetaceans, scientists reporting for The World Conservation Union (IUCN) have stated: '*Removal of live cetaceans from the wild, for captive display and/or research, is equivalent to incidental or deliberate killing...*[72] It has proven extremely difficult to document, much less regulate the extensive international trade in live dolphins. Nearly a hundred scientists working with the IUCN have recommended that dolphin captures should not be undertaken without first instating a rigorous program of research and monitoring to assess wild populations (something which cannot be achieved quickly or inexpensively), which then needs to be reviewed by an independent group of scientists before *any* captures are made. Thus far, those capturing and selling dolphins have shown little willingness to invest any substantial resources to assure that these captures will not harm or deplete the populations they are stolen from. Instead, entrepreneurs usually take advantage of lax or non-existent regulations in small island states or less-developed countries displaying scant concern for the effects of captures.[73] Public response to the capture of wild dolphins often results in tremendous controversy and international media coverage, which in recent years has curbed captures in certain areas. As facts emerge regarding high mortality rates and the potentially devastating effects of captures on wild populations, captures have been prohibited or severely restricted in some countries.[74]

However, so long as there is demand, there will be suppliers. At present, dolphins are still taken from many places including: the Bahamas, South Asia, Cuba, Japan and Siberia.[75] Asia and the South Pacific are becoming increasingly problematic, illustrated distressingly in the politically unstable Solomon Islands, where in 2003 about a hundred dolphins were captured by foreign entrepreneurs, with the intent to sell them off to various captive facilities. Twenty-eight of these dolphins (a number of which have already died) were sold to a popular swim attraction (Parque Nizuc) in Cancun, Mexico.[76]

Swimming with Captive Dolphins

Growing in popularity are tourist attractions, often in tropical locales,* where for a sizable fee, people can interact with captive dolphins (often referred to as "dolphin encounters" or 'swim-with-the-dolphin programs"). Several times each day, the dolphins' pens or pools are invaded by groups of excited tourists, each paying between one and three hundred dollars for an approximately half-hour stint in the water. The ever-increasing numbers of dolphins kept for such purposes have become victims of our consumer culture's unceasing demand for novel entertainment.

Dolphin-swim attractions are making a *killing*, as each captive dolphin is

* Some captive dolphin-swim attractions cater primarily to cruise ship passengers.

capable of pulling in hundreds or even thousands of tourist dollars daily. Advertisements for dolphin-swim-encounters typically come complete with rapturous endorsements from fawning tourists and feature photos of bronzed youngsters grinning and hugging "smiling dolphins," presenting a powerfully seductive fantasy world.

To ensure that everyone has a good time and gets their "money's worth," *swim-with* dolphins are often trained (in addition to the usual pathetic clowning) to "kiss" tourists, hold still, so they can be touched and fondled and of course, are trained to push people around in the water or pull them around on their dorsal fins. For each of these things, the dolphin receives a fish. Because of this system, *swim-with* dolphins tend not to be much interested in enthusiastic tourists at all — but are simply responding to the trainer's commands, while keeping their eyes *fixed* on the fish bucket at all times. As I've clearly observed myself over the years, this is almost invariably the case — however much people might wish it were otherwise.

Dr. Rose, in carefully observing a dolphin-swim-interaction at Orlando's Discovery Cove (a swim-with spin off of Sea World), writes: '*He* [the dolphin] *was focused entirely on his trainer, watching her carefully no matter what the participants were doing or saying. For her part, the trainer kept up a constant high-energy patter, very similar to a magician who attempts to distract her audience from what her hands are doing so they will not witness the reality behind the trick. I was most disturbed by the attitude of the trainers toward the animals. Trainers often know little about wild dolphins... They typically treat the dolphins as they would slightly mischievous, but mentally disabled young children, with a bright cheeriness that condescends and has little sensitivity to the potential abilities that dolphins might have. There is no sense that a dolphin in their care is a fully competent, mature being who, in the wild, would be perfectly capable and self-sufficient... The relationship is one of dominance and submission, however benign. My sense is that the trainer loves her charge, but does not respect him.'* [77]

The public's infamous love affair with dolphins is largely one-sided — but as long as the lucrative façade holds, people continue swarming to these places, oblivious to the fact that the dolphins are only involved because they are hungry and because they have *no choice*. It seems to me we have a word — an ugly word, for those coerced into enduring unwanted physical contact — *forced prostitution*. These places don't educate — they *exploit* — *both* people and dolphins. The popular dream is an illusion — a lucrative lie.

In 1990 there were only four dolphin-swim enterprises in the US, but by 2001, there were more than fourteen, and by 2003, approximately eighteen facilities offered some variation of interactive dolphin encounter in the US.[78] The profitable popularity of US dolphin-swim attractions has set a bad international example, creating an irresponsible incentive and encouraging entrepreneurs in developing nations to imitate them. Mexico has nearly twenty swim-with enterprises. The Dominican Republic has three, Cuba, the Bahamas and Jamaica, all at least two; Venezuela, Columbia, Honduras, Anguilla, Curacao and Tortola all have at least one; while Aruba and The Cayman Islands are all considering opening captive dolphin-swim attractions. Other ventures continue springing up across tourist-frequented areas of Asia and the South Pacific.

Most swim attractions hold wild-caught dolphins, and in order to supply this rising demand created by tourists for more dolphins to swim with, wild populations are continually exploited. Unregulated, substandard conditions are common,[79] as are reports of dolphins typically being overworked, overcrowded and underfed. The saga of the Cubano Dolphins is just one example. Conditions at such interactive captive attractions are inherently stressful and inhumane for the dolphins and potentially dangerous for visitors, as the safety of the participants in these programs cannot be assured.[80]

Studies conducted on captive interactive programs have observed stress-related behaviors in the dolphins involved when in the presence of swimmers, that are related to potentially long-term negative physiological states.[81] Dr. Toni Frohoff began observing and studying captive swim programs in the early 1990s and writes: *'The educational benefits of these interative programs are highly questionable. I must say that after years of watching these programs, they look like little more than glorified petting zoos, using exotic dolphins instead of domestic farm animals. I doubt that people will be any more inspired to work for marine mammal protection after participating in these programs than to become vegetarians after visiting a petting zoo. Not only does the public learn little, if anything, about the* real *life of dolphins, but they actually go home* misinformed, *thinking that the tricks they saw are representive of how dolphins behave in the wild. Finally, captive programs perpetuate the problems facing wild dolphins by implying it is alright to touch and feed dolphins and to treat them like toys or playthings who exist for human amusement.'*[82]

There are further problems inherent with public swim-with attractions. Many interactive programs experience particular trouble with adult male dolphins behaving in an aggressive or sexually inappropriate manner with guests[83] (often resulting in the dolphin's isolation). This is why females are so often preferred over males for swims and one of the reasons why the increase of their capture and removal for swim programs may have particularly harmful consequences for wild populations.

Despite popular public perception, swimming with captive dolphins places humans in potential danger. Even trainers with extensive experience, who are familiar with the dolphins they are working with have been seriously injured[84] (and in the case of captive orcas, have even been killed[85]). Dr. Frohoff is one of many cetacean experts with serious concerns about interactive programs involving dolphins. She writes: *'I have personally witnessed many more injuries than those reported... I have even seen people get bitten by dolphins at petting/feeding pools. Swimmers have been hospitalized for internal injuries, serious wounds and broken bones following 'attacks' by captive dolphins.... Dolphins are not vicious, merely wild. Any wild animal, especially one forced into artificial confinement, must be respected for the animal he or she is — not for how he or she can serve us. When this respect is absent from the relationship, both people and animals can easily get hurt. The very nature of these swim programs prohibits the possibility of developing such a respect. ...When dolphins exhibit signs of agitation or stress around swimmers, the swimmer typically did not recognize them or laughed them off and chose to misinterpret them as signs of fun. Even obvious signals used by dolphins to indicate warning or frustrations to each other (such as open-jaw threats and charges) would frequently go unheeded. Typically, the swimmers would continue doing what they were doing and then be stunned — even offended — if the dolphin forcefully bumped or bit them ...startling results were found not in the communication between the two species, but rather in the extent of miscommunication that was occurring, especially on the part of the swimmers... It was as if they expected them to behave like "Flipper."*[86]

No matter how hard the industry works to promote a glossy image of happy dolphins eagerly attending to paddling humans, the fact remains that swimmer safety cannot be assured and the risks are very real. But encouraged by marine park propaganda and fooled by the popular and entrenched image of "Flipper," people just want to dive right in and hug dolphins, forgetting (or completely unaware) that these are not smiling, peaceful pets, but wild, willful, unpredictable, powerful and potentially deadly predators.

But we *love* our dolphins, comes the inevitable protest from trainers and tourists alike, when critics insist such attractions should be outlawed. For the record, I really do believe that many individuals working as staff and trainers in the captive industry do have an absolutely genuine, albeit *misguided* fondness for the cetaceans they try to care for. Obviously dolphins are beautiful and alluring and marvelous to get close to — but that's hardly the point. Just because we enjoy their company to a fault doesn't mean we are necessarily doing right by them.

Dr. Frohoff writes: *'Educators say that people protect what they love. But if we love dolphins so much, how do we justify taking from them the very things we value most in our own lives: freedom and family? If the bond between humans and dolphins is so sacred then how do we justify exploiting it in such harmful ways?'*[87] Removing a dolphin's freedom and ability to choose whether or not to engage in human company is *not* respect, nor is it love.

Dolphins are not servile spirits, but sensuous, complex, sometimes violent, willful and *wild* creatures who do not belong in pens and pools, being forced to share cramped enclosures with starry-eyed humans. *How*, I wonder, can anyone *really* believe that dolphins could be happier jumping through hoops, taking orders from trainers, endlessly towing people around for rides in pens or pools and eating dead fish?

Some claim that dolphins kept in pens could just jump over the fences any time and escape, but they don't because they really do love swimming with people. As it happens, dolphins *do* occasionally escape and without fail, efforts are immediately mobilized to round them up again. For reasons that are not entirely understood, dolphins are notoriously reluctant to leap over nets, and whether encircled for capture, slaughter or study, it is a rare event, so this can be no useful indicator of contentment.

Popular Fantasy — Bursting the Bubble

Captive dolphin-swim-encounters put a price tag on and make a mockery of something invaluable: the experience of making contact with an intelligent, non-human sentience. When a *wild* dolphin *chooses* to approach and engage in a moment of *actual* communion, it is a great and rare gift of choice and trust. Though unscrupulous business entities may capture, package and sell a pathetic and pale facsimile, the *real* thing can *never* be bought. Such gifts can only be *given* — they cannot be *taken* by force. The delicate, deliberate entwining of interspecies intelligences is not something to *buy* and *consume* between cotton candy, a roller coaster ride and a cheeseburger.

Dr. Rose sums the hype and hypocrisy behind dolphin-swim attractions in this way: *'To me, it appears that the people who support captivity cooperate willingly in their own deception, accepting the architectural illusions as an adequate facsimile of reality. I wonder if their desire to be close to dolphins is so strong that it overwhelms the niggling realization that confining these free spirits is wrong. The very essence that attracts them to these mysterious beings has been confined, modified, controlled and homogenized in captivity. By packaging the magic and making it readily available, marine parks and aquariums seem to blind visitors (let alone trainers, veterinarians, and curators) ...allowing themselves to be manipulated because they want so much to believe that their desire to be with a dolphin is reciprocated.'*[88]

The dolphin slave trade is based on supply and demand. As long as there is a profit to be made, dolphins will be used and abused and will continue to suffer in captivity. Cetacean advocate Richard O'Barry states: "The best way to help is simple: *Don't buy a ticket.*" Speak out — and share what you know. Marine parks and dolphin-swim-attractions thrive on tourist dollars, without which, they will go *extinct*. Each person who walks through a marine park's gates is helping to finance the continued misery and confinement of the dolphins and whales held within — as well as those in the wild who will inevitably replace them when they die. We should be *ashamed* to seek and accept the sacrifice of such beautiful creatures for our own superficial entertainment and gratification.

"Therapeutic" Use of Captive Dolphins

Increasing numbers of captive facilities all over the world are capitalizing on using dolphins for supposedly therapeutic purposes. People suffering from Down's syndrome, cerebral palsy, cancer, autism and other physical and psychological ailments go to these places, seeking healing and hope. While its true that for humans, sharing close company with dolphins is often a wondrous and deeply exhilarating experience, the fact remains: *no credible scientific evidence exists to substantiate the claim that spending time in an enclosure with captive dolphins has lasting healing results.*[89]

However, "dolphin-assisted therapy" (or DAT, as its been dubbed) is proving not only popular, but exceedingly profitable, as distressed people pay large sums of money to the dolphins' owners for "treatment,"[90] two week sessions reputedly running as high as $7,850 USD — not including air fare and accommodations.[91]

Dr. Betsy Smith, one of the initial developers of "dolphin-assisted therapy" no longer works with captive dolphins for ethical reasons. Dr. Smith questioned removing sentient beings from their natural habitat and over time she began to see that these places were capitalizing on vulnerable people, using vulnerable dolphins, while trying to justify their exploitation under the therapy pretext. She writes: '*People profiting from dolphin-assisted therapy do not wish to assemble or sponsor double-blind studies needed to test my exploratory research and no scientific evidence exists that dolphin-assisted therapy is more effective than traditional or other adjunct therapies.*' Dr. Smith ended her therapy research with captive dolphins, after assuring herself that there were many other therapies, including work with domesticated animals providing success stories without imprisoning dolphins.[92]

Dr. Bernard Rimland, director of the Autism Research Institute of San Diego also insists that: *'There is no scientific evidence at all that using dolphins is helpful. The reputable people in the field simply feel the kids like the dolphins and it's a recreational thing.'*[93] A recent scientific study focusing on the possible effects of dolphin-assisted therapy concluded: *'the results of the synthesis do not support the notion that using interactions with dolphins is any more effective than the other reinforcers for improving child learning or social-emotional development. ...Claims of the effectiveness of using dolphins as a procedure for improving the behaviors of young children with disabilities are therefore not supported by available research evidence. ...Currently, there is not enough research evidence available to support the use of this practice.'*[94]

Another study on the use of dolphins for therapeutic purposes, found that the positive results sometimes reported did not necessarily persist and that interacting with dolphins appeared no more effective than using domesticated animals — though far more expensive and carrying much higher risks. This study found a plethora of serious threats to the validity of DAT and similarly concluded: *'the current evidence for the efficacy of Dolphin Assisted Therapy can at best be described as thoroughly unconvincing.'*[95] Yet another recent scientific paper, after reiterating the abundant evidence for injuries sustained by participants in DAT programs, concluded: *'Despite DAT's extensive promotion to the general public, the evidence that it produces enduring improvements in the core symptoms of any psychological disorder is nil. ...there is little reason to believe that DAT is a legitimate therapy or that it constitutes much more than entertainment.'*[96]

Holding dolphins captive for "therapeutic" purposes is just as harmful and wrong as keeping them captive to swim with regular, paying tourists or to amuse crowds at any dolphinarium. There is no need to imprison wildlife to benefit humans. Alternative therapies utilizing high-tech audio-visual virtual representations of dolphins, which can be combined with hydrotherapy, are being investigated, while pet therapy using domestic animals offers better-proven, much more cost-efficient therapeutic help for those who are ill, without harming dolphins.

Positive Changes

Both the idea and practice of keeping of cetaceans captive for entertainment and profit went largely unchallenged for a long time. But as news of traumatic captures, high mortality and the more obvious signs of suffering are revealed and *recognized*, public attitude and ethic in some quarters is changing for the better as reflected in legislative and regulatory initiatives. Though swim-programs are mushrooming in some areas, captive facilities are being closed and outlawed in others.

At the leading edge of this enlightened wave of change, the state of Victoria in Australia in 1985 banned the capture of cetaceans. The state of Queensland in Australia followed suit in 1994. A report by the national Australian Senate Select Committee on Animal Welfare, entitled *Dolphins and Whales in Captivity* stated: *'Many people concerned with animal welfare now question whether humans are entitled to exploit animals and act in a manner which will cause animals to suffer... Critics consider that, even if oceanaria could show that profit and recreation were not the primary motives of oceanaria, the use of captive cetaceans for education and research is not only of dubious benefit, but is also morally questionable. ...The benefit of oceanaria for human and cetacean are no longer sufficient to justify the adverse effects of captivity.'* Similarly, the 1990 Bellerive Symposium on Whales and Dolphins in Captivity, held in Geneva Switzerland, concluded: *'Whales and dolphins are self-aware beings that routinely make decisions and choices about the details of their lives. They are entitled to freedom. Imprisoning them in captivity is quite simply, wrong.'*

In the 1970s, Britain had over thirty different dolphinariums — by 1993, after years of increasing public outcry over substandard facilities, there were *none* left, and this remains the case today. A 1996 MORI public opinion poll stated that up to eighty-five percent of UK citizens opposed keeping cetaceans in captivity.[97]

The Nicaraguan government formalized measures to ban the capture and use of dolphins for commercial display in 2003, while in Cyprus, importing cetaceans has been banned. Mexico, Thailand, Australia, China (including Hong Kong) Indonesia, Laos, The Philippines, Malaysia and Singapore are among nations that have banned or issued moratoriums on the capture of cetaceans in their waters. Italy has also outlawed all swim-with and interactive programs, while in 2005, Chile and Costa Rica both prohibited the public display of most marine mammal species, as well as their import, export and capture from the wild.[98] New Zealand's Conservation Minister stated her opposition to keeping captive cetaceans, specifically directed at the nation's remnant captive display facility in Napier. The Minister stated that she *'welcomes the demise of 'theme parks' where captive dolphins perform tricks in concrete tanks.'*[99]

No dolphin captures have taken place in US waters since 1993, when three were captured by the Chicago Shedd Aquarium, amid intense public outcry. Since then there have been no further capture permits granted in US waters. Between 1990 and 1998 at least twenty North American marine attractions and amusement parks permanently closed or discontinued keeping cetaceans.[100] In 1992 the state of South Carolina became the first US State to outlaw the display of wild caught and captive cetaceans. In 2002, the Hawaiian Island of Maui issued a unanimous county council vote to ban the public display of captive cetaceans, declaring cetaceans: *'highly intelligent and highly sensitive … the council also finds that the exhibition of captive cetaceans leads to distressed living conditions for these animals'*.[101]

These kinds of new regulations are forcing the captivity industry to find other countries — sadly, often those that are in political disarray where the people are destitute and desperate, where legislation on marine mammals is weak or non-existent and where authorities are permissive. Yet heartening news comes from strife-torn Haiti, where in June of 2004, six more captive dolphins were released back into the wild by Richard and Helene O'Barry. This timely release (four more of these dolphins already having died in the tiny, shallow pen holding them) was overseen by Yves-Andre Wainwright, Haiti's Secretary of the Environment. Having deemed the conditions under which the dolphins were held as inhumane, Wainwright commented as the nets were cut and the dolphins swam to freedom: "*In Haiti we want to promote eco-tourism and not tourists who come to see animals who are suffering. We have already, so much suffering in Haiti. We do not want to promote that kind of tourism.*"[102]

As the public becomes aware of the truth, our ethics and policies are evolving. A recent poll found that 68% of Canadians feel it is inappropriate to keep whales and dolphins in captivity.[103] Concerned citizens are taking a critical look at marine parks — authors, school children, teachers, homemakers, scientists, politicians, young, old — and increasingly disturbed by something they recognize as *wrong*, demanding these shamefully exploitative practices be brought to a halt.

Rehabilitation & Release

As public attitude evolves and dolphinariums, marine parks and aquariums close down, the question has been raised over what to do with captive cetaceans made suddenly superfluous to the industry. In the past, the only likely options would have been euthanasia or transfer to another attraction. But despite rabid opposition by much of the captivity industry, an indisputably superior option has been demonstrated to exist for dolphins — rehabilitation and release back into the wild.

In 1990 two captive male bottlenose dolphins were rehabilitated and released back into the Tampa Bay area where they were originally captured.

More than twelve years of subsequent sightings confirmed the dolphins' successful reintegration back into their wild community.[104] Overseen by top American cetacean scientists, Dr. Randy Wells and Dr. Ken Norris, this release project, though not the first of its kind, did much to help establish the success of such endeavors to the scientific community. Since then, other successful cetacean release projects have followed.[105]

A more recent release project involved two bottlenose dolphins that had been abandoned in a tiny dirty pool by their Venezuelan owners in Guatemala when authorities demanded paperwork. Vaunted as "therapeutic" to swim with, the two dolphins had been illegally used as attractions in a traveling show, and then had been left to die. The pair hadn't eaten in five days when Ric and Helene O'Barry, members of the World Society for the Protection of Animals got to the scene. The two dolphins were moved into sea pens at an appropriate coastal location to regain their health and survival skills. In early 2001, after two months of rehabilitation, the dolphins were catching their own fish and after a final health check, were successfully released.[106]

The rehabilitation, release and successful re-adaptation of formerly captive dolphins have made headlines around the world. This change in events and options for captives also forced the cetacean display industry to sit up and pay attention. Members of the captive industry conferred to evaluate the concept of returning dolphins to the wild, and grudgingly admitted that with the correct preparation and conduct it could likely be done.[107]

In reviewing the idea of releasing dolphins, coldly referred to as "surplus" or "un-wanted captive stocks" industry representatives had the *gall* to ask if returning dolphins to the wild was actually *appropriate*. The only sane course to conclude is that as a concept, returning dolphins back to the wild must be more *appropriate* than hunting them down and ripping them away from their families and communities for corporate profit or public entertainment! For the executives, veterinarians, trainers and researchers employed by the captive industry, salaries, careers, reputations and research subjects often *hinge* on holding cetaceans captive — so a skewed and callous spin from this intensely biased direction is not unexpected. The economic motive in the industry's opposition to rehabilitation and releasing of captive cetaceans should not be ignored, as release represents a positive alternative likely to increase the general public's objection to captivity.[108]

The industry has used the excuse that since bottlenose dolphins (the species most commonly held captive) are not considered endangered, there is no compelling reason to consider returning any back to their natural habitats. (*Why*, does a species have to be about to vanish from the face of the planet before anyone sees fit to do something about it?) Ironically, the industry often justifies breeding captive cetaceans in connection with developing successful programs to aid endangered or threatened species. By this reasoning, the industry should *foster* rather than oppose research into rehabilitation and reintroduction, as techniques and methodologies learned with bottlenose dolphins might be used to aid endangered cetacean species.[109]

Instead, the industry claimed that releasing dolphins bequeaths no obvious benefits to either the individuals or the populations they would return to.[110] Rather than being acknowledged as *sentient* individuals that were once part of communities and families, from which they were forcibly stolen and might conceivably be returned to, these beautiful, intelligent creatures, with brains larger than our own, referred to as mere "surplus stocks" exist to the captive industry as mere commodities for the taking (or stocks to be conserved for future plundering). Following this poor lead, Sea World casually calls its' whales and dolphins a *collection*. You collect postage stamps, *not sentient beings*. There is no acknowledgment of anything beyond human utility, no acknowledgment of an intelligent species with its' own purpose and *intrinsic worth*, aside from human economic value. This preoccupation with money and utility reveals a deep disconnection — from compassion and from our fellow beings.

It seems ironic that the captivity industry fully expects dolphins to cope with the violence and trauma of chase, capture, removal from community, family and habitat, incarceration in unnatural conditions, training and acceptance of dead food — but readapting back to where they evolved for over fifty million years, is considered risky and problematic. Deaths and potentially devastating disruption[111] resulting from dolphin captures certainly hasn't stopped industry entrepreneurs from plundering cetacean populations for profit. Yet, once the consideration is put forward to begin putting dolphins *back* where they belong, these same people suddenly become terribly concerned about a plethora of conjured risks that they would otherwise be only too happy to ignore. Worries over disease transmission into wild populations have been raised. As dolphins (particularly males) have large ranges and may roam very far a-field, portions of different populations appear to mix fluidly, causing even industry participants to agree that disease transmission may not necessarily constitute a grave situation.[112]

It goes without saying that wherever possible, captive dolphins should be given a clean bill of health by a marine mammal veterinarian before being released. However, the industry's seemingly conscientious caution over disease transmission dissolves when we realize that some captive facilities simply surreptitiously dump dolphins that become unwieldy or un-wanted, right back into the sea, with never a backward thought for what becomes of them.[113] In 1983 Sealife Park in Hawaii dumped its last surviving spinner dolphin back into the sea after nearly seven years of captivity, while only nine days earlier another of its dolphins had died from chronic hepatitis. More than a few dolphins used by the military have gone AWOL at sea — unremarkably, no one in the industry is screaming over pathology risks incurred in such circumstances, or panicking over open-water swim programs where captive dolphins may easily mix and mate with local wild populations. In fact, a government-condoned export permit for six *Atlantic* bottlenose dolphins to be used in open, *Pacific* waters was granted —recommending merely that the dolphins be properly vaccinated before export.[114]

Risks are ignored or highlighted by the captivity industry, according to its best interests. Though capturing cetaceans is demonstrably traumatic and harmful, no scientific protocols are required — yet the captive industry demands exhaustive research and rationalization before considering returning dolphins back to their communities. The transparency of these hypocritical, self-serving arguments becomes embarrassing. While inflicting outright damage, the industry quibbles over the benefits of reintroduction — though we *know* removing individuals, especially young females, tears at dolphin social fabric.

Through its empty arguments the industry has deemed the reintroduction of dolphins back into the wild "inappropriate," stating that until more data is gathered, returning dolphins to the wild is "inadvisable." Of course, the only way to rectify this lack of data would be to study the release of more dolphins, resulting in a convenient stalemate; the industry opposes further releases, even as it admits that release methodologies need further testing.[115]

While reaping the cash rewards of the public's fascination with cetaceans, the industry assumes a guise of respectability and conservation, claiming that returning dolphins back to their natural habitat is somehow inappropriate — inappropriate, if the name of the game is making money, rather than investigating a positive option for captive cetaceans and rectifying a bad track record perpetuated by a lucrative and utterly superfluous industry.

The method of undoing the damage we inflict on cetaceans by keeping them incarcerated remains in its infancy, but the necessary ingredients for successful rehabilitation and effectual post-release tracking are being rapidly tallied. Naturally, age, disposition and history are important factors in determining how or if any given dolphin can re-adapt to the life nature intended.

Among the most harmful effects of captivity are impoverished social conditions, including the premature separation of young cetaceans from their mothers. The resulting damage can mean not every single captive cetacean is a good candidate for release back into the wild. Certainly the warping that results from detrimental captive conditions can make rehabilitation more challenging. Dolphins who are to be successfully released must recover, enhance or in some cases develop their natural survival skills. Dolphins captured at an age when at least partial self-subsistence had been learned would have a likely advantage. However, as intelligent, social mammals, who learn by watching one another, even captive dolphins with little or no experience, by putting their legendary intelligence and adaptability to its natural use, can likely learn self-sufficiency by watching others with more experience and inclination, should they feel motivated to do so.

For some, their free will has been so subdued, it leaves them unsure of their ability to survive. In order to understand what kinds of damage must be undone before releasing a dolphin back into a successful life in the wild, we must look at what happens when a dolphin is captured. Within weeks of capture, a subtle psychosis begins — with their freedom and choice stolen, their proud wills are broken as they are made completely dependent on their captors — do what I say, and you will receive food.

Dr. Judith Herman, a leading expert on the effects of psychological trauma, describes the warping effects humans may experience when trapped in traumatic or abusive situations: *'People begin to lose their identity, their self-respect. They begin to lose their autonomy and independence.'*[116] It may not be so very different for dolphins, isolated from natural, mutually supportive relationships — typical in captive conditions, where the victims' social ties have been forcibly cut — forcing them to become dependent on the very persons abusing them, in order to survive. Some captives may suffer from a dolphin equivalent of the Stockholm Syndrome; a psychological warping sometimes seen in abducted hostages or those suffering through rape, incest or abuse, where victims refuse freedom or show signs of loyalty to their captors. For those who are taken into this type of tyrannical situation young, or born into such a life, it's even worse because their personalities are formed in the context of an exploitative relationship of coercion and control and subjugation.

In the aftermath of such of brutalization, some victims can have a great deal of difficulty in taking responsibility for their lives — frustrating those trying to help them. Author and expert on slavery, Kevin Bales affirms that being free means more than escaping bondage because freedom is a both a physical and mental state. True liberation, states Bales, is a *process*, not an event, and achieving it can sometimes be a long process. Some former slaves may require a lifetime of care, as their suffering can scar them permanently.[117]

So how do we heal the traumas of captivity and mend a former captive's body, mind and soul? The most important things for an individual's recovery, whether human or dolphin, are the restoration of empowerment and choice.

Richard O'Barry, who over the past thirty-eight years has been involved in the rehabilitation and release of over two dozen dolphins, is one of the few acknowledged experts in this nascent field. O'Barry describes the process leading up to reintroduction as more of a healing art than a science.[118] O'Barry believes that while captivity may dull a dolphin's independence, it rarely destroys it. He feels that though not all dolphins can immediately recover from prolonged warping experienced at human hands and re-adapt successfully to the wild, those who appear to be poor release candidates still deserve retirement in spacious natural surroundings replete with marine life, fresh air, sunlight, tides, appropriate companions, and the option to leave when and if they are deemed ready. None should be subject to forced performances, have food withheld or be made to interact with humans. With time, under such conditions, more heavily damaged dolphins may recover the self-confidence that was stolen or beaten out of them and make a full recovery.

Conversely, certain captive dolphins, perhaps due to short captive duration, detention in natural surroundings or a particularly irrepressible personality, prove themselves more than ready to return to the wild, in some cases simply by jumping the fences that cage them and escaping to freedom. Among these was Bahama Mamma, a female bottlenose dolphin who made a bid for freedom in 1991, after an impressive *seventeen years of captivity*. Subsequent positively identified sightings over a year later confirmed her successful integration into the local wild population.[119] This serves to remind us that a mere generation or two behind human barriers cannot completely undo fifty million years of oceanic evolution.

Dolphins deemed ready for release should be in good physical condition, have a clean bill of health from a certified veterinarian and exhibit normal behavior.[120] This means a dolphin has ceased all begging behavior directed at humans, has working use of their sonar and can reliably demonstrate an ability to catch and eat live fish without depending on human handouts.[121]

At sea dolphins must locate food, deal with inclement weather, disease, hostile sea life, and avoid predators. Though this may sound daunting, millions upon millions of years of evolution exquisitely designed dolphins to overcome all these challenges. In the human realm, hiking, surfing, swimming — even driving to work or crossing the street can all be dangerous. But this doesn't mean everyone should stay home cowering beneath the bed. It is our right to move about freely and we all know the liberty to do so is *well worth* the possible dangers. The idea that wild cetaceans might actually thrive on the challenges of survival, just as humans do, seems to have been ignored by the captive industry.

Our personal freedom is priceless. We are free to swim in the oceans, though there may be sharks, free to go camping, though there may be bears, free to explore the jungles, though there may be tigers, free to drive on the motorways, though every day there are accidents. If we value human freedom so much — how can we be so blind regarding those whom we rob of their liberty to hold captive for our entertainment and pleasure?

Prisons provide food and shelter — yet people aren't willingly lining up and volunteering to spend their lives behind bars. Freedom means *everything* to us — which is why taking it away from an individual is considered such a heavy punishment. Everything I have learned from my years among dolphins has led me to believe that freedom means even *more* to them. For dolphins, liberty is not merely a philosophy or a dream to be achieved after retirement, but an integral, celebrated way of daily life.

Keiko & the Bigger Picture

The killer whale who would one day be known to the world as Keiko was captured in Icelandic waters around 1979, at the tender age of about two. He had the misfortune to end up at Marineland, Niagara Falls where in 1985, he was sold for a whopping $350,000 and shipped to languish in a tiny, overheated tank in Mexico. There in 1993, Keiko starred in the hit anti-captivity movie *Free Willy*, which eventually inspired plans to truly set Keiko free.[122]

In 1996 after much involved preparation, Keiko was moved to a new seawater facility at the Oregon Coast Aquarium to begin readying for re-adaptation to the wild. Initially Keiko was underweight, lethargic and plagued by a chronic skin infection, but eventually a healthy diet combined with immersion in cold, natural seawater cleared up these problems. In September of 1998 amid a furor of controversy, Keiko was returned to his native Icelandic waters to continue his rehabilitation in a natural sea cove pen. By 2000 restored to good health, he was ready for access to the open sea.

Wild Icelandic orcas have huge ranges of hundreds of miles, and because the capture records were so poor, finding Keiko's original family unit would be difficult and daunting at best.

By the summer of 2002, Keiko (tracked by satellite telemetry) was exploring the North Atlantic and by early fall he'd traveled almost 900 miles to the shores of western Norway. During his oceanic forays, Keiko did meet and mingle with passing pods of wild orcas, however after over twenty years of captivity, most of it without the companionship of any other orcas, the twenty-six year old whale probably lacked the social skills to be permanently accepted amongst the tight-knit communities of free ranging orcas. Though Keiko successfully learned to travel and forage, humans could not teach him how to properly integrate into a wild whale community and for such a long-lived species where extended family units comprise both axis and pith, this was a problem for Keiko. Instead, in the absence of other orcas, the lonely whale eventually sought out human company once more. In December of 2003, after five healthy years in the ocean, Keiko died quietly, probably of pneumonia, in the Norwegian bay of Taknes.[123]

Many things were learned during Keiko's saga: among them, that it is easier to capture an orca than to socially reacclimatize him into a complex and tight-knit whale society after a long sentence in captivity. All the more reason we should beware of so casually inflicting damage we do not yet understand how to undo. Though not for lack of trying, humans were unable to fully mend the damage inflicted on Keiko.

Sadly, the question was raised by some: *why even bother?* The answer I think, is that ethically, we owed it to Keiko and all other captive orcas to try. Continual failure to keep captive orcas alive for their normal life span certainly hasn't stopped the captive industry from trying — and their only incentive is money. Keiko's saga was never just about one whale — but discovering hope, and a way back home for so many others who have been stolen from their families and currently languish in concrete pools. Much was learned from Keiko's journey that could one day benefit other captive orcas and while there is much more to be learned, this was a valuable step towards righting one of the terrible wrongs for which we are responsible.

As with bottlenose dolphins, personality and past history will probably have a lot to do with future successes involving the successful release and social re-adaptation of orcas. Because wild orcas appear to remain with their family units for life, their less fluid society would seem to be much more difficult for an awkward stranger to join than bottlenose dolphin society. However, orca clans are known to speak recognizably different dialects,[124] so if the location of a whale's capture is known, it may be possible to locate the original remaining family group (if the captive retains even remnants of his native dialect), where the chances of re-acceptance would be strongest.

A frequent objection raised regarding Keiko's release was why should twenty million dollars have been spent on one whale, when so many people are poor and homeless in the world? One might also ask why should so many *more* millions be spent maintaining captive cetaceans for idle human amusement?

Human priorities have become dangerously skewed. Author Derrick Jensen writes: *'For the price of a single B-1 Bomber, about $285 million, we could provide basic immunization treatments (shots for small pox, diphtheria, measles) to the roughly 575 million children in the world who lack them, thus saving 2.5 million lives annually. For what the world spends on defense every 40 hours — 4.6 billion — we could provide sanitary water for every human being who currently lacks it.'*[125]

Unfortunately, those who control most of the world's wealth and power have proven only too willing to exploit those who are weak, poor, uneducated, voiceless and helpless — humans, animals and ecosystems — in order to make a profit themselves. A complacent, ignorant and indifferent majority whose insatiable consumerism allows these atrocities to continue is the second component responsible for the state of our world.

Captive whales, like vanishing rain forests and poverty-stricken human beings are victims of greed and ignorance. Injustices and atrocities need to be recognized, addressed and rectified in *ALL* quarters! We, the everyday people of the developed nations carry enough collective clout, that we should *all* be making efforts to improve the state of our world, whether helping animals, protesting war and outrageous defense expenditure, tackling human rights violations, clear-cut logging practices or toxic poisoning of the environment — the list goes on. Each of us should as a matter of daily course put restorative effort into making the world a better place. Compassion, respect and responsibility towards cetaceans, the environment and our fellows are inexorably linked and these efforts translate to a kinder, cleaner, better and happier world for *everyone*. A wiser, kinder humanity would know this, and understand that Keiko should never have been torn from his family in the first place.

Future & Alternatives

Though seeing live captive cetaceans up close may be exciting — their freedom is not something we are entitled to take from them. As increasing numbers of people come to realize this, some marine parks are shifting focus away from live animal exhibits to thrill rides. We don't need clowning hoop-jumpers in order to take the knowledge we've already gained about cetaceans and put it to use helping occasional sick or stranded animals or to encourage youth towards active, useful, responsible marine conservation initiatives.

Exciting and truly educational alternatives to keeping live, suffering cetaceans in captivity are expanding along with our technology. Imax films can produce leaping whales, large as life in all their gargantuan, pelagic majesty, while 3-D films can bring dolphins surging right into your lap — all without harming individuals or removing them from their natural habitat. TV documentaries, the internet, DVDs and a plethora of books, nature magazines and science journals can all offer further entertaining education about cetaceans. Museums use no live animals, relying instead on audio-visual displays, models and animatronics to foster knowledge about the natural world, which can be made far more informative and beneficial than any poor dolphin living a false, forced existence in a concrete tank. Fresh documentary footage from the world's oceans can broadcast dolphins and whales right into your living room for you and your family's educational enjoyment, without removing a single cetacean from its oceanic home. As technological strides continue to advance, high-tech, interactive, holographic, virtually simulated dolphins can be made available to the public arena, without harming any live cetaceans.

Whale Watching

For those inspired, careful and adventurous souls, there are of course also the world's boundless oceans to explore where one can *responsibly* meet cetaceans first hand, in *their* world and on *their* terms. There's no reason why people who will happily fork out hundreds of dollars and travel cross-country to visit over-priced, over-crowded theme parks, can't manage a trip to the seaside to go whale watching.

Seeing cetaceans or any of Nature's other great wonders should not necessarily be a matter of convenience. If you want to gaze upon and *truly* appreciate the Grand Canyon with your own eyes, you will have to go to it; if you want to see a real blue whale, the largest animal on the planet, you will have to go to sea!

In fact, the amazing expansion and popularity of whale and dolphin watching indicates that increasing numbers of people are doing just this. Hundreds of destinations in some *eighty-seven* countries now offer whale and dolphin watching opportunities, which attract over ten million people globally each year, in a billion-dollar industry.[126]

However, a few key areas have become over-popular, swamped with too many boats, trying to get too close, wreaking havoc on the lives of the whales that people are crowding to see (an example of which can be found in the San Juan Puget Sound areas of the North Pacific). Not the least of this problem is the terrible noise from so many water craft. Scientist and orca expert Dr. Alexandra Morton writes: *'No automotive manufacturer would consider making a car or truck that produces as much noise as boat engines make underwater. Such a vehicle would be banned from all townships. However, the shrieking blare of boat engines is contained below the water out of human earshot, and so 'quiet' was never considered.*[127] On the Pacific Northwest Coast, more than seventy-five tour operators take some 472,000 people whale watching each year and though more than half (some 265,000) watch from land-based locations, this still may leave too many on the water.[128]

However, only a few specific whale-watching sites are over-crowded. Some seventy percent of this planet is ocean. North America alone has something like 190,000 miles of coastline — more than any other continent. Whale watching is a relatively new kind of tourism and so novel ways of dealing with these issues are starting to be addressed by researchers and legislators. Solutions include thinning crowds in over-taxed areas by issuing limited licenses to *responsible* whale watch boats, and by improving and enforcing protective regulations in heavily trafficked areas.[129]

With new ventures starting in a growing number of locations, cetacean enthusiasts seeking wild encounters have increasing options to spread out into tolerable numbers. In parts of the world where whale watching is new, it is important that both legislators and excursion operators carefully examine what is happening in established whale-watch "hot spots" in order to better learn what to do — and what not to do. Guidelines and codes of conduct are readily available for adoption by the tourism industry and government agencies.[130] The tendency toward too many boats, trying to get too close should be avoided and rules that maximize cetacean comfort and minimize human interference, adopted. Strategic land-based watching sites have the lowest human impact on cetaceans and their growing popularity should be encouraged. As in any interaction with wild places or animals, people should seek knowledgeable guides or tour operators who are familiar with the area and its inhabitants, who tread as softly and respectfully as possible on both the environment and the animals.

Overall the development of whale watching is a positive thing for both humans and cetaceans alike. Author Jim Nollman writes: *'Whale watching is founded on the economic premise that wherever whale-watching flourishes, whaling inevitably withers. Recent studies have made it clear, that the growth of ecotourism in Japan is influencing that whale-consuming culture to appreciate living whales more effectively than twenty years of foreign protest ever accomplished.'*[131]

Wild Swims

A dizzying variety of tours are available in an expanding number of countries and locations, featuring encounters with wild dolphins. As with whale watching, some areas have become over-taxed, and there are other problems to consider.

As I've found out, even at sea among wild dolphins, an unhealthy residue from the captive industry's "Flipper Myth" lingers. People seeking out wild dolphins need to become better informed and realize that the lives of *real*, wild dolphins have little relation to humans, unless imposed. What dolphins find most thrilling, interesting and engaging are each other — not us. This doesn't mean we may not at times be welcomed with curiosity, or that mutual, profound exchanges don't happen — but the dolphins' lives don't revolve around it. The lives of wild dolphins are full, valid and richly textured without us. Though close encounters among wild cetaceans are unarguably touching and wondrous for us, it is often inappropriate and even outright disruptive when humans thoughtlessly crash in on wild dolphins without the appropriate respect or sensitivity.

A popular spot to both watch and swim with dolphins is off New Zealand's Kaikoura peninsula. Scientists studying dolphins' reactions to in-water tourists and the presence of tour boats found that dolphins did not always choose to interact and when given the choice, bottlenose dolphins approached swimmers only thirty-four percent of the time. The rest of the time the dolphins were observed to continue engaging in the activities they had been involved in prior to swimmers entering the water, leading researchers to state that the majority of the time dolphins appear to prefer going about their normal lives rather than engaging swimmers. Unfortunately instances of both tour boat operators and swimmers acting in an intrusive and aggressive manner were not rare: *'People leap off the side of their boats directly on top of dolphins, lunge for them as they swim past and drive at high-speed circles in an attempt to get them to jump.'* This study concluded that not all dolphins are interested in engaging human activity, and that they prefer to choose whether or not to interact among swimmers. While these results may sound like commonsense, studies have demonstrated that in their effort to appease the desire to get closer to dolphins, humans often fail to act in a respectful, responsible way.[132]

Problems with peoples' insensitivity and over-eagerness to swim with dolphins are as ubiquitous as the misleading image of "Flipper." Dr. Kathleen Dudzinski, who studies wild dolphins on the other side of the world from New Zealand, in the Bahamas, writes, *'I could not help but witness the aggressive tendencies of the swimmers towards dolphins. Mostly people thought they could catch a dolphin and, once caught, the dolphin would just love to be touched all over.'* Dudzinski understands that the popular desire to interact personally with dolphins is only likely to grow and states that the best way to deal with the expanding demand for wild dolphins' company is to make every effort to ensure people are properly educated on how to act *responsibly* in the presence of wild cetaceans.[133]

On the big island of Hawaii, researchers working with the Ocean Mammal Institute led a project to study the effects of swimmers, kayaks and motorboats on pods of spinner dolphins. From cliff-tops one hundred and fifty feet above the water, researchers were able to follow the movements of human activity and the dolphins' resulting behaviors. It was observed that locals and those with experience usually swam with the spinners in early morning, just after the dolphins had come into the bay, after a busy night of deep diving and feeding, to seek shallow sandy areas in which to socialize and rest. But by nine or ten, boats, zodiacs, tourist kayaks and dolphin-swim workshop tours began to converge, all eagerly pursuing the spinner dolphins. Though the next several hours were when the dolphins most needed quiet, it was also the height of demanding and ceaseless human presence, often causing the spinners to take evasive action. This study concluded: *'Respecting wild dolphins could be one small step toward our deeper evolution. If we can learn to respect them, realizing that they exist for themselves, not to benefit us, and if we can learn to interact with them as equals, our worldview may begin to shift. If we can learn to listen, we may be able to save ourselves as well as other species.'*[134]

It is unfortunate that visiting humans find it so difficult to exercise self-restraint, especially when they've paid "good money" for a popularly preconceived experience like "swimming with dolphins."

Responsible, sustainable tourism — *true* eco-tourism — requires people to approach cetaceans in a careful informed and respectful manner, preferably in smaller numbers. To reduce disruption experts advise selecting smaller tour vessels with an experienced, naturalist or biologist on board to better interpret cetacean behavior. Experienced, considerate and reputable tour operators who are familiar with an area and its inhabitants will err on the side of caution when approaching cetaceans and a good skipper is knowledgeable in maneuvering around cetaceans safely with due care and attention. An accidental encounter with the propeller blades of a boat can leave a dolphin or whale injured or dead. Vessels under sail create far less noise pollution and are much less likely to disrupt or injure cetaceans. Over-trafficked areas should be avoided. A number of conservation organizations offer educational opportunities for the public to participate in scientific research with wild cetaceans. While viewing wild dolphins and whales up close, much may be learned about their lives, biology and behavior at sea, enhancing the experience considerably and making these options among those most highly recommended.

For those encountering cetaceans without the recommended benefit of an experienced and responsible guide, taking the time to absorb some factual, practical knowlege regarding cetacean signals, behavior, habits and ettiquette is also highly advisable. As a general rule, small, quiet groups of swimmers have the lowest impact and are the least disruptive. Employing a thoughtful, informed and respectful approach only impoves the likelihood of prolonging a close encounter. Essential recommendations when encountering wild dolphins include:

- Never feed wild dolphins.
- Do not approach dolphins too closely in boats — they will come to you, if they want to investigate.
- If dolphins do approach your boat, avoid abrupt changes in speed and direction.
- Do not separate or scatter dolphins, especially mothers and young.
- Do not interrupt or interfere with dolphins that are resting, feeding, mating or fighting.
- Do not enter the water abruptly if dolphins are nearby and avoid loud noises or sudden movements.
- Never pursue or chase dolphins, either in boats or by swimming.
- Do NOT grasp, grab or clutch at wild dolphins and *never* try to impede or restrict a dolphin's movements in any way!
- If a dolphin does choose to initiate touch, avoid sensitive, delicate areas — blowhole, eyes, face, genital region, fins and flukes.
- Leave the water immediately if dolphins exhibit violent or sexual behavior.
- Do not swim with dolphins if you are feeling ill or recovering from viral or bacterial infection.
- Never dump litter, especially plastic garbage or chemical waste into the water.[135]

In a world where whales and dolphin remain very much at risk from numerous human practices, tourism that is *truly* educational and respectful rather than exploitative, appears to encourage an increasing empathy toward cetaceans and their marine environment, without removing any dolphins or whales from their oceanic communities and reducing them to captives. Though the potential for harm should not be ignored, when managed and conducted properly, such wild encounters represent an overall hopeful turn in the human-cetacean relationship.

Humans evolved embedded in the natural world and there remains within us a deep, abiding longing to *reconnect* with wild places and wild creatures. It is this profound desire for contact that is exploited by captive institutions like marine parks. The human species needs to rediscover that we can have a positive place in Nature, instead of always imagining ourselves existing apart, above or removed from it. As such, opportunities to *respectfully* reconnect with the wild are essential!

Having studied wild dolphins for a quarter of a century, Dr. Denise Herzing writes: *'When we deny participation with others, we deny our relationship with them as well.'*[136] Dolphins incorporating sensitive human participants into their lives exemplifies a kind of consanguinity between human and Nature that is at once new and ancient. An essential part of this involves forging *elective* bonds of trust, because the dolphins always have the choice to leave. Of course even careful and respectful human presence will have some effect on wild cetaceans. *Everything* in Nature from a typhoon to a tiny grain of eroded coral sand has an effect. Everything in Nature affects everything else; everything eats and is eaten, while elements shift within a constantly changing dynamic — that *is* Nature!

When one swims in the sea, nearly naked, without gadgetry or weapons, one is at risk, and may potentially become predator or prey. This is the way for both humans and cetaceans to meet: by mutual, respectful *choice* in the oceans, as equals. Only here, amid Nature's danger and glory, are we finally back in the balance.

CHAPTER TWENTY-EIGHT

INTELLECTUAL PROPERTY

"On the planet Earth, man had always assumed that he was more intelligent than dolphins because he had achieved so much – the wheel, New York, wars and so on – whilst all the dolphins had ever done was muck about in the water having a good time. But conversely, the dolphins had always believed that they were far more intelligent than man – for precisely the same reasons."
Douglas Adams, *The Hitchhiker's Guide to the Galaxy.*

How intelligent are dolphins *really*? Most people are unaware of just how loaded this frequently asked question is, or how difficult the concept of *intelligence* is to define and truly quantify. As a species, we're infamous for annihilating each other and poisoning the earth, air, water and other living creatures upon which we depend, and thus in many ways, humans are a poor example of a highly intelligent life form. Our so-called intelligence has brought us to the brink of disaster and perhaps extinction. Other creatures who do not indulge in such thoroughly destructive activities may have found ways to enjoy their intelligence with more *wisdom* than we.

What *IS* Intelligence?

Intelligence is a nebulous concept, and we have a difficult time defining, clarifying and measuring it, even in ourselves. Intelligence tests rely on human context, experience and manipulation and are limited by the questions we can devise and the human perspectives and systems within which those questions are meaningful. Dictionaries generally define intelligence as the ability to acquire and apply knowledge and skills. Science has loosely defined intelligence as a flexible capacity for reason and understanding which goes beyond purely instinctive responses. Acclaimed behavioral scientist, Dr. Donald Griffin defined intelligence as *'versatile adaptability of behavior to novel challenges.*[1]An intelligent creature is said to be able to learn and retain knowledge, reason on the basis of such acquired knowledge and with it, adapt to new circumstances. Biology Professor Dr. Marc Bekoff further adds that intelligence also includes an ability to learn from the past in order to anticipate and plan for the future.[2]

There are a number of different ways of assessing intellectual ability in humans, the results of which can often be frustratingly ambiguous or even questionable. IQ tests are frequently criticized for being culturally and even gender biased, and such bias is certainly magnified when scientists attempt to measure an animal's mind by comparing it somehow to the human IQ. If we have yet to fully develop any valid, universal measure of intelligence in the human species, we are that much further away from definitively quantifying it in non-human animals.

Most standard IQ tests measure *Analytical Intelligence*, centered on abstract thinking, logical reasoning and linguistic/mathematical skills. But there are many kinds of intelligence. *Creative Intelligence* involves generating new ideas to deal with novel situations; *Contextual (or Tacit) Intelligence* involves street smarts, or the ability to *apply* knowledge in order to both shape and choose one's environment.

Psychologist Dr. Howard Gardner developed the *Theory of Multiple Intelligences,*[3] consisting of a number of distinct types of recognizable intelligence. *Linguistic* and *Logical-Mathematical* intelligence tend to be valued most highly in our current western world and questions pertaining to these kinds of intelligence usually make up the bulk of IQ tests.

Other types of recognized intelligence include *Musical Intelligence* (identifying, composing, performing and appreciating pitches, tones and rhythms in musical patterns). *Bodily-Kinesthetic Intelligence* involves movement coordination (as in dancers or athletes), or the ability to physically solve problems or fashion products using one's body (as in craft persons and surgeons). *Spatial Intelligence* is the ability to recognize, manipulate and navigate patterns of wide space (as in pilots or sailors, or in confined space — sculptors, surgeons, engineers and architects.) More difficult to study and quantify are *Interpersonal Intelligence* (understanding the intricacies, motivations and intentions in relating to others) and *Intra-personal Intelligence* (being aware and in control of one's inner states and desires). Dr. Gardner also recognizes *Naturalist Intelligence* (expertise in recognizing, identifying and classifying flora and fauna in one's environment and interacting with nature).[4] Someone exhibiting the abilities of a full-blown naturalist, Gardner writes, may go well beyond taxonomic capabilities, additionally possessing talents of caring for, taming or interacting subtly with a variety of living creatures.[5]

Gardner also speculates on other kinds of highly elusive intelligence. *Spiritual* or *Existential Intelligence* (perhaps no more abstract than the realm of advanced mathematics), may also qualify as a distinct, intellectual capacity. Spiritual/Existential intelligence recognizes those who are skilled in achieving and teaching certain psychological or meditative states; mastery of an internal craft — possibly as a form of gathering knowledge, leading to deeper or higher truths; or those who exhibit facility, clarity or depth in thinking about or engaging in transcendental concerns ('ultimate' issues such as the meaning of life and death and the fate of physical and psychological worlds) (like Lao Tzu or J. Krishnamurti). Gardener further speculates on the existence of *Moral*, or *Philosophical Intelligence,* for which Spiritual/Existential intelligence may pave the way. Advanced Moral Intelligence may involve a strong sense of and enduring commitment to uphold justice, truth, compassion and the sanctity of life in the world we inhabit. Those displaying Moral intelligence show a heightened awareness and concern for the effects of their actions on others[6] (like Albert Schweitzer or Gandhi).

That we fail to place our highest value on intelligence qualities relating to nature, social relationships, inner states or ethical recognition is quite telling. Rather, emphasis is often on manipulating logistics, linguistics and technology, demonstrated clearly throughout our species' innovative, violent and destructive history.

Dr. Gardner writes that the theory of Multiple Intelligence is applicable to non-humans and admits that species like dolphins, with very different sensory capabilities, may have valid kinds of intelligence unknown or undeveloped in humans.[7] Non-human creatures like dolphins may have evolved recognizing and valuing some of the very kinds of intelligence that we often do not. In dolphins, the laborious semantics of word-based language and the manipulating of constrained, linear logic, like the accumulation or manufacture of items may hold little enough interest, while acoustic, bodily kinesthetic and interpersonal abilities are plainly of great use and interest. Dr. Diana Reiss, a researcher who studies dolphin intelligence, argues that intelligence cannot properly be conceived solely in human terms and disagrees with the typical assumption that only our kind of intelligence is *real* intelligence.[8]

Shades of Grey Matter

Evolutionary continuity indicates our intelligence must have evolved from that of other animals' just like any other attribute. Varied and rapidly accumulating scientific evidence is revealing emotional and intellectual abundance in non-human animals and is calling for a re-evaluation of the previous assumption that intelligence, emotion and sentience has been granted to man alone.

Brain tissue is as metabolically expensive as muscle, *and* it is active day and night. Though the human brain accounts for only about 1.5% of our body weight, it demands about 20% of our energy supply.[9] Thus, the evolution of large, metabolically expensive brains would only have been developed and maintained for *very* compelling reasons of vital importance — reasons conferring major advantages that outweigh the costs incurred in having such an organ. Unlike the human species, cetacean births are not impeded by their mothers' body frames. In cetaceans, the infant passes entirely through soft tissue, which has allowed their brains to expand with an unrestricted ease that has been limited in our species by the human pelvic shape. Cetacean researcher Dr. Alexandra Morton points out that even simple brains require a constant and plentiful supply of oxygen. Dolphins and whales spend their lives holding their breath and are generally in almost constant motion. Because such muscular motion demands so much oxygen — already in limited supply for a diving, swimming mammal — the diversion of so much precious oxygen to maintain the colossal brains of cetaceans, tells us that those huge brains must be crucially earning their keep somehow.[10]

Exactly how brains relate to cognition, mind and consciousness is still not definitively understood and the correlation between how brain size and complexity reflects intelligence remains a point of considerable discussion. One way scientists gage the question of intelligence is by examining the obvious physical correlation between brain size and intelligence, as larger brains are generally thought to produce more sophisticated intellects. Gorilla brains average 500 grams, chimpanzees about 400 grams, orangutans 333 grams,[11] and humans 1,370-1,400 grams. The brain weight of the bottlenose dolphin is *higher* than in humans, 1,587grams[12] — and up to 1,700 grams.[13] The mean brain mass in bottlenose dolphins is 1.6kg and 1.5kg in humans, but this pales in comparison to the 5.6kg of orcas (killer whales), 4.8kg of African elephants and 7.8kg of sperm whales.[14]

The connection between *brain* and *body* size is important in calculating the *Encephalization Quotient*, or *EQ*. EQ is the ratio of brain weight to body weight, the measure of which is also frequently correlated with intelligence. EQ measures the amount of "excess" brain not devoted to controlling and maintaining bodily functions and thus presumed to be available for intellectual functions like memory, perception and problem solving. Chimpanzees have an estimated EQ of about 2.3, humans about 7.0, while dolphins have EQs ranging from 4.95[15] up to 5.31,[16] suggesting the level of intelligence or cognitive processing in dolphins is much closer to the human range than our nearest primate relatives.[17] However, it has been pointed out that straight comparisons of EQ between humans and dolphins fail take into account the high proportion of mass in cetaceans that is insulative blubber, a tissue that requires no brain mass to maintain. If the dolphin EQ were to be reconfigured without the weight of insulating blubber, it becomes *much* more closely comparable to that of humans.[18] Moreover, human brain/body weight ratios actually cover a wide range and numbers would obviously appear more impressive in persons who are of slight build, than those who are obese.

Some scientists argue the ratio of brain weight to spinal cord weight is a better measurement of mammalian intelligence: 8 to 1 in most apes, 40 to 1 in bottlenose dolphins and about 50 to 1 in humans.[19] Again, such ratio comparisons may be misleading, as human spines are of course tailless, while the elongated spines of dolphins extend down into their powerful flukes.

In any case, size does appear to matter, particularly for critical portions of the brain. At least some of the physical structure believed to underlie consciousness (in mammals) are found in the cerebrum and especially its outer layer, which is called the *cerebral cortex*, where information is thought to be received, organized, analyzed and stored. In humans the cerebral cortex is about 2,200 square centimeters and in chimpanzees about 500.[20] The bottlenose dolphin cortex covers an enormous 3,700 square centimeters and its surface is more convoluted than in humans. However, because the dolphins' cortex is about half as thick, its volume ends up about eighty-five percent of the human cortex (560 cubic cm to our 660 cubic cm).[21]

In terms of volume, weight, cell count and sheer complexity, the dolphins' brain certainly favors the development of intelligence.[22] Neurologist John Lilly wrote: *'The result of careful neuro-anatomical and extensive neurophysiological studies indicates that our brains' only decisive difference from the apes is in the size of our cerebral cortical 'silent' areas on the frontal, parietal and temporal lobes. Silent areas have no direct-input connections and thus are devoted to central processing thinking, imagination, long-term goals, ethics etc.)... These cortial areas are the ones we use for understanding justice, compassion and the need for social interdependence... This may make us pause when we consider the brains of cetacea. Excellent controlled neurological studies of cetacean brains show that the silent areas are larger in the cetaceans, whose brains are bigger than ours... all of the additional mass is in the silent areas. Microscopic analysis shows that their cellular densities and connections are quite as large and complex as ours.*[23]

Whatever the connection between brain-cortex-size and intelligence in mammals, it must be noted that certain species of birds (particularly parrots, ravens and crows) with brains the size of a shelled walnut, lacking any substantial cerebral cortex, are also proving to be *highly* intelligent.[24] Birds seem instead to use *striatal* brain regions specific to avians, suggesting that complex cognition is *not* dependent upon a cerebral cortex and that anatomical equivalents have evolved in other species.[25]

Although comparable in size to the human brain, dolphin brains differ greatly in organization, far more than ape brains do. While the human species is thought to have had its current brain structure for roughly one hundred thousand years — dolphins have had brains comparable and larger than ours for about fifteen *million* years.[26] Another striking difference is that dolphin brains do not appear to be organized for binocular vision. Dolphin eyes move independently, bringing in two largely different sets of information for processing from a visual field that overlaps only minimally in their broad panoramic view encompassing at least 180 degrees. The two hemispheres of a dolphin's brain appear to visually operate largely independently and this hemispheric independence seems to carry over into dolphin sleep, as they seem to rest one hemisphere at a time, in order to remain partially alert at all times and to allow conscious breathing.

Unsurprisingly the amount of a dolphin's brain devoted to auditory processing is much larger than that of humans and also much *closer* to the areas devoted to visual processing. Because of the highly integrated nature of the dolphin's audio-visual perception, they likely interface with their physical and social environments in a manner quite unlike humans.[27] Despite inhabiting different elements and our vastly differing evolutionary histories and perceptual worlds, limited linguistic (and arguably substantial non-verbal) communication *has* been possible, indicating an overlap of cognitive ground between humans and dolphins.*

Social Intelligence

Elephants, parrots, cetaceans and apes, despite their many differences, are all considered to be highly intelligent animals. Scientists, wondering how

* For a more comprehensive look at the impressive qualities of the dolphin brain, associated cognitive abilities—and the ethical implications, see: *In Defense of Dolphins: The New Moral Frontier*, by Thomas I. White, Blackwell Publishing 2007.

such impressive intellectual abilities separately arose in such different creatures, have isolated something shared by these species. Apes, parrots, dolphins and elephants all have long life spans and all live in socially complex communities — and oddly, this may be the reason these animals all became so intellectually developed. The pressures of social living are now thought to be a major selective force driving the evolution of intelligence. A telling correlation reveals that animal species with the largest brains tend to live in large social groups involving ongoing, long-term and diverse relationships that require complex levels of communication and cooperation. The more extensive and complex the relationships, the more brain-power is required to keep track of the social milieu.

Primatologist Dr. Roger Fouts logically affirms human intelligence did not spring full-blown from nowhere, but rather, was *inherited* from our primate ancestors and many scientists now believe the impressive powers of reasoning shared by apes and humans emerged in order to handle the complex dynamics of close-knit family-life and the intricacies of a highly complex social community.[28]

The first humans are thought to have lived in social groups, much like chimpanzees or bonobos (our closest genetic relatives, both sharing 98.4 of human DNA, making them more closely related to us, than they are to gorillas).[29] Our ape-like ancestor was almost certainly an intensely political and social creature. By cooperating to forage and defend themselves from predators, they were able to overcome many of the ecological challenges they faced. With pressures from predation and starvation lessened, the primary challenges facing ancient proto-humans became *each other* — members of their own or other social groups. Such *intra*-species competition, it is postulated, forced clans of hominids to cooperate ever more intensely and in ever more complex ways against other cooperating groups, thus honing the intellectual social tools needed navigate a complex social landscape. It was this escalating "intellectual arms race" that scientists speculate provided the impetus to evolve ever more sophisticated social intelligence.

Humans are apt social problem-solvers (and, it must be pointed out, problem-causers) and though we direct our intelligence more and more toward technological things, much of what goes on in our minds, directly or indirectly, is still social. Social-Political, or *Machiavellian**intelligence has come to the fore as an explanation for the development of advanced intelligence in a number of species, including chimps, bonobos and dolphins, which all seem to have responded similarly to the demands of social

---

* After Niccolo Machiavelli — 1469-1527, a Florentine political-philosopher of the Renaissance.

pressures. Researchers are finding that it is in their complex interpersonal relationships where the subtle nuances of affection and conflict, requiring such mental alacrity come into play — and where big brains are required to navigate social competition for sex, resources and even for influencing the rest of a group favorably, as competitors use social skills to garner support, outsmart, manipulate, work together, enforce rules of conduct, forge and maintain alliances, keep track of favors or insults, play out social scenarios in their heads and so forth. Such "political intelligence" allows individuals to predict and make accurate assessments of others' behavior in diverse, ever-shifting social situations and circumstances.

After having closely observed wild dolphins in Australia for over a decade, researcher Dr. Rachel Smolker writes of the connection between mental alacrity and the complexities of dolphin social life, observing that many male bottlenose dolphins form cooperative alliances, which compete with other male alliances for access to female dolphins. These male dolphins go through a lengthy process of assessing one another before forming alliances. While Smolker thinks size and health are likely factors taken into consideration, she strongly suspects the dolphins have a sense of one another's intelligence, loyalty, fairness, reputation and status in the community and that they can assess such characteristics both through direct personal experience and by monitoring the opinions and interactions of others.[30] Scientists consider the level of complexity observed in these dolphin alliances unequalled in any other species other than humans.[31]

Mind & Consciousness

Mechanistic science commonly views consciousness as merely incidental patterns resulting from physical and chemical activity in the cerebral cortex, implying mental activity is nothing but the subjective experience of brain activity. Though we know there is some kind of close interconnection between mental activity and brain activity, there's very little evidence behind the idea that the mind is solely the result of brain activity. Consciousness affects the brain and the brain affects consciousness, and changes in the brain can lead to changes in consciousness, but this does not prove that the mind *is* the brain.[32]

The *International Dictionary of Psychology* tells us that consciousness *'is a fascinating but elusive phenomenon: it is impossible to specify what it is, what it does, or why it evolved.'*[33] Which doesn't help us much, while the *Concise Encyclopedia of Psychology* tells us that *consciousness* is synonymous with *awareness,* while admitting this term is no less ambiguous or difficult to understand.[34]

A major part of the difficulty in defining and recognizing consciousness is providing an acceptable scientific definition of conscious mental experience based on observable properties that are objectively identifiable. But consciousness being essentially a subjective and ephemeral thing, renders the acquisition of such evidence a high challenge indeed, one that *Homo sapiens* has yet to solve. At present, we don't yet have a complete sense of what "consciousness, self and self-identity" mean even for humans, much less in non-human species.

However, the archaic notion that all animals are thoughtless, unfeeling robots is being rapidly dismantled — and indeed, this narrow view never had any place among many non-occidental cultures. Acclaimed Behaviorist Dr. Donald Griffin employed a common-sense approach in addressing the subject of consciousness in non-human animals and felt that by relying on the same criteria of reasonable plausibility that leads us to accept the reality of consciousness in other humans, it could be safely extrapolated that many animals participate in comparable mental awareness.[35]

Dr. Marc Bekoff sheds further light on these matters, suggesting that social complexity may have led not only to higher *intelligence,* but also the evolution of *consciousness* itself. He writes: *'It has been suggested that consciousness evolved in social situations where it is important to be able to anticipate the flexible and adaptive behavior of others. If this is true, then complex social skills might be taken as evidence of consciousness.'*[36]

Biologist Dr. Bernd Heinrich writes: *'We'll never find proof for the existence of consciousness by picking the animal apart, or by looking at its parts in isolation. ... Every living thing is, like a book, more than ink and paper. It is a record of history spanning over two billion years. The more we dissect and look at the parts disconnected, the more we destroy what we are trying to find — the more we destroy what took millions of years to make... Consciousness is not a thing, it is a continuum without boundaries.'*[37]

We are a young species and our science is younger still. The more we learn, the more we find there is to learn. Every question science painstakingly answers leads to a further, dizzying array of questions. Honest science admits it is far from definitive answers in many areas of discovery and truth. It has been postulated that the "mind" upon which we focus so much study, may be no more than a stage in the evolution of consciousness. Perhaps author Jim Nollman in his book *The Charged Border* is correct in musing that: *'The brain may not be the seat of the mind, but rather the conduit of consciousness.'*[38]

Self-awareness & Sentience

Detecting and measuring sentience or self-awareness in non-humans seems just as challenging as defining consciousness. However, scientists are beginning to design ingenious methods of inquiry into this difficult realm. The Gallup* test for self-recognition has become the acknowledged "gold standard" for visual self-recognition in non-human animals and human children. The Gallup test involves, after familiarization with mirrors, the dabbing of an odorless, tasteless red dot on the subject's forehead, following which, if the subject looks into the mirror and then touches the dot — on their own forehead, rather than the mirror image — they are said to recognize themselves in the mirror's reflection, and therefore to be psychologically "self-aware." No human child less than fifteen months old has ever passed this mirror self-recognition test. The percentage of successful children increases from fifteen to twenty-four months. Chimps as young as two and a half years old have also passed,[39] as have other species of great apes.

The Gallup test has been adapted for dolphins — who have also passed, demonstrating self-recognition and self-awareness.[40] Dolphins have also shown themselves able to distinguish between live video feeds and taped recordings of themselves,[41] and have demonstrated aspects of self-awareness by proving themselves able to repeat behaviors recently performed, when requested to do so, thus indicating an awareness of their own recent behavior, complimenting the Gallup-type tests.[42] Other indications that dolphins have a sense of self is their use of individual-unique whistles, known as signature whistles — the dolphin equivalent of a name — strongly implying dolphins have a sense of "self' and "other." Even the fact that dolphins routinely make purposeful (perhaps even ethical) choices is thought by some scientists to be a measurable indication of their sentience.[43]

Dolphins have had their impressive, larger brains for many millions of years longer than man. Finding self-awareness in creatures whose evolutionary history separated from ours over sixty million years ago may say something fundamental about the evolution of intelligence and sentience on earth: that it can and has developed convergently in other, perhaps many other forms.

---

* Named after psychologist, Dr. Gordon Gallup.

Pride & Prejudice

Having named ourselves Homo sapiens sapiens — wise, *wise* man, the notion that man is the most intelligent life form on the planet (indeed, the universe) is deeply ingrained in the Western mind. Thus, it is perhaps not surprising that evidence of non-human intelligence sometimes meets with resistance. Our concepts of what it means to be intelligent, sentient, conscious or self-aware may not always be sufficiently neutral to guarantee philosophical objectivity towards evidence for it in other species. In addition to each of us preserving a uniquely subjective perspective, we all carry a number of biases, some of which we may be more aware of than others. Such bias may be sexist, class-based, political, cultural, academic, Western, religious, or even human — all or any of which will affect how we report on any so-called objective reality. Despite the value of objectivity in scientific methods, honest scientists admit it is inevitable that the experiences, beliefs and preferences of researchers will affect the interpretation and results of findings.[44] Dr. Bekoff comments, '*Numerous biases are embedded in scientific training and thinking. Scientists, as human beings, have individual agendas — personal, social, economical and political.*'[45] Researcher and marine mammal scientist Dr. Denise Herzing continues: '*Scientists are first human, then researchers, despite the fact that many will argue this point! To be truly objective, to disregard all our cultural filters and biases, is impossible...*'[46]

Because of this human bias, when the question "How intelligent are dolphins?" is asked, this often translates into *How much are they like us?* Much current debate over non-human intelligence boils down to argument over how similar animal abilities are to ours. Issues often focus on if or how well animals can use tools, comprehend human speech, use human designed languages, and even perform on human intelligence tests. Such bias makes it difficult for us to recognize or measure intelligence in a species like dolphins, who have a very different evolutionary history than ours, lack both hands and vocal cords, and living in water, would be unable to develop technologies based on fire and electricity. Investigating and understanding dolphin intelligence requires a profound conceptual shift away from our usual biased modes in order to make comparisons across species that are fair, accurate and useful.[47]

Fortunately, a host of behavioral ethologists, psychologists and field biologists are rewriting the old elitist mind frame regarding animal intelligence and awareness, thanks to an emerging science driven by a genuine wish to better understand the richness of non-human lives. Dr. Bekoff affirms that studying animal intelligence challenges our own, as we find new ways to investigate and document it.[48]

Anthropomorphism

Anthropomorphism — attributing human-like thinking or emotions to animals — has often been considered one of the worst sins of animal science. In his book, *Animal Minds*, Behaviorist Dr. Donald Griffin stated that in order to properly understand any species it is important to try and learn as much as possible about what they think and feel because we cannot understand an animal fully without knowing what their subjective lives are like. Griffin felt it was unfortunate that students of animal behavior are often constrained by guilty feelings that inquiry into the subjective feelings or conscious thoughts of non-humans is somehow "unscientific."[49]

Lawyer and author Steven Wise logically asks: '*Why should it be considered reasonable to start by assuming that only humans are conscious and then label any contrary claim as anthropomorphic?*'[50] As the study of animal behavior progresses and expands, this narrow and limiting consensus view has begun to shift in many quarters. Dr. Bekoff insists that engaging in anthropomorphism allows those studying animal behavior to access other animals' worlds, making their emotions, thoughts and feelings more available and thereby, their behaviors more comprehensible.[51] Acclaimed, long-term studies, like those of chimpanzees by Dr. Jane Goodall, are demonstrating that a certain amount of anthropomorphism is merely a common sense approach. When educated observers attempt to better understand the lives of animals, it is not such a far leap to imagine what a given animal might know, feel or think in certain situations, helping to bridge important gaps of understanding.

Primatologist Dr. Frans De Waal suggests that perhaps anthropomorphism isn't to be avoided at all costs, but rather used as a logical starting point, because of the evolutionary past humans share with other animals. De Waal observes it is not because anthropomorphism interferes with science, but rather because it acknowledges *continuity* between humans and animals, that it has met with such criticism. De Waal points out that the absence of consciousness or sentience is about as hard to prove as its presence; hence using caution in ascribing it to animals would be entirely acceptable — if human behavior were held to the same standard, which of course is not the case.[52]

Animal Language and Communication Studies

Numerous studies involving a growing number of scientists and animal species are expanding the understood parameters of animal intelligence. A limited number of great apes, parrots and dolphins have been taught, through elaborate, long-term scientific experiments, to communicate elements of language through verbal, gestural, or symbolic codes. Once an animal acquires sufficient command of a human language code, interspecies exchange can reveal aspects of non-human intelligence, cognition and self-awareness.

The use of symbolic and gestural languages have ended up providing researchers a fascinating venue through which we can communicate with animals, and they with us. Of particular interest is how symbolic and gestural languages provide insight into animals' *inner worlds* that under normal circumstances remain inaccessible. Over the last forty years or so, language studies with non-human animals have changed human perspective, showing us that animals are intellectually and emotionally capable of much more than science ever previously suspected. Great apes, dolphins and parrots have been taught to understand how words, signs or symbols can function as mental representations of items, objects, actions, questions, requests or foods. They've also been taught that these communicative systems can be used to request absent items and have learned the difference between requesting and identifying objects.[53]

Dr. Irene Pepperberg, Professor of Evolutionary Biology, Psychology and Neuroscience at the University of Arizona, observes that researchers studying cognition in animals that have learned to use human devised languages often lose sight of the resulting interspecies communication as an *investigative* tool and instead, focus arguments on comparing human and animal linguistic abilities. Thus, evidence of animal cognitive capacities may be lost amidst endless debates about the extent to which an animal has acquired "language" or demonstrates linguistic competence in human terms. Such debates are based on the assumption that an animal's learning and use of such human devised languages are indicative of its cognitive ability — which Dr. Pepperberg feels is unlikely.[54] In humans, the study of cognitive behavior is closely tied to the study of language development. Some researchers suggest that because most animals seemingly lack the ability to learn human languages, they must be cognitively inferior. Pepperberg argues that language training (or its lack) likely affects only the *ease* with which researchers can test for animal learning on certain concepts, not *whether* such learning occurs or can occur. Pepperberg adds that direct, cross-species comparisons of competence using a *human-based* language are neither always possible nor useful.[55]

Dr. Pepperberg notes that part of the problem in devising methods that demonstrate the *true* extent of animal cognitive competence involves the abilities and limitations of human researchers, rather than the limitations of the animal subjects. Not only must an animal's inherent and *perceptual* capabilities be taken into consideration, but experimental designs must allow the subject not only to learn a task, but also to *express* its knowledge effectively.[56]

Captive Dolphin Studies

Unfortunately the best-known comparative studies involving dolphins have severely limited the avenues available for them to demonstrate or express the full extent of their comprehension and cognitive abilities. Dr. Bekoff states that often research studies on behavior, cognition and communication in captive animals are so controlled, they can produce misleading results. Animals that are being studied in artificial, physical environments (typical captive dolphin pools, tanks and laboratory conditions) may be so stressed or tainted from living in captivity, that data may be compromised from the start. Thus, the limitations scientists encounter may be inherent in captive methodologies, rather than an accurate indication of animals' actual capacities. Bekoff comments: *'In many cases animals are as smart as our methods of study allow them to be. We just need to be clever enough to tap into how they do things in their worlds, not ours.'*[57]

Much dolphin research done in labs has been hampered by using animals captured at an age likely too young to have learned the full use of their species' communication modes. Additionally, cetaceans who are born or grow up in captivity, develop bereft of the rich intellectual nectar which wild dolphins' societal fabric provides, leaving captives deficient in numerous ways that we are only just beginning to appreciate. Stress inherent in captive conditions has added further deformation to research efforts, while the limitations of the human hearing range and resulting equipment restrictions have also proved problematic.

In many cases, scientific credibility rests on the need to offer only what can be demonstrated under controlled, repeated, conditions. Biologist Lyall Watson points out that everything we know about dolphins' awareness and sociability suggests that they are likely to be bored by programs which require that they perform repetitive and meaningless tasks,[58] especially in isolated conditions, away from the "distraction" of peers or playthings. Thus, traditional scientific captive studies have provided dolphins with a less than optimum environment in which to display their intellectual abilities to us.

Nevertheless, despite less than optimum conditions, dolphins have shown very high levels of problem solving ability, flexible behavior, inventiveness, forward planning, learning and an ability to utilize new knowledge.

The Dolphin Institute

Beginning in the 1970s, Dr. Louis Herman professor of Psychology at the University of Hawaii, conducted cognitive and language studies on dolphins. Using two bottlenose dolphins, he studied their vision, hearing, learning, intelligence and memory and found that in tasks involving auditory memory the dolphins were able to out-perform humans.[59]

However, almost from the start, Herman's dolphin research was dogged by controversy. In 1977, two lab attendants, former students of Herman's, loaded the two research dolphins into a van and set them free in the ocean. Unfortunately, they were *Atlantic* bottlenose dolphins and were released in the *Pacific* Ocean. One of the freedom crusaders was quoted in a 1979 issue of *National Geographic*: *'We were giving them what every animal or person truly deserves in life – his own freedom.'* Herman's former students claimed the two dolphins were frustrated by repetitious experiments, conducted in a barren concrete tank only fifty feet in diameter and a paltry five feet in depth (less than a dolphin's body length). They also claimed Herman would deprive them of toys and companionship and criticized that these conditions were having adverse effects on the dolphins. They concluded that leaving the dolphins to spend the rest of their lives under such conditions was immoral, stating humans had no right *'to hold intelligent, feeling beings like dolphins in captivity.'*[60]

Immoral or not, Herman soon replaced the original two dolphins with another pair, captured in the Gulf of Mexico at the tender age of two or three years old. These two dolphin research subjects were dubbed *Akeakamai* and *Phoenix*.[61]

Akeakamai learned a gestural language, distantly related to American Sign Language, while Phoenix learned an acoustical language of computer-generated whistles. Each dolphin was taught about thirty words, including verbs and nouns, names for themselves, various objects, like ball and net, directions like right, left, surface, bottom, over, under and concepts of yes and no. These words could be strung together to form either instructions or questions. Both dolphins learned to understand sentences expressed through these simple artificial languages and demonstrated their understanding by succeeding at task instructions involving *novel* sentences. Both also learned to report on the absence or presence of objects in the tank.[62] After working with two or three word sentences, the dolphins learned at once to comply with four word sentences and later, those with five words.[63] By 1990, the dolphins had demonstrated their understanding of more than two thousand different sentences, using about sixty words.[64] Herman was careful to control for non-linguistic cues and used novel sentences to assess the dolphins' comprehension. In particular, the dolphins' ability to handle *new* sentences on the first try was a critical indicator of just how impressive their cognitive abilities were. In fact, this was one of Herman's most significant findings because such comprehension was considered a hallmark of human language ability.[65]

Word order meaning lies at the core of syntax (the difference between *man eats fish* and *fish eats man*) and formal linguists proclaim syntax the quintessential component of human language, allowing for virtually unlimited forms of meaning.[66] The reversibility of such sentences like "take the ball to the surfboard" significantly revealed that both dolphins were also very aware of the syntactic rules governing their language,[67] and demonstrated that dolphins are capable of comprehending how syntax and semantics change sentence meaning.[68] Before these results, it was claimed that humans were the only species with the intellectual sophistication to handle such concepts.[69]

Not only did Akeakamai and Phoenix prove their ability to understand the imposed grammar of complicated human sentences using both acoustic and visual codes, they also learned to understand the holding up of replicas in place of object-word-gestures, to understand human pointing in place of object referral and to spontaneously imitate human actions and vocalizations[70] — all of which require very sophisticated cognitive capacities. Herman also tested the dolphins' responses to "nonsense" sentences and these opened an opportunity for the dolphins to display some creative thinking. When asked to take one object to another that was not actually present in the tank, the dolphin spontaneously solved this seemingly impossible request by taking the only item present to the NO panel.[71] This kind of problem-solving ability demonstrates *extremely* impressive and creative reasoning!

Both dolphins also learned the sign for "creative act of choice" where they were required to create new and spontaneous behaviors — another cognitively impressive feat. They were later taught the concept of *"creative tandem"* where they had to make up a spontaneous behavior and demonstrate it *together*. Not only were Ake and Phoenix able to grasp and demonstrate these difficult concepts, but video documentation appeared to reveal the two dolphins briefly "conferring" together just before executing these spontaneous, synchronous, creative tasks.[72] How exactly the arrangement for such spontaneous performance was made, or what signals passed between the two dolphins in coordinating behaviors that require rapid, simultaneous responses, remained admittedly beyond their captors' perception.[73]

Phoenix and Akeakamai (among others) also proved themselves capable of spontaneously understanding gestural instructions given through televised images, with no prior training or demonstration.[74] They subsequently responded accurately to increasingly abstract images, such as arms or hands gesturing on black background. The dolphins proved their understanding of these TV relays as representations of real requests through the accuracy of their responses, which were on par with fluent human responses.[75]

So astute and sophisticated were the dolphins' abilities, it was discovered they could infer which objects were being referred to by human pointing gestures or even eye gaze — findings that were then replicated at another facility.[76] This implies the dolphins were able to understand the *intention* behind these human gestures, referring to varying objects at a distance, which is considered an *extremely* sophisticated mental operation, involving abstract, conceptual thinking.[77]

Other scientists have commented that probably the most remarkable and striking implications of Herman's language research stems from the dolphins' capacity to comprehend human language to the extent they do, pointing out that within the parameters of such research, the dolphins are operating in a *foreign cognitive environment* and their proven ability to adapt to a human created language demonstrates an even more sophisticated intellectual capacity than handling syntax commands containing abstract terms. They continue: '*Even though there is nothing obviously parallel to human language among dolphins, it is highly unlikely, considering the age of the dolphin brain, that the cognitive capacities that dolphins evidence in language research were sitting unused until human researchers came along... That dolphins demonstrate the capacity to operate within an artificial representational and rule-governed system is highly suggestive that they employ the capacity in their own lives, (the details of which, have yet to be identified) that is as cognitively complex as the human capacity for language without being analogous in structure and form.*'[78]

Full language competence usually involves both production and comprehension, but cetacean studies have predominantly involved comprehension without much allowance for production. Unlike a number of other acclaimed communication projects with other animals, including parrots, chimpanzees and gorillas, Herman's language experiments did not invite or enable the dolphins to make requests, comments, express themselves, or initiate communicative exchanges themselves. Through the specific codes Herman devised, the dolphins were unable to communicate except by responding to commands via direct action or answering questions via Yes/No paddles and so, while Akeakamai and Phoenix demonstrated linguistic *comprehension*, they were not *allowed* to *produce* language. Dr.

Herman's experiments were perfect for giving orders, but not for two-way communicative or expressive interchanges.

Dr. Herman has worked under contract for the US Navy and used dolphins previously used or procured by the Navy in his experiments.[79] Herman's experiments have also yielded the kinds of results likely to be of great military interest; indeed, it would be foolish to suppose that teaching dolphins to report on the absence, presence or nature of underwater objects and to follow precise, varied, complex orders given by humans, would *not* be of immense interest and use in the military's much-criticized, classified deployment of cetaceans in its projects.

Controversy over Herman's captive dolphin experiments continued: in 2000, when one of Herman's dolphins died prematurely from an infection, Hawaiian animal advocates called for an end to his repetitive experiments in "cruel" conditions, and for the remaining dolphins held at his lab to be rehabilitated and released back to their ancestral waters. Under increasing criticism, Herman defended his work with the familiar rhetoric so-often used by the captivity industry, insisting the dolphins he kept were ambassadors — a misnomer, as lawyer and author Steven Wise points out, because the dolphins had *no choice* in the matter and did not represent their sovereigns, making the word "ambassador" inaccurate.[80]

Concerning his experiments, Herman wrote: *'The work we have carried out with dolphins has expanded our understanding of the perceptual world of this species and certainly has demonstrated that the dolphin's reputation for intelligence is well-earned.'*[81] Sadly, the dolphins' well-earned reputation for intelligence was not such that it exempted them from capture or life-incarceration in Herman's tiny tanks. Despite their impressive intellects, captive dolphins are still considered human property.

Perhaps what Dr. Herman's research *should* have taught him (and other associated public or academic entities) is that these intelligent, sophisticated, sensitive, sonic, sentient, social and naturally wide-ranging creatures do *not* belong in tiny concrete tanks, being ordered around or endlessly barraged with repetitive instructions by curious or even well-meaning humans. Examining the implications of their own research, other scientists before Herman have found their way to similar conclusions.[82]

Finally, Dr. Herman's research has satisfied some human curiosity, but at what cost? Despite expert care, all the dolphins at Herman's research facility, including Akeakamai and Phoenix have died prematurely from illnesses.

At present we persist in assuming that we are perfectly entitled to *use* cetaceans for our purposes, whether as research subjects to feed our curiosity (or as it is so often grandly expressed, "to further science"), as entertainment in marine parks, or to turn profits in swim programs. Despite the deaths of over seven million dolphins, some tuna fishermen *still* feel they have every right to continue using dolphins to catch tuna. People need to realize that it is *exactly* the *same* underlying mindset responsible for all of these things — which result in dolphins suffering and dying because of unchallenged human desires. Thus, captive institutes, while insisting they promote research, education and conservation, ignore their own very *real* roll in supporting and encouraging the kind of mindset that perpetuates harmful human acts against cetaceans.

Finally, it is very worth noting that while dolphins have proven their ability to learn relatively sophisticated artificial languages, humans remain unable to decode the majority of dolphin vocalizations, which may themselves constitute a kind of previously unknown language. It is interesting to observe that in terms of understanding and utilizing foreign communication codes, the dolphins appear to be displaying capabilities superior to our own.

Project Delphis

Dr. Kenneth Marten, a cetacean biologist studying dolphin awareness in Hawaii, set out to gather evidence that dolphins are self-aware beings, in order to encourage positive changes in human perception and treatment of dolphins, particularly on the legislative level.

Dr. Marten video taped dolphins engaging in self-examination in front of mirrors, twisting and posturing, even looking into their own mouths and tongue curling (the dolphin equivalent of making faces). The dolphins watched themselves blowing bubbles and sometimes brought objects to manipulate in front of their reflections — all of which *strongly* suggested *self-awareness*. The dolphins appeared to respond to the mirror quickly and Marten speculates an explanation may lie the presence of windows in the tanks, which appear to provide adequate reflective surfaces (the quality of which likely varied with changing light at different times of day).[83] Wild dolphins may also be familiar with their own reflections, as the ocean on a calm day, creates a beautiful mirror, just below the surface.

To combat a lack of novelty, the dolphins were marked on their backs (a blind spot) with spots of zinc oxide sunscreen cream. This was Dr. Marten's version of the Gallup dot test: and he videotaped the results of five bottlenose dolphins' reactions and behavior through a one-way mirror. Again, the dolphins were observed twisting, turning, contorting and rhythmically posturing to examine these new marks.[84]

To be sure that these postures related to displays of self-awareness, rather than social reaction, Dr. Marten compared the dolphins' behaviors to their reactions when encountering a *real* stranger (through an underwater gate) and also by recording the dolphins watching themselves on TV in real-time and play back modes for comparison. Results from these experiments concluded that the findings were consistent with self-examination rather than social behavior and that the data in its entirety, makes a compelling case for self-recognition and self-awareness in the bottlenose species.[85] Dr. Marten's work was subsequently repeated, testing two bottlenose dolphins at the New York Aquarium, by marking them with temporary black ink on parts of their bodies they could see only with a mirror. The dolphins were filmed as they interacted with a plexiglas mirror and the glass walls of their tank, again clearly demonstrating self-recognition behaviors. Analyzed data was described as "definitive evidence" of mirror-self-recognition, and thus, self-awareness, furthering the strength of Dr. Marten's conclusions.[86] Yet another similar study concluded that several other cetacean species, like bottlenose dolphins (but unlike California sea lions), also appear to possess the cognitive abilities required for self-recognition.[87]

At present it appears scientific measure has yet to map the upper or outer limits of dolphin mental capabilities. It has, perhaps quite reasonably, been volunteered that with our younger, smaller brains, we simply may not be able to. As scientists devise new, creative, technological ways to investigate their intellectual capacity, dolphins gracefully rise to the challenge.

Wild Research

Over the past fifty years, the number of research projects studying wild animals in their natural environments has sky rocketed, led by an intrepid and innovative breed of field scientist into every corner of the globe, studying increasing numbers of animal species, including cetaceans. It is the collective, ever-evolving discoveries of these wild studies that mark the way of the future in useful, non-invasive human inquiry into the lives of non-human animals.

Long-term behavioral studies are shedding unprecedented light on cetacean societies, communication, cognition, life history, behavior and ecology. Recognition of free-ranging individuals by researchers is the breakthrough that allows the description of social relationships in wild animals. Individuals are usually identified and recognized using photographs of natural markings and it is important for researchers to maintain a photo-catalogue of individuals in the study area. As many individuals as possible must be identified, including age, sex and if possible the genetic relationships between the "cast of characters" in the study area. Known individuals are followed over hours, weeks, months or years, while specific behavioral information is recorded in a systematic fashion. Thus, researchers are eventually furnished with a comprehensive perspective on individuals' social lives. The meaning of behavior and relationships is determined through detailed observation and documentation of the context and history of interactions between individuals and groups. With time and patience, non-invasive studies on wild cetaceans have been developed, including habituation to the presence of research boats or even swimmers. Studies of cetacean behavior have increased in number and scope in recent years and although dolphins and whales are often difficult to observe at length, reliable techniques for doing so now exist and are being improved upon. Technological advances, like satellite imagery and temporary suction cup tags are opening new windows for studying cetaceans in the wild and can produce a wealth of high-resolution data about their lives.[88]

Within the context of such studies, known animals cease to be regarded as anonymous members of a merely statistical population, and instead become recognized as *individuals* with identities and life histories. When this happens wild animal communities can no longer be exploited with perfect impunity — because individuals are recognized and named and if harm or death occurs — especially due to human activity — they are missed! Through such long-term affiliations, scientists and researchers are increasingly recognizing the important roll they can play in conservation initiatives, helping to identify and call attention to threats and problems, turning learned experts into responsible advocates on behalf of species and ecosystems.[89]

Ethology

Science is developing new ways of investigating the inner worlds of non-human animals. Researchers, often behavioral biologists, ecologists, or psychologists who study animal minds *through* animal behavior, especially in field situations, are known as *cognitive ethologists*. Ethology is the study of animal minds, how they think, what they think about and how they remember and process information; striving to better understand the nature of animal consciousness and emotions by observing their behavior, usually in a natural environment.[90] Primatologist Dr. Roger Fouts feels that ethology at its best, takes a very humble approach towards nature, putting theories, assumptions and scientific dogma aside, and focusing on observation, rather than manipulation.[91] Dr. Denise Herzing describes cognitive ethologists as *'patient observers'* and writes: *'The difference between ethology and psychological behavioral studies lies mostly in ethology's strong emphasis on spontaneous behavior in the natural environment — waiting to see what animals do of their own accord, instead of encouraging a particular kind of behavior for experimental purposes.'*[92]

Much serious contemporary inquiry into the study of animal minds and behavior has come through the work of behaviorists like Dr. Donald Griffin, who took a common sense view that animals are likely to think about what they are doing and the results they expect from their actions. To the careful and informed observer, studying how individuals adapt to novel or rapidly changing situations offers great insight about what may be happening in their minds. Dr. Griffin wrote: *'Cognitive Ethology presents us with one of the supreme scientific challenges of our times and it calls for our best efforts of critical and imaginative investigation.'*[93] Dr. Bekoff affirms that by using a combination of careful observation and educated intuition, we can learn a lot about our animal kin and about ourselves.[94]

Animal Culture

Humans like to think of themselves in a class all their own — that it is only we who use tools, experience emotion, are conscious and have culture. These boundaries have been repeatedly crossed by animals and for Western science, this began with Jane Goodall's pioneering work and discovery in the 1960s that wild chimpanzees use tools.[95] A growing mountain of evidence demonstrates that varied animal species transmit culture between generations, are self-aware, use insight (not just trial and error), to solve problems, understand the effects of their actions, learn and cooperate, use and make tools; and given appropriate opportunity and motivation, can teach, deceive, empathize and even self-medicate.[96]* Dr. Bekoff writes: *'Researchers have now discovered that tool use, language use, self-consciousness, culture, art and rationality no longer can reliably be used to draw species boundaries*

---

* There is mounting evidence for self-medication, widespread in a number of animals: see Frans De Waal's *The Ape and the Sushi Master: Cultural Reflections of a Primatologist,* Basic Books, New York 2001 (pp. 254-5).

that separate humans from other animals... Claims that only humans use tools or language, are artists, have culture, or reason are no longer defensible given the enormous growth in our knowledge of our animal kin.'[97]

Primatologist Dr. Frans De Waal defines *culture* as the habits and innovations of a group, transmitted non-genetically to successive generations. Traits passed on through learning can be regarded as traditions and a set of group-specific traditions can be regarded as culture.[98] Dr. Roger Fouts observes that culture — whether art, tool making, or language — is always transmitted through *learning*, rather than genetics.[99] A broad definition of culture is defined simply as non-genetic behavioral transmission of knowledge and habits *learned* from others, which explains why two groups of the same species may behave differently. Such definition applies easily to both animals and humans without the exclusion of either.[100]

Rather than occurring through random mutation, habits often result from *deliberate choices*: thus, culture can be *consciously created*. Students of animal behavior are widely treating culture as a complex phenomenon with its own dynamics, most of which, have barely been explored. There exists a complex interplay between genetic and cultural transmission and the study of "cultural biology" occurs where the fields of anthropology and zoology meet and overlap.

Regarding culture in non-humans, de Waal suggests that the proverb, '*It takes a village to raise a child*' probably applies just as much to dolphins, baboons, elephants and many other animals. In his excellent book, *The Ape and the Sushi Master*, de Waal writes of his conviction that, '*the more we look for culture in animals, the more we will find it. ...The rapidly growing literature gives the impression that we have only scratched the surface: cultural diversity in the animal kingdom probably takes on vast proportions. ...The world is full of feathered and furry animals that learn their life's lessons, habits and songs from one another...*'[101]

Cultural-Cognitive Complexity in Cetaceans

Cetacean societies are among the most complex in the mammalian world, however scientific research into this fascinating realm is in its infancy, as field studies on free-ranging cetaceans only began about thirty years ago. Though significant gaps remain in our understanding of these creatures, intriguing illumination continues to issue from long-term studies focusing on the societies of wild cetaceans. Many researchers favor an ethological or ethnographic approach, understanding that the full complexity and dynamic of cetacean cultures can only be observed and appreciated by studying them in the context of their natural settings and social groupings. Researchers who spend days and nights on and in the water, year after year alongside dolphins and whales, are among those who know cetaceans best, recording the intimate details of their lives, learning about who they really are and the subtleties of the societies they live in.

Insight into the complexities of cetaceans' natural societies is essential for understanding the minds of dolphins and whales. There are likely critical differences in how an aqueous intelligence manifests itself, as compared to terrestrial intelligence, and scientific inquiry continues to chip away at the edges of this mystery. Researcher Dr. Rachel Smolker notes: '*Certainly our best measure of dolphin intelligence comes from watching what they do, rather than looking at their brain anatomy and guessing how they might use such an organ. ...ultimately we must go out to the oceans and see what they do, how they live. It is out there, after all, that they evolved those large brains, over millions of years, and it is there that they must make use of them.*'[102]

It has been noted that though modern Western culture tends to emphasize the independent individual, other cultures place much more emphasis on an individual's relationship to family and community, which makes for a far more *interconnected* concept of "self." Some scientists speculate that in cetaceans, the concept of "self" may be an inherently social one.[103] For orcas *family* is central to all aspects around which their lives revolve, living in stable matrilineal family groups consisting of up to four generations of whales, which may live up to sixty or even eighty or ninety years of age.[104]

Social living appears not only to have goaded intellectual expansion in cetaceans, but has also led to the development of culturally specific traditions in a number of species. Researcher and whale expert Dr. Hal Whitehead considers it very likely that culture is widespread among cetaceans, perhaps taking some forms rarely found in non-human terrestrial animals. He speculates: '*The ocean would seem to be an excellent medium for the evolution of vocal, social and foraging cultures – although not material cultures, with no hands and few suitable materials.*'[105] Scientists have compiled a list of around twenty behavior patterns in cetaceans that are influenced by local tradition and show cultural variation.[106] Bottlenose dolphins, orca whales and sperm whales (among the best-studied species) are culturally diverse. Little-studied species like pelagic dolphins, river dolphins and beaked whales likely have still other social systems about which we know very little. Cultural transmission occurs through observational social learning, through teaching, mimicry and the synchronization of behavior during exposure to the many activities comprising social life. Cetacean society forms a repository of experience, traditions and information that can be passed from older to younger dolphins, or shared fluidly and dynamically between all age groups.[107]

Like humans, cetaceans possess biological attributes that favor social learning and culture: long lives, advanced cognitive abilities and prolonged parental care.[108] Evidence is accumulating that in some cetacean species, mothers transmit important information to members of their family line by instruction and social learning in a manner that appears rare outside of human society. Both orcas and pilot whales possess matrilineal social systems and (like human females) may live decades after the birth of their last offspring. Scientists suspect cultural processes may have played a part in this phenomenon. Pilot whales may suckle their young for up to fifteen years and cease to ovulate at around forty, though their maximum life span exceeds sixty years, which means twenty-five percent of an adult female's life may be post-reproductive.[109] Extended menopausal persistence is rare in the animal kingdom, however, if the cultural teaching role of older, experienced cetacean females as living sources of information is very important, post-menopausal continuance could be highly adaptive, significantly increasing the fitness and survival of family descendants. It may be that the extended infancy and adolescence of dolphins and whales is required to learn extensive culturally and cognitively complex behaviors from parents and community. These ideas are also relevant to our understanding of human prehistory, as such cultural development may closely parallel early human evolution.[110]

In cultural animal societies, individuals with important cultural knowledge can carry exceptional significance in their community, far in excess of their reproductive value. Because a species can be culturally as well as genetically diverse, with differing habits, customs and knowledge which allows animals adapt to changes in their immediate environments — science is beginning to realize that cultural diversity can affect issues of species conservation.[111]

Orcas

Orcas, or killer whales, inhabit in all the world's oceans and are the apex predators of the oceanic food chain, enjoying an extreme range in food items.[112] One of the obvious distinguishing cultural variances between orca tribes can be seen in the quarry they pursue, the hunting techniques they employ and how they pass these skills onto their young. In some areas, female killer whales are known to spend years showing their youngsters how to hunt elephant seals according to local custom.[113]

Another distinct cultural variant among orcas are the different vocal dialects used by each clan, which are so distinctive that astute researchers can tell passing orca families apart merely by listening to their haunting underwater calls on strategically placed hydrophones.[114]

Like other cetacean researchers, Dr. Alexandra Morton found that orcas seem to enjoy creating and adopting less functional behaviors that for all practical purposes appeared to be what we would call "fads." *'Each year certain behaviors get started in one pod, move through the entire northern resident community, then disappear by the next summer. In summer 1980 it was headstands.'*[115] Other kinds of cultural behavior appear more formalized and enduring, including community specific "greeting ceremonies" which have been observed when different orca pods meet up.[116]

Dr. Morton also observed how orcas appear to gain satisfaction, even joy from creating and perfecting actions *together*, which led her to state that *synchrony* is a founding principal of orca society. She wrote that in many instances, it appeared the behavior itself was secondary and that what mattered was acting in synchrony with someone else.[117] My experiences have led me to this same conclusion; that *synchrony* is an integral cornerstone of cetacean relations, culture, thought and delight.

After decades of closely observing wild killer whales, Dr. Morton cannot shake the suspicion that orcas represent a sentience to be reckoned with. Regarding the degree of intelligence possessed by orcas (with a brain almost four times the size of a human's) she writes: *'Their intelligence has yet to be adequately analyzed; indeed their powers of cognition may be too complex for us to accurately quantify. In brain power they may surpass us.'*[118]

The Largest Brain on the Planet

It is the sperm whale that lays claim to the largest brain on this planet, having a mass five or six times greater than our own, with a mean of 7.8kg and a maximum of 9.2kg — compared with about 1.5 kg in humans.[119] In his book *The Charged Border*, Jim Nollman speculates on the topic of intelligence as it pertains to men and sperm whales, pointing out that if fives times the brain does in fact mean five times the mind, the human capacity to test the claim may simply not exist. *'If the Sperm whale possesses a fivefold intellect, then the human mind is too puny an instrument to confirm it. ...Even if brain size is not a reliable indicator of intelligence, the extent of our own ignorance can be amply demonstrated by the fact that until recently humans related to this potential wisdom keeper only as a repository of oil.'*[120]

Dr. Hal Whitehead, considered the foremost scientific authority on sperm whales, addresses the question of their intelligence and culture, in his book *Sperm Whales: Social Evolution in the Ocean*. Dr. Whitehead notes that the architecture of the sperm whale's brain suggests strengths in acoustic processing, conscious mental processes, intelligence, personality and sensory processing, pointing out that the neo cortex is particularly large, and in primates, this is the area of the brain most closely associated with social intelligence. The lives of sperm whales strongly appear to be organized along cultural lines and cultural structuring has thus-far been found in all of the best-studied cetacean species.[121]

An interesting area of study includes the different patterns of clicks that sperm whales utilize, some for hunting (and probably navigation) and others specifically for communication. Like orcas, sperm whales appear to possess stable, group-specific vocal repertoires. Social units possessing similar click repertoires, have been classified into "clans" with each clan's differing repertoire known as its' "dialect," which probably represent cultural variants and may also be markers of important cultural divides.[122] Scientists investigating the whales' use of rhythmic inter-sound pulse-intervals, suggest these exchanges may affirm social relationships and possibly advertise the identities of clans and individual members.[123]

A precise understanding of how sperm whales communicate using their complex, rhythmic patterns of clicks remains unknown at present. It is possible that the whales' complex vocalizations relate to the syncopated, rhythmically encoded communication systems described at length by biologist Dr. Peter Beamish in his book, *Dancing with Whales*[124] as an example of what may be Nature's Morse Codes.

Dolphins

Socially, emotionally and intellectually, dolphins are highly sophisticated beings.[125] Almost anyone who has worked with or watched dolphins at any length can recount examples of their intelligence and creative thinking. In addition to the information presented here and elsewhere, there is plenty of circumstantial evidence, and these anecdotes* paint an increasingly clear

---

* A Note on Anecdotes: We should be cautious about dismissing anecdotes because such isolated observations may represent critical clues regarding animal intelligence. Anecdotal observations can indicate important starting points for rigorous scientific study and when many anecdotal accounts point independently to consistent patterns, anecdotes are transformed into natural history; the plural of anecdote becomes data.

picture of dolphins as conscious, conceptualizing creatures of impressive and intricate intellect.

An anecdote of which I am fond describes a researcher gazing through the underwater viewing window at an aquarium observing the dolphins beyond. While he was puffing on a cigarette, a baby dolphin came over to investigate, peering through the glass back at him. The researcher exhaled a cloud of smoke right before the eyes of the baby dolphin, who followed its rising trail. After a moment, the baby dolphin swam over to its mother and nursed, immediately after which it returned to the viewing window and before the astonished eyes of the researcher, released it's mouthful of milk — which underwater almost exactly resembled the cloud of cigarette smoke![126] The implications of this dolphin's communicative-imitative gesture are very much worth noting as such imitation actually involves abstract, complex, communicative skills, demanding very high cognitive abilities. Scientific experiments have since proven dolphins capable of both extensive physical *and* vocal mimicry.[127] It is speculated that these abilities may derive from the high degrees of synchronicity and cohesion present in dolphin society.[128] In fact, cetaceans and certain bird species are among the only animals that display vocal learning and mimicry, which is otherwise glaringly rare among terrestrial animals. Since such imitative vocal learning is so vital to human language and communication, its lack in other primate species is striking.[129]

Research has found that dolphins are equipped to analyze situations and to learn and solve problems by making considered judgments about the possible consequences of their actions. Dolphins have impressive, accurate memories, phenomenally complex relationships, an ability to grasp abstract concepts and inexplicably, a capacity to comprehend the fundamental principles of language (including syntax and names).[130] They are also among the few non-human animals able to recognize, and even examine themselves in a mirror, which is considered a cognitive milestone, inferring self-awareness and sentience.

Like humans, dolphins seemed to have responded intellectually to social pressures. Given the correlation between brain size and social complexity, Dr. Smolker says dolphins *should* have the very large brains they possess. She writes that in the dolphins' world, *'it is easy to imagine the advantages of a little political savvy, diplomatic skills, an ability to outsmart or manipulate others; to envision the consequences of your behavior before taking action, to empathize with others and assess what they may or may not know and how they feel, and perhaps even to reflect on one's self in relation to other group members.'*[131] Smolker believes that like us, dolphins' minds are on each other and is convinced that this is the driving force behind dolphin intelligence. She thinks it likely and that they spend much of their brainpower keeping track of who does what with whom, engaging in rivalries and social politics and figuring out what others might be thinking, while competing and cooperating in complicated, shifting, multi-leveled alliances.[132]

During a protracted period of development and dependence, young dolphins participate in an extensive enculturation process, familiarizing them with the rules and conventions of their society and with cooperative and collaborative activities, while learning the identities and personalities of other dolphins in their extended community. This process begins as baby dolphins learn to decipher the repertoire of social signals they are exposed to, while observing the contextual social interactions and reactions of their mothers, siblings and community; young primates, including humans, learn in a similar manner. The correct meaning and application of acoustic, visual, tactile and social signals are likely refined and confirmed by older, experienced dolphins during daily social activities like foraging, courtship, fighting and play.[133]

Obviously, dolphins don't build or write anything — and have no need to, and yet they have developed brains, which not only compare with ours, but in some species, may outstrip ours. The human dependence on tools means that a large part of human culture exits outside of the individual, whereas in dolphins it is still embodied within the individual's brain and behavior, which likely creates a substantial difference in how human and cetacean perceive and interact with their worlds.

However, instances of dolphin tool-use appear to be among the cultural-type behaviors passed on to offspring through their mothers, an example of which can be seen in bottlenose dolphins of Shark Bay, Australia. Out of a population of about sixty or so dolphins, a few individuals, all females, have been observed using sea sponges lodged on their rostrums using these apparent tools to protect their snouts as they scour the sea floor for prey.[134] Author Dr. Thomas White notes that the cognitive sophistication demanded by the complexities of dolphin social life makes the ability to use natural objects as tools look simple by comparison.[135]

Culturally, dolphins employ diverse and complex foraging strategies, efficiently tailored to specific species, situations and group-sizes, involving a high degree of cohesion and cooperation.[136] In some parts of the world these strategies have even come to include humans, resulting in some interesting instances of interspecies cooperation. Since at least 1847 in Laguna, Brazil, the local wild bottlenose dolphins have cooperated closely with local fishermen. Following a strict, almost ritual protocol, involving no training or verbal commands, humans and dolphins coordinate their actions. A distinct rolling dive from the dolphins signals to the men when they must throw their nets, while the dolphins rush forward, driving fish into them and eating their fill in the confusion.[137] The men cannot see the fish in the muddy water and daily rely on the dolphins' cues to make a successful catch. Similar practices are known in other parts of the world and have been reported since antiquity. This example of cooperative fishing in Brazil is a clear case of both dolphins and humans passing a distinctive *interspecies* cultural tradition down through generations.

Of course dolphins don't just use their savvy for foraging. Dolphins can also be infamously playful and utilize their intelligence in *creative* and playful ways. As conscious breathers, dolphins can control their underwater exhalations to create bubble rings. The production of stable bubble rings requires not only practice and expertise, but also forethought. Younger dolphins seem to learn to produce bubble rings by watching older dolphins and the quality and complexity of bubble ring development seems to increase with age and experience. When playing with bubble rings, dolphins appear to demonstrate anticipatory planning by consistently positioning themselves low in the water column before commencing ring creation. Dolphins have frequently been observed to monitor and manipulate their bubble ring creations, using their bodies or by generating vortices around the rings, which can cause them to turn vertically 90 degrees or flip orientation by 180 degrees. They may also conjoin one bubble ring to another, forming a single, larger ring, blow smaller rings through bigger rings, or swim right through their shimmering, hoop-like creations. After carefully following the bubbles' trajectory and manipulating them in various ways, the dolphins' most frequent final response is to bite the silvery rings, thereby destroying them! Researchers observing these shimmering, spontaneous acts of creation by the dolphin mind are fascinated.[138]

Humans have great difficulty in perceiving, recording and thereby appreciating the full scope of the acoustic world in which cetaceans are immersed. The dolphin hearing range is up to ten times that of humans. A dolphin's echolocation click train may be made up of hundreds or even thousands of sound pulses per second[139] and the extensive auditory processing areas of their brains are capable of separating those pulses and decoding the contours of each individual echo, all the while still interrogating a target. To the human ear, such sound pulses fuse together in our minds at a mere twenty-to-thirty clicks per second. In the past, recording technologies were too limited to make the full bandwidth utilized by dolphins available to researchers limiting the full spectrum of information. The development and application of high-speed digitizing has increased the human ability to document the full acoustic repertoire of signals being used, opening up a rich store of potential information for scientific decoding in many band frequencies used by dolphins.[140]

Acoustically, dolphins can discriminate pitch, duration, amplitude, frequency, contour, sequencing patterns, octave adjustment and inter-sound intervals. Features such as rhythmic spacing between signals may be particularly relevant, as rhythmic signal sequences may play a *crucial* role, especially when combined with synchronous body motions, in the social interactions of many species, including dolphins. Such universal rhythmic modes of communication infer evolutionary continuity between species, though at present, this is a neglected area of behavioral analysis.[141] Continuing on this important aside, eminent cetacean researcher Dr. Ken Norris noted that because the differing layers of water temperature and density of oceanic conditions can create distortions in pitch, information encoded in the precise *timing* of acoustic communications is more easily deciphered over distance.[142]

Dolphins appear able to perceive, process and transmit a wider range of sensory information than humans. Their sense of echolocation provides three-dimensional information on the texture, internal structure, density and composition of objects, environment and other living creatures.[143] Dolphins also appear to have highly integrated audio-visual perception that may synchronously generate visual images from auditory information and vice versa. Other little studied dolphin senses may include an ability to tactilely receive and interpret acoustic information with their bodies through skin receptors. It appears dolphins can also use echolocation in a tactile manner, effectually enabling them to reach out and touch or investigate items of interest (including each other) via pure sound.[144]

Set amid their dizzying social milieus, dolphin dialects are rapid, rhythmic, almost musical, and research technology is only just allowing us to detect and decipher the full range of their acoustical complexities. Studies of dolphins in varied social contexts report dolphins produce a wide variety of whistles, some which appear unique to individuals (like signature whistles), and others that are shared between social groups.[145] Field research on wild dolphin populations is beginning to reveal differences in dialect — the types and structure of whistles used by different groups of dolphins.[146] Recent research examining the complexity of cetacean vocalizations has discovered that the information-carrying capacity of dolphin whistles is similar to many human languages, which suggests that they could potentially be speaking their own language.[147] In a recent preliminary study, Information Theory (originally designed to mathematically examine the information capacity and organization of communication systems) was applied as an objective tool for examining and comparing the organization, informational complexity and development of human and dolphin vocal repertoires. This method yields statistical information for objectively analyzing and clarifying communicative repertoires of unknown structure or function (as in the case of dolphin whistles, about which so little is known).[148]

Using Information Theory, diverse human languages have been analyzed and graphed, all measuring a statistical balance using signals neither too repetitious nor too random, optimizing the amount of potential communication conveyed from speaker to receiver. A communication system exhibiting such balance indicates a high potential for a complex signaling (or language). Preliminary comparative analysis of adult dolphin whistle data showed a balance of -0.95, closely matching the optimum -1.00 balance in human language.[149]

Further research and evaluation along this avenue will require analyzing larger samples of dolphin whistle data. Continued advances in bio-acoustic technology are beginning to permit efficient analysis and categorization of large samples of acoustic data for such sequential and statistical analysis. Further investigation could eventually allow the reconstruction of dolphin whistle sequence structure (successfully accomplished with human language), possibly leading to eventual insights on *contextual* information within dolphin whistle repertoires.[150]

If dolphins do have a language, it likely shares more differences than similarities to human languages. Author Robin Brown speculated that dolphins don't need our kind of vocal language — an awkward and inefficient communication method underwater[151] — instead, they may have evolved their own complex, multifaceted communication system. These are areas of scientific inquiry we are just barely beginning to broach, and they hold the possibility of radical and wonderful discoveries.

After many years of studying different aspects of dolphin intelligence, neuroscientist Dr. John Lilly, concluded: *'It would be presumptuous to assume that we, at the present time, can know how to measure their intellectual capacity.'*[152] According to the standard definition of intelligence, dolphins' ability to acquire and apply knowledge and skills is of a high caliber — and thus, by our own human definition, they are to be considered *extremely* intelligent. Of course people always want to know if dolphins are "smarter than us" unaware that such facile comparisons may not be possible or useful.

One thing about which we can be certain is that the dolphins' intelligence has led them to flourish for millions of years without degrading their environment (a claim we certainly cannot make). They also appear to have developed non-lethal ways of dealing with each other. Thus, it would seem that in many ways, dolphins give the appearance of being "smarter" in their world than we have proven to be in ours.

From Observer to Participant

Dr. Jane Goodall was one of the first pioneers to become a *cultural observer* of non-human lives. Primatologist Frans De Waal describes this: *'Much like cultural anthropologists who document how one human population differs from another...this method is now being applied to other animals, most successfully, dolphins and whales.'*[153]

Some ethologists are just beginning to take this role as cultural *observer* in non-human societies a step further (where appropriate or invited), into *cultural participant*. Dr. Denise Herzing, who has studied the social complexities of wild dolphins for over a quarter of a century, feels this approach can open up an enormously powerful new science of *participatory* research involving other species. She writes: *'The development of a participatory science or epistemology is already underway, specifically in the area of cognitive ethology and interspecies communication. Like other paradigms, boundaries must be crossed and a new way of thinking about possible methodologies and experimentation in science must emerge. Viewing non-human subjects as mutual, full participants in discovery, is likely to increase our understanding of other species, much like cultural anthropology has attempted to do with different human cultures.'*[154]

Careful, participatory ethology can involve researchers sharing daily life with other species, learning cultural nuances and habits, as they gradually learn to appropriately adopt, interpret and apply non-human communication systems. Universal, possibly rhythmic modes of communication may exist in the animal realm and while most humans may have forgotten the use of these signals, it may be possible to relearn, remember and reconnect via such communicative channels. Dolphins incorporating sensitive researchers into their lives and teaching adherence to their social rules, exemplify a new kind of consanguinity between human and *Other*, with a particular focus on forging *elective* bonds of trust. Insight and information stems and builds from long-term, respectful relationships where the animals always have the choice to leave or to invite interaction.

Despite our many differences, dolphins seem to recognize us as beings similar to themselves — beings who are intelligent and curious about other intelligences. Interspecies interaction satisfies none of the dolphins' basic survival needs — they appear to receive gratification solely from social interaction.[155] By partaking in the lives of other species and sharing experiences, we may create relationships and over time, mutual knowing; things that are *understood* between species. The ability to establish channels for interspecies communication is a very sophisticated intellectual operation and for generations many dolphins have been doing just this.

Dr. Herzing affirms that: *'Our ability to acknowledge them as full participants in mutual interactions could enhance our understanding of who they are in their environment. This is not to the exclusion of normal objective science. Instead it represents a complimentary approach to it, providing richness and aspects not attainable through the limited methodologies that we have used in the past.... The acceptance of interspecies interaction as a valid and important scientific area of inquiry will be dependent on the acceptance of a larger phenomena: That of a non-anthropo-centric relationship with nature. Expanding our ethical boundaries to include non-humans... The emerging paradigm that will allow interspecies interaction is larger than the current scientific one. It is not a paradigm about the potential intelligence and sentience of one species — in this case dolphins. It is about our appropriate interaction with the living world; of "being in relation with" rather than in control over.'*[156]

Wordless Connection

For many people their greatest ideas come to them in a pure, wordless form. Pictures, images, concepts, feelings, signs, symbols, smells, memories and even music can exist meaningfully in the mind, beyond words — which serve to elaborate (and sometimes obfuscate), one's range of thoughts. Not only can humans communicate thoughts and feelings without words — wordless exchanges comprise some of the most profound elements shared between people, frequently surpassing spoken exchanges.

Biologist Dr. Bernd Heinrich writes: *'We can and do think with words, but that's not because thinking requires words, but rather because we're social animals who have evolved to use words to communicate... I suspect the great gulf or discontinuity that exists between us and other animals, is ultimately less a matter of consciousness than of culture.'*[157]

Jim Nollman suggests that aspects of interspecies communication may not be a science so much as an art. Nollman has found that he is able to communicate with cetaceans and other animal species through music and rhythm. He writes: *'Science thrives on the careful replication of data. It seeks absolute answers, best expressed through the language of mathematics. Its tools are objectivity, observation, rigor and skepticism. By contrast, music with whales honors the axiom that there can be no absolute meaning in a work of art because everyone who experiences it gets to discover their own meaning. The process thrives on subjectivity, participation and improvisation.'*[158]

Other, non-musical kinds of interspecies communication may also defy analysis, just as a deft, private emotional exchange between two familiar human beings might. As subjective as such communication may be, in order to be understood, the worlds of any two communicators (of whatever species) must overlap, thus creating a realm (however fleeting) where different worlds can touch. Interspecies communication then becomes a delicate balancing act between the observer and participant, the subjective and objective; of experiencing and recording; of applying the intuitive to the rational. Dr. Konrad Lorenz, one of the founders of the study of ethology wrote that *'understanding seems quite separate from the methodology of the natural sciences. To marry intuitive insight with systematic data collection is both the challenge and the joy of studying animal behavior.'*[159]

In the realm of wordless, creative, often emotional exchanges, human and *Other* may meet and despite sometimes deep differences, find common ground where we can share of ourselves with one another. Emotional connections burst across the barriers between species in shared play, laughter, silliness and friendships, as well as other more subdued empathies.

Innumerable texts carry astonishing, touching stories of interspecies communion. When the barriers fall away, we may touch the richness in the hearts, minds and souls of *Other*, even if only for an incredibly illuminated instant, through the humble and poignant vehicle of shared experience.

The Future: Other into Us

Dr. Marc Bekoff uses the term "deep ethology" to describe the recognition that humans are not only an integral *part* of nature, but also our unique human responsibility to care for the natural world; sensitivity and humility being essential components of this guiding ethic.[160] Dr. Bekoff and his colleagues are among growing numbers of scientists whose work demonstrates that identifying intimately with a studied species does *not* compromise rigorous data collection and analysis, revealing that "hard" science can be compatible with compassionate socially-environmentally responsible science.

A worthy idea Dr. Bekoff puts forward, suggests scientists studying a particular species become advocates for that species and that this stewardship be considered of equal or even greater importance than obtaining peer-reviewed scientific results. He points out that scientists like Dr. Jane Goodall have exemplified this ethic. Dr. Bekoff refuses to take a reductionist and impersonal scientific view of our world, writing: *'I am in awe of how much nature has to offer when we take leave of our heads and open our hearts to her boundless and breathtaking splendor... Science can make nature less majestic and less magical by impeding our truly sensing, feeling and understanding the scope of the amazing world in which we live. ...Holistic, heartfelt science reinforces a sense of togetherness and relationship, family and community and awe. It fosters the development of deep and reciprocal friendships among humans, animals and nature. It helps us resonate with nature's radiance and lessens our tendency to think egocentrically, that we are at the center of everything. ...Saturating science with spirit, compassion, humility, grace and love can help bring science and nature together into a unified whole.'*[161] Similarly, Dr. Denise Herzing openly states her motivation emerges from a personal passion about the Earth. She writes: *'Instead of controlling the world through mechanistic science, a mature science would participate with the world in hopes of perceiving its subtleties.'*[162]

So often we find scientific writings devoid and dispassionate, with a glaring separation forced between the "seer and the seen." Dr. Bekoff writes: *'Science does not allow for expressions of sentimentality or spirituality. Unchecked, science can easily produce a soul-less society and a loss of human dignity and free will.'*[163] It has certainly produced a loss of dignity and free will for many non-humans. In her galvanizing and ground-breaking book *Silent Spring,*[164] Rachel Carson noted that the human drive to conquer and dominate nature sits at the root of our substantial and growing environmental problems. With this in mind, a science that encourages humans to detach themselves from their animal origins and regard nature as mere subjects or resources, does not offer much hope for the future.

Dr. Herzing affirms that a mature, evolved science views power as a grave responsibility, rather than license to dominate and indulge supremacy. *'It acknowledges intrinsic rights, interconnectedness and the need for respecting Earth and all its systems' needs. It seeks to improve the human-nature relationship...'*[165] For me, my years among the Cubano Dolphins have taught me that only by acknowledging non-humans as beings who are both feeling and aware can we hope to enter into their lives with true insight and comprehension, rather than forever remaining ignorant spectators.

And so we return to the question: *How smart are dolphins, really?* While it may be a long while before science presents us with irrefutable and definitive answers, at present, it would appear the experts' general consensus is: ***Very.***

In fact, we may yet determine that in some important ways cetaceans outstrip us in certain kinds of intelligence and thus, they may have a lot to teach us about becoming better social mammals and better beings.

Often, the question *"How intelligent are dolphins?"* translates as: *How much should they to be valued?* If they are determined to be very intelligent — (usually by being more like us), then they are more likely to be deemed worthy of our respect and thereby more deserving of life. Determining a non-human intelligence that matches (or exceeds) our own would have profound implications on many levels, some which we may not be ready to acknowledge.

To most humans, the most important criteria for personhood are intellectual. *Person*, as philosophical term, defines someone exhibiting advanced traits of intelligence and self-awareness, often synonymously confused with *Human*, or Homo sapiens — a biological concept. Persons must be able to think analytically and conceptually and their behavior must demonstrate sophisticated cognitive capacities like innovative problem solving. In reviewing the collectively demonstrated intellectual capacities of dolphins, some scientists are now of the opinion that they should be recognized as *Persons* — along with humans, as members of a community of equals.[166] As such, dolphins would be entitled to basic considerations such as freedom from harmful human interference.

Such opinion is increasingly supported[167] and these conclusions immediately raise dynamic ethical questions. If cetaceans are so intellectually and socially sophisticated that they warrant recognition as persons, there is a pressing and profound need to discontinue using them as we do, to their detriment, for selfish human purposes.

CHAPTER TWENTY-NINE

ETHICAL EVOLUTION

Our great moral test is revealed in our treatment of those who are at our mercy.

As scientific evidence increasingly demonstrates dolphins' capacity to think, feel and reason consciously, a number of important ethical dilemmas arise, including the idea that our exploiting or causing pain and suffering to other conscious, conceptualizing creatures is morally wrong.

The scientific research that is currently available suggests a strong case for recognizing dolphins as nonhuman *persons* — individuals of intrinsic worth, with a right to life, independent of human utility. Currently we use dolphins simply as objects to advance our own interests, demonstrating no respect for their moral standing. We treat dolphins as if they were *property*, not *persons*. Recognized as persons, with a sophisticated, individual awareness of the world — *beings*, rather than objects — means dolphins share the same fundamental grounds for moral consideration as humans. The implications then are that humans have a *moral responsibility* to refrain from acting in a manner that does — or even *might* harm them.[1] As such, limiting, compromising or interfering with a dolphin's freedom of choice constitutes harm.

Creating a moral pecking order based on our limited understanding of an animal's capacity for intelligence or sentience may be an ethically crude model; however, legally expanding the circle of human compassion towards non-human life has to begin somewhere and because of their communicative intelligence and our inclination to relate to it, cetaceans (like great apes) do look like a promising place to ignite and strengthen this vital process. To invite cetaceans into the community of ethical concern would mean acknowledging their equal moral entitlement to life, bodily integrity (the prohibition of torture) and freedom, enforceable by law.[2] I believe this is something well worth working toward.

The evidence for dolphin intelligence and sentience implies a sobering capacity for physical, mental and emotional suffering.[3] At present, many thousands of cetaceans continue to suffer fear, pain and death because of human activities.[4] Official discussion of negative human impacts on dolphins focuses on "stocks," entire species or populations. If dolphins are acknowledged as individual *persons* with intrinsic worth — rather than mere resources or property with a prescribed price — it means that the human-induced suffering of each and every dolphin is of moral and legal concern, not just activities that threaten the extinction of entire species.[5]

The capacity to suffer is increasingly viewed as sufficient grounds for moral and compassionate consideration of living creatures. Regarding suffering inflicted upon non-human animals, world renowned primatologist, humanitarian and environmentalist Dr. Jane Goodall writes: *'Even if we only suspect that they might have rich, emotional lives, that they might have self-awareness, that they might be capable of mental as well as physical suffering, then we cannot fail to be deeply disturbed by the way our own species inflicts so much suffering on so many animal species.'*[6]Author and Scholar Thomas White writes that even if there is only a reasonable *possibility* (which indeed, there is) that dolphins may qualify as persons with intrinsic worth, our moral obligation is clear, and requires that we "do no harm" until the situation can be clarified.[7]

The first campaigns to win independence for American colonists, emancipation for slaves, and civil rights for various minorities were all met with incredulity, skepticism, dismissal and hostility. All these human groups were once considered to be so inferior in intellect, ability and value by the white patriarchal ruling class, that they were viewed as being beneath moral consideration. Abolitionists faced an ethical and political atmosphere comparable to that presently confronting people fighting for the freedom from oppression and exploitation of non-humans in general and dolphins in particular.

Lawyer Steven Wise notes that human slavery was as firmly and widely entrenched as non-human slavery is today and we face the same kinds of arguments repeated by those in favor of the continued use and ownership of animals and ecosystems. The current, disconnected, elitist human attitude toward Nature is largely one of utility and ownership, which has been embedded and solidified in our laws and customs for a very long time. The obstacles to rectifying this situation are major and real, yet we have made the same necessary kinds of profound moral shifts in the past, even when abolition conflicted with strong economic interests.[8]

Today it is hard to comprehend why human slavery was accepted from antiquity and not seriously challenged as a fundamentally unethical practice until the late 1700s. The institution was so basic that the evolution of genuine anti-slavery attitudes required a *profound* shift in human moral perception.[9]

Books illuminating atrocities or injustices and bringing them into public awareness have played an integral part in effecting this shift. The writings of Olaudah Equiano popularized and fueled the abolition debate in England, while Harriet Beecher Stowe's *Uncle Tom's Cabin* (1852) was credited (by Lincoln himself, among others) with igniting the American Civil War.

Today, a vast majority believes human slavery is wrong, but three hundred years ago that belief was rarely encountered, and three thousand years ago it did not exist. It appears humans have now risen to an ethical point where we find ourselves setting out upon a similarly perilous and controversial road regarding our treatment of non-human animals and this process of moral exclusion, then partial and increasing acceptance is firm in history.

In a world where unrestrained human greed and ignorance has put the survival of all earthly life at risk, increasing standards of compassion and ethical concern may be *crucial* for our survival. The human capacity to *evolve ethically* may hold the key; it may be our only hope.

Acts of cruelty tarnish and diminish us as human beings and the insistence that such injuries are beneath our moral concern betrays something terribly ugly in our species. Certainly such a view is severely lacking in noble and compassionate humanitarian qualities that we claim to value so highly.

Such sacred principles as freedom from slavery or torture and freedom of choice are among the most basic kinds of legal considerations, ones to which cetaceans, like human beings (and perhaps many other life forms) may be most strongly entitled. Lawyer, author and animal advocate Steven Wise defines "liberty" as the basic building block of legal rights. Today (ironically, many observe) liberty is vaunted as the supreme value of the Western world. Human liberty is understood to exist, not as a grant from any state, but as an inherent quality, deriving from human life; something described as being *inherent, immutable, inalienable* and *self-evident* — a veritable law of nature. Such intrinsic "rights" cannot be waived and their violation can (supposedly) never be excused. They are considered to be the foundation of freedom, justice and peace in the world.[10]

The Economics of Slavery

A slave is someone who is the legal property of another person, whether by capture, purchase or birth; someone who has been completely divested of freedom and personal rights and forced to obey. Human slavery was made possible by the legal rule that humans could be owned as *property* — a concept that today we understand as profoundly wrong. However, contrary to popular belief, human slavery is *not* a horror safely consigned to the past. Though modern slavery is a crime with many millions of victims,* most people don't even realize it exists. Slavery is no longer about *legal* ownership, but involves people controlled by violence and denied all personal freedom, forced to make money for someone else; the common denominator is poverty. Cheap goods and foods that are harvested or made by slaves are imported directly to North America and Europe. Slaves may have made the shoes on your feet, the clothes you are wearing or the tea that you drink. When shopping for bargains, people don't usually stop to ask why a product is cheap, unaware that a terrible price *is* being paid — but it is being kept hidden from us. We're facing an epidemic of slavery that is tied to our own comparatively comfortable lives in developed countries through the expanding global economy.[11]

Under international trade agreement* rules, environmental laws and social considerations become subordinated to international trade. These trade policies encourage growth of sales and increased profits, regardless of the impact on life — human, animal or ecosystem.[12] The benefits of global expansion are highly concentrated in the hands of large multinational corporations and their owners, bringing immense wealth and power to an elite few and increasing poverty for the majority. This system makes little distinction as to how a profit is made; whether people or animals were exploited or killed; whether ecosystems or human communities were depleted or poisoned.[13]

In his crucial book, *Disposable People: New Slavery in the Global Economy*, Kevin Bales points out that if responsibility for the continuing existence of slavery is extended to those who profit from it, we must confront a *shocking* ethical problem — that it is *all* of us living in developed nations who are responsible for the continuation of these atrocities. What we call "the free world" currently feeds on slavery of all sorts. We need to recognize that this is not a distant "third world" issue, but a global reality in which we are *already* involved and implicated. However, when an educated public brings pressure to bear, corporations can learn to worry about problems usually considered beneath them. Putting pressure on profits is a key public strategy for ending slavery, along with other similarly reprehensible practices.

* Author Kevin Bales estimates some *27 million* slaves worldwide — other estimates are as high as *200 million*.
* Particularly The General Agreement on Tariffs and Trade — GATT, and the North American Free Trade Agreement — NAFTA.

Slaveholders will violently defend their lucrative enterprises, but they will walk away from the slaves and the business if they stop making money.[14] And this holds true whether those enslaved are humans or dolphins.

Dr. Denise Herzing observes that ideas that require people to reorganize their world usually provoke hostility and ferocious resistance from traditional quarters. Many "rights" movements have initially had to go outside the law, facing repression and ridicule, intensely polarized public discussion and finally, acceptance. The problem has always been that certain groups of people benefit from the denial of rights to others and are reluctant to relinquish those benefits. Even though many people supported more humane and improved conditions for oppressed black slaves, slaveholders remained unwilling to give them up as property until forced to do so. We see the same kinds of arguments and compromises proposed today for captive cetaceans[15] yet a well-treated captive dolphin is still a prisoner, bereft of liberty and freedom of choice.

When change is demanded, conflicts inevitably arise, as those untouched by increasing compassion and likely benefiting from its absence, try to maintain the regime in place. Additionally, most people initially experience great difficulty in accepting that they may be involved in something wrong or exploitative. In defense of their accustomed habits, many lash out — usually at the wrong targets.

I have known the horror of captured lives that were destroyed to feed the greed of slaveholders and their ignorant customers. I have watched these slaves suffering as they were crushed, through brutality and indifference. That they were dolphins rather than humans makes no difference.

I see little difference between the abuse, exploitation and enslavement of humans and dolphins, because a clear view of our tangled global economical substrate reveals that these issues are one and the same. Both are symptoms of the system in place where the greedy and powerful routinely subjugate the poor, the weak and the vulnerable for profit. Reformist philosopher Henry Salt wrote: *'The emancipation of men from cruelty and injustice will bring with it in due course the emancipation of animals also. The two reforms are inseparably connected, and neither can be fully realized alone.'*[16] Salt understood that the emancipation of humans and animals alike from oppression and cruelty would depend on human beings reaching their *full ethical potential*. He felt that what was lacking in human attitudes was a true sense of *kinship* with non-human beings and that this development concerned our very *humanity*. Salt had no doubt that injustice to non-human beings was part of a general social malaise and understood that a social system where commercial profit is the main object of work will never give appropriate consideration to the well being of men and women — much less to that of animals.[17]

Because the oppression of humans and animals is so inextricably linked, eradicating it will require changes on extremely profound levels. In his daring and pivotal book, *The Culture of Make Believe*, Derrick Jensen writes: *'What's at stake here goes to the heart of our civilization. What's at stake here is life itself.'*[18] Comparing the killing or enslavement of dolphins (or other non-human life) to the exploitation of human beings upsets some people, but we need to realize is that in both cases, suffering and death are made acceptable and inevitable by a utilitarian worldview, blinding us to our true, interconnected relationship, making it impossible to perceive others (whether whales, trees or child prostitutes in Thailand) as individuals of *worth*. Death and ruin occur because the desire for material wealth, comfort and convenience has become more important than communities, more important than ecological health, more important than happiness — and more important than life. The pursuit of profit and pleasure routinely subordinates morality and compassion; business does not acknowledge the devastating legacy of toxins, strife and suffering it passes on to future generations. As long as we value money more highly than living beings and our relationships with them, we will continue to regard *Others* only as resources to be used, objectified, discarded or killed.

Jensen observes that we protect ourselves from painful realizations by dismissing or ignoring evidence that we participate in atrocities — even though the facts may be staring us in the face. We allow ourselves to be blinded, to believe the state of our world isn't slipping past critical. Evils are regularly watered down before they are brought before the public eye, often until they are no longer recognizable. War and world domination become, "protecting the free world" and clear cutting entire forests and strip-mining the oceans becomes "developing natural resources" — all justified in the name of progress and good business. Though we might prefer to imagine that animals and ecosystems are merely resources to be conserved or consumed — in reality they have worth and purpose entirely independent of human use.[19]

We humans imagine ourselves as *separate*, set above and against other cultures, tribes, races and species. Because we see ourselves as separate from the rest of the world, we start to see every other being as a mere thing, existing for our use, amusement or disposal. One of the most profound differences commonly seen between many Industrialized and Indigenous ways of viewing and interacting with our world is the belief that everything exists merely for man's use (or abuse), whereas many aboriginal peoples understand the world is *alive*, filled with the many voices of thinking, feeling beings that are as worthy and valuable as themselves.

The idea that humans, animals and the ecosystems they live in constitute a single society remains central to the beliefs of many indigenous cultures: Animals and elements are treated with appropriate respect and courtesy and when a life is taken to sustain one's own, it is done with *true* reverence and gratitude. Ownership of Nature is often a foreign concept: an idea as unthinkable and morally reprehensible as selling a mother or brother into slavery. Similarly, many ancient eastern philosophies assume the ultimate oneness of all Nature's components and this view causes the gulf between humans and Nature to vanish — *both* being regarded as sacred and imbued with divinity.[20] These wise and ancient beliefs place humans as a *part* of the web of life, not standing in lofty dominion above or beyond it, and they hold lessons we are in *dire* need of.

We desperately need to understand the reality of the lives that are affected by our consumer culture; to realize what luxuries come at the expense of others' suffering — and thus, at the expense of our very humanity. We must *recognize* the inherent inhumanity of our current system and in order to *evolve* beyond it, we must cease valuing commodities over life.

Slavery is unquestionably an abomination that denies the sanctity of life. Author Kevin Bales asks: *'If there are still slaves, how can you be proud of your freedom?'*[21] Author Derrick Jensen insists its time to begin asking some fundamental questions: *'What sort of democracy can be based explicitly on the misery of others? And what sort of people would desire and claim a luxury which has cost the hopes and lives of a race of slaves?'* In order to avoid inner conflict, Jensen points out people must live in a state of denial — denying their involvement in perpetuating atrocities and exploitation. The parts of our humanity that normally should connect us to these Others have been cut off. Our empathies have been deadened, or we would naturally recoil at the thought of directly or indirectly causing such harm. Instead we have created a deeply disconnected society that rewards exploitation and continues to make the wrong choices. We forget that we even have the choice to make in the first place — but we *do*.[22]

Behavior cannot change without a fundamental change in consciousness — but how can we change human consciousness? I believe it must begin with certain profound *realizations,* only one of which is: we *cannot* go on indefinitely as we have. If we cannot introduce *profound* changes into our current ways of thinking and behaving, we have no future. We need to realize that we don't have to live in a society based on the rich and powerful exploiting the poor and the weak and the silent, where the few draw their extreme luxuries from the toil and sweat and suffering of the many. We can find ways to live without the enslavement and abuse of our fellows, human and animal. We can live without rapaciously destroying Nature — indeed this is the only way the human species can ultimately endure on this planet. Ultimately, safeguarding human welfare necessitates extending compassion and moral consideration to entire ecosystems and upholding the sanctity of all life. We need to realize that the true emancipation of humans, of animals, and of Nature are *inseparably* connected. Those who oppress and destroy, knowingly or otherwise, need to recognize the oppressed as members of their greater community, worthy of real compassion and respect.

Author Dr. Roderick Frazier Nash writes that from the perspective of intellectual history, environmental (and interspecies) ethics are revolutionary and arguably the most dramatic expansion of morality in the course of human thought.[23] Historically, the evolution of ethics has come from the inclusion of other races or genders into the community of moral concern, and thus has our humanity grown and evolved. Faced with the dawning realization that other species have intrinsic worth and that our morality ought to include our relationship and dealings with animals and ecosystems, our humanity is again struggling to *evolve ethically* on a deep level. Choosing compassion over utility and profit appears to be one of the most profound choices we are struggling to move towards.

There are those who appear unable or perhaps profoundly unwilling to grasp this concept, or move towards the necessary kinds of change. For a long time, much human morality has been mired in narrow self-interest, but as our ethical standards evolve, what once appeared reasonable may no longer seem that way.

Returning to Dr. Howard Gardener's Theory of Multiple Intelligences, (from the previous chapter), he postulates over the existence of a philosophical or *Moral Intelligence*. At present, a moral awareness or intelligence appears to have manifested only incompletely in our species. The ethical evolution of humankind involves reaching a kind of *moral maturity*, both as individuals and as a species. Many people do not seem to perceive this evolutionary step. We seem caught in the middle; a dual species, with some individuals becoming aware of profound truths and opposing unjust laws and destructive, harmful practices — and others remaining steadfastly self-absorbed, and unconcerned with any larger fate. Each seems incomprehensible to the other.

It is our own *self-awareness* that should allow us to recognize other self-aware beings when we meet them — and to then act appropriately. Many people appear to be able to recognize dolphins as fellows immediately — others seem to lack this ability. Interestingly, dolphins *do* seem to recognize humans in this way — and to act accordingly. Throughout two thousand years of recorded contact, dolphins have normally behaved toward humans in a non-aggressive fashion, even in the face of provocation,[24] while reports of dolphins rescuing and assisting humans are well known. Wild dolphins tend to treat humans in a respectful manner and their repeated actions appear to indicate they consider our lives worth saving. So which species is more ethically evolved and morally mature?

The peak position humans currently occupy on this planet conveys *enormous* responsibility — not only for our own continued survival, but for the well being of all other species and their living ecosystems that now lie under our power. Only by restoring our severed links with the living world around us, can we restore our own lives. In order to do this, in order to face a future that holds any hope, a new declaration is needed; what is increasingly called a Declaration of *Interdependence,* to acknowledge our interconnectedness, affirm our respect for other living beings, and to guide and teach us how to appropriately change our ways before it is too late.[25]

Our present, consumer-driven society is based on the exploitation of *Others* who are made all but invisible and therefore irrelevant to us. Governments do not act to protect animals or to right social or ethical wrongs, especially those perpetrated by powerful organizations, unless there is public pressure to do so. Each one of us can help to bring about positive changes in this system by making informed, ethical choices in what we buy, and perhaps even more importantly, what we do not buy or buy into, because, as Dr. Marc Bekoff reminds us, in a consumer-driven society, buyers are powerful![26] We the people are *not* impotent and should never forget the cash register is our daily voting booth in a capitalist system. We don't have to support companies that cause destruction and harm. We *do* have a choice and we *can* consciously choose to support social, ethical and environmental values through our daily purchases and activities.

Author of the astounding *The Ecology of Commerce*, economist Paul Hawken feels our understanding of the role of commerce in society is stuck at a primitive level. Hawken states that ethical and ecological thinking needs to be injected into every aspect of society, particularly our economic institutions. Hawken's *restorative economics* challenge the assumption that we can continue on, unburdened by *real* connection and responsibility to Nature and social conscience.[27]

'Indifference is deadly' insists Dr. Bekoff — 'do something — anything to make this a better planet.'[28] Mahatma Gandhi offered the incomparable wisdom: *You must BE the change you wish to see in the world.* As she travels tirelessly around the globe, Dr. Jane Goodall spreads a similarly essential message: *Every individual matters, every individual has a role to play and every individual makes a difference.*[29] Whether that difference becomes part of the problem or part of the solution, is up to each of us.

Dr. Bekoff urges that our behavior toward others be motivated not by profit, but by morality, compassion, love and respect, and asks: *'Could anyone reasonably argue that a world with less cruelty and destruction and more compassion and love would not be a better place in which to live and raise children? I don't think so.'*[30]

Philosopher Arnold Schopenhauer wrote that compassion is the basis of all morality. Aldo Leopold wrote: *"A moral being, respects a living thing."*[31] Like Henry Salt, he understood that as moral creatures, human beings carry a responsibility to articulate and defend the worth and treatment of the other living occupants of our planet. Albert Schweitzer felt that the most fundamental principle of ethics is a *"Reverence for Life"*[32] and thus the preservation, restoration and enhancement of life in general becomes the anchor of our *Ethical Evolution.* The powerful and privileged status humans enjoy on this Earth entails, not a *right* to exploit, but a *responsibility* to protect.

Where we fight for the freedom of dolphins, we fight for the freedom of the Earth and *all* its peoples, because the destructive system that ensnares and harms dolphins, also harms us all. They are a supremely apt symbol, for the polarized human relationship with Nature and the internal struggle we are facing within human nature itself.

"The dolphin," wrote author Robin Brown, *"is a test, not just of our intelligence, but of our awareness, our courage and our humanity."*[33]

CHAPTER THIRTY

OTHER INTO US

"Man stands in his own shadow and wonders why it is dark."
Alan Watts, *The Spirit of Zen*.

A s a species and as a bio-system, we are in trouble. In fact we appear to be slipping alarmingly past critical. Consumption in developed nations has grown to monstrous proportions and obesity is rampant — while over twenty percent of the earth's peoples are chronically hungry or starving. Corporations create billions of tons of hazardous waste every year and toxic chemical pollution now affects every forest, every ocean, the soil of every continent and the entire upper atmosphere — while cancer has reached epidemic proportions.

We have decimated ninety-seven percent of the ancient forests in North America, and are losing 27,000 species a year, seventy-four a day, *1 every twenty minutes*, while 500,000 trees are cut *every hour* in tropical forests.[1] Our problems are vast and complex, but come down to some six billion people breeding exponentially. The process and manner of fulfilling human desires and needs is stripping the earth of its capacity to sustain life. In biological terms, we have become a parasite, and we are devouring our host.

So, what can be done? To simplify an answer to a tremendously complex and vital question:

Realization
Responsibility
Reconnect
Restoration

The first step is *Realization* — of the existence, reality and *dire* enormity of the problems we are at this very instant facing. We need to realize our daily complicity and contribution toward the declining state of things — the facts about which most people simply have no idea and very little interest.

Instead, we allow corporate media to pacify and distract us and after the daily grind, most folk come home and stupefy themselves with television, video games, drugs, booze, junk food, shopping or whatever, and try not to think about it all. Much time, energy and money are expended, groping for things to distract us and help us forget a deep misery and foreboding that for some strange reason just will not go away.

People need to realize the reasons why they should care about clear-cutting, oil spills, social responsibility, factory farming, slavery, cruelty, animal testing, genetically modified foods, ethics, dying dolphins, toxic pollutants, poverty, strife, famine, war, over-population and so many other issues connected to needless death, destruction and suffering — because we are *responsible* for it happening, both by actively supporting it through the things we purchase or invest in and by passively or ignorantly standing by and letting atrocities occur. We need to realize that these things are of concern to all of us, because we are ALL accountable for the diminishing and destruction of life on Earth and we are ALL paying the price.

We must *realize* how corporate greed and public ignorance fuel the poisoning of the planet and of ourselves. We must *realize* it is WE who are being sold, stolen, extracted, mined, abused, impoverished, sickened, enslaved and exploited. And we must realize that it doesn't have to be this way.

In our arrogance and ignorance, we imagine that the laws which apply to the rest of Nature do not apply to us. But like gravity, these laws of Nature cannot be changed or erased by any human vote. On our present course, we are in the process of eliminating ourselves and taking a lot of other innocent life forms with us. The human species is *not* exempt from the biological realities that govern all life and just like any other species, when we outstrip and poison our food and water resources, our population will experience a decline until it is once again in balance with available resources.

Responsibility

Once we realize the state of things and acknowledge the part we play, it is time to accept responsibility for the situation. As humans, we are all responsible. Those of us that have been born to developed nations have inherited a colossal and grave debt from the rampant and excessive exploitations of our forefathers — and it has fallen to us to make amends. As comprehension dawns, it becomes clear that the onus rests upon the people of the developed nations to rectify the damaging results of the current global imbalance, as it is of our own making. It is our only hope for a sustainable future. The position we occupy, of power and of privilege, compared the majority of human beings living on earth engenders a responsibility to initiate positive, restorative changes in *all* quarters.

Responsible existence does not mean having no impact on one's environment (as this is impossible), but making efforts and taking steps to reduce the harmful imprint of human activity, while increasing actions and activities that are restorative. Ecological principles of balance and sustainability point the way: Take no more than what you need and leave the rest alone; leave the world better than you found it; try not to cause harm and make amends if you do; take life only when in need, with increasing care and with true reverence and gratitude.

Restoration

Realizing and understanding our responsibility is not enough. After realization, it is easy to become overwhelmed, but we must not remain indifferent in our responses, or fall prey to the paralysis of guilt! Instead, we must educate ourselves and find ways of taking positive, restorative action. We must avidly, creatively and determinedly seek solutions. Until governments, corporations, political and religious establishments prove willing to initiate the necessary changes, the onus falls squarely on the shoulders of each of us as individuals and communities, to start living a different way; to think globally and act locally to make things a little better each day, instead of worse. We can break our previous patterns and *most* importantly, teach our children to walk on the earth with lighter and more loving steps. We can daily strive to become more aware, more conscious, more mindful moment by moment, of the subsequent effects of our actions. Nothing less than a world of changed minds can save us all.

For those who think the Herculean tasks facing humanity are beyond their means, to stop and pick up garbage, to plant a tree, to refuse certain choices (like attending captive dolphin-swim encounters or taking the family to a marine park), when we *know* the immediate effects are detrimental — doing or not doing these things are within easy reach. Making educated choices on what you buy and buy into; what you eat, where you go and what you are supporting — directly or indirectly, are within the means of every person who can read and get to a library or computer — and probably plenty of those who can't. Share what you know. Each one of us can and must make a difference. Never forget, when the money flow stops, harmful practices cease — and that puts the reins of power squarely in the hands of ordinary citizens.

Reconnect

In order to summon the effort, the time and the energy for restorative actions, we have to *want* to — we have to *care*. This means more than simply engaging our heads with grim facts and figures. We must engage our hearts. When things get personal, we get motivated. In order to care, we need to reconnect, with Nature and with each other! This an integral and *entirely* accessible component of restoration — inspiring us to help restore and support living, thriving, diverse, sustainable communities of all kinds, through direct involvement.

Human Beings evolved embedded in the natural world and there remains within us a deep and abiding longing to reconnect with wild places and wild creatures. Derrick Jensen writes: *'Our separation from the natural world affects every aspect of our lives, from the most intimate to the most global.'* Many aboriginal cultures demonstrate how humankind may live so intimately within the environment that they enter into *relationship* with the animals and the Earth. Jensen feels that one reason humans are so destructive is that as a whole, we do not recognize, participate in, value or respect such relationships.[2]

It appears that individuals of indigenous cultures, like the Yequana tribe of South America, who live closer to Nature, experience lives that are more satisfying and meaningful to them. Such increasingly rare cultures, where they remain relatively un-spoilt by influences from our own, are not riddled with crime, mental illness, suicide, drug addiction, cruelty, poverty, injustice and corruption. They are not plagued with anxiety, depression, self-hatred, nor seething with anger and discontent. They do not live in terror of one another or go crazy because their lives seem empty, lonely or pointless. They do not need to buy a constant stream of junk items to insulate and numb themselves from the world. Instead, such people see themselves as an active, healthy part of their human communities and of the larger natural community they are invariably integrated into. Such people tend to value the richness conveyed through *relationships*, rather than material objects.[3]

For most people life is indisputably busy, with never enough hours in the day. We rush along and time flies by. By the time we realize we should have spent more time with our kids, our parents, grandparents, spouse or siblings — it may be too late. Emphasis in modern society often seems to ignore the importance of cultivating positive relationships with our family, friends and community members. Nothing you can buy prepackaged can replace the kind of deep satisfaction that comes from enjoying an active and positive roll in one's neighborhood and community. Usually, this is not very difficult: Smile, talk, offer to help, get involved and away you go!

As we have seen, captive institutions may actually serve to distort our understanding of relationships with animals and ecosystems, encouraging us to perceive ourselves as separate from and superior to non-human life. We do not need to rely on zoos or marine parks in order to reconnect with Nature, nor need we travel to the farthest corners of the earth or sea. Rather, we can foster and develop these relationships right where we live, in our own backyards, gardens or local parks and woodlands. Derrick Jensen describes this, not as abstract connections to abstract nature, but as cultivating *specific* connection with a *particular* stream, tree, bird or stone. He further affirms that if we work to create habitats with local species in mind, we can encourage wildlife to live and flourish alongside us.[4]

Connection stems from appreciation. This includes both the inhalation of detail and the sweep of the broad view. A mountain sunrise may be awe inspiring — but so is the tiny tendril of green defiantly growing out of a crack in the pavement. Breathing in the colors, the scents, the songs, the beauty; feeling the earth under your feet — these things encourage us to open ourselves to the wonders around us. It's easy, profoundly enriching and joyful — and all it takes is a little time.

It is of utmost importance that our affinity with Nature be cultivated in ways that are _responsible_ and _respectful._ This requires that we re-define ourselves in a more humble, compassionate position within the natural order by changing the human role from conqueror to community member. In turn, such relationship leads to challenging entrenched ideas that trees, animals, rivers, mountains, oceans and fields exist as mere resources to be used, managed, conserved, discarded, polluted or expended with impunity. Only when we embrace Nature as *family* can we understand our human responsibility to protect and nurture it. Without this profound transformation of human spirit and consciousness, without a *rekindling* of this sacred covenant with Nature and within ourselves — the world's suffering cannot end. In this crucial respect, we must either evolve or go extinct.

Deep, ethical changes in society follow a known process of recognition and then correction of perpetrated wrongs. At first only radicals recognize the problems and speak out — and are predictably condemned, ignored and derided. Eventually however, marginalized opinion becomes mainstream and reform is instated. Always, those who profit most refuse to change until outdated practices are firmly outlawed (and enforced).

It is the same regarding our treatment of cetaceans — the so-called radicals have lifted their voices and now the populace begins to murmur. Those individuals and establishments profiting from the captivity industry and other practices that harm cetaceans continue to try and hide or obfuscate the truth in order to quell the voices of distention, but eventually the murmur will rise to a roar.

Growing evidence of dolphins' considerable intellect is raising dynamic ethical questions and eliciting a call for change towards the way in which we regard and treat our fellows. Ultimately, the message moves beyond the pedantic realm of self-serving arguments, euphemisms, legalities and statistics. There is no argument that can vindicate our ill-treatment of these creatures. There are only those do or do not have the willingness to look at what we have wrought, the courage to take responsibility for it, and the conviction to do something about it.

The suffering, the grave iniquities, the detrimental trials that humans, animals and ecosystems endure at ignorant or greedy human hands will only be redressed if the human species finds a way:

To *realize* the effects of our actions and inaction; to take *responsibility* for perpetrating positive changes; to *reconnect* with each other and the living world around us, and thus inspired, find *restorative* solutions — in short, we must *Rekindle*. It bears repeating, that as one of the world's most beloved and beleaguered creatures, it is perhaps fitting that dolphins have become a kind of focal point in seeking to achieve this end.

Other, into *Us;* become that which you love.

Spotted dolphins, wild and free.

NOTES

Chapter 27: Deconstructing the Velvet Cage

1. US Animal Welfare Act Regulations, Subpart E, Marine Mammals.
2. Wells, R., Scott, M. D., "Bottlenose Dolphins (Tursiops truncatus)", *Handbook of Marine Mammals*, Vol. 6 of the *Second Book of Dolphins and Porpoises*, San Diego, CA: Academic Press, 1999 (pp. 137-182).
3. Rose, Naomi, Farinato, Richard & Sherwin, Susan (editors), *The Case Against Marine Mammals in Captivity*, HSUS/WSPA Document, 2006 (pp. 11).
4. Waples, Kelly. A. & Gales, Nicholas, J., "Evaluating and minimizing social stress in the care of captive bottlenose dolphins (Tursiops truncatus)", *Zoo Biology* 21(1): 5-26, 2002 (pp. 6, 7, 18).
5. *Marine Mammal Inventory Report*, cited in "Effects of Confinement: Causes of Mortality", WDCS document.
6. *"Biting the Hand that Feeds: The Case Against Dolphin Petting Pools"*, WDCS & HSUS Investigative Report, 2003.
7. Rose, Naomi, Farinato, Richard & Sherwin, Susan (editors), *The Case Against Marine Mammals in Captivity*, HSUS/WSPA Document, 2006 (pp. 30).
8. Frohoff, Toni, "The Kindred Wild", in *Between Species: Celebrating the Dolphin-Human Bond*, Edited by Toni Frohoff, Ph.D., and Brenda Peterson, San Francisco: Sierra Club Books 2003 (pp. 67).
9. Frohoff, Toni, "Interacting with Captive Dolphins", in *Between Species: Celebrating the Dolphin-Human Bond*, Edited by Toni Frohoff, Ph.D., and Brenda Peterson, San Francisco: Sierra Club Books 2003 (pp. 333).
10. Frohoff, Toni, *Report on Observations and Preliminary Assessment at Boudewijn Seapark Dolphinarium in Brugge, Belgium*, Brugge & Brussels, Belgium: TarraMar Research 2005 (pp. 3).
11. Frohoff, Toni, *Report on Observations and Preliminary Assessment at Boudewijn Seapark Dolphinarium in Brugge, Belgium*, Brugge & Brussels, Belgium: TarraMar Research 2005 (pp. 6).
12. Rose, Naomi, Farinato, Richard & Sherwin, Susan (editors), *The Case Against Marine Mammals in Captivity*, HSUS/WSPA Document, 2006 (pp. 3).
13. Frohoff, Toni, "The Kindred Wild", in *Between Species: Celebrating the Human-Dolphin Bond*, edited by Toni Frohoff, PhD., and Brenda Peterson, San Francisco: Sierra Club

Books 2003 (pp. 67).

14. O'Barry, Richard, *To Free A Wild Dolphin*, Los Angeles: Renaissance Books 2000, (pp. 19)

15. Bearzi, Giovanni, "At Home with the Dolphins", in *Between Species: Celebrating the Dolphin-Human Bond*, edited by Toni Frohoff, PhD., and Brenda Peterson, San Francisco: Sierra Club Books 2003 (pp. 108).

16. Alliance of Marine Mammal Parks and Aquariums, Annual Report to Congress 2003. AMMPA website: www.ammpa.org

17. Rose, Naomi, Farinato, Richard & Sherwin, Susan (editors), *The Case Against Marine Mammals in Captivity*, HSUS/WSPA Document, 2006 (pp.4).

18. Alliance of Marine Mammal Parks and Aquariums website: www.ammpa.org, Frequently Asked Questions: *How is positive reinforcement used to train marine mammals?* [accessed March 2008].

19. Baird, Robin, W., "the Killer Whale: Foraging Specializations and Group Hunting" in *Cetacean Societies: Field Studies of Dolphins and Whales* edited by Janet Mann, Richard Connor, Peter Tyack and Hal Whitehead: University of Chicago Press 2000 (pp.138).

20. Morton, Alexandra, *Listening to Whales: What the Orcas Have Taught Us*, New York: Ballentine Books 2002 (pp. 56).

21. Jensen, Derrick, *Thought to Exist in the Wild: Awakening from the Nightmare of Zoos*, Santa Cruz, CA: No Voice Unheard 2007 (pp. 9, 88, 96).

22. Jensen, Derrick, *Thought to Exist in the Wild: Awakening from the Nightmare of Zoos*, Santa Cruz, CA: No Voice Unheard 2007 (pp. 87, 90, 92, 129).

23. O'Barry, Richard, *To Free A Wild Dolphin*, Los Angeles: Renaissance Books 2000.

24. Getty, F. 1991 November 25, NMFS presentation, public meeting on killer whales in captivity, cited in: "Captive orcas: Dying to Entertain You", by Vanessa Williams, WDCS report 2001, www.wdcs.org/submissions_bin/orcareport.pdf [accessed April 5, 2008].

25. Rose, Naomi, Farinato, Richard & Sherwin, Susan (editors), *The Case Against Marine Mammals in Captivity*, HSUS/WSPA Document, 2006 (pp. 4).

26. Bettinger T. and Quinn, H. "Conservation funds: How do zoos and aquaria decide which projects to fund?" in *Proceedings of the AZA Annual Conference*, St. Louis: AZA, 2000 (pp. 52-54).

27. Rose, Naomi, Farinato, Richard & Sherwin, Susan (editors), *The Case Against Marine Mammals in Captivity*, HSUS/WSPA Document, 2006 (pp. 19, 20).

28. Jensen, Derrick, *Thought to Exist in the Wild: Awakening from the Nightmare of Zoos*, Santa Cruz, CA: No Voice Unheard 2007 (pp. 92-93).

29. Rose, Naomi, "Sea Change", in *Between Species: Celebrating the Dolphin-Human Bond*, edited by Toni Frohoff, Ph.D., & Brenda Peterson, San Francisco: Sierra Club Books 2003 (pp. 227-228).

30. Rose, Naomi, Farinato, Richard & Sherwin, Susan (editors) *The Case Against Marine Mammals in Captivity*, HSUS/WSPA Document, 2006 (pp. 5, 7, 8).

31. Reeves, Randall R., Smith, Brian D., Crepso, Enrique A., and Notarbartolo di Sciara, Giuseppe, *Dolphins, Whales & Porpoises: 2002-2010 Conservation Action Plan for the World's Cetaceans,* 2003, IUCN/SSC Cetacean Specialist Group (pp. 47-48).

32. Vail, Courtney S. & Risch, Denise, *Driven By Demand: Dolphin drive hunts in Japan and the Involvement of the Aquarium Industry,* WDCS Document, edited by Cathy Williamson, April 2006.

33. Vail, Courtney S. & Risch, Denise, *Driven By Demand: Dolphin drive hunts in Japan and the Involvement of the Aquarium Industry,* WDCS Document, edited by Cathy Williamson, April 2006 (pp.15).

34. Vail, Courtney S. & Risch, Denise, *Driven By Demand: Dolphin drive hunts in Japan and the Involvement of the Aquarium Industry,* WDCS Document, edited by Cathy Williamson, April 2006 (pp.15, 32); & N. Rose, R. Farinato & S. Sherwin (editors), *The Case Against Marine Mammals in Captivity,* HSUS/WSPA Document, 2006 (p. 6).

35. Vail, Courtney S. & Risch, Denise, *Driven By Demand: Dolphin drive hunts in Japan and the Involvement of the Aquarium Industry,* WDCS Document, edited by Cathy Williamson, April 2006 (pp. 15, 21, 32).

36. Vail, C & Risch, D., *Driven By Demand: Dolphin drive hunts in Japan and the Involvement of the Aquarium Industry,* WDCS Document, edited by Cathy Williamson, April 2006 (pp. 33) & *"Held Captive: Developing Nations"*, HSUS website article: www.hsus.org/marine_mammals/what_are_the_issues/marine_mammals_in_captiv ity/held_captive_developing_nations.html [accessed April 4, 2008]

37. Rose, Naomi, Farinato, Richard & Sherwin, Susan (editors), *The Case Against Marine Mammals in Captivity,* HSUS/WSPA Document, 2006 (pp.5).

38. Rose, Naomi, Farinato, Richard & Sherwin, Susan (editors), *The Case Against Marine Mammals in Captivity,* HSUS/WSPA Document, 2006 (pp. 4, 12).

39. Mayers, S. PhD. *A Review of the Scientific Justifications for Maintaining Cetaceans in Captivity,* Report for WDCS 1998.

40. Mooney, J. *Captive Cetaceans: A Handbook for Campaigners,* WDCS document 1998.

41. Rose, Naomi, Farinato, Richard & Sherwin, Susan (editors), *The Case Against Marine Mammals in Captivity,* HSUS/WSPA Document, 2006 (pp. 14).

42. Whitehead, Hal, Reeves, Randall and Tyack, Peter, "Science and the Conservation, Protection and Management of Wild Cetaceans" in *Cetacean Societies: Field Studies of Dolphins and Whales,* edited by Janet Mann, Richard Connor, Peter Tyack, and Hal Whitehead: University of Chicago 2000 (pp. 311-12).

43. Mayers, S., PhD. *A Review of Scientific Justifications for Maintaining Cetaceans in Captivity,* report for WDCS 1998.

44. Mayers, S., PhD. *A Review of Scientific Justifications for Maintaining Cetaceans in Captivity,* report for WDCS 1998.

45. Kraus, S. D., Read, A. J., Solow, A., Baldwin, K., Spraudlin, T., Anderson, E., & Williamson, J., (1997) "Acoustic Alarms Reduce Porpoise Mortality". *Nature* 388:525.

46. Mayers, S., PhD. *A Review of Scientific Justifications for Maintaining Cetaceans in Captivity*, Report for WDCS 1998 & *Arguments Against Captivity*, WDCS document.

47. Rose, Naomi, Farinato, Richard & Sherwin, Susan (editors), *The Case Against Marine Mammals in Captivity*, HSUS/WSPA Document, 2006 (pp. 15).

48. Rose, Naomi, Farinato, Richard & Sherwin, Susan (editors), *The Case Against Marine Mammals in Captivity*, HSUS/WSPA Document, 2006 (pp. 15, 60).

49. Rose, Naomi, Farinato, Richard & Sherwin, Susan (editors), *The Case Against Marine Mammals in Captivity*, HSUS/WSPA Document, 2006 (p.26).

50. Mooney, Jerye, *Captive Cetaceans: A Handbook for Campaigners*, WDCS document, March 1998 (pp. 22); website: www.wdcs.org/submissions_bin/captivityhandbook.pdf [accessed April 4, 2008].

51. Lavigne, D. M., Woodley, T.H., Hannah, J. L., "A Comparison of Survival Rates for Captive and Free-Ranging Bottlenose Dolphins, Killer Whales and Beluga Whales", IMMA Technical Report, 97-02 & Small. R and DeMaster. D. P. 1995. "Acclimatization to Captivity: A Quantitative estimate based on survival of bottlenose dolphins and California sea lions." *Marine Mammal Science* 11: 510-519.

52. Wells, Randall S., Connor, Richard, Mann, Janet, and Read, Andrew, "The Bottlenose Dolphin: Social Relationships in a Fission-Fusion Society" In *Cetacean Societies: Field Studies of Dolphins and Whales*, edited by Janet Mann, Richard Connor, Peter Tyack, and Hal Whitehead: University of Chicago 2000 (pp. 95).

53. Rose, Naomi, "Sea Change", in *Between Species: Celebrating the Dolphin-Human Bond*, edited by Toni Frohoff Ph.D. & Brenda Peterson, San Francisco: Sierra Club Books 2003 (pp. 222-223).

54. St. Aubin, D.J., & Dierauf, L. A., "Stress and Marine Mammals" In *CRC Handbook of Marine Mammal Medicine*, New York & London CRC Press 2001 (pp. 253-271).

55. DeMaster, D. & J. Drevenak, 1988: "Survivorship Patterns in Three Species of Captive Cetacean", *Marine Mammal Science* vol. 4 No. 4 (pp. 297-311).

56. Baird, Robin, W., "the Killer Whale: Foraging Specializations and Group Hunting" in *Cetacean Societies: Field Studies of Dolphins and Whales* edited by Janet Mann, Richard Connor, Peter Tyack and Hal Whitehead: University of Chicago Press 2000 (pp. 145). & Olesiuk. P. F., M. A. Bigg & G. M. Ellis, 1990 "Life History and population dynamics of resident killer whales (orcinus orca) in the coastal waters of British Columbia and Washington State." Report for the IWC, special issue 12, pp. 209-244. & Ford, J. K., G.M. Ellis & K.C. Balcomb, *Killer Whales*, Vancouver: UBC Press, 1994 (pp. 1-102).

57. Mooney, Jerye, *Captive Cetaceans: A Handbook for Campaigners*, WDCS document, March 1998 (pp. 36); website: www.wdcs.org/submissions_bin/captivityhandbook.pdf [accessed April 4, 2008].

58. Lavigne, D. M., Woodley, T. H., Hannah, J. L., "A Comparison of Survival Rates for Captive and Free-Ranging Bottlenose Dolphins, Killer Whales and Beluga Whales", IMMA Technical Report, No. 97-02.

59. Lavigne, D. M., Woodley, T. H., Hannah, J. L., "A Comparison of Survival Rates for Captive and Free-Ranging Bottlenose Dolphins, Killer Whales and Beluga Whales", IMMA Technical Report, No. 97-02. & Small. R and DeMaster. D. P. 1995. "Acclimatization to Captivity: A Quantitative estimate based on survival of bottlenose dolphins and California sea lions." *Marine Mammal Science* 11: 510-519.

60. Lavigne, D. M., Woodley, T. H., Hannah, J. L., "A Comparison of Survival Rates for Captive and Free-Ranging Bottlenose Dolphins, Killer Whales and Beluga Whales", IMMA Technical Report, 97-02.

61. Lavigne, D. M., Woodley, T. H., Hannah, J. L., "A Comparison of Survival Rates for Captive and Free-Ranging Bottlenose Dolphins, Killer Whales and Beluga Whales", IMMA Technical Report, 97-02.

62. Rose, Naomi, Farinato, Richard & Sherwin, Susan (editors), *The Case Against Marine Mammals in Captivity*, HSUS/WSPA Document, 2006 (pp.5).

63. Small, R.J., & DeMaster, D. P., "Acclimatization to Captivity: A quantitative estimate based on survival of bottlenose dolphins and California sea lions." *Marine Mammal Science* 11: 1995 (pp. 510-519).

64. Rose, Naomi, "*The Solomon Islands Dolphins: The Myth of "Good" Marine Parks*, July 2003, HSUS website article: www.hsus.org/marine_mammals/marine_mammals_news/ the_solomon_island_dolphins_the myth_of good_marine_parks.html [accessed April 4, 2008].

65. *Florida Sun-Sentinel*: "Marine Attractions: Below the Surface", by Sally Kestin, May 23, 2004.

66. Williams, V., *Captive Orcas: Dying to Entertain You*, WDCS report 2001(pp. 17), website: www.wdcs.org/submissions_bin/orcareport.pdf [accessed April 5, 2008].

67. Cousteau, Jacques-Yves & Philippe Dole, *Dolphins*, New York: Doubleday 1975.

68. Cousteau, Jacques-Yves & Philippe Dole, *Dolphins*, New York: Doubleday 1975.

69. Lusseau, David & Newman, M. E. J., "Identifying the role that individual animals play in their social network." *Ecology Letters, Proceedings of the Royal Society, London B* (Suppliment), doi: 10. 1098/rbl.2004.0225 (2004).

70. Rose, Naomi, "Sea Change" in *Between Species: Celebrating the Dolphin-Human Bond*, edited by Toni Frohoff Ph.D. & Brenda Peterson, San Francisco: Sierra Club Books 2003 (pp. 223).

71. Frohoff, Toni, "The Kindred Wild" in *Between Species: Celebrating the Dolphin-Human Bond*, by Toni Frohoff Ph.D. & Brenda Peterson, San Francisco: Sierra Club Books 2003 (pp. 60).

72. Reeves, Randall R., Smith, Brian D., Crepso, Enrique A., and Notarbartolo di Sciara, Giuseppe, *Dolphins, Whales & Porpoises: 2002-2010 Conservation Action Plan for the World's Cetaceans,*2003, IUCN/SSC Cetacean Specialist Group (pp. 17).

73. Reeves, Randall R., Smith, Brian D., Crepso, Enrique A., and Notarbartolo di Sciara, Giuseppe, *Dolphins, Whales & Porpoises: 2002-2010 Conservation Action Plan for the World's Cetaceans,*2003, IUCN/SSC Cetacean Specialist Group (pp. 17, 72).

74. Rose, Naomi, Farinato, Richard & Sherwin, Susan (editors), *The Case Against Marine Mammals in Captivity*, HSUS/WSPA Document, 2006 (pp.47).

75. Reeves, Randall R., Smith, Brian D., Crepso, Enrique A., and Notarbartolo di Sciara, Giuseppe, *Dolphins, Whales & Porpoises: 2002-2010 Conservation Action Plan for the World's Cetaceans*, 2003, IUCN/SSC Cetacean Specialist Group (pp. 17, 47, 72).

76. Rose, Naomi, "*The Solomon Islands Dolphins: The Myth of "Good" Marine Parks*, July 2003, HSUS website article: www.hsus.org/marine_mammals/marine_mammals_news/the_solomon_island_dolphins_the myth_ofgood_marine_parks.html [accessed April 4, 2008].

77. Rose, Naomi, "Sea Change" in *Between Species: Celebrating the Dolphin-Human Bond*, edited by Toni Frohoff, Ph.D. & Brenda Peterson, San Francisco: Sierra Club Books 2003 (pp. 225-226).

78. Frohoff, Toni, "Interacting with Captive Dolphins" in *Between Species: Celebrating the Dolphin-Human Bond*, by Toni Frohoff PhD. & Brenda Peterson, San Francisco: Sierra Club Books 2003 (pp. 332).

79. "*Held Captive: Developing Nations*", HSUS website article: www.hsus.org/marine_mammals/what_are_the_issues/marine_mammals_in_captivity/held_captive_developing_nations.html [accessed April 4, 2008]

80. Rose, Naomi, Farinato, Richard & Sherwin, Susan (editors), *The Case Against Marine Mammals in Captivity*, HSUS/WSPA Document, 2006 (pp. 29).

81. Frohoff, Toni, "Interacting with Captive Dolphins" in *Between Species: Celebrating the Dolphin-Human Bond*, by Toni Frohoff PhD. & Brenda Peterson, San Francisco: Sierra Club Books 2003 (pp. 331) & Frohoff, Toni, "Behavior of Captive Dolphins and Humans During Controlled In-Water Interactions" (Master's Thesis, Texas A&M University 1993); Samuels, A., and T. Spradlin, "Quantitative Behavioral Study of Bottlenose Dolphins in Swim-With-the-Dolphins Programs in the United States," *Marine Mammal Science 11 (1995)*.

82. Frohoff, Toni, PhD. "Close Encounters with Dolphins: a Call for Peace Between Species" in *Evergreen Monthly* 03/01.

83. Kellert, Stephen, *American Perceptions of Marine Mammal Conservation and Management*. HSUS report 1999.

84. Norris, Kennth, "Aggressive behavior in Cetacea", *Aggression and Defense: Natural Mechanisms*, edited by C.D. Clemente and D.B. Kindsley, University of California Press: Berkeley 1967 (pp. 225-241).

85. Hoyt, Erich, "Dangers to Trainers: The Performing Orca — Why the Show Must Stop" in *Frontline: A Whale of a Business*, WDCS 1992.

86. Frohoff, Toni, "The Kindred Wild" in *Between Species: Celebrating the Dolphin-Human Bond*, edited by Toni Frohoff PhD. & Brenda Peterson, San Francisco: Sierra Club Books 2003 (pp. 63-65).

87. Frohoff, Toni, "The Kindred Wild" in *Between Species: Celebrating the Dolphin-Human Bond*, edited by Toni Frohoff & Brenda Peterson, San Francisco: Sierra Club Books, 2003

(pp. 69).

88. Rose, Naomi, "Sea Change" in *Between Species: Celebrating the Dolphin-Human Bond,* edited by Toni Frohoff & Brenda Peterson, San Francisco: Sierra Club Books 2003 (pp. 224-5).

89. Marino, Lori and Lilienfeld, Scott.O., "Dolphin-Assisted Therapy: More Flawed Data and More Flawed Conclusions." *Anthrozoos* 11(4): 2007 (pp. 239).

90. Humpfries, T.L. PhD., "Effectiveness of Dolphin-Assisted Therapy as a Behavioral Intervention for Young Children with Disabilities," *Bridges,* Vol. 1, No. 6, May 2003.

91. Brakes, Philippa & Williamson, Cathy, *Can You Put Your Faith in DAT?* Report for WDCS, October 2007 (pp. 14).

92. Smith, B., PhD. "The Discovery of Dolphin Assisted Therapy", in *Between Species: Celebrating the Dolphin-Human Bond,* by Toni Frohoff & Brenda Peterson, San Francisco: Sierra Club Books 2003 (pp. 245-6).

93. Rossiter, William, "What About Dolphin-Assisted Therapy?": *CSI Whales Alive!* Vol. VII, No. 2, April 1998.

94. Humpfries, T.L. PhD. "Effectiveness of Dolphin-Assisted Therapy as a Behavioral Intervention for Young Children with Disabilities", *Bridges,* Vol. 1, No. 6, May 2003.

95. Marino, Lori & Lilienfeld, Scott O., "Dolphin-Assisted Therapy: Flawed Data, Flawed Conclusions." *Anthrozoos:* 11 (4) 1998 (pp. 194-200).

96. Marino, Lori and Lilienfeld, Scott, O., "Dolphin-Assisted Therapy: More Flawed Data and More Flawed Conclusions," *Anthrozoos,* 11 (4): 2007 (pp. 239-249).

97. Mooney, J., *Captive Cetaceans: A Handbook for Campaigners,* WDCS Document 1998 (pp. 29-30).

98. Rose, Naomi, Farinato, Richard & Sherwin, Susan (editors), *The Case Against Marine Mammals in Captivity,* HSUS/WSPA Document, 2006 (pp. 47).

99. Cetacean Society International, *Whales Alive!* Newsletter, Vol. X No. 2, April 2001.

100. Mooney, J., *Captive Cetaceans: A Handbook for Campaigners,* WDCS Document 1998.

101. Rossiter, William, *Whales Alive! Cetacean Society International newsletter,* Vol. XII, No.2 April 2003.

102. See Dolphin Project web-site: www. dolphinproject.org, "Dolphins in Haiti" & Wozo Productions web-site: wozoproductions.org, "Dolphin Rescue film", June 3, 2004.

103. Rose, Naomi, Farinato, Richard & Sherwin, Susan (editors), *The Case Against Marine Mammals in Captivity,* HSUS/WSPA Document, 2006 (pp. 10, 56).

104. Bassos-Hull, Kim M.Sc., "Echo and Misha Update: Twelve Years Back in the Wild", Sarasota Dolphin Research Program.

105. Balcomb, Kenneth, *Cetacean Releases: A List of Examples,* 1995, The Center for Whale Research.

106. O'Barry, Richard, with Keith Colbourne, *To Free A Dolphin,* Los Angeles: Renaissance Books, 2000.

107. Brill, R., "Return to the Wild as an Option for Managing Atlantic Bottlenose Dolphins", 1994 AZA conference paper & *Soundings* magazine no. 20(3) IMATA. 1994.

108. Rose, Naomi, Farinato, Richard & Sherwin, Susan (editors), *The Case Against Marine Mammals in Captivity,* HSUS/WSPA Document, 2006 (pp.13).

109. Rose, Naomi, Farinato, Richard & Sherwin, Susan (editors), *The Case Against Marine Mammals in Captivity,* HSUS/WSPA Document, 2006 (pp.12).

110. Brill, R., "Return to the Wild as an Option for Managing Atlantic Bottlenose Dolphins", 1994 AZA conference paper & *Soundings* magazine no. 20(3) IMATA. 1994.

111. Forney, K.A., St. Aubin, D. J., & Chivers, S. J., "Chase and Encirclement Stress Studies on Dolphins Involved in Eastern Tropical Pacific Purse-Seine Operations During 2001". Southwest Fisheries Science Center, NMFS, NOAA, Administrative Report, June 2002.

112. Brill, R., "Return to the Wild as an Option for Managing Atlantic Bottlenose Dolphins", 1994 AZA conference paper & *Soundings* magazine no. 20(3) IMATA. 1994.

113. O'Barry, Richard, with Keith Colbourne, *Behind the Dolphin Smile,* Berkley Publishing Group, 1991.

114. Twiss, J., 1995 September 7. Letter to NMFS, cited in: *Captive Cetaceans: A Handbook for Campaigners* by J. Mooney, WDCS document, 1998.

115. European Association for Aquatic Mammals (EAAM): *Position Statement on the Release of Long Term Captive Cetaceans,* www.eaam.org/position_statement_on_releases/ [accessed March 19, 2008].

116. Jensen, Derrick, *A Language Older Than Words,* New York: Context Books, 2000.

117. Bales, Kevin, *Disposable People: New Slavery in the Global Economy.* London: University of California Press 1999 (pp. 253, 256).

118. O'Barry, Richard, *To Free A Dolphin,* Los Angeles: Renaissance Books, 2000 & Richard O'Barry, "A Healing Art" Dolphin Project Website: www.dolphinproject.org/a-healing-art.html [accessed March 10, 2008].

119. Balcomb, Kenneth, *Cetacean Releases: A List of Examples,* Center for Whale Studies document 1995.

120. Barnett, James, *Evaluation of Rehabilitation as an Option for Stranded Dolphins, Porpoises and Whales*: Winston Churchill Memorial Trust Travel Fellowship, 2002 (pp.50-51).

121. O'Barry, Richard, "*Protocol for the Rehabilitation and Release of Captive Atlantic Bottlenose Dolphins (tursiops truncatus),*" 2003 website article: www.dolphinproject.org/the-protocol.html [accessed March 10, 2008]

122. Cousteau, J.M., *Keiko's story: The Timeline,* Ocean Futures Society website article: www.oceanfutures.org/keiko/keiko_history.php [accessed March 6, 2008].

123. Cousteau, J. M., "*Keiko Died in Freedom",* Ocean Futures Society feature story, December 2003, website: www.oceanfutures.org/dispatch_12_16_03_keiko.asp [accessed March 10, 2008].

124. Ford. J.K.B., 1991: "Vocal Traditions Among Resident Killer Whales (Orcinus orca) in Coastal Waters of British Columbia, Canada." *Canadian Journal of Zoology,* 69, 1454-1483.

125. Jensen, Derrick, *A Language Older Than Words,* New York: Context Books, 2000 (pp. 225).

126. Hoyt, Erich, *A Blueprint for Dolphin and Whale Watching Development*, Humane Society International, 2007 (pp.1, 3). & *Whale Watching 2001, Worldwide Tourism, Numbers, Expenditures and Expanding Socioeconomic Benefits*, International Fund for Animal Welfare (IFAW) special report, August 2001.

127. Morton, Alexandra, *Listening to Whales: What the Orcas Have Taught Us*, New York: Ballentine Books 2002 (pp. 234).

128. Hoyt, Erich, "Towards a New Ethic for Watching Dolphins and Whales", in *Between Species: Celebrating the Dolphin-Human Bond*, edited by Toni Frohoff & Brenda Peterson, San Francisco: Sierra Club Books, 2003 (pp. 174).

129. Hoyt, Erich, *A Blueprint for Dolphin and Whale Watching Development*, Humane Society International, 2007 (pp. 4, 25).

130. Reeves, Randall R., Smith, Brian D., Crepso, Enrique A., and Notarbartolo di Sciara, Giuseppe, *Dolphins, Whales & Porpoises: 2002-2010 Conservation Action Plan for the World's Cetaceans,*2003, IUCN/SSC Cetacean Specialist Group (pp. 25).

131. Nollman, Jim, "Talking to Beluga", in *Between Species: Celebrating the Dolphin-Human Bond*, edited by Toni Frohoff & Brenda Peterson, San Francisco: Sierra Club Books, 2003 (pp. 91).

132. Constantine, Rochelle and Susan Yin. "Swimming with Dolphins in New Zealand," In *Between Species: Celebrating the Dolphin-Human Bond*, edited by Toni Frohoff and Brenda Peterson, San Francisco: Sierra Club Books, 2003 (pp. 257-262).

133. Dudzinski, Kathleen, "Letting Dolphins Speak: Are We Listening?" In *Between Species: Celebrating the Dolphin-Human Bond*, edited by Toni Frohoff & Brenda Peterson, San Francisco: Sierra Club Books, 2003 (pp. 291-293).

134. Calvez, Leigh, "Dolphin Lessons", In *Between Species: Celebrating the Dolphin-Human Bond*, edited by Toni Frohoff & Brenda Peterson, San Francisco: Sierra Club Books, 2003 (pp.247-256).

135. Frohoff, Toni, "Interacting with Dolphins in the Wild", In *Between Species: Celebrating the Dolphin-Human Bond*, edited by Toni Frohoff, PhD., and Brenda Peterson, San Francisco: Sierra Club Books 2003 (pp. 339).

136. Herzing, Denise, *Dolphins in the Wild: An Eight Year Field Study on Dolphin Communication and Interspecies Interaction,* Behavioral Biology & Environmental Studies Doctoral Thesis, 1993.

Chapter 28: Intellectual Property

1. Griffin, Donald R., *Animal Minds*, University of Chicago Press 1992.

2. Bekoff, Marc, *Minding Animals: Awareness, Emotions, and Heart,* New York: Oxford University Press 2002 (pp. 91).

3. Gardner, Howard, *Frames of Mind: The Theory of Multiple Intelligences*, New York, Basic

Books 1983.

4. Gardner, Howard, *Intelligence Reframed: Multiple Intelligences for the 21st Century*, New York: Perseus Books, 1999 (41-43, 47-49) & Howard Gardner, *Multiple Intelligence: Theory in Practice*, New York: Basic Books 1993 (pp. 8-9).

5. Gardner, Howard, "Are there additional Intelligences? The Case for Naturalist, Spiritual and Existential Intelligences." In *Education, Information and Transformation: Essays on Learning and Thinking*, Jeffrey Kane (ed), New Jersy: Upper Saddle River, 1999 (pp. 115).

6. Gardner, Howard, *Intelligence Reframed: Multiple Intelligences for the 21st Century*, New York, Perseus Books, 1999 (53, 55-57, 59, 60, 62, 67-71, 74-76).

7. Gardner, Howard, *Intelligence Reframed: Multiple Intelligences for the 21st Century*, New York: Perseus Books, 1999 (pp. 110-111).

8. Reiss, Diana. "The Dolphin, an Alien Intelligence" in, *First Contact: The Search for Extraterrestrial Intelligence*, by Ben Bova & Byron Preiss, New Amer Library Trade 1990 (pp. 39).

9. Heinrich, Bernd, *Mind of the Raven*, New York: HarperCollins, 1999 (pp. 327).

10. Morton, Alexandra, *Listening to Whales: What the Orcas Have Taught Us*, New York: Ballantine Books, 2002 (pp. 135, 306).

11. Wise, Steven, M., *Drawing the Line: Science and the Case for Animal Rights*, Cambridge MA: Perseus Books 2002 (pp.134).

12. Kaiser, David A., *Linguistic Behavior in Nonhuman Species: A Paradigm for Testing Mental Continuity*, Los Angeles: University of California 1990.

13. Linehan, E. J., "The Trouble with Dolphins", *National Geographic*, vol. 155 no. 4, April 1979 (pp. 538).

14. Whitehead, Hal, *Sperm Whales: Social Evolution in the Oceans*, Chicago: University of Chicago Press, 2003 (pp. 322-23).

15. Marino, Lori, "Convergence of Complex Cognitive Abilities in Cetaceans and Primates." *Brain, Behavior and Evolution*, **59**, 2002 (pp. 21-32).

16. Klinowska, Margaret, "Brains, Behavior and Intelligence in Cetaceans," in: *High North: 11 Essays on Whales and Man*, 2nd edition, Research Group in Mammalian Ecology and Reproduction, Cambridge University, September 1994.

17. Reiss, Diana, McCowan, Brenda and Marino, Lori, "Communicative and other cognitive characteristics of bottlenose dolphins", *Cognitive Sciences*.Vol. 1 (**4**) 1997 (pp. 140-141).

18. Marino, Lori, "A Comparison of Encephalization between Odontocete Cetaceans and Anthropoid Primates," *Brain, Behavior, and Evolution*, **51**, 1998 (pp. 236).

19. Ridgway, Sam H., "The Central Nervous System of the Bottlenose Dolphin," in Stephen Leatherwood & Randall R. Reeves (eds) *The Bottlenose Dolphin*, San Diego: Academic Press, 1990 (pp. 87).

20. Wise, Steven M., *Rattling the Cage: Toward Legal Rights for Animals*, Cambridge, MA:

Perseus Publishing 2000 (pp. 133).

21. H. Elias and D. Schwartz, "Surface areas of the cerebral cortex of mammals determined by stereological methods". *Science*, **166**, 111-113 (1969).

22. Smolker, Rachel. *To Touch a Wild Dolphin*, New York: Ballentine Books, 2001.

23. Lilly, John C., "Toward a Cetacean Nation," in *Between Species: Celebrating the Dolphin-Human Bond*, edited by Toni Frohoff & Brenda Peterson, San Francisco: Sierra Club Books, 2003 (pp. 80).

24. Pepperberg, Irene. M., *The Alex Studies: Cognitive and Communicative Abilities of Grey Parrots*, Cambridge, MA: Harvard University Press 1999 & Heinrich, Bernd, *Mind of the Raven*, New York: HarperCollins, 1999.

25. Pepperberg, Irene. M., *The Alex Studies: Cognitive and Communicative Abilities of Grey Parrots*, Cambridge, MA: Harvard University Press 1999.

26. Herzing, Denise, L., & White, Thomas, "Dolphins and the Question of Personhood" in *Etica &Animali*, 9/98, 1999 (pp. 64-84).

27. Marino, Lori, "Brain-Behavior Relationships in Cetaceans and Primates: Implications for the Evolution of Complex Intelligence," PhD dissertation, State University of New York at Albany, 1995 (pp. 387), Cited in: Thomas White, *In Defense of Dolphins; The New Moral Frontier*, Oxford: Blackwell Publishing 2007 (pp. 38).

28. Fouts, Roger, *Next of Kin: My Conversations With Chimpanzees*, New York: Avon Books, 1997 (pp. 45).

29. Fouts, Roger, *Next of Kin: My Conversations With Chimpanzees*, New York: Avon Books, 1997 (pp. 55).

30. Smolker, Rachel, *To Touch a Wild Dolphin*, New York: Doubleday 2001 (pp. 246).

31. White, Thomas I., *In Defense of Dolphins: The New Moral Frontier*, Oxford: Blackwell Publishing 2007 (pp. 33, 35).

32. Sheldrake, Rupert, *The Sense of Being Stared At*, New York: Three Rivers Press 2003 (pp. 13, 14).

33. Cited in: Wise, Steven M., *Rattling the Cage*, Cambridge MA: Perseus Publishing 2000 (pp. 129).

34. Corsini, Rayond J. and Auerbach, Alan J., (ed) *The Concise Encyclopedia of Psychology*, 2nd Edition, John Wiley & Sons, 1996 (pp. 183).

35. Griffin, Donald, *Animal Thinking*, Cambridge MA, Harvard University Press, 1984 (pp. 28)

36. Bekoff, Marc, *Minding Animals: Awareness, Emotions, and Heart*, New York: Oxford University Press 2002 (pp. 95).

37. Heinrich, Bernd, *Mind of the Raven*, New York: HarperPerennial 1999 (pp. 339).

38. Nollman, Jim, *The Charged Border: Where Whales and Humans Meet*. New York: Henry Holt and Company, Inc. 1999.

39. Wise, Steven M., *Rattling the Cage: Toward Legal Rights for Animals*, Cambridge MA: Perseus Publishing 1999 (pp. 199).

40. Marten, Kenneth and Suchi Psarakos, "Evidence of self-awareness in the bottlenose dolphin (Tursiops truncatus)", In: *Self-Awareness in Animals and Humans: Developmental Perspectives*, edited by Sue Taylor Parker, Robert W. Mitchell, and Maria L. Boccia, Chapter 24, pp. 361-379, New York, Cambridge University Press, 1995 & Reiss, Diana and Lori Marino, "Mirror self-recognition in the bottlenose dolphin: A case of cognitive convergence". *Proceedings of the National Academy of Sciences, 98*(10), 5937-5942 (2001). & Lori Marino, Diana Reiss and Gordon G. Gallup Jr. "Mirror self-recognition in bottlenose dolphins: Implications for comparative investigations of highly dissimilar species," In *Self-Awareness in Animals and Humans: Developmental Perspectives*, edited by Sue Taylor Parker et al, Cambridge University Press 1994 (pp. 380, 386-390).

41. Marten, Kenneth and Suchi Psarakos, "Using Self-View Television to Distinguish between Self-Examination and Social Behavior in the Bottlenose Dolphin (Tursiops truncatus)." In, *Journal of Consciousness and Cognition*, volume 4, No.2, June 1995 (pp. 205-224), Orlando, Academic Press.

42. Herman, Louis, "Exploring the Cognitive World of the Bottlenosed Dolphin." In *the Cognitive Animal*, edited by Marc Bekoff, Colin Allen & Gordon Burghardt. Cambridge MA: MIT Press, 2002 (pp. 275-283).

43. Herzing, Denise, L., & White, Thomas, "Dolphins and the Question of Personhood" in *Etica &Animali*, 9/98, 1999 (pp. 64-84).

44. Whitehead, Hal, Reeves, Randall R., and Tyack, Peter, "Science and the Conservation, Protection, and Management of Wild Cetaceans." In *Cetacean Societies: Field Studies of Dolphins and Whales*, edited by Janet Mann, Richard Connor, Peter Tyack and Hal Whitehead: University of Chicago Press 2000 (pp. 329).

45. Bekoff, Marc, *Minding Animals: Awareness, Emotions and Heart*, New York: Oxford University Press, 2002 (pp. 181).

46. Herzing, Denise, *Dolphins in the Wild: An Eight Year Field Study on Dolphin Communication and Interspecies Interaction*, Behavioral Biology & Environmental Studies Doctoral Thesis, 1993.

47. Herzing, Denise, L., & White, Thomas, "Dolphins and the Question of Personhood" in *Etica &Animali*, 9/98, 1999 (pp. 64-84).

48. Bekoff, Marc, *Minding Animals: Awareness, Emotions and Heart*, New York: Oxford University Press, 2002.

49. Griffin, Donald, *Animal Minds*, University of Chicago Press, 1992.

50. Wise, Steven, *Rattling the Cage: Towards Legal Rights for Animals*, Cambridge, MA: Perseus Books 2000 (pp. 124).

51. Bekoff, Marc, *Minding Animals: Awareness, Emotions and Heart*, New York: Oxford University Press, 2002.

52. De Waal, Frans, *The Ape and the Sushi Master: Cultural Reflections of a Primatologist*, New York: Basic Books, 2001 (pp. 41, 64, 65).

53. Pepperberg, Irene M., *The Alex Studies: Cognitive and Communicative Abilities of Grey*

Parrots, Cambridge MA: Harvard University Press, 1999 (pp. 43, 44).

54. Pepperberg, Irene M., *The Alex Studies: Cognitive and Communicative Abilities of Grey Parrots,* Cambridge MA: Harvard University Press, 1999 (pp. 34-35).

55. Pepperberg, Irene M., *The Alex Studies: Cognitive and Communicative Abilities of Grey Parrots,* Cambridge MA: Harvard University Press, 1999 (pp. 129-130).

56. Pepperberg, Irene M., *The Alex Studies: Cognitive and Communicative Abilities of Grey Parrots,* Cambridge MA: Harvard University Press, 1999 (pp. 153, 155).

57. Bekoff, Marc, *Minding Animals: Awareness, Emotions, and Heart,* New York: Oxford University Press 2002 (pp. 50, 51, 68).

58. Watson, Lyall, *Whales of the World,* London: Hutchison, 1981 (pp. 49).

59. "The Trouble with Dolphins", *National Geographic,* vol. 155, No. 4 April 1979 (pp. 533).

60. Wise, Steven, M., *Drawing the Line: Science and the Case for Animal Rights,* Cambridge MA: Perseus Books, 2000 (pp. 135) & "The Trouble with Dolphins", *National Geographic,* vol. 155, No. 4 April 1979 (pp. 536-539).

61. White, Thomas I., *In Defense of Dolphins: The New Moral Frontier,* Oxford: Blackwell Publishing 2007 (pp.96).

62. Herman, Louis, "What the dolphin knows, or might know in its natural world." In *Dolphin Societies: Discoveries and Puzzles,* Karen Pryor, and Ken Norris (ed.), University of California Press 1991, (pp. 351, 354-355).

63. Wise, Steven, M., *Drawing the Line: Science and the Case for Animal Rights,* Cambridge MA: Perseus Books, 2000 (pp. 141-142, 144).

64. Herzing, Denise, L., & White, Thomas, "Dolphins and the Question of Personhood" in *Etica &Animali,* 9/98, 1999 (pp. 64-84).

65. White, Thomas I., *In Defense of Dolphins: The New Moral Frontier,* Oxford: Blackwell Publishing 2007 (pp. 103).

66. Hillix, W. A, and Duane Rumbaugh, *Animal Bodies, Human Minds: Ape, Dolphin and Parrot Language Skills,* New York: Kluwer Academic/Plenum Publishers, 2004 (pp. 161).

67. Herman, Louis, S. A. Kuczaj and Holder, M.D., "Responses to anomalous gestural sequences by a language-trained dolphin: evidence for processing of semantic relations and syntactic information." In *Journal of Experimental Psychology,* General, 122 (2) 1993 (pp. 184-194). & Hillix, W. A, and Duane Rumbaugh, *Animal Bodies, Human Minds: Ape, Dolphin and Parrot Language Skills,* New York: Kluwer Academic/Plenum Publishers, 2004 (pp. 222).

68. Herman, Louis, "Exploring the Cognitive World of the Bottlenosed Dolphin." In *the Cognitive Animal,* edited by Marc Bekoff, Colin Allen & Gordon Burghardt. Cambridge MA: MIT Press, 2002 (pp. 275-283).

69. White, Thomas I., *In Defense of Dolphins: The New Moral Frontier,* Oxford: Blackwell Publishing 2007 (pp. 100, 110).

70. Herman, Louis and Robert Uyayama, "The dolphin's grammatical competency: Comments on Kako" In *Animal Learning and Behavior* 27 (1) 1999 (pp. 18-23). & Herman,

Louis, "Exploring the Cognitive World of the Bottlenosed Dolphin." In *the Cognitive Animal,* edited by mark Bekoff, Colin Allen & Gordon Burghardt. Cambridge MA: MIT Press, 2002 (pp. 275-283).

71. Wise, Steven, M., *Drawing the Line: Science and the Case for Animal Rights,* Cambridge MA: Perseus Books, 2000 (pp. 145-147).

72. Freeman, Macgillivray, *Dolphins* (IMAX film), Macgillivray Freeman Films 2000.

73. Herman, Louis M., "Intelligence and Rational Behavior in Bottlenose Dolphins," in *Rational Animals?* Susan Hurley & Matthew Nudds (eds), Oxford; New York: Oxford University Press 2006 (pp. 454).

74. Herman, Louis, "Exploring the Cognitive World of the Bottlenosed Dolphin." In *the Cognitive Animal,* edited by Marc Bekoff, Colin Allen & Gordon Burghardt. Cambridge MA: MIT Press, 2002 (pp. 275-283).

75. Herman, Louis, Palmer Morrel-Samuels, and Adam Pack, "Bottlenosed dolphin and human recognition of veridical and degraded video displays of an artificial gestural language." *Journal of Experimental Psychology*: General, 119(2) 1990 (pp. 215-230) & Kaiser, David, *Linguistic Behavior in Nonhuman Species: A Paradigm for Testing Mental Continuity,* Los Angeles: University of California 1990.

76. Herman, Louis, M., Pack, Adam A. et al., "Dolphins (Tursiops truncates) Comprehend the Referential Character of the Human Pointing Gesture," *Journal of Comparative Psychology*, 113(4) 1999 (pp. 347) & Alain Tschudin, Josep Call, R.I.M. Dunbar, Gabrielle Harriss and Charmaine van der Elst, "Comprehension of Signs By Dolphins (tursiops truncates)," *Journal of Comparative Psychology*, 115(1) 2001 (pp.100-105).

77. White, Thomas I., In Defense of Dolphins: The New Moral Frontier, Oxford: Blackwell Publishing 2007 (pp. 68-71,75).

78. Herzing, Denise, L., & White, Thomas, "Dolphins and the Question of Personhood" in *Etica &Animali*, 9/98, 1999 (pp. 75-76).

79. Wise, Steven, M., *Drawing the Line: Science and the Case for Animal Rights,* Cambridge MA: Perseus Books, 2002 (pp. 136-137).

80. Wise, Steven, M., *Drawing the Line: Science and the Case for Animal Rights,* Cambridge MA: Perseus Books, 2000 (pp. 139-140).

81. Herman, Louis, "Exploring the Cognitive World of the Bottlenosed Dolphin." In *the Cognitive Animal,* edited by Marc Bekoff, Colin Allen & Gordon Burghardt. Cambridge MA: MIT Press, 2002 (pp. 275-283).

82. Nash, Roderick Frazier, *The Rights of Nature: A History of Environmental Ethics,* The University of Wisconsin Press, 1989 (pp. 185).

83. Marten, Kenneth and Suchi Psarkos, "Evidence of self-awareness in the bottlenose dolphin (Tursiops truncatus)" In: *Self-Awareness in Animals and Humans: Developmental Perspectives,* edited by Sue Taylor Parker, Robert W. Mitchell, and Maria L. Boccia, New York: Cambridge University Press, 1995 (Chapter 24, pp. 361-379).

84. Marten, Kenneth and Suchi Psarkos, "Evidence of self-awareness in the bottlenose

dolphin (Tursiops truncatus)" In: *Self-Awareness in Animals and Humans: Developmental Perspectives*, edited by Sue Taylor Parker, Robert W. Mitchell, and Maria L. Boccia, New York, Cambridge University Press, 1995 (Chapter 24, pp. 361-379).

85. Marten, Kenneth, and Suchi Psarkos, "Using Self-View Television to Distinguish between Self-Examination and Social Behavior in the Bottlenose Dolphin (Tursiops truncatus).", *Journal of Consciousness and Cognition*, volume 4, No.2, June, Academic Press, Orlando, 1995 (pp. 205-224); & Kenneth Marten and Suchi Psarkos, "Evidence of Self-awareness in the Bottlenose Dolphin (Tursiops truncatus)" In: *Self-Awareness in Animals and Humans: Developmental Perspectives*, edited by Sue Taylor Parker, Robert W. Mitchell, and Maria L. Boccia, New York: Cambridge University Press, 1995 (Chapter 24, pp. 361-379).

86. Reiss, Diana and Lori Marino, "Mirror self-recognition in the bottlenose dolphin: A case of cognitive convergence." In *Proceedings of the National Academy of Sciences, 98*(10), 2001 (pp. 5937-5942). & Lori Marino, Diana Reiss and Gordon G. Gallup Jr. "Mirror self-recognition in bottlenose dolphins: Implications for comparative investigations of highly dissimilar species," In *Self-Awareness in Animals and Humans: Developmental Perspectives*, edited by Sue Taylor Parker et al, New York: Cambridge University Press 1995 (pp. 380, 387-390).

87. Delfour, Fabienne and Marten, Ken, "Mirror image processing in three marine mammal species: killer whales (Orcinus orca), false killer whales (Pseudorca crassidens) and California sea lions (Zalophus californianus).", *Behavioral Processes* 53(3) 2001 (pp. 181-190).

88. Samuels, Amy, Tyack, Peter, Mann, Janet, *Cetacean Societies: Field Studies of Dolphins and Whales*, edited by Janet Mann, Richard Connor, Peter Tyack and Hal Whitehead: University of Chicago Press 2000 (pp. 42, 44, 45, 46, 56, 64, 334).

89. Whitehead, Hal, Reeves, Randall R. and Tyack, Peter, "Science and the Conservation, Protection and management of Wild Cetaceans." In *Cetacean Societies: Field Studies of Dolphins and Whales*, edited by Janet Mann, Richard Connor, Peter Tyack and Hal Whitehead: University of Chicago Press 2000 (pp. 329).

90. Bekoff, Marc, *Minding Animals: Awareness, Emotions, and Heart*, New York: Oxford University Press 2002.

91. Fouts, Roger, *Next of Kin: My Conversations With Chimpanzees*, New York: Avon Books, 1997 (pp. 28).

92. Herzing, Denise, *Dolphins in the Wild: An Eight Year Field Study on Dolphin Communication and Interspecies Interaction*, Behavioral Biology & Environmental Studies Doctoral Thesis, 1993.

93. Griffin, Donald, *Animal Minds*, Chicago: University of Chicago Press, 1992 (pp. 260).

94. Bekoff, Marc, *Minding Animals: Awareness, Emotions, and Heart*, New York: Oxford University Press 2002 (pp. 92).

95. Goodall, Jane, *In the Shadow of Man*, New York: Houghton Mifflin Company, 1971 (pp.

277-280).

96. Wise, Steven M. Drawing the Line: Science and the Cage for Animal Rights, New York: Perseus Books 2002 (pp. 4).

97. Bekoff, Marc, *Minding Animals: Awareness, Emotions, and Heart,* New York: Oxford University Press 2002 (pp. 13).

98. De Waal, Frans & Frans Lanting, *Bonobo: The Forgotten Ape,* Berkley CA: University of California Press, 1997 (pp. 42).

99. Fouts, Roger, *Next of Kin: My Conversations With Chimpanzees,* New York: Avon Books, 1997 (pp. 241).

100. De Waal, The Ape and the Sushi Master: Cultural Reflections of a Primatologist, New York: Basic Books, 2001 (pp. 6, 237).

101. De Waal, *The Ape and the Sushi Master: Cultural Reflections of a Primatologist,* New York: Basic Books, 2001 (pp. 29, 25, 267).

102. Smolker, Rachel, *To Touch a Wild Dolphin,* New York: Doubleday, 2001 (pp. 13).

103. White, Thomas I., *In Defense of Dolphins: The New Moral Frontier*, Oxford: Blackwell Publishing 2007 (pp. 175-178).

104. Baird, Robin W., "The Killer Whale: Foraging Specializations and Group Hunting" In *Cetacean Societies: Field Studies of Dolphins and Whales,* edited by Janet Mann, Richard Connor, Peter Tyack and Hal Whitehead: University of Chicago Press 2000 (pp. 145).

105. Whitehead, Hal, *Sperm Whales: Social Evolution in the Ocean,* Chicago: University of Chicago Press 2003 (pp. 355, 356).

106. Rendell, Luke, & Whitehead, Hal "Culture in Whales and Dolphins" In *Behavioral Brain Sciences* 24 (2), 2001 (pp. 309-382).

107. Herzing, Denise, L., "Acoustics and Social Behavior of Wild Dolphins: Implications for a Sound Society." In *Hearing by Whales and Dolphins,* edited by W. Witlow et al. New York: Springer 2000 (pp. 225-272).

108. Rendell, Luke & Whitehead, Hal, "Culture in Whales and Dolphins", *Behavioral Brain Sciences* 24 (2) 2001 (pp. 309-382).

109. Mann, Janet and Whitehead, Hal, "Female Reproductive Strategies of Cetaceans: Life Histories and Calf Care." & Peter Tyack, Richard Connor, Janet Mann and Hal Whitehead, "The Future of Behavioral Research on Cetaceans in the Wild." In *Cetacean Societies: Field Studies of Dolphins and Whales,* edited by Janet Mann, Richard Connor, Peter Tyack and Hal Whitehead: University of Chicago Press 2000 (pp. 233, 243, 246, 337).

110. Rendell, Luke & Whitehead, Hal, "Culture in Whales and Dolphins", *Behavioral Brain Sciences* 24 (2) 2001 (pp. 309-382).

111. Whitehead, Hal, Rendell, Luke, Osborne, Richard W., and Wursig, Bernd, "Culture and conservation of non-humans with reference to whales and dolphins: review and new directions," *Biological Conservation* 120, 2004 (pp. 432, 433, 438).

112. Baird, Robin W., "The Killer Whale: Foraging Specializations and Group Hunting" In

Cetacean Societies: Field Studies of Dolphins and Whales, edited by Janet Mann, Richard Connor, Peter Tyack and Hal Whitehead: University of Chicago Press 2000 (pp. 131, 138).

113. Bekoff, Marc, *Minding Animals: Awareness, Emotions, and Heart,* New York: Oxford University Press 2002 (pp. 13).

114. Tyack, Peter, "Functional Aspects of Cetacean Communication" In *Cetacean Societies: Field Studies of Dolphins and Whales,* edited by Janet Mann, Richard Connor, Peter Tyack and Hal Whitehead: University of Chicago Press 2000 (pp. 297). & John Ford, "Vocal traditions among resident killer whales (Orcinus orca) in coastal waters of British Columbia" *Canadian Journal of Zoology,* 69: 1991 (pp. 1454-1483).

115. Morton, Alexandra, *Listening to Whales: What the Orcas Have Taught Us,* New York: Ballantine Books, 2002 (pp. 307).

116. Rendell, Luke and Whitehead, Hal, "Culture in Whales and Dolphins," *Behavioral Brain Sciences* 24(2) 2001 (pp. 309-382) .

117. Morton, Alexandra, *Listening to Whales: What the Orcas Have Taught Us,* New York: Ballantine Books, 2002 (pp. 55, 106).

118. Morton, Alexandra, *Listening to Whales: What the Orcas Have Taught Us,* New York: Ballantine Books, 2002 (pp. 3).

119. Whitehead, Hal, *Sperm Whales: Social Evolution in the Ocean,* Chicago: University of Chicago Press 2003 (pp. 322).

120. Nollman, Jim, *The Charged Border: Where Whales and Humans Meet,* New York: Henry Holt & Co. 1999 (pp. 55).

121. Whitehead, Hal, *Sperm Whales: Social Evolution in the Ocean,* Chicago: University of Chicago Press 2003 (pp. 323, 325, 354, 358).

122. Whitehead, Hal, *Sperm Whales: Social Evolution in the Ocean,* Chicago: University of Chicago Press 2003 (pp. 134, 292, 315, 340).

123. Schulz, Tlyer, M., *The Production and Exchange of Sperm Whale Coda Vocalizations,* Thesis Abstract, Dalhouse University Department of Biology, September 21, 2007.

124. Beamish, Peter, *Dancing with Whales,* St. John's Newfoundland: Creative Publishers 1993.

125. Herzing, Denise, L., & White, Thomas, "Dolphins and the Question of Personhood" in *Etica &Animali,* 9/98, 1999 (pp. 64-84).

126. Smolker, Rachel, To Touch a Wild Dolphin: A Journey of Discovery with the Sea's Most Intelligent Creatures, New York: Doubleday, 2001 (pp. 14).

127. Herman, Louis M., Pack, Adam A., & Morrel-Samuels, Palmer, "Representational and Conceptual Skills of Dolphins," in *Language and Communication: Comparative Perspectives,* edited by H.L. Roitblat, L. M. Herman, P. E. Nachtigall, Hillsdale, NJ: Lawrence Erlbaum Associates, 1993 (pp. 403-442); Richards, Dougals G., Wolz, James P., and Herman, Louis M., "Vocal Mimicry of Computer Generated Sounds and Vocal Labeling of Objects by a Bottlenosed Dolphin, Tursiops truncatus," *Journal of*

Comparative Psychology, 98(1) 1984 (pp. 10-28).

128. Herman, Louis, "Exploring the Cognitive World of the Bottlenosed Dolphin." In *the Cognitive Animal,* edited by Marc Bekoff, Colin Allen & Gordon Burghardt. Cambridge MA: MIT Press, 2002 (pp. 275-283).

129. Tyack, Peter L., "Functional Aspects of Cetacean Communication" In *Cetacean Societies: Field Studies of Dolphins and Whales,* edited by Janet Mann, Richard Connor, Peter Tyack and Hal Whitehead: University of Chicago Press 2000 (pp. 305-306).

130. Herman, Louis, M., et al., "Bottlenose dolphins can generalize rules and develop abstract concepts." *Marine Mammal Science* 10, 1994; pp. 70-80).

131. Smolker, Rachel, To Touch a Wild Dolphin: A Journey of Discovery with the Sea's Most Intelligent Creatures, New York: Doubleday, 2001 (pp. 243).

132. Smolker, Rachel, To Touch a Wild Dolphin: A Journey of Discovery with the Sea's Most Intelligent Creatures, New York: Doubleday, 2001 (pp. 254).

133. Herzing, Denise, L., "Acoustics and Social Behavior of Wild Dolphins: Implications for a Sound Society." In *Hearing by Whales and Dolphins,* edited by W. Witlow et al. New York: Springer 2000 (pp. 252-254).

134. Rendell, Luke & Whitehead, Hal, "Culture in whales and Dolphins", *Behavioral Brain Sciences* 24 (2) 2001 (pp. 309-382).

135. White, Thomas I., *In Defense of Dolphins: The New Moral Frontier*, Oxford: Blackwell Publishing 2007 (pp. 150).

136. White, Thomas I., *In Defense of Dolphins: The New Moral Frontier*, Oxford: Blackwell Publishing 2007 (pp. 78-79).

137. Rendell, Luke & Whitehead, Hal, "Culture in whales and Dolphins", *Behavioral Brain Sciences* 24 (2) 2001 (pp. 309-382).

138. McCowan, Brenda, Marino, Lori, Reiss, Diana, Vance, Eric and Walke, Leah, "Bubble Ring Play of Bottlenose Dolphins (tursiops truncatus): Implications for Cognition", *Journal of Comparative Psychology* Vol. 114 (1) 2000 (pp. 98-106) & Marten, Kenneth, Shariff, K., Psarakos, S., and White, D. J., "Ring Bubbles of Dolphins, "*Scientific American* 275, 1996 (pp. 83-87).

139. Whitlow, W. L. Au, "Instrumentation for Dolphin Echolocation Experiments", *The Journal of the Acoustical Society of America,* Vol. 83, Issue S1 (pp.S15).

140. Herzing, Denise, L., "Acoustics and Social Behavior of Wild Dolphins: Implications for a Sound Society." In *Hearing by Whales and Dolphins,* edited by W. Witlow et al. New York: Springer 2000 (pp. 257, 259, 262).

141. Herzing, Denise, L., "Acoustics and Social Behavior of Wild Dolphins: Implications for a Sound Society." In *Hearing by Whales and Dolphins,* edited by W. Witlow et al. New York: Springer 2000 (233, 249, 256).

142. Norris, Kenneth, S., *Dolphin Days: The Life & Times of the Spinner Dolphin*. New York: Avon Books 1991 (pp. 208).

143. White, Thomas I., *In Defense of Dolphins: The New Moral Frontier*, Oxford: Blackwell

Publishing 2007 (pp. 22, 26, 40).

144. Herzing, Denise, L., "Acoustics and Social Behavior of Wild Dolphins: Implications for a Sound Society." In *Hearing by Whales and Dolphins,* edited by W. Witlow et al. New York: Springer 2000 (pp. 237, 244, 247, 248, 251, 255).

145. McCowan, Brenda, and Reiss, Diana, "The fallacy of 'signature whistles' in bottlenose dolphins: a comparative perspective of 'signature information' in animal vocalizations." *Animal Behavior* 62(6) 2001 (pp. 1151-1162) & Reiss, Diana, McCowan, Brenda, and Marino, Lori, "Communicative and other cognitive characteristics of bottlenose dolphins" *Trends in Cognitive Sciences,* Vol. 1 (4) 1997, (pp. 142).

146. Ding. W., Wursing, B., and Evans, W. E., "Whistles of bottlenose dolphins: comparisons among populations." *Aquatic Mammals,* 21, 1995 (pp. 65-77).

147. Rose, Naomi, Farinato, Richard & Sherwin, Susan, *The Case Against Marine Mammals in Captivity,* HSUS/WSPA report, 2006 (pp. 40).

148. McCowan, Brenda, Hanser, Sean F., & Doyle, Laurance R., "Quantitative tools for comparing animal communication systems: information theory applied to bottlenose dolphin whistle repertoires," *Animal Behavior* (57), 1999 (pp. 409-419).

149. McCowan, Brenda, Hanser, Sean F., & Doyle, Laurance R., "Quantitative tools for comparing animal communication systems: information theory applied to bottlenose dolphin whistle repertoires," *Animal Behavior* (57), 1999 (pp. 409-419).

150. McCowan, Brenda, Hanser, Sean F., & Doyle, Laurance R., "Quantitative tools for comparing animal communication systems: information theory applied to bottlenose dolphin whistle repertoires," *Animal Behavior* (57), 1999 (pp. 409-419).

151. Brown, Robin, *The Lure of the Dolphin,* New York: Avon Books, 1979 (pp. 110).

152. Lilly, John. C., "Towards a Cetacean Nation", in *Between Species: Celebrating the Dolphin-Human Bond,* edited by Toni Frohoff & Brenda Peterson, San Francisco: Sierra Club Books, 2003 (pp. 81).

153. De Waal, Frans, *The Ape and the Sushi Master: Cultural Reflections of a Primatologist,* New York: Basic Books, 2001 (pp. 25).

154. Herzing, Denise, *Dolphins in the Wild: An Eight Year Field Study on Dolphin Communication and Interspecies Interaction,* Behavioral Biology & Environmental Studies Doctoral Thesis, 1993.

155. Herzing, Denise, L., & White, Thomas, "Dolphins and the Question of Personhood" in *Etica &Animali,* 9/98, 1999 (pp. 64-84).

156. Herzing, Denise, *Dolphins in the Wild: An Eight Year Field Study on Dolphin Communication and Interspecies Interaction,* Behavioral Biology & Environmental Studies Doctoral Thesis, 1993.

157. Heinrich, Bernd, *Mind of the Raven,* New York: Cliff Street Books, 1999 (pp. 342).

158. Nollman, Jim, *The Charged Border: Where Whales and Humans Meet,* New York: Henry Holt & Co. 1999 (pp. 66).

159. Lorenz, Konrad, *The Foundations of Ethology,* New York: Simon & Shuster, 1981.

160. Bekoff, Marc, "Troubling Tursiops" in *Between Species: Celebrating the Dolphin-Human Bond*, edited by Toni Frohoff & Brenda Peterson, San Francisco: Sierra Club Books, 2003 (pp. 271).

161. Bekoff, Marc, *Minding Animals: Awareness, Emotions, and Heart*, New York: Oxford University Press 2002 (pp. 9, 10, 172, 181, 185, 192).

162. Herzing, Denise, *Dolphins in the Wild: An Eight Year Field Study on Dolphin Communication and Interspecies Interaction*, Behavioral Biology & Environmental Studies Doctoral Thesis, 1993.

163. Bekoff, Marc, *Minding Animals: Awareness, Emotions, and Heart*, New York: Oxford University Press 2002 (pp. xviii).

164. Carson, Rachel, *Silent Spring*, New York: Houghton Mifflin, New York 1962.

165. Herzing, Denise, *Dolphins in the Wild: An Eight Year Field Study on Dolphin Communication and Interspecies Interaction*, Behavioral Biology & Environmental Studies Doctoral Thesis, 1993.

166. Herzing, Denise, L., & White, Thomas, "Dolphins and the Question of Personhood" in *Etica &Animali*, 9/98, 1999 (pp. 64-84). & White, Thomas I., *In Defense of Dolphins; The New Moral Frontier*, Oxford: Blackwell Publishing, 2007.

167. White, Thomas I., *In Defense of Dolphins; The New Moral Frontier*, Oxford: Blackwell Publishing, 2007.

Chapter 29: Ethical Evolution

1. White, Thomas I., *In Defense of Dolphins: The New Moral Frontier*, Oxford: Blackwell Publishing 2007 (pp. 50, 185, 186, 187, 188, 195).

2. Bekoff, Marc. *Minding Animals: Awareness, Emotions, and Heart*. New York: Oxford University Press, 2002 (pp. 142-143).

3. White, Thomas I., *In Defense of Dolphins: The New Moral Frontier*, Oxford: Blackwell Publishing 2007 (pp. 49, 51, 54, 68, 74, 80).

4. Whitehead, Hal, Reeves, Randall R., Tyack, Peter, "Science and the Conservation, Protection, and management of Wild Cetaceans" in *Cetacean Societies: Field Studies of Dolphins and Whales*, edited by Janet Mann, Richard C. Connor, Peter L. Tyack and Hal Whitehead. Chicago: The University of Chicago Press 2000 (pp. 332).

5. White, Thomas I., *In Defense of Dolphins: The New Moral Frontier*, Oxford: Blackwell Publishing 2007 (pp. 185, 186, 193).

6. Goodall, Jane, "Foreword" in *Minding Animals: Awareness, Emotions, and Heart*, by Marc Bekoff, New York: Oxford University Press, 2002 (pp. xi).

7. White, Thomas I., *In Defense of Dolphins: The New Moral Frontier*, Oxford: Blackwell Publishing 2007 (pp. 188).

8. Wise, Steven, M. *Drawing the Line: Science and the Case for Animal Rights*. Cambridge,

MA: Perseus Books, 2002 (pp.17, 239, 240).

9. Wise, Steven, M. *Drawing the Line: Science and the Case for Animal Rights.* Cambridge, MA: Perseus Books, 2002 (pp. 23).

10. Wise, Steven, M. *Rattling the Cage.* Cambridge, MA; Perseus Publishing, 2000 (pp. 54-55, 80-81).

11. Bales, Kevin, *Disposable People: New Slavery in the Global Economy.* London, University of California Press, 1999 (pp. 3, 4, 5, 6, 8, 9, 10, 11, 32, 237, 238).

12. Hawken, Paul, *The Ecology of Commerce: A Declaration of Sustainability,* New York: HarperCollins 1994 (pp. 96, 97, 98, 100).

13. Bales, Kevin, *Disposable People: New Slavery in the Global Economy.* London, University of California Press, 1999 (pp. 10, 32, 143,) & Hawken, Paul, *The Ecology of Commerce: A Declaration of Sustainability,* New York: HarperCollins 1994 (pp.10, 135).

14. Bales, Kevin, *Disposable People: New Slavery in the Global Economy.* London, University of California Press, 1999 (pp. 33, 236, 238, 240, 241, 246, 261).

15. Herzing, Denise L., *Dolphins in the Wild: An Eight Year Study on Dolphin Communication and Interspecies Interaction,* Behavioral Biology & Environmental Studies Doctoral Thesis, 1993: (pp. 56, 57, 169).

16. Salt, Henry S., "Humanitarianism: Its General Principles and Progress," in, *Cruelties of civilization: program of Humane Reform,* London: 1897 (pp. vii) cited in: Roderick Frazier Nash, *The Rights of Nature: A History of Environmental Ethics.* London: The University of Wisconsin Press, 1989 (pp. 29).

17. Nash, Roderick Frazier, *The Rights of Nature: A History of Environmental Ethics.* The University of Wisconsin Press, 1989 (pp. 28-30) & Henry S. Salt, *Animal Rights: Considered in Relation to Social Progress,* New York: Macmillan & Co. 1894.

18. Jensen, Derrick. *The Culture of Make Believe.* New York, Context Books, 2002 (pp. 551).

19. Jensen, Derrick. *The Culture of Make Believe.* New York, Context Books, 2002 (pp. 353, 570-571).

20. Nash, Roderick Frazier, *The Rights of Nature: A History of Environmental Ethics.* The University of Wisconsin Press, 1989 (pp. 113, 117, 118).

21. Bales, Kevin, *Disposable People: New Slavery in the Global Economy.* London, University of California Press, 1999 (pp. 261-262).

22. Jensen, Derrick. *The Culture of Make Believe.* New York, Context Books, 2002 (pp. 94, 137-138, 224).

23. Nash, Roderick Frazier, *The Rights of Nature: A History of Environmental Ethics.* The University of Wisconsin Press, 1989 (pp. 7).

24. White, Thomas I., *In Defense of Dolphins: The New Moral Frontier,* Oxford: Blackwell Publishing 2007 (pp. 220).

25. See: www.davidsuzuki.org/fils/Declaration.pdf [accessed April 9, 2008]. & Hawken, Paul, *The Ecology of Commerce: A Declaration of Sustainability,* New York: HarperCollins 1994 (pp. 219).

26. Bekoff, Marc. *Minding Animals: Awareness, Emotions, and Heart.* New York: Oxford University Press, 2002 (pp. 153).

27. Hawken, Paul, *The Ecology of Commerce: A Declaration of Sustainability,* New York: HarperCollins 1994 (pp. xiv, 2, 11).

28. Bekoff, Marc. *Minding Animals: Awareness, Emotions, and Heart.* New York: Oxford University Press, 2002 (pp. 32).

29. See: www.janegoodall.org

30. Bekoff, Marc, "Troubling Tursiops: Living in Harmony with Kindred Spirits." In *Between Species: Celebrating the Dolphin-Human Bond.* Edited by Toni Frohoff and Brenda Peterson, San Francisco, Sierra Club Books, 2003 (pp. 271, 274).

31. Leopold, Aldo "Some Fundamentals of Conservation in the Southwest," *Environmental Ethics,* ed. Eugene C. Hargrove, Vol 1, No. 2, Summer 1979 (pp. 139).

32. Schweitzer, Albert, *Teaching of Reverence for Life,* translated by Richard and Clara Winston, New York: Holt, Rinehart & Winston, 1965 (pp. 26, 32).

33. Brown, Robin, *The Lure of the Dolphin.* New York, Avon Books 1979 (pp. 185).

Chapter 30: Other Into Us

1. Hawken, Paul, *The Ecology of Commerce: A Declaration of Sustainability,* New York: HarperCollins 1994 (pp. 29).

2. Jensen, Derrick & Tweedy-Holmes, Karen, *Thought to Exist in the Wild: Awakening From the Nightmare of Zoos,* Santa Cruz CA: No voice Unheard (pp. 4, 89, 93, 95).

3. Liedloff, Jean, *The Continuum Concept: In Search of Happiness Lost,* DaCapo Press, 1998.

4. Jensen, Derrick & Tweedy-Holmes, Karen, *Thought to Exist in the Wild: Awakening From the Nightmare of Zoos,* Santa Cruz CA: No voice Unheard (pp. 125, 126, 128).